HOOKED ON OFFICIATING

CHARLIE LENNOX

All rights reserved. No part of this book shall be reproduced or transmitted in any form or by any means, electronic, mechanical, magnetic, photographic including photocopying, recording or by any information storage and retrieval system, without prior written permission of the publisher. No patent liability is assumed with respect to the use of the information contained herein. Although every precaution has been taken in the preparation of this book, the publisher and author assume no responsibility for errors or omissions. Neither is any liability assumed for damages resulting from the use of the information contained herein.

Copyright © 2013 by Charlie Lennox

ISBN 978-0-7414-9702-4 Paperback
ISBN 978-0-7414-9703-1 Hardcover
ISBN 978-0-7414-9704-8 eBook
Library of Congress Control Number: 2013911057

Printed in the United States of America

Published July 2013

INFINITY PUBLISHING
1094 New DeHaven Street, Suite 100
West Conshohocken, PA 19428-2713
Toll-free (877) BUY BOOK
Local Phone (610) 941-9999
Fax (610) 941-9959
Info@buybooksontheweb.com
www.buybooksontheweb.com

This book is dedicated to all the past and present Referees and Linesmen of the Ontario Hockey Association who have worked so hard to make this great game safe and fair for all who play.

Table of Contents

Introduction		v
Chapter 1	-They Said It...Best Advice	1
	-Where are they Now-Bob Nadin	8
	-Quiz # 1	13
Chapter 2	-Officiating Humour	15
	-Where are they Now-Ken Bannerman	21
	-Quiz # 2	29
Chapter 3	-They Said It On...Best Official	31
	-Where are they Now-Jim Lever	37
	-Quiz # 3	40
Chapter 4	-It Really Happened	41
	-Where are they Now-Sam Sisco	45
	-Quiz # 4	48
Chapter 5	-Poetry in Motion	49
	-Where are they Now-Ralph Sparks	59
	-Quiz # 5	62
Chapter 6	-Did You Know?	63
	-Where are they Now-Bryan Lewis	69
	-Quiz # 6	74
Chapter 7	-Quotes Worth Repeating	75
	-Where are they Now-Bill Devorski	80
	-Quiz # 7	83
Chapter 8	-OHA Moments	85
	-Where are they Now-Craig Spada	95
	-Quiz # 8	98

Chapter 9	-More Worth Repeating	99
	-Where are they Now-Mel Huctwith	104
	-Quiz # 9	106
Chapter 10	-Heyref Fan Heckles	107
	-Where are they Now-Matt Pavelich	110
	-Quiz # 10	112
Chapter 11	-OHA Officiating Awards	113
	-Where are they Now- Ivan Locke	122
	-Quiz # 11	128
Chapter 12	-Why Did You Hang Them Up?	129
	-Where are they Now-Bob Morley	131
	-Quiz # 12	137
	-Quiz Answers	138
	-Lest We Forget	139
Chapter 13	-Remembering Hugh McLean	141
	-Remembering Gord Fevreau	144
	-Remembering Blair Graham	147
	-Remembering Frank Slota	150
	-Remembering Roger Neilson	152
Chapter 14	-OHASupervisors' Tips	167
Chapter 15	-Past and Present Officials	303
	-OHA Officials 2013-1912	303
Index		455
Acknowledgements		461
About the Author		463

Introduction

HOOKED ON OFFICIATING

For forty-four years I have been "Hooked on Officiating" as a member of the Ontario Hockey Association. I have been a Referee, a Supervisor, a Supervision Co-Coordinator and for the last 22 years, their Referee Assignor. During that time there have been thousands of officials who have come through Minor hockey to the Junior Leagues with the dream of making it to the NHL. Some make it but, there are also thousands of officials who don't go on to the NHL. They have good jobs, young families and are able to stay close to home. They just go out there night after night and do the job to the best of their abilities. These are their stories, their opinions and their game experiences.

This book is a compilation of questionnaires, research, interviews and experiences passed on by hockey officials. It is a small part of the OHA's Officiating history filled with the officials' best advice, their choice as to who was the best official, some amazing game moments, humorous stories, officiating quotes and even poetry sent in by the officials. You will also find some 'Where are they Now' stories on Past and Present officials. Each chapter starts with a Hey Ref heckle from the many fans who watch the games and there is a short quiz at the end of each chapter to test your rule knowledge.

In a special tribute, we remember four of the OHA's character referees and our favourite coach.

The historic year by year lists of the Past and Present OHA officials range from 1912-2013. Many players were also officials in the early years. The great Hockey Hall of Fame goaltender, George Hainsworth, was once an OHA official in the 1922-23 season. Canada's Outstanding Athlete of the Year is named after Lou Marsh who was an OHA official from 1912 to 1933. You will recognize many more players who became officials as you browse through the year to year lists.

This book is also about their supervisors. They are a group of dedicated men, all highly qualified former officials, who are just trying to give back. There is a section on "Supervisors' Tips" that reflect the many elements that make up the job of being a top official. These "Tips" were taken **right off the evaluation sheets** which the supervisors fill out after they have observed the officials work a game. The supervisors all give real assessments of what they consider sincere, honest feedback to help each official reach their full potential.

We strongly feel there would be a terrific benefit for officials in other parts of the country to know what the Supervisors are telling the OHA officials. Their evaluation "Tips" come from the many years of experience they have gained while officiating at higher levels of hockey.

As well, it is our hope that this will serve as an eye opener for the fans as to what the referees have to contend with in each game and add some insight into what the supervisors are looking for in an official.

Enjoy and, **"May All of Life's Penalties be MINORS."**

Charlie Lennox

"Hey Ref, you couldn't make a call from a phone booth."

Chapter 1
THEY SAID IT...BEST ADVICE

This question was very popular and there was a good response to it by many officials. Some of these officials have gone on to the NHL and the OHL. We believe their answers are valuable to all officials who strive to better themselves.

Mark Vines: "Like anything, the more you put into it, the more you get out."

Kerry Fraser: "People don't come to watch you officiate. It's the players' game and it's a privilege for us to be on the ice with the players and to skate on their ice."

Ken Bannerman: "You can't make a fair call if you are not in the proper position."

Al Dawe: "When you are a Linesman, keep your mouth shut and speak when you are spoken to. Never bad-mouth another official."

Norm Ball: "John Willsie once told me to take charge and never look back."

John Kalar: "They are yelling at the stripes. Don't take it personal."

Dave Stortz: "Kalvin Forrest once told me it's okay to have fun out on the ice, but don't smile after a tough call."

Scott Driscoll: "Think before you talk, never get into a pissing match with a skunk and don't point your finger at a player when you are talking to him."

Ian Nichols: "Know the rules but leave the rule book in the dressing room."

Derek Amell: "Ivan Locke told me to never lie to a player or coach. They may not like the answer, but they will respect you for it."

Jim King: "Pat Patterson once told me to make an effort to listen to the Captain and the Assistants instead of going off half cocked and pig headed."

Clarke Pollock: "Hugh McLean once told me if you are going to live by the sword, you had better be prepared to die by it."

Frank Robinson: "Jim Lever told me to work hard and have fun."

Chris French: "Don't let the fans get to you; they are actually paying for your services."

Glenn Sherwood: "Hustle on every move you make; no one can ever fault you if you are in position make the call."

Tom Lundy: "If you say you are going to do something, DO IT."

Dwayne Phillips: "Keep a positive attitude and don't let a blown call ruin the rest of your game."

Matt Manor: "I was once told it is about the game, not the officials, always remember that, but never forget it is not about the coach either."

Bob Hodges: "Art Skov told me to read the rule book then use common sense."

Jim Steeves: "Jim Lever always told me to anticipate the situation and questions before they happen."

Mike Lucas: "Let the players know you see what's going on by talking to them."

Brian Harasymchuk: "Andy Van Hellemond once told me to never try to appease a team because you will only be 50% right."

Dave Mikolasek: "Chuck Farkas told me to be myself and have fun every game."

Steve Percy: "When working with different officials, try to pick up their good attributes and use them in your game."

Kevin Ryan: "Byron Jackson once told me to be myself, be fair and try to be consistent and call my own game."

Michael Nomi: "Treat every game with respect."

Wayne McDonald: "Have fun and work hard out there."

Art Connor: "Know the rules and use common sense (there is too much grab/hold and stick work). Stick to the rules and earn respect."

Dave Hornsby: "Be honest, be yourself and have fun working the game."

George Boorman: "You must be the calmest person on the ice. A player arguing loudly with you will continue to do so if you respond the same way."

Dave Ogilvie: "Don't take it personally and have fun."

Jeff Edwards: "Always look interested and keep 100% concentration on the game and, a smile doesn't hurt."

Bryan Lewis: "Pat Patterson once told me to get a haircut and pull up my pants."

Dave Stortz: "Harry Deline once told me to always wear BLACK pants to a game. You never know who will forget their ref pants or when a seam will split."

Don Daigle: "Ken Griffen advised me to always keep my cool and don't show anger."

Doug Robb: "Jim Lever once told me to know the rules and know how to stick-handle around them."

Ted Reid: "Gerry Blodget once told me to remember how you treat people on the way up the ladder because you will see them again on the way down."

Tony Schlegel: "Put in your best effort every game because every game is important to someone otherwise they wouldn't be playing it."

Steve Dick: "Keep your eyes and ears open and your mouth shut."

Gus Bambridge: "Look clean and tidy on and off the ice. Know the rules and try not to be seen."

Jim Hawthorne: "Don Koharski told me to make sure your first call makes a statement and is an impact penalty. There is nothing worst than having the first call a marginal penalty."

Jim LeBlanc: "Hugh McLean once told me if a player is trying to ruin your game, get rid of him."

Will Norris: "You only get out of officiating whatever you put into it. If you give it a 110% effort, the rewards or assignments will be there."

Tim Dolbear: "John Willsie once told me "an ICING is always an icing."

Chuck Farkas: "John Blackwell once told me to expect the unexpected, this game can throw any situation at you when you least expect it."

Bryan Edgar: "Respect and be honest with the players."

Mike Duggan: "Be Humble."

Tom Taylor: "Do the best you can and listen to any and all advice."

Paul Jones: "John Searle told me you must concentrate and focus from the drop of the puck to the final buzzer."

Bob Spence: "If you make a mistake, admit it. If you didn't see it, admit you didn't see it."

Darryl Matthews: "Rick Morphew once told me if you work on game flow, you will have game control."

Scott Lavender: "Keep your ears shut when you are near the benches."

Colin Town: "Leave your personal life in the room. Don't take it out on the players."

Tom Jukes: "Try to always officiate the same way no matter what level of hockey you are working."

Sandy Proctor: "Scotty Morrison once told me to always dress, act and look like an official."

Ed Butler: "Know the rules, be in proper position and bring your common sense to the game."

Scott Rasenberg: "Officiating is not always about the calls you make, it is sometimes about the calls you didn't make."

Martin Porteous: "Keep your eye on the "play" behind the play for the referee."

Ron Asselstine: "Work every game as if it was your last one because you never know who is in the building watching your game."

Bill Brethauer: "Do the job to the best of your capabilities. Be honest and fair with the players and team officials and you'll get along just fine."

Greg Campbell: "Don Koharski told me coaches will try to be your friend but remember you are there to do a job, not make friends."

Lyle Lloyd: "Davey Jones of the old Belleville MacFarlands once told me to close my ears after I called a penalty because the player is likely going to give me a quick verbal shot. He's just upset with himself and you should give him the benefit of the doubt."

Dave Montgomery: "Charlie Lennox told me to make the call and stay calm; show conviction and always hustle."

Tom Smith: When you finish a game and nobody can remember who refereed, you've done a good job."

George Wilson: "Be confident about your abilities. Remember there are a ten million Chinamen who really don't care a hoot about your performance."

John May: "Gus Gordon once told me, call the game on the ice and keep your nose out of the politics."

John McCutcheon: "Be yourself out there and referee a safe but fair hockey game."

Ben Craig: "No matter what happens, never second guess yourself. When in a tough game "Keep Calling."

WHERE ARE THEY NOW?
Bob Nadin

Bob Nadin retired from teaching in 1994 after 36 years as head of the Boys' Physical Education Department at Weston Collegiate. He resides with his wife Nancy in Etobicoke, Ontario. Bob was the Referee-in-Chief of the CAHA (now Hockey Canada) from 1976 to 1986. He also supervised for the NHL from 1992 to 1996. Since 1984, Bob has been a member of the International Ice Hockey Federation's Rules and Referee Committees. At present, he is an Honorary Member of the IIHF Officiating Committee and Canada's Representative. He is also known for having initiated the Referee Certification Program for the CAHA and introduced the Officiating Rule Case Books for both Canadian and International hockey.

In 1972 he was a referee at the Olympics in Sapporo Japan. He has also supervised at eight other Olympic Games and many other World Championships over the years. When he is home, he supervises the junior games for the OHA (Ontario Hockey Association). He was inducted onto the OHA's Referee Honour Roll in 1981 and awarded the OHA Gold stick in 1984.

Bob was presented with the Paul Loicq Award for outstanding contributions to the IIHF at a special ceremony in Russia in 2007. It is the highest personal recognition given by the IIHF.

In May of 2013, at the World Championships in Stockholm, Sweden, the Olympic Committee presented Bob with the Pierre de Coubertin Medal. It is a special medal given to those individuals who demonstrate the spirit of sportsmanship in Olympic Events. This is one of the noblest honours that can be bestowed upon any individual.

Remember When With...Bob Nadin

CL: Tell us about the time you had a problem with a Goal Judge in Niagara Falls.

BN: Well, it seemed every time the Goal Judge put the light on to signal a goal, I saw it differently and waved it off. Actually it happened three times. After the last one, the Goal Judge quit and threw the cord for the light over the boards.

CL: How about the time you got hit with an egg at the old Barton St arena in Hamilton?

BN: Yes, that was one of the pleasures of not wearing a helmet in those days. This guy hit me right in the back of the head. I remember you asked me if you could wipe it off but I wouldn't let you. I didn't want to give the guy the satisfaction. I skated the rest of the period with the egg running down my neck.

CL: In the old days, the OHA officials worked the Montreal Junior Canadians at the Montreal Forum. Do you have any fond memories of those games?

BN: I remember the guy with the box of ice-cream bars. Every time Montreal needed a delay, he would throw a couple of ice-cream bars over the boards usually when there was a stoppage at the opposite end of the ice. The linesman would have to skate the length of the ice to pick them up. Finally near the end of the third period, he threw the whole box over the boards.

CL: Any other stories about those great Montreal Junior teams?

BN: I remember one night when they were the visiting team in St Catharines. The lights went out for the National Anthem with both teams standing on their bluelines. When the lights came back on after the Anthem, there were a dozen live frogs hopping all over the ice. The two linesmen looked pretty funny trying to catch all the frogs.

CL: What about the famous lemon pie hit in Barrie?

BN: The Linesmen really set me up for that one. They had a pie in the spare linesmen's bag and when the game was over they asked if they could take a picture of me with the linesmen who worked the game. When the picture was taken they spun me around right into the lemon pie. They hit me so hard with it the pie plate cut my nose. The dressing room was very small and there was lemon pie on everything, our clothes, the floor, the ceiling. I almost made the little buggers walk home that night.

CL: Did you ever turn the tables on the linesmen?

BN: In Peterborough, they used to throw "Fish Eyes" at the officials. I know several linesmen who took some home in their skates. Unfortunately, they didn't discover them until the next morning and by that time their house didn't smell very good.

CL: I understand you are partial to live "Guppies."

BN: We had an official's party at my house and as usual the wives were in the rec room and all the officials were in bar which was the room with my tropical fish tanks. While I was upstairs answering the phone, someone put one of my prize Guppies in my glass of beer. When I came back down everyone was proposing toasts to the OHA and as the story goes, it took four toasts before I swallowed the fish. I have never seen so many guys rolling on the floor laughing. I didn't even realize that I had swallowed anything until they started to offer me fish food.

CL: You have worked many big games in your career, is there one in particular that you remember?

BN: On May 12, 1971, I was fortunate enough to work the final game of Junior hockey for Marcel Dionne of St. Catharines against the Quebec Remparts with Guy LaFleur. They played it at Maple Leaf Gardens before a full house. St Catharines won the game 6-3 but refused to go back to Quebec because their bus had been attacked by irate fans after game four. Quebec was awarded the series and went on to defeat Edmonton for the Memorial Cup.

CL: Who was the best official you ever worked with?

BN: Gord Fevreau, he let the players play and didn't call fringe or marginal penalties. He had the respect of the players and the coaches.

CL: What determines a good official?

BN: The quality of his work as an official will be determined as much by his attitude as by his skill.

CL: Do you have any advice for a young official?

BN: If you tell the truth, you don't have to remember anything.

Bob Nadin Lemon Pie Attack

Rules Quiz # 1 (answers on page 138)
Questions from Hockey Canada Rule Book

1. What is the determining factor for an offside when the puck has completely crossed the blue line?

   A. The position of the puck
   B. The position of the player's stick
   C. The position of the player's body
   D. The position of the player's skates

2. Which official in the two referee system is responsible for conducting the line change procedure?

   A. The official dropping the puck
   B. Either official can perform the procedure
   C. The official who is not dropping the puck
   D. Both officials to ensure the teams get the message

3. What is the referee's decision when a player charges a goaltender while he is in his crease?

   A. Major penalty
   B. Minor penalty
   C. Major penalty and a game misconduct
   D. Stop play, make sure that the goaltender is not injured and conduct the face-off in the neutral zone

4. When does the referee use the line change procedure?

   A. At each stoppage of play
   B. When the visiting team conducts a change
   C. When the face-offs are in the end zone

"Hey Ref, you're missing a good game."
REF: "Yah I know, but they sent me to this one."

Chapter 2
OFFICIATING HUMOUR

Do You Understand?

At one point during the game, the coach said to one of his young players, "Do you understand what co-operation is? What a team is?"
The little boy nodded in the affirmative.
"Do you understand that what matters is that we play together as a team?"
The little boy nodded yes.
"So," the coach continued, "When a penalty is called, or you're offside, you don't argue or curse or attack the Referee. Do you understand all that?"
Again the little boy nodded.
"Good," said the coach, "Now go over there and explain it to your parents."

Heavenly Refs

Al and Harry loved to referee and one night after a game they were discussing and wondering if there was any hockey in Heaven. "Yes," Al said, "there must be otherwise it wouldn't be called Heaven." So they agreed that whoever died first would somehow notify the other to let him know if there was indeed hockey in Heaven.

Harry passed on a few years later and one morning when Al was walking to work he was tapped on the shoulder. He turned around and didn't see anyone but heard Harry's voice saying, "Al, yes there is hockey in Heaven". Al said, "Great- I thought so." Harry said, "Al that's the good news...the bad news is you're refereeing Friday."

No Home Life

Three guys meet St Peter at the Pearly Gates in Heaven and are waiting to get in. St Peter explains that heaven is very big and they will need some transportation to get around. He asks the first guy if he has any sins to confess. He says, "I was twice unfaithful to my wife." St Peters says "Ok, you get that little Volkswagen over there." The second guy says, "I was only unfaithful once to my wife". St Peter says, "You get that middle size car." The third guy says," I was a Hockey Referee and I was away a lot but I was never unfaithful to my wife." "Good," said St Peter, "You get that luxury Cadillac."

A few days later, all three meet on the same cloud and they see the Referee in the Cadillac deeply sobbing. "What is the matter?" they asked. The Ref replies through his tears, "I just saw my wife and she was on a skateboard."

Poor Referee

A Referee's dilapidated car broke down on the way home from a hockey game. The next morning he managed to get the vehicle towed to a garage for repairs. "I hope you'll go easy on the cost," he told the mechanic. "After all, I'm just a poor Referee." "I know," came the reply, "I was at the game yesterday."

The Challenge

It seems the Devil was always challenging St Peter to a game of hockey and St Peter always turned him down. One day St Peter was walking around the big practice rink in the sky and he noticed that he had some pretty good hockey players out there. So he decided to take the Devil up on his challenge. He got on the "Hot Line" to the Devil and said he would accept his challenge to play a hockey game. The Devil said, "Okay, but you'll lose," St Peter replied. "Lose, how could we lose, we have the best players to ever play the game." "Doesn't matter," said the Devil, "you'll still lose." St Peter exclaimed, "We have Sawchuk, Horton, Harvey, Richard, how could we lose?" "Because" said the Devil, "I've got all the Referees down here."

What's The Score?

When the irate coach confronted the Referee in the hallway at the end of the second period, the Referee calmly replied, "You're just upset because we're winning by three goals!"

Every hockey coach should be married because sooner or later he is going to have to blame someone other than the officials.

Two peanuts went to Referee a hockey game, one was a salted.

Hockey Hero

Two boys are playing hockey on a pond in a Toronto suburb, when one is viciously attacked by a Rottweiler. Thinking quickly, the other boy grabs his hockey stick, wedges it down into the dog's collar and twists, immobilizing, stunning and rendering the dog unconscious.

A reporter who was passing by sees the incident and rushes over to interview the boy. He starts writing in his notebook, "Young Maple Leaf Fan Saves Friend from Brutal Dog Attack."

"But I'm not a Maple Leaf fan," the little hero said.

The reporter replied, "Sorry but since we are in Toronto, I just assumed you were."

He starts over..."Little St Michaels Majors Fan Rescues Friend from Horrific Attack."

The boy stopped him again saying, "I'm not a St Mikes fan, either."

"Well," said the reporter, "I assumed everyone in this part of Toronto was either for the Maple Leafs or St Mikes. What team DO you root for?"

"I don't root for anyone," the little boy replies, "I'm a HOCKEY REFEREE."

The reporter starts a new sheet in his notebook:
"Little B---ard Kills Beloved Family Pet."

Who's The Greatest?

Four women were having coffee and bragging about their children.

The first mother says, "My son is a priest. When he walks into a room, everyone calls him Father."

The next woman tries to top her, "Really? My son married the princess of a small European country and when he walks into a room, people call him your Highness!"

The third woman chirps, "Well, my son is a cardinal of the church. Whenever he walks into a room, people call him your Eminence!"

The fourth woman is just sitting there sipping her coffee silently, and the other three look at her in a subtle way, as if to say, Well?

She smiles and says, "Oh well. My son is a very large and handsome hockey Referee. Whenever he walks into a room, women say OH MY GOD!

Ref Talk

Two Referees are talking after a game. "My wife thinks I favour Officiating over Marriage even though we are celebrating our third season together."

You're the Best

I was coming off the ice after a game and a fan came up to me a said, "Stefan, I think you are the 2nd best referee in the OHA." I said thank you! He replied by saying, "But every other referee is tied for first!"

Submitted by Brent Stefan

The Call

There are three hockey referees talking. One is young, one is middle-aged, and one is older. They are discussing the way they call a play. The young Referee brags, "I call it the way it is." The Middle-aged Referee boasts, "I call it the way I see it." The older one looks at the other two and quietly declares, "It's nothing until I call it."

Linesman's Cake

"My wife made a cake for the Linesmen." Harry said to his friend.

"How do you know it's a cake for the Linesmen?" his friend replied.

"NO ICING"

WHERE ARE THEY NOW?
Ken Bannerman

Ken Bannerman was an OHA referee for 27 years from 1978 to 2005. A Barrie resident, he retired from Barrie Parks and Recreation in 2010 after 36 years. He is presently an active partner in Great Outdoor Gym Fitness equipment during the summer and works the Ski Lifts at Snow Valley Resort in the winter. He was inducted into the Barrie Sports Hall of Fame in 2010 and is now on their Board of Directors.

Ken has been an OHA Supervisor for 17 years (1990 to 2001 and 2007 to 2013). He was awarded the Jack Clancy Award in 1988 as the Most Dedicated Official in the OHA for that season and in 2000 was awarded the John Blackwell Award for Most Deserving Official. In 2005, he was inducted onto the OHA's Referee Honour Roll.

Remember When With...Ken Bannerman

CL: How did you get involved in officiating?

KB: A friend asked me to help out a long time ago. I started with the kids on half ice and worked my way up through the Hockey Canada officiating program. I received my Level 6 Certification in 1988 at a Hockey Canada Clinic in North Bay.

CL: Your boys, Korey and Kevin were on the OHA staff and Korey is presently a referee on the OHL staff as well as one of the top referees in the OHA. Korey received the Hugh McLean Award as the

OHA's Most Promising Official in 2009. Did you ever get a chance to work with either of them on the ice?

KB: Yes, Korey worked the lines for me one night in an OHA game in Stayner. My Mom and Dad got to see us work together. It was a very emotional night for all of us. My final game as a referee was with my two sons Korey and Kevin on the lines in a Bantam game in Barrie. It was a big night with the media there and lots of friends and fellow officials from all around the area.

CL: You worked many International games during your long career including trips to Tokyo, Japan (90) Klagenfurt, Austria (92), and Bolzano, Italy (94). In addition, you refereed eight Team Canada games in Canada as well the Dudley-Hewitt Cup (95). In 1992, you were selected by Hockey Canada to work the World B Pool Championship in Austria. Can you tell us about that final game in Austria?

KB: It was the Gold Medal game and it was so loud in the rink that when I gave the numbers to the timekeeper for goals and assists, I had to write them down.

CL: You received a special gift while goal judging in Austria?

KB: When you are at an International Tournament all the officials have to take a turn at goal judging. You are required to wear your referee sweater when you are the goal judge. During the game a local man in a uniform came over to talk to me. He was a fireman and we chatted at the end of the first period. He told me he was going to get me a special present. Apparently, he ran home and brought me back a bottle of home-made schnapps. I couldn't refuse his offer so I ended up goal judging for the rest of the game with a bottle of alcohol on my knee at a World Championship.

CL: You went to Japan in 1990 and I understand you were able to take your Dad along with you. That must have been a very memorable moment?

KB: It was definitely a special trip and I was glad we had that trip together. He had a great time and they treated him with honour and gave him special treatment everywhere we went. It is a memory I think of often.

CL: Did you have any other special games as an official?

KB: Yes there were many, but I would say working my first game at Maple Leaf Gardens; refereeing two games between Team Canada and Team Russia in my hometown of Barrie; refereeing at a Team Canada tryout camp game and dropping the puck between Wayne Gretzky and Steve Izerman.

CL: What was the toughest game you ever refereed?

KB: I would have to say it was a JrB playoff game in Bramalea. It was an awful mean game but we knew in advance it was going to be that type of game. It was a challenge for all the officials and it took all I could muster to control the teams and the fans.

CL: Did you ever have any problems with spectator abuse?

KB: Can't say I had any real problems in the OHA but in minor hockey some parents would wait for you outside the arena to let you know what they thought of your officiating.

CL: What do you miss about not being on the ice?

KB: I miss the challenge and the feeling of a job well done. Of course, I miss the guys on the ice. We had a lot of fun over the years.

CL: In your opinion, what determines a good official?

KB: The best officials are the ones who understand the game and can master the skill of communication and know how to apply the rules at the appropriate time.

CL: Who was the best official you ever worked with in the OHA?

KB: Sandy Proctor was the best. He is the one who taught me how the skill of communication can help you avoid problems on the ice.

CL: Is there anything you would like to pass along to young officials?

KB: Listen to everything and learn from everyone. There is always something you can pick up no matter how many years you have been officiating.

Ken Bannerman Retires

The following article was written by Mike Dodd, writer for "Orillia Today" and appears here with his permission.

His departure from the game of hockey was reflective of his officiating style, quiet and orderly, with very little fanfare.

When Barrie resident Ken Bannerman slipped off his stripped sweater for the final time recently, the veteran Ontario Hockey Association referee brought to an end a career spanning 27 years.

Bannerman worked a minor hockey game alongside his two sons and then slipped quietly into the night.

No boos, no jeers and sadly no applause.

When it came to offering an evaluation of his refereeing style, there was no middle ground when it came to Ken Bannerman.

Many a night, fans in rinks from Huntsville to Markham questioned his mental capacity and yet he kept on working. There's an old phrase that's always made me chuckle and sums the situation up best.

"When you blow the whistle, you're the only sane person in the building."

You either admired him or hated him outright.

I happened to be one of those who admired him for the work he did and the way in which he conducted himself when he was on the ice.

In all the times I saw him work games, I never saw him lose his composure and goodness knows there were enough insults hurled his way over the years to throw him over the emotional edge.

I don't know what it was, but I seemed to hit it off with Ken the first time I chatted with him.

Our first conversation was somewhere around 20 years ago, when I spotted him sitting in the stands watching a practice. The two of us had seen a lot of each other before that, with him working games and me wandering the halls looking for quotes after a game. He sensed pretty quickly that I wasn't someone who was going to give him grief over his officiating and simply enjoyed talking about hockey.

Say what you want about his ability, but Ken Bannerman was, and still is a man of principle.

Good friends with many NHL officials, Ken turned down an invitation to work Pro games as a replacement official, when the NHL officials went on strike years ago.

Some 15 years ago, I remember covering a game seven playoff game, featuring Couchiching and Collingwood in what had been an emotional series between these two teams.

Ken worked the game and when it appeared early that both teams were going to stick to hockey, he all but stuffed his whistle in his pocket and let the two teams play.

There were a few "near infractions" on both sides, but Ken decided it would be smarter to let the two teams play on. He has a sense of the flow of a game, something only a select few officials have. Play went back and forth for three periods, with both teams enjoying excellent scoring chances. Collingwood ended up scoring two late goals to pull out a 3-2 victory and win the series. A total of three penalties were called in the game.

To this day, it still ranks as the best live hockey game I've ever watched. I ended up writing a column about the series and sent a copy of it along with a thank you card to Ken letting him know how much I appreciated his work. It's the only time in 28 years of journalism I've been motivated to do that.

Three years ago, I ended up in Huntsville on a Friday night, arriving at the rink long before game time. There in the corridor was Ken, sipping a coffee and getting himself mentally ready for the task at hand.

What we talked about was hockey and his continuing love for the game. He talked about incidents in hockey when things get a little heated and nights when fighting his way to a rink through difficult weather conditions made him think twice about whether he wanted to continue officiating.

As luck would have it, I landed in Kitchener in 2000 at the OHA Awards Luncheon where I was presented with OHA Media Award by President, Brent Ladds.

At the same luncheon, Ken Bannerman received the "Most Deserving Official Award" in the OHA for the year 1999-2000. He was clearly emotional when he was handed the Award. Members of his family were in attendance, adding to the significance of the moment. I later sent Ken a photo copy and he went out of his way to say thanks.

In recent years, Ken said he hoped he could stay in the game long enough to be able to work a Junior game with one of his sons. That wish came true when he worked a JrA game in Couchiching with his son, Korey. Prior to the game, he stopped me in the hall and asked if I'd snap off a few photos of he and his son on the ice.

With that dream realized, I had the feeling Ken was beginning to count down the final months in his whistle-blowing career. He ended up working a year longer than I figured he would and retired from the OHA February 05, 2005.

Unlike officials who stay on too long and then suddenly find themselves struggling to keep up with the play, Ken elected to go while he still was well-respected and still had his health.

In recent years, there's been talk amongst hockey officials that the level of officiating has slipped, and we're asking too many young officials to work games and make tough calls with only limited experience behind them.

But with the abuse they take at times, who'd want to stay in officiating for 25 years?

Ken Bannerman gave more to the game of hockey than he took out of it. He was as skilled an official as you will find and someone other officials need measure themselves by.

He ended up on the receiving end of more than a few errant puck blasts and had the bruises to prove it. But, in the end, he performed his duties with class and dignity.

Thanks for the memories Ken.

Rules Quiz # 2 *(answers on 138)*
Questions from Hockey Canada Rule Book

1. During a penalty shot, the player performs a spin-o-rama move. Is it legal?

    A. No, because the player proceeded the puck
    B. No, because the puck must always be moving forward
    C. Yes, as long as this is a continuous motion
    D. Yes, if the player has crossed the blue line.

2. What penalty shall be assessed any player who deliberately attempts to or deliberately injures an opponent with a slash, high stick or cross-check?

    A. Double minor
    B. Minor or major at referee's discretion
    C. Minor penalty
    D. Match penalty

3. Any player who is assessed a second misconduct penalty in the same game shall automatically be assessed a game misconduct penalty?

    A. True
    B. False

4. The rule aimed at the third player to enter a fight only applies to situations where at least one player has been assessed a major penalty for fighting.

    A. True
    B. False

"Hey Ref, if you were my husband, I'd feed you poison." REF: "Lady if I was your husband, I'd take it."

Chapter 3
THEY SAID IT...ON BEST OFFICIAL

There was a good response to this question and everyone had their own opinion as to who they thought was the best official. Of course they could only comment on the officials they had actually worked with in games. I think the most important part of this exercise is to understand WHY they considered their choice as the BEST OFFICIAL.

Will Norris: "Andy Van Hellemond, he knew what had happened, he knew what was happening and he knew what was going to happen."

John May: "Ralph Sparks was an extremely dedicated official and an outstanding crew chief. He was a very supportive referee from a linesman's point of view."

Dave Hornsby: "Rick Morphew, his presence on the ice changed a difficult game into an easy one."

Lyle Lloyd: "Red Gravelle, he always gave 100%. He was small and an excellent skater who knew the game because he had played it."

Clarke Pollock: "Mark Vines, he was an excellent Linesman."

Don Daigle: "Gil Neuwendyk, he was the most honest and competitive person I knew."

Bill Brethauer: "Lou Maschio and Hugh McLean were both veteran NHL officials who had the ability to let you do your game (2man system) without taking over or overshadowing you on calls and backed you up 100%"

Eric Schwippi: "Clarke Pollock, he had a great knowledge of the game."

Brent Casselman: "Wally Harris, he had respect."

Jim Steeves: "Jim Lever, he was always unpredictable."

Peter Balsdon: "Justin Winter, he had great command of the rule book combined with practical application on the ice."

Brian Coles: "Jim Lever, Ralph Sparks and Tom Brown for their imparted knowledge from working with them and the countless hours in their cars and watering holes discussing and receiving advice."

Jeff Caplan: "Ralph Sparks was an honest, fair, dedicated official who told it as it was and pulled no punches."

John Sullivan: "Gord Fevreau had a great feel for the game and he seemed to make the right call at the right time."

Tom Taylor: "Bob Nadin, he could look after any situation and always gave 100%."

Terry Garbutt: "Wally Harris and Bruce Hood both had a tremendous feel for the tone of the game."

Gus Bambridge: "Al Dick had a great knowledge of the game. He had the ability to control games allowing both teams an equal opportunity to win."

Bryan Richards: "Al Dawe for his excellent rapport with the coaches and the players, and Clarke Pollock as the best referee for game management."

Norm Ball: "Glen Grice, he was a big, strong, honest linesman who was the type of guy you always wanted with you. He supported you 100% and was able to develop the best rapport with the players in the shortest time I have ever seen."

John McCutcheon: "Bill Devorski, when working with him, you knew you were going to have a hoot. He always talked to the players and the fans."

Sandy Proctor: "Scotty Morrison, Bob Nadin, Blair Graham and Gord Fevreau each brought a different perspective to the game to learn from."

Larry Clark: "Bob Nadin, he was the best official I ever had the pleasure of working with."

Tom Lundy: "Bob Nadin and Jim Lever, they both had an excellent feel for the game and the respect of all participants, coaches, players, owners, and fans."

Don Van Massenhoven: "John Willsie, he had a great feel for the game. Most people thought he didn't call enough penalties, but if the players didn't want to play, he could fill the penalty sheet very quickly."

Ron Asselstine: "Andy Van Hellemond was consistent, dedicated, and had a great feel for the game, he had excellent judgment and never bluffed."

Jim LeBlanc: "Bob Nadin earned the players' respect by knowing how to talk to them. He never had to raise his voice."

Bob Spence: "Don Van Massenhoven, he always had control and he knew when to let them play and when to take back control of the game."

Dave Mikolasek: "Gene Kusy made your night fun and comfortable and always made the game exciting. He made you want to go back out the next night."

Mike Duggan: "Ralph Sparks for his sense of fair play and great knowledge of the rules and game experience."

Scott Driscoll: Andy Van Hellemond in pro hockey had the utmost respect of his colleagues, players and management. He had a great feel for the game and was an excellent communicator."

Bob Hodges: "Andy Van Hellemond, he had the best feel for the game."

Dave Montgomery: Ralph Sparks was fearless and very supportive of his linesmen. He was committed to giving his best effort."

Frank Robinson: "Terry Landon, he was a big, strong excellent skater who had tremendous respect from the players."

Charlie Lennox: "Bob Nadin, he was a school teacher and knew how to talk to the players."

Art Connor: "Hugh McLean, Bob Nadin and Gord Fevreau; they all earned the respect of the teams."

Dave Ogilvie: "Mike Lucas, he was well respected by players and the coaches."

Mitch Osborne: "Dave Stortz, he handled the game with ease and care. He was smart, loved the game and could make any situation positive."

Scott Driscoll: "John Willsie in amateur hockey was a great referee and an even better human being."

Sam Sisco: "Metro Martinello in games where the two man system was used. He was the best at covering the ice and we had great communications with each other."

Darryl Matthews: "Doug Martin, he focused on coaching young officials and their development."

Jim Lever: "Bob Nadin referee and Bob Morley linesman."

Derek Amell: "Dave Lynch, he taught me how to respect players and how to communicate without yelling."

Doug Robb: "Bob Nadin was a great teacher of the game and always had advice on becoming a good official. He kept you well informed on and off the ice in all situations."

Jim King: "Jack Shropshire had everything on the ball; style, class and personality."

Norm Ball: "Pat Hagarty, he was fair, consistent and principled in his approach to officiating and supervising. He always took the "high road". He was the most nonpolitical man I have ever met. He had my respect."

Ian Nicholls: "Mark Dumesnil had the best rapport with players and coaches. He was consistent and a good team leader."

Ben Craig: Bryon Jackson and Jack Clancy made you feel part of a team and would always ask for your input.

John Cane: "Don Goodridge as a referee and two linesmen who I was happy to have work the games with me. They were Darryl Dawson and Derek Amell."

WHERE ARE THEY NOW?
Jim Lever

Jim Lever was a long time employee of the Toronto Transit Commission and resides with his wife Joan in their Toronto home. Jim, was an OHA Level VI referee, has been selected to referee many International hockey games including the 1984 Olympics in Sarajevo. He also officiated at the 1981 World Championship in Tokyo, Japan. He worked the World Juniors in Finland and Germany as well as the Ivestia Tournament in Russia. Jim is a former THL Referee-in-Chief and is presently an OHL supervisor. Jim was inducted onto the OHA's Referee Honour Roll in 1989. He is proud of his OHA roots as an official and a supervisor and believes the OHA to be a great training ground for young officials.

Remember When With... Jim Lever

CL: Tell us about the time you had to fight your way ONTO the ice in a JrA game at London Gardens.

JL: London had a fan by the name of "Crazy George" I think he was a garbage man, who was just brutal on referees. He would stand right at the referee's dressing room door and call them everything he could think of as they were coming off the ice. Of course, he had about 25 cronies behind him to back him up. This particular night, Oshawa were the visiting team and right near the end of the first period, the Oshawa goalie raced out to the blueline to clear the puck. A London forward jumped right into the goalie and an Oshawa defenseman came to the rescue of his goalie. After the fight ended, I gave the London forward an extra five for Charging. When we went off at the end of the period, "Crazy George" was going nuts. We ignored him and went into the dressing room. Old Arnold Etcher, the Oshawa timekeeper, had accompanied the team to London for this game. He came into the room to bring up some apples. Arnold always had apples for the officials. Anyway, when we out to start the second period, "Crazy George" and his boys jumped us in the hallway. They forced us against the boards so we couldn't open the door to get on the ice. We got in a few good shots before security finally arrived. Poor, old Arnold ended up in the middle of it. Hugh McLean was there and wouldn't restart the game until the OPP came and got "Crazy George" out of the building. I understand they eventually banned him from the arena.

CL: Once upon a time you were a Goal Judge.

JL: I remember it was a Senior AAA playoff game in Orillia and we used to take turns Lining one game and Goal Judging the next. It was my turn to Goal Judge. If you have ever been to Orillia, you would know the Goal Judge doesn't sit right behind the net. He actually stands off to the left. The arena was packed and spectators were standing all around the glass. It was really difficult to know who the Goal Judge was.

Late in the game, Orillia appeared to score a goal that would have put them ahead in the game. I didn't think it went in and I didn't put the goal light on. The fans were screaming in the stands directly behind the net. They were all looking for the Goal Judge. I pointed to a guy right behind the net. They threw everything at him. The guy ended up completely covered with pop and coffee. Fortunately, there were no more goals scored at my end of the rink.

CL: Tell about the phantom hole in the net in a JrB game in the old Metro JrB League.

JL: I suppose it is a little trick that probably saved my hide a few times. An attacking forward let go a shot that in my opinion went through the mesh on the net. I called it a goal. The team that had been scored on complained bitterly that there was no hole. I called a linesman over and told him to go down to the net and find a hole. He didn't find a hole but he put on a good show of tying one up.

CL: How about that unforgettable airplane trip to Ottawa.

JL: The stewardess brought me a coffee and put it down on the tray but it was broken and the coffee spilled in my lap. I had my seatbelt on and couldn't get up. It burnt my groin badly. When we got to the arena, the Ottawa Trainer gave me some ointment to put on it. The whole game I just skated between the bluelines. Brian Kilrae, the Ottawa coach, said later that he didn't notice any difference in my positioning.

CL: I understand you were in the fertilizer business?

JL: We were young linesmen and we liked to have some fun with the senior referees in those days. One night we went to the stockyards about midnight and loaded a pick-up truck with pure cow manure. We backed the truck on Bob Nadin's lawn and quickly shoveled it out. We then took a 'For Sale' sign from across the road and stuck it in the pile. When we got home, we phoned the Globe and Mail and placed a classified ad for' free manure'. We also had the Globe bill him for the advertisement. Bob later said that it burnt his grass all to hell but in the spring, he had the best lawn on the street.

Rules Quiz #3 *(answers on page 138)*
Questions from Hockey Canada Rule Book

1. An attacking player is standing in the goal crease. The puck is shot, hitting the player in the crease and drops down in the crease. The attacking player gets out of the crease, and then shoots the puck into the goal.
    A. The goal is disallowed
    B. The goal is allowed

2. What penalty is assessed to a player who persists in disputing or shows disrespect for the ruling of an official?
    A. Bench minor or a misconduct penalty
    B. Ten minute misconduct penalty
    C. Bench minor and a game misconduct
    D. Gross misconduct

3. A player in the penalty box hands his stick to a teammate on the ice whose stick has been broken. What is the penalty?
    A. Minor to player receiving stick, no penalty to player in box
    B. Minor to both players

4. The correct line change procedure allows the visiting team five seconds to make a single line change of players before the referee puts his arm up.
    A. True
    B. False

"Hey Ref, you left your white cane in the car with your seeing-eye dog."

Chapter 4

IT REALLY HAPPENED...

These are incidents that actually happened in games and caught our interest.

Catch It If You Can...

Clarke Pollock: "Every year in the first Listowel JrB playoff game, a faithful fan would throw a live rooster out on the ice. The Linesmen always had a difficult time trying to catch him to the delight of the crowd."

Did You See That?

Bryan Richards: "At a Bradford JrC game in 1990, during an opposition breakaway, a young lady in the glassed in end of the rink elected to lift up her shirt and expose her breasts. This caused a big roar and the player lost control of the puck. The team complained but little could be done as the young lady disappeared, although I am sure a search was conducted."

Tiny Bubbles...

Will Norris: "One of my fellow officials put shampoo in my whistle and the first time I blew it for a stoppage of play......bubbles came out."

Oops, I Forgot...

Ron Asselstine: "Playoff game ... the arena was full and I fell on my ass because I forgot to take off my skate guards. I wasn't too amused ... but my partners and the crowd thought it was hilarious."

Knock, Knock...
Curtesy of **Jim Proudfoot,** *Toronto Star*

Three NHL officials had just worked a game in Los Angeles and agreed to go out afterwards and get something to eat. Greg Madill, the referee, showed up at Linesman Ron Finn's room and they sat down to wait for Ron Asselstine. There was a knock at the door.

"That'll be Ron," said Finn as he walked over to the door. Upon opening the door, he was confronted by a serious looking dude pointing a .357 Magnum at his chest.

"This is a stick-up," the thug announced. "Go to hell," Finn retorted and slammed the door shut.

A huge explosion ensued and a bullet crashed through the door, zipped past Finn, ricocheted off the ceiling and the metal window frame and eventually bounced onto the floor. Finn said he could feel the air being sucked dry as the bullet went by his hand.

"It's not Asselstine," Finn shouted amid the clatter. His fingers were bruised from the bullet's passage. The police found the bullet later and showed Finn how the gunman had filed an "x" into the top to make it explode on contact.

The intruder and his colleagues were arrested in the parking lot outside the hotel. They were security guards from a nearby hotel doing a little moonlighting.

Finn and Madill testified at the trial the following summer. The two would-be robbers, who had long records, were sentenced to nine years apiece in jail."

Sucked In...

Larry Baxter: "I remember going to pick up an extra puck that was on the ice at the far end of the arena. It was tied to a fishing line and the guy reeled it in as I tried to grab it, of course, to the delight of the crowd."

Who Did That?

Referee John Sullivan was skating down the ice, near the boards when a lady leaned over and whacked him with her purse. The blow messed up the only two or three strands of hair referee Sullivan had on his head. He turned and pointed at her as the play moved out of the end zone. At the next stoppage of play, he skated over to where the lady was sitting. She was now surrounded by many supportive fans. He pointed his finger at her and said, "Lady, you know that purse you hit me with"? She said, "Yes"? He said, "You wouldn't happen to have a comb in there so I can fix my hair?"

It Couldn't Happen...

Charlie Lennox: "I was supervising an OJHL JrA game between Buffalo and Mississauga at the beautifully renovated Port Credit arena on October 20, 2112, when linesman Aaron Neely had something unbelievable happen. Late in the game, Aaron was getting set for an end zone corner face-off when one team called for a timeout. The practice is for the linesman to put the puck on the ice during the timeout. The purpose is to keep it from getting warm in his hand which would prevent it from sliding properly when play resumed. Aaron dropped the puck from his waist and it landed on its edge and stayed that way right in the middle of the face-off dot. He could not believe it and left it there and signaled his partner, Chris Ferreira, to come and see it. What are the odds of that happening?"

WHERE ARE THEY NOW?
Sam Sisco

Sam Sisco was well known in IHL circles as he worked as a Linesman and a Referee in the League for over 20 years. He retired after the 1981-82 season and began to focus his efforts towards the betterment of the profession. Often regarded as one of the finest instructors of hockey officials, he spent ten years as a supervisor of officials in the NHL.

Sam Sisco is a native of Windsor, Ontario and served many years as a mathematics teacher at a local high school. He retired from teaching in 1992 and began supervising on a more regular basis in the NHL. He has been involved in officiating for 40 plus years and has scouted games and evaluated officials and their performances for the NHL, IHL, AHL, ECHL, OHL and OHA Leagues. He was an OHA supervisor from 1975-1994.

In 2008, he was awarded the Legacy Award as the Windsor and Essex Sports Person of the year. He said he was surprised, humbled and very honoured to receive the award.

In his younger days, he played JrB hockey for the Blenheim Bobcats and then moved up to play a season with the Senior AAA Windsor Bulldogs.

In 1957 he turned to officiating and had an outstanding career working every League in the area. He was one of the first local referees to officiate in the NCAA.

Sam also served as Referee-in-Chief for the IHL and the Windsor and District Referee's Association.

He was always available to assist at the annual OHA Referee School to help select officials for the staff and to pass on his wealth of experience to the young officials. In 1996, he was inducted onto the OHA's Referee Honour Roll.

Remember When With...Sam Sisco

CL: Do you have any career hightlights?

SS: "I had a career in officiating that included a lot of championship games," One of the highlights was a tournament in 1974 involving Canada, the U.S., Russia and the Czechs. It was the same Russian team that played Canada in 1972, Vladislav Tretiak was in goal and Valeri Kharlamov was there."

CL: Did you really give "Superman" a penalty?

SS: Yes I did. Ted Gavin was a former NHL coach with Detroit and a wild man behind the bench who was known to litter the ice with debris of every description. In 1979, while coaching Toledo in the IHL, terrible Ted became upset with one of my referee decisions. After waving his arms frantically like some prehistoric bird and uttering odd yelping noises, Garvin climbed onto the boards and began to disrobe. When he was got down to his undershirt, I saw it was emblazoned with a large Superman crest. I gave him a two minute unsportsmanlike conduct penalty.

CL: I hear you got a real wakeup call.

SS: I had a habit of letting the linesmen drive to the game while I had a little sleep in the back. One night, the linemen brought two flashlights and on a lonely stretch of road, the driver slammed on the brakes and yelled "Lookout", while the other linesman shone the two flashlights in my face. Damm near had a heart attack.

CL: You have a good story about haircuts.

SS: Bobby Knight, the great Indiana basketball coach, was a disciple of short hair. He once told a player to get his hair cut and to his surprise the player retorted, "Jesus had long hair." Bobby took the player outside to a pond behind the arena and told him "Walk across that or get your hair cut."

CL: Do you have any advice for hockey officials?

SS: Listen to any and all advice. Your ears will never get you into trouble.

CL: Give us one of your famous Sam Sisco "Success in Life" quotes.

SS: "If you fail to prepare, you prepare to fail."

Rules Quiz #4 *(answers on page 138)*
Questions from Hockey Canada Rule Book

1. What penalty shall be assessed if a player closes his hand on the puck within the confines of the goal crease?

    A. Minor penalty
    B. Major penalty
    C. Penalty shot
    D. Major penalty and game misconduct

2. A slashing penalty shall be assessed to a player who swings his stick at an opponent without actually hitting him?

    A. True
    B. False

3. Can the linesman stop play when the puck has been hit by a high stick and the referee did not see it?

    A. Yes
    B. No

4. What penalty is assessed to a goaltender who leaves his crease and becomes the first player to intervene in a fight?

    A. Minor penalty for leaving his crease
    B. Major penalty for leaving his crease
    C. Minor for leaving his crease plus a game misconduct for third man in

"Hey Ref, I though clowns wore polka dots not stripes."

Chapter 5

POETRY IN MOTION

In this section we ran a contest for the best poem with the winner getting a heyrefs.com t-shirt. We did not include Vern Buffey's mother or Ted Reeve in the contest.

I Don't Get No Satisfaction

I think that I shall never see,
A satisfactory Referee.
Above whose head a halo shines,
Whose merits rate reporter's lines.
One that calls them as they are,
Not as the fans might wish by far.
A gent who leans not either way,
But lets the boys decide the play.
A guy who'll sting the Coach who yaps,
From Vancouver Isle to Halifax.
Poems are made by fools like me,
But only God could referee.

Vern Buffey's Mother

There's Hope

I stood there at the Pearly gates,
My face was worn and old.
And meekly asked the Man of Fate,
Admission to the fold.

"What have you done", St Peter asked,
"To seek admission here?"
"I was a hockey referee on earth" I said,
"For many a weary year."
The gate swung sharply open then,
As St Peter punched a bell,
"Come in", he said "and take a harp,
You've had your share of Hell".

Brent Ladds, OHA Past President

It's Not In

End to end with blinding speed,
To the net, a scripted read.
A look behind, no lamp is lit,
So from the sound, a post it hit.
While hoards of players scream and fuss,
An obvious time, we might discuss.
For if it entered the yawning cage,
It might explain the festered rage.
But what I've seen and what I heard,
Will deafen me to a player's word.
To the judge I turn and seek,
Praying his eyes had the smallest peek.
But in my travel, he can't be found,
He is only there for the final round.
So in disgust, I am offered heat,
Not from the players shall I retreat.
"It hit the post" so plain to see,
I am standing here, it's in front of me.
From everyone the whine is served,
100%, and not unnerved.
I issue how it is going to be,
So...get the puck away from me.

Scott Hutchinson

There Are Nights...

Hack, whack, spear and spit,
There are nights I think, "I don't need this s..t."
Can't give a check, can't take a hit,
And throw a tantrum when the red light is lit.

But then you meet a goalie with a toothy grin,
Or a speedy centre who scores with a nifty spin.
And a team that gracious after a win,
And you realize that being a ref is not a sin.

Rob Mills

Who Is To Blame?

Behold each playoff hockey coach in language loud and clear,
Puts all the blame of losing on the G.D. referee.
The referee made two mistakes against each sloppy crew,
Each player made 12 booboos and the coach made thirty-two.

Ted Reeve, Toronto Telegram

The Linesman

The official who is an assistant to the Referee in charge,
You will find he is usually fast, tall and large.
His job is to control face-offs, offsides and the occasional fight,
And never to question whether the Referee is right.

He must anticipate every stoppage of play,
So he can get to the game action right away.
To stop any problems before they arise,
And to try to get between players using his size.

He separates players when they get in a bunch,
And many times, unfortunately, steps into a punch.
Most players don't want to see him when they are fighting mad,
Except if they are losing, then suddenly they are glad.

He is severely restricted in the penalties he can call,
Even though he is probably in the best position to see them all.
This is his time to watch and learn from all that he sees,
Because he knows the "Best Linesmen think like Referees".

Charlie Lennox

That's All It Takes

He worked all day under the gun,
Then rushed to the rink, they said it would be fun.
The League had rated him one of the best,
But tonight was going to be a critical test.

He had a game plan at the start of the day,
To make the game safe for all to play.
However it became evident the players didn't care
If an opponent was injured, no respect did they share.

After the whistles, he called the glove in the face,
What the players were doing was a total disgrace.
He called hooking and slashing most of the night,
The fans couldn't believe what he was doing was right.

He kept tight control and wouldn't let go,
And without knowing it became the centre of the show.
He was ruining the game some would say,
He wouldn't let the players play.

They continued to harass him on ever call,
The players were dreadful, showed no respect at all.
The abuse was almost more then he could take,
But fortunately his confidence they did not break.

The game wore on way too long,
By the final buzzer most fans were gone.
If only they had received the message and showed they could play,
He would have backed off and stayed out of the way.

Finally the long game was over and done,
He couldn't remember who lost or who won.
He had called what was necessary in a terrible game,
And endured the abuse time and again.

Why does this happen, why do they rant and rave,
Should they not be cheering the goalkeeper's save.
The referee reacts to what he sees,
He is not there to argue or to hear pleas.

When he had showered and was leaving the rink,
He started to have doubts and it made him think.
Why does he take it and for such little pay,
Surely he can find exercise in some other way.

Then he passed a parent on his way out the door,
Her comment was something he couldn't ignore.
She said in a sincere voice that only he could hear,
"Thanks Ref, have a good year".

Charlie Lennox

It's Gone

Another season has passed and a new one to begin,
The years that have preceded are wearing within.
My old knees are sore and my back feeling stiff,
But the aches fade away at the end of the first shift.

A reliable Linesman that I've known for years,
A lot of miles between us with late nights and beers.
His partner's a Rookie who's supposed to be hot,
I see the hunger in his eyes, as I was once in his spot.

This Rookie's excitement makes me remember,
Twenty-one years ago in my first September.
With the future ahead and dreams of the show,
My presence and hard work for sure I'd be a pro.

A higher League found me and I worked quite a few seasons,
The dream still alive and yet within reason.
My opportunities were plenty and I took full advantage,
But during the big game I sustained ligament damage.

Two player collided and in an awkward fall,
I lay on the ice knowing I had lost it all.
During my rehab others got their shot,
I then fully realize that I had lost my spot.

One more year in the League and my time is done,
With the unwritten rule it will be a chance for someone.
To step back hurts as I forfeit my dreams,
But I will still officiate as part of a team.

Passion for this game is why I remain,
The Rookie on my lines one day will feel my pain.
I sincerely hope that all his goals will be met,
But having dreams come true is not a sure bet.

I will pass on to these young men all that I know,
Perhaps aiding a prospect at making the show.
Memories and friends with stories from the past,
Enjoy every game and treat it like it was your last.

Paul Jones

Where The Heck Is He?

Where in the heck could that referee be?
It's 130 am and he hasn't phoned the score to me.
Did he take the Linesmen out for a beer
To celebrate a good job late in the year?

It's 230 now the world waits on the Net,
Still no score has been phoned in yet.
Maybe the game was long and he got home late,
He'll probably phone when he gets up at eight.

I'll put in all the scores that I got
Twenty-three remembered, one did not.
No use waiting, he has gone to bed,
Phoning in the score is not in his head.

I hate to whine about the scores of a game,
But I really do need them all the same.
Everyone wants to know right away,
They don't want to wait until late in the day.

A check at 8 on extensions 0,1, 2 and 3,
Still no score has been phoned into me.
I'll have to call long distance to his home,
And hope he will answer his #*&@# telephone.

Just give me the scores that's all I ask,
So I can try to get back to sleep real fast.
Thanks to all the refs who phoned right away,
You'll live to ref another day.

Charlie Lennox

We Need Them

I've heard it said but can't agree
That hockey must get a better referee.
The kind that will in the winter wear
The helmet of black upon his hair.
Who'll run his games and make decisions
With infinite wisdom and great precisions.
Eliciting arguments from neither factions
On close plays and rule infractions.
Paragons of virtue and above reproach
Respected and admired by parents and coach.

I'm sad to say that I've got to report
We really don't want referees of that sort.
For when the game is over and done
We never believe that the best team won.
We must have someone on which to blame
Other than our sons for the loss of the game.
The referee did this but he didn't do that
He favoured the other team and more such crap.
We just can't accept that our sons didn't play
Well enough to win on that given day.

A referee knows that and accepts with a grin
The fact that you blame him when you don't win.
He rarely gets angry and just calls what he sees
You must learn to accept this from your referees.
So the next time the game is not going so great
And parents on both sides are expressing their hate.
Remember the referee just volunteered for the job
But he volunteered to referee, not to be God.

When it's over and he's skating away
Why not compliment him on his call of the play.
Tell him you appreciate the work that he's done

And if you'd played better perhaps you'd have won.
He may not believe it when he hears what you say
But it may help him feel better at the end of the day.
And in his room while he is changing his gear
He may reconsider quitting at the end of the year.
Remember it matters not a wit what we do
But we will always need a ref or two.

Author Unknown

Ralph Sparks

WHERE ARE THEY NOW?
Ralph Sparks

Ralph retired from the Etobicoke Fire Department and with his wife, Helen, moved to their winterized cottage in beautiful Muskoka in the Bracebridge area. After several years at the cottage they moved into town and bought a house in Gravenhurst.

Ralph was a Level 6 referee and he had an outstanding career as an on-ice OHA official for 37 years. He also supervised officials in Toronto and the Barrie areas and is a former GTHL Referee-in-Chief.

Ralph was selected to work the CIAU finals in Calgary in 1985 and in the same year, he represented Canada at the Izvestia Tournament in Moscow, Russia.

In 1991, Ralph received the John Blackwell Award as the Most Deserving Official. He was inducted onto the OHA's Referee Honour Roll in 1998.

Remember When With...Ralph Sparks

CL: In your long career, you must have had many difficult calls. Do you recall one in particular?

RS: I do remember having to call a penalty in triple overtime in the OCAA final game. The non-offending team scored on the power play.

CL: You often use your wife as a Goal Judge in the playoffs.

RS: Yes, she is very knowledgeable about hockey and has worked as the Timekeeper for several Junior teams.

CL: Tell us about that Senior game in Dundas.

RS: We were working a SRA game in Dundas against Cambridge when a defenseman from Cambridge fired a shot from the point that went over the net striking the glass startling the Goal Judge who flipped on the light. I blew the play dead to check on why the light had been turned on and Brian "bugsy" Crichton from Camridge started to yell some derogatory remarks about some 'broad working the light'. I quickly told him that it was my wife and without any hesitation, he came back with **"and not a bad Goal Judge either."**

CL: She had a little trouble at a U of Toronto game too?

RS: Yes, there was a scramble around the U of Toronto net and suddenly the goal light came on. I could see the red light out of the corner of my eye and since I knew the puck was not in, I blew my whistle to stop play. The Toronto goalie was yelling at me and a defenseman was rushing at me to tell me the same thing. I motioned for her to come around the boards to the door so I talk to her. I asked her why she had put the light on. She said that she had leaned forward to better see the puck and one of her "boobs" had touched the switch and the light went on. I asked her how I was going to explain that to the players. She said, "That's your problem, not mine" and closed the door.

CL: Did you ever have anyone throw anything at you?

RS: Many times, but I do remember a game in Stratford where a spectator apparently did not like one of my calls. He hurled a 26oz whisky bottle from the stands that hit the ice and slid across the width of the ice and came to rest at my feet...unbroken.

CL: Did you ever have trouble with hecklers?

RS: In Kitchener, during a game, one particular fan was giving me a hard time by coming down to the glass, yelling and screaming at me. Then he would go back to the exit and stand by a concrete wall. After one incident, a player skated up and told me to forget about it. He said he would take care of it. I said don't worry about it. Moments later, the play was in the end zone and the puck was passed back to this player at the point. He turned to face the stands and fired the puck which hit the concrete wall about 6 inches above the heckler's head. Needless to say, that fan did not bother me again.

CL: What is the Best Advice you ever received about officiating?

RS: Make sure you know the rulebook/casebook so when a situation happens in a game (which might be once in your career), you will have an answer for it.

CL: Who was the best official you ever worked with?

RS: Gord Fevreau. He was the type that could let the game go until all hell was about to break loose and then he would make one call and order was restored.

Rules Quiz #5 *(answers on page 138)*
Questions from Hockey Canada Rule Book

1. A defending player shoots the puck out over his defending blue line. It then deflects off a teammate back into his defending zone while an attacking player is in that zone. The linesman must signal a delayed off-side.

    A. True
    B. False

2. What penalty is assessed a goaltender who intentionally takes part in the play in any manner while beyond the centre red line?

    A. Major penalty
    B. Minor penalty
    C. Major plus game misconduct

3. What penalty is assessed a defenseman who deliberately knocks his goal net off its moorings with only 15 seconds remaining in a full ten minute overtime period?

    A. Minor penalty
    B. Major penalty
    C. Penalty shot
    D. Awarded goal

4. The puck is kicked by a player and then deflects off a teammate's skates and goes into the opposing goal. Does it count?

    A. Yes
    B. No

"Hey Ref, you're making a fool of yourself." Ref: "Maybe, but at least I'm getting paid to make a fool of myself."

Chapter 6

DID YOU KNOW- About the Game

First Face-off by Dropping the Puck-It wasn't until 1913 that referees began dropping the puck on face-offs? Prior to that they placed the puck between the sticks of the players facing off and yelled,"Play!"

The Official's Sweater- NHL officials have not always worn black and white vertical striped jerseys. As early as the "Roaring Twenties", a referee's jersey sported a large "R" on the front. White sweaters were donned until the 1953-54 season, when an orange jersey with black trim was introduced. This new style lasted only two and a half seasons. At a meeting of the NHL governors in December 1955, addressed concerns about that particular uniform. The orange proved to be confusing to players and fans, particularly when red uniforms were worn by either team.

Furthermore, on black and white television screens, the jersey appeared entirely black. In an attempt to solve this confusion, the NHL changed it to today's rational black and white vertical stripes. The "zebra" sweater was immediately adopted during mid-season.

The First Major Rule Change in NHL History goes on the books Jan 09, 1918, when the League removed the stipulation that a minor penalty be assessed to any goalie who leaves his feet to stop the puck.

The Goal Line-In 1903, the CAHA adopted the use of a Goal Line to help Goal Umpires determine if the puck crossed the between the posts.

Icing the Puck-On Dec08 1931, the New York Americans iced the puck 61 times during a 3-2 game at Boston. Bruins owner, Charles Adams, demanded the NHL introduce a rule calling for a face-off in the defending team's zone when it elects to shoot the puck the length of the ice to relieve the pressure. When his pleas fell on deaf ears, Boston made a mockery of its next game against the Americans, Jan03 at New York, icing the puck 87 times in a 0-0 tie. Despite the tactics, the icing rule was not adopted by the NHL until the 1937-38 season.

Minor Penalties-In the 1956-57 season the NHL introduced a rule that a player who received a minor penalty would return to the ice as soon as the opposition scored a goal. Previously, the teams spent the full two minutes short-handed which was of great benefit to the talent laden teams who often scored more than once during a minor penalty.

Helmets Needed-The Ontario Hockey Association's Junior A series ruled Thursday, October 09, 1969 to make helmets compulsory for all players next January 01. Junior B and lower divisions of the OHA already require players to wear helmets.

Did You Know- In the OHA

Lou Marsh Award-Christine Sinclair was awarded the Lou Marsh Award as Canada's Outstanding Athletic for 2012. But do know who Lou Marsh was?

He was an OHA referee from 1912 - 1934 and was selected to work the Winter Olympics in Lake Placid, New York in 1932. He also was an NHL referee and worked the 1929 playoffs.

Syl Apps Raps Rough Play-"At what point do you consider fighting a part of hockey?" asked Mr. Apps to representatives of the OHA, OMHA and the THL In 1965.

Allstars play Russians-bolstered by Bobby Orr, Andre Lacroix and Danny Grant before a crowd of 14,886 in Toronto on Dec14/65, the Russians nipped the Juniors 4-3 on a third period goal. The referee who handled the game was OHA official Blair "Bugsy" Graham.

Flyers Defeat Petes Despite Disputed Goal-Before 2,700 hometown fans in Niagara Falls in 1969, the Flyers took a narrow win despite a disputed goal by Rick MacLeish that delayed the game 20 minutes while Flyers argued with referee Bob Nadin.

OHA Secretary Manager Bill Hanley announced on Wednesday, January 23, 1967, that the OHA had approved an application from an Ottawa group for a new JrA franchise.

Tinted or Mirrored Visors are Banned –they are not CSA approved and are NOT to be worn in the OHA. It is a safety issue, especially the mirrored ones. The fear is if a player is hurt, the Trainer can't see the player's eyes without removing his helmet which is something he might not want to do.

OHA Referee Co-Ordinators over the Years

Bill Hanley	1947-1968
Larry Clark	1968-1970
Barry Fraser	1970-1974
David Branch	1974-1976
Steve Ferris	1976-1977
Brent Ladds	1977-1978
Brian Rennie	1978-1978
Garey Wilson	1978-1980
Terry Fallis	1980-1982
Neil Downs	1982-1986
Will Norris	1986-1989
Charlie Lennox	1989-2011
Bob Morley	2011-

Did You Know-In the Hall of Fame

Hall of Fame Linesmen- There are only five Linesmen in the Hockey Hall of Fame. They are: Neil Armstrong, Matt Pavelich, George Hayes, John D'Amico and Ray Scapinello. All five are OHA alumni.

Did You Know-In the IIHF

Deliberate Attempt to Injure-There is no "Deliberate Attempt to Injure" penalty in the IIHF. It is called "Excessive Rough Play" because the words "Deliberate Attempt" implies guilt in a court of law.

Did You Know- In the NHL

George Hayes Fired in 1965-The NHL fired Linesman, George Hayes for refusing to take an eye examination. Hayes an NHL Official for 19 years said it is against his principles. "I feel I should be judged by the job I do on the ice and not by some report from an eye doctor."

Stanley Cup Finals 2004-The officials for the fifth game of the 2004 Stanley Cup finals between Calgary and Tampa Bay were all members of the OHA alumni. The referees were Bill McCreary and Stephen Walkom. The linesmen were Scott Driscoll and Ray Scapinello.

Who Officiated Most Periods in 2012 Final?-In the six games between Los Angeles and New Jersey in the 2012 NHL finals, all 4 referees and all 4 linesmen were scheduled to work 3 games each or 9 periods. However Pierre Racicot was injured and Derek Amell replaced him for the third period of game 6.

Ferguson suspended in 1967-The NHL suspended Montreal Canadian forward, John Ferguson for punching Linesman Brent Casselman. He received a 3 game suspension and a $25.00 fine.

Johnny Bower Complains in 1967-Toronto Maple Leaf goaltender, Johnny Bower complains about the new rule that states a fully-dressed goaltender must be on the bench to replace the playing goalie "immediately" should he be injured. "You freeze," Bower said. "Your pads feel 10 pounds heavier and your feet go numb. You get so you can't feel a thing. I just don't feel right".

Ron MacLean refereed one NHL period of an exhibition game between Buffalo and Pittsburgh at the Mellon Arena in 2006. MacLean was paired up with Stephen Walkom, a former referee and the NHL's Senior Vice-President and Director of Officiating. (Walkom has since returned as an on-ice referee).

This was in response to MacLean being outspoken at times last year over his opposition to the NHL's crackdown on obstruction.

After the game MacLean said he used to have a problem when the referee out at centre ice made a call in the corner. MacLean now understands that the back guy has an easier time of seeing things because the game is moving a little slower and he has a wider scope.

MacLean said because of the experience, it will help him scale back some of his criticism of the new rules.

WHERE ARE THEY NOW?
Bryan Lewis

Bryan was born in Alliston, Ontario and currently resides in Georgetown with his wife Elaine. He has three children, Janelle, Duane and Alyson. He began officiating during the late 1950s. He was an OHA referee from 1962-66. He worked his first NHL game in 1970 and he ended his on-ice career after the 1985-86 season to become a member of the NHL Supervisory staff. He was appointed NHL Director of Officiating in 1989, a position he held until after the 1999-00 season. In 1989, Bryan was inducted onto the OHA's Referee Honour Roll and in June, 2009, he was awarded the OHA Gold stick.

He currently is the Referee-in-Chief of the Central Hockey League of which his son Duane is the Commissioner of the League. He is also the Referee-in-Chief of the Ontario University Association and a Supervisor for the Ontario Hockey Association.

In his spare time, Bryan is an elected councillor for the Town of Halton Hills.

Remember When with Bryan Lewis

CL: How did you get involved in officiating?

BL: I got involved in Officiating as an extra way of getting ice time to improve my skating and when we finally got paid for youth games, it was extra spending money...better than delivering papers. (I did that also).

CL: I understand you kept up your OMHA registration even while in the NHL?

BL: Yes, it was a way of getting back onto the ice in a manner to say "thank you" to an organization and town that provided me with the skills to become a professional official. To do youth games you had to have an OMHA card...so I attended their annual re-certification clinics and earned mine for many years even when I was a pro.

CL: In your long career, are there any games that stand out as highlights?

BL: I would have to say game 1,000 in the NHL. It was the only time my mother ever saw me officiate in person. I was also in a Supervisor capacity at the Winter Olympics in Nagano, Japan in 1998. The trip to entertain the troops in Kandahar, Afghanistan with other former NHL players in 2011 changed my life and I have gained the greatest repect for our troops in Afghanistan. All these events were a big thrill.

CL: What was your toughest call?

BL: My toughest calls were not on the ice. They were making decisions on releasing officials from the NHL staff. It was done with the ultimate input of the Supervisory Staff, but it still was never easy. The appeal process following was most difficult.

CL: Do you have a humourous story you could tell us?

BL: Had a fellow official tear the ass out his pants and I made him take all the face-offs for balance of the period until repairs were available. There were many off-ice fun times with/to fellow officials which will forever remain within the fraternity.

CL: Did you ever have any problems with spectator abuse?

BL: Someone put a note under my hotel room door advising me that the next time I skated out to referee in New York, I would be shot.

CL: Were you ever heckled by fans while officiating?

BL: In Amateur hockey it was, "Hey Lewis, we'll cut your tires" and "Hey Lewis, we'll put sugar in your gas tank." I always hoped they never saw where I parked my car.

CL: What do you miss about not being on the ice?

BL: Mostly the inter-reaction with players. I still get some now while doing benefit games...same players.

CL: You have always said the NHL means "No Home Life." Was that true in your case?

BL: Yes, you are definitely on the road for long stretches and you do miss many family functions. But that's the nature of the job. However, in spite of all the travel, it was still a great career path and I would do it all again.

CL: You still have a very busy schedule, Referee-in-Chief for the CHL and the OUA, supervising for the OHA, speaking engagements and Town Councillor. How is your home life any different?

BL: The difference is most of the time; I get to go home at night. It is a different set of priorities. I make every effort to attend all family events. Hockey, Politics, and Volunteering are still important, but not first.

CL: You met an important person while supervising for the ECHL in Alaska?

BL: Yes, I met and had my picture taken with Sarah Palin. We spoke re small town politics (where she started and I am). She is a hockey fan. I bought her book following the meeting.

CL: When the new playing rules were implemented several years back you pointed out that there would be a dramatically different emphasis on the rules. What were the two main points?

BL: The new rules deal with the use of the stick. The stick will not be allowed to, in any way, impede a player's progress, and; It is imperative that coaches teach the players that the stick can only be used to play the puck.

CL: You had a hand in the new positioning system with two Referees and two Linesmen.

BL: We started the 2 x 2 system in the NHL. It was designed, refined and nurtured by myself and all NHL staff members, both on and off the ice. That system is now widely accepted throughout the hockey world.

CL: Getting the OHA Gold Stick in 2009 had a special meaning for you?

BL: Yes, I was thrilled to join my late father-in-law, Dixie Beehive Owner, Howard Pallett, who was honoured in 1975 by the OHA with a Gold Stick.

CL: You must be very proud that your son and your son-in-law are both involved with Professional Hockey Leagues?

BL: I am very fortunate to have my son Duane as the Central Hockey League Commissioner and my son-in-law, Rod Pasma as Senior Manager in Hockey Operations for the National Hockey League. Some time ago our daughter Janelle worked in the Office of the Hamilton Canucks and in the PR Department (part-time) of the NHL. When family events occur, hockey is not allowed to be discussed.

CL: What officials helped you the most when you were just starting out in the NHL?

BL: I have respect for most current and former NHL officials, but one who shared all information and answered my every question as a rookie, was Art Skov. A Linesman of equal assistance was John D'Amico.

CL: In your opinion what determines a good official?

BL: A good official is determined by his strong skating skills and his ability to handle pressure. He must display good judgment on and off the ice and have a willingness to listen and accept the coaching of his Supervisors.

CL: Do you have any advice you would like to pass along to a young official?

BL: Be patient in your career development. If you are worthy of a professional career, the Pros will find you. There are no secrets. Take the coaching advice of all provided. I do not ever recall coaching or being coached to be bad.

Rules Quiz #6 *(answers on page 138)*
Questions from Hockey Canada Rule Book

1. Only one measurement of any kind will be allowed per team, per stoppage of play.

    A. True
    B. False

2. The referee has signaled a double minor penalty for spearing and the opposing team scores before play is stopped. What is the referee's call?

    A. No penalty washed out, player serves 4 minutes
    B. The double minor is washed out
    C. Goal cancelled and double minor is served
    D. Two minutes is washed. Player serves two minutes

3. Can a player slide along the ice and knock the puck off an opponent's stick prior to making contact with that player and not receive a penalty?

    A. Yes
    B. No

4. Any player or goaltender incurring a major penalty shall be assessed an automatic game misconduct and sent to the dressing room?

    A. True
    B. False

"Hey Ref, did you buy that shirt or did you win it in a Cracker Jack Box?"

Chapter 7

WORTH REPEATING...

David Branch: "There is no such thing as a Legal Head Check."

Dennis Parrish: "The ECHL is looking for people with character, not people who are characters."

Bob Nadin: "Bad habits are like a comfortable bed, easy to get into, but hard to get out of."

Dan Marouelli: "You must have a positive attitude or you will succumb to the negativity."

Terry Gregson: "The difference between the best and the rest is between the "ears."

Stephen Walkom: "Try to get along on your ability not someone else's inability."

Ryan Hutchinson: "Don't be content with AVERAGE because AVERAGE is just as close to the bottom as it is to the top."

Rob Mills: "A non-call is still a call; you've just penalized the wrong team."

Sam Sisco: "You're only as good as your next call, and don't lose any sleep over your last call."

John McCauley: "If a referee's mind wanders, he's going to be in a jackpot right away."

Bob Nadin: "There is no failure except in no longer trying."

Ken Miller: "Being a good linesman is a good but not a perfect indicator of one's ability to referee."

Bob Nadin: "Nothing makes an official feel better than having his judgment vindicated."

Ed Butler: "They may call you a bum, but you're only a bum for a moment, you can always skate away."

Bob Nadin: "You don't need to shout if you use the right words."

Bryan Lewis: "When I stepped on the ice, I was 50% wrong no matter what I did."

Bob Nadin: "Don't write a report to be understood. Write it so that it cannot be misunderstood."

George Wilson: "Work hard and if that isn't enough, work harder."

Bob Nadin: "The real fault of an official is to have faults and not try to mend them."

Scott Hutchinson: "Officiating is much like marriage...you are at least 50% wrong all the time."

Bob Nadin: "Any fool can criticize and complain, and most of them do."

Scott Hutchinson: "It is much easier to learn from the wisdom of others, than from the lack of ones own."

Bob Nadin: "Good supervision is the art of getting average people to do superior work."

Ken Miller: "Remember, longevity is not a guarantee of promotion."

Sam Sisco: "The difference between a good call and a bad call is a matter of 6 inches...the distance between your ears."

Bruce Hood: "I'm never wrong, but I can think of a thousand times that I wished my arm was cut off at the shoulder."

Ted Baker: "A referee's greatest strength develops at the point where he overcomes his greatest weakness."

Dan Marouelli: "Treat disrespect with respect."

Bob Nadin: "Officials rarely succeed unless they are having fun doing it."

Scott Hutchinson: "The best way to gain experience is to make mistakes. The best way to find yourself out of work is to keep making them."

Bob Nadin: "The best way to get the last word is to apologize."

Brain Wareham: "Do it for the kids."

Scott Hutchinson: "To be a successful official, one must learn that being in CONTROL is far more acceptable then being in POWER."

Ken Miller: "Be competitive. Tell yourself, I am not going to let this game get away from me, I am better than that."

Bob Nadin: "An official with a chip on his shoulder usually means there is more wood higher up."

Ron Wicks: "We strive for perfection; then again, we'd all like to be married to Bo Derek."

Bob Nadin: "You can often change things if you just change your attitude."

John Sullivan: "Any Referee can put players in the box, but it takes a good one to keep them out."

Bob Nadin: "One thing you can give and still keep is your word."

Scott Hutchinson: "Utilize your strengths, improve upon your weaknesses and listen to those who travelled before you."

Ken Miller: "Silence can't be misquoted."

Rick Schaly: "It's not what you call, it's what you don't call that counts."

Ken Miller: "Confidence should be like thermal underwear, it keeps us comfortable but nobody really sees it."

Ted Baker: "A good attitude requires a hockey official to be in complete control of everything above his neck."

Mickey Ion: "Remember once the puck drops, you are only sane person in the building."

Doug Hayward: "Feel for the Game is like holding a bird in your hand. If you squeeze it too tight, you will kill it. If you don't hold it tight enough, it will get away."

Pat Scarlett: "If officiating was easy, everyone would do it."

Ken Miller: "If an official wants a job where the crowd watches only him, he should get a job driving the Zamboni."

Scott Russell: "The greatest officials are the ones who escape the notoriety of the media."

WHERE ARE THEY NOW?
Bill Devorski

Bill took the "package" from the University of Guelph after 20 years and with his wife Bernie they look after the family home in Guelph. Bill retired from the OHA in 1984 after 35 years as an on-ice official. In 1989, Bill was added to the OHA Referees' Honour Roll. This award was created in 1979 to honour referees who have had International or National championships officiating experience. He was a supervisor for the OHA for 15 years. If my math is correct, that's 50 years of service to the OHA.

Remember when with ... Bill Devorski

CL: Tell us about that Sutherland Cup JrB final?

BD: It was at St Michael's arena with Sarnia as the visiting team. A brawl broke out in the third period at the players' bench while I was reporting a penalty. Before it was over there were cops all over the ice trying to break up fights. We sent the players to the dressing room for 20 minutes to cool them out. I then cleared the building and we played the last 5 minutes with no fans in the building. The police sergeant advised both teams that if there were any more fights he was going to take everyone down to the station in the "Paddy Wagon"...skates and all. There was no more trouble after that.

CL: What happened to your hat at a JrB Tournament?

BD: Somebody got my good hat from the dressing room and gave it to Dick Robinson, theSarnia JrB coach. When I went out to start for the start of the third period, he yelled, Devorski, 'If you make one more bad call I'm going to throw my hat on the ice." I replied, "You do that buster and I'll run you right....hey wait, that's **MY** hat...how did you get that?" I later learned that Pat Doherty, the then Chairman of the OHA, was having some fun with me. The coach didn't throw the hat, I didn't have to throw him out and I got my hat back.

CL: Will Norris tells a story about a rainy day in Owen Sound.

BD: We were working a Junior B game in Owen Sound and it was pouring rain outside. The puck went over the boards and I signaled for the face-off inside the blueline. One of the players came over and said, "Hey ref the face-off should be outside." I said, "Listen son, it is raining outside, we're staying inside."

CL: What is the best advice you ever received?

BD: Set your game tone early in the game and call all the high risk penalties.

CL: I understand you missed a game in Owen Sound?

BD: No I didn't, but I did drive all the way to Owen Sound on a Friday night only to find out the game was to be played on Saturday night. I marked it wrong on the calendar. I heard about that one for a long time.

CL: You worked a lot of those Detroit Tier II games?

BD: Yes, and I had some real adventures on the 401 drive home. One night we hit a snowstorm outside of Windsor and didn't get home until 7:00 am the next morning. It would have made things a lot easier if I had been smart enough to make a simple telephone call home.

Another time after a game in Detroit, the electrical system went out in my old car and I had to drive from Windsor to Guelph on the 401 with no lights. We were very fortunate there was a full moon and we never got stopped by the police.

CL: Who was the best referee you ever worked with?

BD: Hugh McLean, he had the respect of all the teams.

CL: You must be awful proud of your sons Paul and Greg in the NHL and now two grandsons, Ben and Ryan Wilson, in the OHA and OHL?

BD: I am proud of all my children and grandchildren, but it does give a great deal of pleasure to know I might have passed on some of the things I learned about officiating to them.

Rules Quiz #7 *(answers on page 138)*
Questions from Hockey Canada Rule Book

1. A player is identified as wearing his helmet and/or facial protector in an offset position during play. What action should the referee take?
   A. Instruct the player to leave the ice
   B. If this is first incident, a warning is issued to team. Any subsequent incident the player will be assessed a Misconduct
   C. Instruct the player to put his helmet/visor down
   D. Assess a minor penalty

2. Any player that incurs a total of three or more stick infractions penalties during the same game shall be ejected from the game. For the purpose of this rule, what infractions are considered stick infractions?
   A. high-sticking, spearing, slashing, crosschecking, hooking
   B. high-sticking, crosschecking, slashing, spearing, butt-ending
   C. slashing, hooking, tripping, high-sticking, spearing
   D. spearing, tripping, butt-ending, hooking, high-sticking

3. A defending player shoots the puck out over his defending blue line. It then deflects off a teammate back into his defending zone while an attacking player is in that zone. The linesman must signal a delayed off-side.
   A. True or B. False

4. A goaltender can be a team captain?
   A. Yes or B. No

"Hey Ref, I've seen better eyes on a potato."

Chapter 8

OHA MOMENTS...

Once in a Lifetime

Level VI Referee, Scott Hutchinson, had an amazing once in a lifetime playoff game on March 02, 2000. It was the fifth game of a Provincial JrA playoff series between Collingwood and Couchiching. The game went to the 19:21 mark of the third overtime period and took exactly four hours to play. The amazing thing about this game?

THERE WAS NOT ONE PENALTY CALLED IN THE ENTIRE GAME.

Pass the Plate

On January 02, 1999, referee Garey Wilson along with his two Linesmen, Bob McKellar and Scott Taylor, were assigned to a JrA game in Durham. While the game was in progress, the town was hit by a huge snowstorm. By the time the game was over, the OPP had closed all the roads out of town. Wexford, the visiting team, spent the night on their bus in the Tim Hoton's parking lot. The officiating crew was forced to spend the night in the local Anglican Church. Garey said, "It was hard sleeping on those benches but at least they didn't pass the collection plate."

Turn Out the Lights the Party's over

The 1931 OHA Intermediate series between Collingwood and Penetang was heating up. In the second game of the playoffs in Penetang, a huge fight broke out on the ice.

The Penetang arena had no end mesh or glass along the boards. Soon the fans were over the boards and there were fights everywhere. The police were called and they went on the ice in an attempt to break up the fights.

The referee, John Dobson of Barrie, had the arena staff turn off the lights, but that had little effect. Finally, he ordered the public announcer to start playing the National Anthem. This strategy worked and the fans and players began to break off their fights to stand at attention on the ice. The Anthem was played several times before everyone cleared out and order was restored.

Will It Ever End

On March 10, 1999, Pt Colborne played the St Catharines in the third game of the Golden Horseshoe JrB playoffs. The series was tied 1-1. This game started at 7:30 p.m. and ended at 2:13 a.m. after 8 periods of hockey. It is the longest recorded game in OHA history. The length of the game was 143 minutes and 47 seconds. St Catharines won the game 3-2 and went on to win the series 4-1.

Regular | Overtime
20 +20 +20 + 10 +20 +20 +20 +13:47

The referee was Steve Webb. The Linesmen were Todd Coopman and Jay Warren. The OHA paid all three officials an additional game fee for this super effort.

The longest game in hockey history was played March 24, 1936 between Detroit and Montreal Marons at the Forum. It lasted 176 minutes and 30 seconds.

Another Interesting Game

Veteran referee, **Bob Bell**, of Picton had an interesting JrC playoff game on March 17, 2007 between Colborne Cobras and the Amherstview Jets. He was required to call four (4) Penalty Shots, 3 of them were in overtime. Three were called against Amherstview and one against Colborne. No goals were scored on any of the Penalty Shots.

Amherstview won the game in the 3rd overtime period to make the series 3-2 in favour of Colborne. Amherstview went on to win the next 2 games to take the series 4-3 after being down 0-2.

Longest OHA Game

On February 11th, 2007, Toronto JR Canadians played the Pickering Panthers in the 2nd game of the Provincial JrA first round of playoffs. The game started at 730pm and finished at 140am with a goal in the 6th period of overtime. It is believed to be the longest recorded game in OHA history. The length of the game was 154 minutes and 32 seconds. This surpassed the March 10, 1999 game in a JrB playoff game in Pt Colborne that lasted 143 minutes and 47 seconds.

20 + 20 +20 + 10 + 20 + 20 + 20 + 20 + 4.32

The referee for this game was **Rob Padt** and his Linesmen were **Tom Jukes** and **Nial Smith**. The OHA also paid all three of these officials an additional game fee for the super effort.

Steve Baker...Thanks

In the third period of a JR Development game Thursday, November 25, 2004, between Lambeth and Thamesford, a Lambeth player was injured. He was in fact about to receive a penalty for hooking. As the penalty was being called both players flipped to the ice. The Lambeth player went to his players' bench seeming not knowing he was penalized. When told, he went quietly to the penalty box. Play resumed for about six seconds before the Lambeth bench got the referee's attention about the player in the penalty box. The referee, Steve Baker, who is a fireman by profession, immediately went over to see the player. He learned the player had some pain at the base of his neck and was disoriented. Steve sat with the player in the penalty box for 45 minutes while the E.M.S. people were summoned. Steve was clearly the ranking person in the building during the interim and he fulfilled his/our responsibility with his normal professionalism.

It is important in these situations to have professional, well trained people that know exactly what is needed in providing the right care at the right time for the players.

As the referee in charge the OHA wants to commend Steve for the care and compassion he demonstrated towards the injured player.

A Positive Story Surrounding a Tragic Event

This is a great example of two OHA officials that gave it their best in a tragic situation.

On Sunday Jan11, 2009, James Bradshaw from Guelph had picked up fellow official Jim Brudz in Brantford. They were on their way to a 200pm OHA JrC game in Norwich, when they came upon an accident scene, involving a SUV and a snowmobile. They were approximately 30 seconds behind the accident and first ones on the scene. They stopped their vehicle to aid in any way they could. With training through S.C. Johnson in Brantford, Jim Brudz provided CPR to the victim and tried his best along with another person to attempt to revive the accident victim until emergency crews arrived.

The willingness to stop and help a seriously injured accident victim, who later passed on in the hospital, takes great courage and knowledge to try to help in an intense pressure situation.

Even though this recognition does not involve a hockey game directly, the OHA and all of its members should be proud of the two officials who came to the aid of a person in need.

OHA Officiating First

An OHA first happened last Tuesday, Jan25, 2005, when a female official work the lines in an OHA JrA game. The game between Syracuse and Bancroft had been rescheduled and the office was not notified of the new date. A frantic General Manager was advised he could use minor hockey officials if both teams would agree to it. They did and signed the game sheet to indicate their approval. After a hurry-up search the following officials worked the game.

Bob Vance, a former Level III was the referee and **Barb Stewart** (a current Level III) and Brent Anderson worked the Lines. The game went well with no major incidents. The OHA sent a letter to each official thanking them for helping us out in an emergency.

Referee's Sweater Makes Hall of Fame -09

The sweater of former OHA official and Ayr Centennial Hockey player, Steve Cruickshank, has made its way into the Canadian Hockey Hall of Fame in Toronto.

Forty-one year old Steve Cruickshank, who grew up on a farm in Paris, Ontario had his sweater placed into the Hockey Hall of Fame as he is the longest tenured referee in the Central Hockey League.

Late last year, Steve officiated in his 900th game in the CHL and hopes to officiate1000 games before hanging up his whistle for retirement.

The entry in the Hall of Fame displays the referee jersey he wore during games two and five of the 2007 CHL Ray Miron President's Cup championship series between Laredo Bucks and Colorado Eagles.

Steve, who owns a home in North Little Rock, Arkansas, travels extensively in the United States officiating games. He visits his home area in the summer.

He played minor hockey in Paris and later joined the Centennials. He was an aggressive and skilled player who was a top scorer in his youth. He was a strong skater which makes him a good on-ice official. His refereeing career began in Paris when he as close to 20 years old. He joined the Ontario Hockey Association in 1990 and left to join the CHL in 1997.

Congrats T.J. Luxmore

Hockey Canada is pleased to announce today, April 26, 2007, the awarding of scholarships to seven top young officials in Canada. The scholarship program, the first of its kind in amateur sport, was initiated by the founding ownership group of the NHLs Calgary Flames, with a goal of enhancing officiating at all levels of the game in Canada.

The Ken Stiles Officiating Scholarship Awards were announced by the Calgary Flames founding ownership group, named for the late Ken Stiles, a President of the Flames Project 75.

Congratulations to OHA Official, T.J. Luxmore on his scholarship award.

Scott Oakman in China

OHA Level 6 referee Scott Oakman was given an opportunity of a lifetime when Bob Nadin asked him if he would be willing to go to China to officiate at the Chinese Winter Games. Scott accepted and was flown to Harbin, North China. They paid all his expenses, took him on tours and he got to referee the championship final. Here is his report:

It was great. They treated me like a king. The hockey was slightly higher quality then top end University hockey. It was faster and much more physical than I expected. For instance in the championship game I called 4 boarding penalties and 2 elbowing penalties. The two teams in the final were made up of all the Men's national team, essentially a 50-50 split in players. The other obvious difference was that on every infraction, the player stayed down like he was injured. Even on penalties like holding. It was really bizarre. The players never argued for a major penalty, no trainer would come out, but the player would stay down for several minutes while his team-mates stood over him, then they would eventually pick him up and help him off the ice.

The crowd was also very different. The arena probably had double number of people then the actual capacity of the arena was designed for but for most of the game you could hear a pin drop. The only time there was cheering or noise was when the host team would move the puck up the ice over centre and into the attacking zone for a scoring opportunity. Once that scoring opportunity ended, the crowd went silent, and I mean silent, until the next rush up the ice.

I was able to visit the Great Wall, Tiananmen Square and the Ancient Forbidden Palace. The food was a bit of a challenge but we found a pizza place the second day so I ate there as much as I could.

Thanks to Bob Nadin for giving me this tremendous opportunity which I enjoyed immensely.

Mike Pearce Reports on his trip to Turkey

When Michael Pearce became a hockey official, he didn't suspect an atlas would someday be as handy as his rulebook.

The longtime referee from Chatham begins working Thursday at the World University Games in Erzurum, Turkey.

He didn't even know hockey was played there when the International Ice Hockey Federation came calling.

"When I first got the assignment, I didn't think they had snow," he said.

It turns out Erzurum has the highest elevation in Turkey, approximately 2,000 metres above sea level. The temperature was expected to dip to -14 C on Wednesday.

Pearce's first assignment from the IIHF was also in an unlikely locale. In 2004, he called games at the Mexican national championship in Mexico City.

"Turkey's not a place I would probably go on my own," he said. "I've been to a few places around the world, but it's certainly a unique opportunity. I look forward to the officiating challenge but also visiting a few sites."

I returned home yesterday from the World University Games in Erzurum, Turkey.

The trip was awesome. I worked 10 games in 11 days. It was a heavy schedule as we were also stand-by officials for games and we only had one day off. I worked two extra games in the tournament: one referee fell sick in the preliminary round, and another was injured 5 minutes into his quarter-final game between Canada/Slovakia. I skated the rest of his game and then my scheduled quarter-final game between Russia/Czech Republic right after. The Russia/Czech game was a notable game that resulted in 340 minutes in penalties including 6 match penalties. Four players were banned from the remainder of the tournament. The IIHF supervisor put on my supervision sheet that it was the "game of the year". It generated a lot of talk, but the supervisors were very happy how it was handled. Andrew Hubbard and I were given the gold medal game between Russia and Belarus. Russia won 1-0. Canada won bronze, beating Kazakhstan.

I met a lot of great people and thoroughly enjoyed myself. Turkey is not somewhere I would have likely visited on my own, so it was a fantastic opportunity to see their culture. I now have friends in Finland, Sweden, Turkey, and Slovakia.

The World University Games bring together athletes from 58 countries playing 11 sports. They're held every two years.

WHERE ARE THEY NOW?
Craig Spada

Craig was born in Welland, Ontario and grew up in Ridgeway, Ontario. He officiated in the OHA from 1994-2001 and joined the OHL in 1998 until 2001. He obtained his Level 6 Certification in 2001 at a Hockey Canada Clinic in Halifax. Craig received the Ivan Locke Award in 1999 as the OHA's Most Improved Official. In 2001, he was signed to an AHL/NHL contract. He worked his first NHL game Mar 22, 2002 in Detroit with Blaine Angus and Linesmen Darren Gibbs and Lyle Seitz.

In 2003, he became one of only 32 full-time NHL Referees. It meant a lot of work, including long stretches of travel away from his wife, Allison, and two children, which is always tough on a young family.

Remembering with Craig Spada

CL: Looking back, how did you get involved in officiating?

CS: After I finished playing, I wanted to stay involved in the game so I thought I would try officiating.

CL: In your officiating career, are there any games that stand out as highlights?

CS: In 2003, I did the game 7 final in Hamilton when Houston Aeros defeated the Hamilton Bulldogs to win the Calder Cup. Game sevens are always exciting.

CL: What was the toughest game you ever refereed?

CS: Two come to mind. One would be an AHL game that broke all the AHL penalty records and then there was a semi final OHL game Barrie at Sudbury that was extremely aggressive.

CL: What was your toughest call?

CS: I guess it would be the missed call when Matt Sundin threw his broken stick into the crowd. It made all the papers and we were even fined by the League.

CL: Do you have any humourous stories you could tell us?

CS: Some of the OHA boys after the above missed call stuck about 10-12 broken sticks in my front lawn. It was very funny.

CL: As a young NHL referee did you feel any extra pressure as a referee at that level?

CS: It's a pretty intense job and It puts a different prospective on officiating than when you're doing it as a hobby. You're getting paid to make sure things go properly, but you are able to train full-time and, mentally it became easier.

CL: What was the best fan heckle you ever heard?

CS: I recall as I was skating off the ice a fellow official said to me about a heckling fan, "Did you bring your dad again?"

CL: What do you miss about not being on the ice?

CS: I don't really miss being on the ice at all but, I miss the guys and the conversations.

CL: In your opinion what determines a good official?

CS: Best I ever heard it described is, "A great official is made not born." So I would say it comes down to experience.

CL: You have always had your Real Estate License?

CS: Yes, When I realized there wouldn't be a NHL season in 2004, I returned to being a Real Estate Agent in Fort Erie, something I always did in addition to the officiating. I've have had my real estate license since I was 19 and I always kept it up, so it was nice to have that to fall back on.

CL: During the NHL Lockout you did some Supervising for the OHA?

CS: Yes, I would watch them officiate a game and then give them some constructive feedback on their performance. I was basically coaching the officials. Guys did it for me, so it was a good opportunity to give back. I would never be where I am if it wasn't for good coaching, just like any hockey player. I think we have some quality Referees and Linesmen in the Niagara area."

CL: Do you have any advice for young Linesmen?

CS: Just remember; "**The best Linesmen think like Referees.**"

Craig retired from the NHL in 2007 after five years and 247 games and returned to his Real Estate career. He rejoined the OHA Officiating Program as a Supervisor for the 2012-13 hockey season.

Rules Quiz # 8 *(answers on page 138)*
Questions from Hockey Canada Rule Book

1. After a line change, the Linesman drops the puck to start play. Immediately the Referee notices that one team has too many players on the ice. What course of action should the Referee take?

    A. Stop play immediately and assess a Bench Minor penalty.
    B. Stop play immediately, no penalty.
    C. Let play continue
    D. Blow play down and assess a Minor penalty

2. How long does the home team have to initiate a line change after the Referee has raised his arm?

    A. No change would be allowed
    B. 5 seconds
    C. 10 seconds
    D. 15 seconds

3. Can a player on the ice carry two sticks so that he can give one to a teammate who has lost or broken his stick?

    A. No
    B. Yes

4. A player loses his helmet while play is in progress. Before replacing the helmet, he participates in the play. The referee shall:

    A. Signal a delayed penalty and assess a minor penalty.
    B. Stop play immediately and assess minor for ineligible player.
    C. Stop play and allow the player to pick up his helmet.

"Hey Ref, if your IQ was any lower, you'd trip over it."

Chapter 9

MORE "WORTH REPEATING"

"Everyone can make a mistake; to repeat it depicts a lack of intelligence."

"The reward of a thing well done; is to have done it."

"Competent officials have confidence in themselves and their abilities."

"By the time a man finds greener pastures, he might not be able to climb the fence."

"Life is just mind over matter. If you don't mind, it doesn't matter."

"If you spend your whole life waiting for the storm you'll never enjoy the sunshine."

"Common sense, judgment and discretion used correctly will lead to the proper level of acceptability."

"When we focus on solving problems, we avoid placing blame."

"Nothing will ever be attempted if all objections must first be overcome."

"Competition doesn't create character; it exposes it."

"Consistency results from applying a uniform rule interpretation to each separate competitive action."

"Do what you love, love what you do, and try to give back more than you offered."

"Confident officials remain in control during adversity."

"Only the man who is ready to help has the right to criticize."

"When all else fails; try thinking."

"Don't let your peers set your standards; be yourself."

"Obstacles are things a person sees, when he takes his eyes off his goal."

"Most people will agree with you if you just keep quiet."

"The hardest thing to learn in life is which bridge to cross over and which to burn."

"Most referees say that they did not see; when in fact they weren't even looking."

"Good officiating requires a lot of hard work, dedication and practice."

"The trouble with referees is that they just don't care which team wins."

"Nothing is as self-blinding as being self-righteous."

"If you keep doing what you have been doing; you will keep getting what you have been getting."

"The most profitable development of all is self-development."

"Decisiveness requires good concentration skills and proper focus attention."

"The road to success is always under construction."

"There must not only be control; it must seem to be there."

"The quieter you become, the more you can hear.

"The most effective command is the one made to sound like a request."

"No one can make you feel inferior without your consent."

"It's not what you know that gets you into trouble. It's what you think you know; that isn't so."

"Consistency results from applying a uniform rule interpretation to each separate competitive action."

"The mind is like a parachute, it works best when it's open."

"The greatest mistake a man can make is to be afraid of making one."

"You learn the rules by study; and the exceptions to the rules by experience."

"You will never know what you can do unless you attempt what you think you can't do."

"If you don't believe in yourself, chances are that nobody else will."

"Integrity refers to calling a game in an unbiased, honest manner regardless of the reactions of players, coaches or spectators."

"Listen to others but make up your own mind."

"Your self-worth must be stronger than anyone's rejection."

"The difference between genius and stupidity is there are limits on genius."

"Put brain in gear before opening mouth."

"Don't be afraid to go out on a limb; that's where the fruit is."

"A professional is someone who can do his best work when he doesn't feel like it."

"Tact is knowing how far is too far to go."

"Negative thinking is mental malpractice."

"When you're in a hole; stop digging."

"Understanding does not necessarily mean agreement."

"There is never too much communication in a hockey game, the problem lies with too much at one time."

"If you can accept that you are okay the way you are, then you can stop trying to prove you're okay."

"Good judgment begins with a thorough and complete understanding of the rules."

"You can only reason someone out of what they have been reasoned into."

"Respect cannot be demanded, or bought: it must be earned."

"Don't let what you can't do interfere with what you can do."

"If you make the decision, your subconscious will make the provision."

"Everything a referee does becomes a part of his officiating image and his total image is often the determining factor for acceptability."

WHERE ARE THEY NOW?
Mel Huctwith

Mel Huctwith has been a Supervisor of Officials in the London area since 1979. He became a member of the OHA Referees' Honour Roll in 1990 and was awarded the President Certificate for Excellence in 2006. Mel is a former school teacher and put together the following guideline for game control.

1. A referee should consider the possible advantage of anticipating the nature of the game he is preparing to officiate. This can be done without forcing an outcome.

2. Early in the game the referee should be aware that he is establishing his definition for that game via call selection; i.e. rule emphasis/level, etc.

3. The best definition guide is reflected in the advice. Do not get any farther into a game than you are prepared to stay all night. There is no different weighting for goals scored in the first period as compared to the third, why should there be any different level of judgment relating to penalties?

4. In our higher levels of hockey the most useful definition line will be the difference between play and non-play actions. We must work to remove the latter from our game. Non-play actions are best summarized as actions likely to Injure, cheat, embarrass some other participant in the game.

5. In lower levels of competition the definition line will be the difference between low-skilled and low-focused actions. In addition to the earlier questions, perhaps

the guiding questions could be. What was the player trying to do? What did he do? What was the consequence of his action? Generally a correct call will involve a strong Yes to one of these questions and a partial Yes to one of the others.

6. High-risk infractions are never to be considered as possible non-call traders. Players and coaches will not accept this type of non-call, nor should they be expected to.

7. If the game has coaching staffs of extremely different philosophies/capabilities, it is unlikely that we can safely involve ourselves in deliberate non-calls.

8. If a team has opened up a wide score differential that score differential may well lead the referee to re-state his definition, within the earlier one.

9. It is critical that the referee maintain his control function to the end of the game. He must be in a position to call infractions against either team equally with the expectation that those calls will improve the operation of the game, and that these calls are necessary and appropriate, as seen by an objective third party.

10. As a referee grows into his function, his game-to-game definition becomes his reputation. It is important, however, that our veterans do not begin to substitute their reputation for good definition. When an official begins riding his number, his game operation will soon start to deteriorate.

Mel retired as a supervisor in 2006 and lives with his wife in London.

Rules Quiz # 9 *(answers on page 138)*
Questions from Hockey Canada Rule Book

1. A goaltender deliberately removes his helmet during the course of a Penalty Shot. What is the Referee's call?

    A. Penalty Shot over plus Minor penalty
    B. Penalty Shot over plus Misconduct penalty to Goaltender
    C. Penalty shot over plus Gross Misconduct to Goaltender
    D. Award a goal

2. Team A ices the puck. The goaltender from Team B comes out of his crease to potentially play the puck, but decides not to play the puck. The linesman must signal icing.

    A. True or B. False

3. A player who has been awarded a penalty shot is also assessed a Match penalty on the same play. How does the Referee handle this?

    A. No penalty shot and assessed Match
    B. Player can take Penalty Shot then leave
    C. Player not allowed Penalty Shot but any other player can take it
    D. Player not allowed Penalty Shot, Captain shall designate player on the ice.

4. When shall the Referee blow his whistle when he has signaled a delayed penalty?

    A. When the offending team touches the puck
    B. When the official's arm get tired
    C. When the offending team gains possession and control of the puck.

"Hey Ref, You must be pregnant, you have already missed two periods."

Chapter 10

MORE HECKLES...

Officiating can be very rewarding and a lot of fun and, it has its challenges. Yes, appearance, skating and attitude are important to being successful, but the most important ingredient is a thorough and complete understanding of the rules. If you don't know the rules you are going to make mistakes. When you make mistakes everyone gets upset. Players, coaches, parents and fans will make life miserable for you and you will get heckled.

There are penalties for players and coaches who heckle an official, but there is not much you can do when a fan waits until it is all quiet and then in a loud voice comes out with a one liner. Some hecklers are actually funny and some are disgusting. It is a definite form of harassment but like it or not, if you are going to be an official, you are going to hear it.

Perhaps if you see it here or at the beginning of each chapter, it won't bother you when you hear it on the ice. It is all in good fun.

We have included some more of our best heckles here for your enjoyment.

Hey Ref, *you're denying your village of its idiot.*

Hey Ref, *how does someone get to be a referee with no brains and no talent.*

Hey Ref, *I am captivated by your delusions of adequacy.*

Hey Ref, *I like you, you remind me of when I was young and stupid.*

Hey Ref, *I looked up "stupid" in the dictionary and your picture was there.*

Hey Ref, *I think you have been working with glue too much.*

Hey Ref, *you mind is as sharp as a marble.*

Hey Ref, *bring your mom and dad next game and I'll marry them at centre ice.*

Hey Ref, *5,000 refs quit each year and you are one who chose to stay.*

Hey Ref, *do you still get mileage if you go home on their bus.*

Hey Ref, *don't wake up, I've got a bet on you.*

Hey Ref, *even your dog thinks you're an idiot.*

Hey Ref, *how can a know-it-all be so incredibly stupid?*

Hey Ref, *if you had another eye, you would be a Cyclops.*

Hey Ref, *if you were a building, you'd be condemned.*

Hey Ref, *I heard you started working out, but I guess you gave it up.*

Hey Ref, *put your arm up if you're an idiot (just prior to a line change).*

Hey Ref*, take your sweater back to Foot Locker.*

Hey Ref, *If I knew you were coming, I'd have set the arena on fire.*

Hey Ref, *I love what you have done with your hair. How did you get it to come out of your nose like that?*

Hey Ref, *we don't have to go home for turkey, we have one right here on the ice.*

Hey Ref, *you mind me of a toothache I once had.*

Hey Ref, *you weren't blind last night, what happened on the way home?*

Hey Ref*, you won't need a nap tonight, you've been asleep since the second period.*

Hey Ref, *You know I paid to watch you officiate.*

Ref: *Yes and I have it right here (slaps his wallet).*

Hey Sparks, *the brightest thing about you is your name.*

WHERE ARE THEY NOW?
Matt Pavelich

On behalf of the OHA Board of Directors and the Referee Executive Committee, OHA Referee-in-Chief, Gary Moroney, announced the retirement of Windsor Area Supervisor, Matt Pavelich at the end of the 2012-13 season.

The Windsor native began officiating at the age of 14 in minor hockey before being named Referee-in-Chief of the Northern Michigan Intermediate League.

Pavelich worked in the American Hockey League in 1955-56 before making the leap to the NHL the following year. During his 31 years on the ice, Matt worked an amazing 1,727 regular season games and 245 playoff games. He also was selected to be a linesman in 9 NHL All-Star games.

When Matt retired he ranked second only to Neil Armstrong in regular season games worked and his 245 playoff games ranked second behind John D'Amico.

After he left the ice, Matt became an NHL Supervisor of Officials. In 1987, he was the first Linesman ever to be inducted into the Hockey Hall of Fame.

Matt joined the OHA Supervisory Staff for the 1994-1995 season and was inducted onto the OHA's Referee Honour Roll in 1996.

Clearly an accomplished Official himself, Matt might be most proud of his work with young Officials, helping many to reach their goals in the OHA, OHL and Professional Leagues throughout North America.

Matt was honoured by the Great Lakes Jr. C League on January 13, 2012, prior to the Junior C game between Belle River and Essex. He was recognized by the League for his service as an OHA supervisor of officials over the past 12 years.

"I don't recognize the game," Pavelich said. "Because of all the equipment technology and the size of the players, I see kids shooting the puck harder in Junior C now than some NHLers did back then."

CL: You always enjoyed the fans. What was the best heckle you heard?

MP: There was a guy in Boston who would yell, "Hey Pavelich, we named a town after you. Marblehead!"

CL: In all your years in the NHL, who would be your choice as the best referee?

MP: Without a doubt, Andy Van Hellemond had the best feel for the game of any referee that I ever worked with. He was always in tune and control. The teams had faith and trust in his standard. There were never any surprises in the way he was going to call a game.

Although retired, Matt is still in demand as a referee for NHL Alumni Old-Timers' games across the country.

Rules Quiz #10 *(answers on page 138)*
Questions from Hockey Canada Rule Book

1. What would happen if a second puck was thrown on the ice while play was in progress?

    A. Play stopped immediately
    B. Play continue until a stoppage
    C. Play continue but stopped if it became mixed up with real game puck

2. When a team calls for a timeout, why does the Linesman put the puck down on the ice?

    A. To keep his hand from freezing
    B. So the players will know where the face-off will take place after the timeout.
    C. To keep the puck from getting warm and not sliding properly when play continues.
    D. All of the above

3. Can a goalkeeper use a broken stick as long as it is not dangerous?

    A. Yes
    B. No

4. The puck is shot by an attacking player and deflects off the crossbar and goes out of bounds. Where does the face-off take place?

    A. At the either corner face-off dots
    B. At centre ice
    C. At the neutral zone face-off dot of the defending team
    D. At the neutral zone face-off dot of the attacking team.

"Hey Ref, if you were any dumber, you'd have to be watered twice a day."

Chapter 11

OFFICIATING AWARDS

The **"Hugh McLean Award"** was created in 1990 to be presented annually to the Most Promising Official in the OHA.

1990	Scott Driscoll,	Seaforth
1991	Bob Hooper,	Stoney Creek
1992	Ryan Renaud,	Belle River
1993	Kevin Pollock,	Kincardine
1994	Steve Cathcart,	Toronto
1995	Ken Gallagher,	Brantford
1996	Brent Pye,	Essex
1997	Allan Madill,	Creemore
1998	Wes McCauley,	Georgetown
1999	Kevin Hastings,	Aurora
2000	Dan Kordic	Mississauga
2001	Todd Dawdy	Ridgeway
2002	Jason Goldenberg	Markham
2003	Ryan Lachine	Windsor
2004	Brett Punchard	Scarborough
2005	Ross Bain	Toronto
2006	Matt Traub	Thornhill
2007	Joe Monette	Belle River
2008	Drew Williams	Thorold
2009	Korey Bannerman	Barrie
2010	Jesse Wilmot	Hamilton
2011	Kyle Flood	Essex
2012	Justin Knaggs	Brooklyn
2013	Justin Herrington	Holland Landing

The **"John Blackwell Award"** was created in 1990 to be presented annually to the Most Deserving Official in the OHA

1990	Rick Singleton,	London
1991	Ralph Sparks,	Weston
1992	Bob Morley,	Hamilton
1993	John Willsie,	London
1994	Cam Rundle,	Brighton
1995	Gus Bambridge,	Cobourg
1996	Jim Harwood,	Toronto
1997	Brad Fagan,	Guelph
1998	Ron Maclean,	Oakville
1999	Bill Beveridge,	Petrolia
2000	Ken Bannerman	Barrie
2001	Brent Thompson	Bowmanville
2002	Al Detlor	Stirling
2003	Rob Anderson	Strathroy
2004	John Searle Jr	St George
2005	Steve Baker	London
2006	Wayne Tmbers	Aurora
2007	Steve Gould	London
2008	Dave Regan	Kingston
2009	Darcy Burchel I	Hamilton
2010	Glen McBryde	Morriston
2011	Mike Pearce	Chatham
2012	Pete Kostyk	Niagara Falls
2013	Darren Purnell	Stoney Creek

The **"Ivan Locke Award"** was created in 1990 to be presented annually to the Most Improved Official in the OHA.

1990	Don VanMassenhoven,	Strathroy
1991	Bob Beatty,	Kitchener
1992	Lee Rodgers,	Orangeville
1993	Kevin Leaman,	Woodbridge
1994	Steve Miller,	Stratford
1995	John Stephenson,	Streetsville

1996	Darryl Dawson,	Oshawa
1997	Dave Wright,	Mississauga
1998	Scott Hutchinson,	Alliston
1999	Craig Spada,	Ridgeway
2000	Bill Waye,	London
2001	Sean McQuigge	Alliston
2002	Greg Campbell	Windsor
2003	Chris Hodgins	Markham
2004	Rob Palm	Newmarket
2005	Steve Percy	Sarnia
2006	Brent Holdsworth	Hamilton
2007	Kendrick Nicholson	Sauble Beach
2008	Dave Lewis	Pickering
2009	Tim Cox	Chatham
2010	T.J. Luxmore	Waterloo
2011	Ben Wilson	Guelph
2012	Tyson Orlie	Toronto
2013	Pat Myers	Thorold

The "**Jack Clancy Award**" was created in 1980 in the memory of OHA Supervisor, Jack Clancy and is presented annually to the OHA official who demonstrates a dedicated and responsible attitude towards his duties and the Association.

1980	Ian Huffman,	Toronto
1981	Frank Robinson,	Kingston
1982	Bob Good,	Kitchener
1983	George Boorman,	Barrie
1984	Ivan Bryce,	Watford
1985	unknown	
1986	Allan Dawe,	Aurora
1987	Pascall Zaitz,	Markdale
1988	Gary Kipfer,	Brampton
1989	Ken Bannerman,	Barrie
1990	Brian Marshall,	Hamilton
1991	Jim Hawthorne,	Ridgetown
1992	Dave Wedlake,	Pickering
1993	Larry Baxter,	Burlington

1994 Bob Clifford, Leamington
1995 Kalvin Forrest, Wainfleet
1996 Ken Harris, Kingston
1997 Jim Maitland, Sarnia
1998 Dave Davey, Hagersville
1999 Bob Morley, Hamilton
2000 Garey Wilson Toronto
2001 Rob Reid Pt Dover
2002 Dave Stortz Welland
2003 Doug Crawford Chatsworth
2004 Bill MacAlpine Brigden
2005 Sean McQuigge Alliston
2006 Bob Bell Picton
2007 Steve Stasiuk Stoney Creek
2008 Ed Munroe Toronto
2009 Ray McManus London
2010 Jonathan Wallace Toronto
2011 Steve Brown Oshawa
2012 Walter Araujo Brampton
2013 Greg Campbell Essex

Officials who were Awarded OHA Gold Stick

2009 Bryan Lewis, Georgetown
2006 Gary Moroney, Aurora
1994 Ivan Locke, Oshawa
1993 Larry Clark, Scarborough
1984 Bob Nadin, Toronto
1984 Ross Magnus, Toronto
1980 Hugh McLean, London
1977 Frank Slota, Kitchener
1958 Dinty Moore, Pt Colborne
1947 Fred C. Waghorne, Toronto

Officials who were Awarded OHA Crystal Puck

2012 Frank Robinson, Oshawa
2009 Charlie Lennox, Oakville

OHA Referees Honour Roll

This award was created in 1979 to honour referees who had International or National Championship officiating experience such as the Memorial Cup, Centennial Cup, Allan Cup, the Olympics or any OHA official who has ten years experience and then progresses on to the NHL. All of the criteria is to be maintained at the discretion of the OHA Referee's Executive Committee prior to selection.

2007 Stephen Walkom, North Bay
2005 Ken Bannerman, Barrie
2005 Bob Morley Hamilton
1998 Ralph Sparks, Toronto
1996 Terry Gregson, Elora
1996 Matt Pavelich, Windsor
1996 Sam Sisco, Windsor
1990 Mel Huctwith, London
1990 Will Norris, Guelph
1989 John McCauley, Georgetown
1989 Bryan Lewis, Georgetown
1989 Bill Devorski, Guelph
1989 Frank Chase, Welland
1989 Jim Lever, Toronto
1984 Art Casterton, Kingston
1984 Vern Goyer, Belleville
1982 Frank Slota, Kitchener
1981 Bob Nadin, Toronto
1980 Gord Fevreau, Oakville
1980 Blair Graham, Oakville
1980 Gerry Olinski, Kitchener
1979 Lou Maschio, Guelph
1979 Hugh McLean, London

Officiating Achievement Recognition

The following OHA officials have been recognized as having achieved the highest Level in Amateur Hockey officiating across Canada. They have achieved a Level VI standing in the Hockey Canada Officiating Program.

This program was started back in 1973 and its purpose was to prepare referees to officiate at National Championships and designated IIHF Competitions (Memorial Cup, Royal Bank Cup, Allan Cup, Hardy Cup, CIS University Cup, CCAA finals, World Championships, and the Olympics).

The Ontario Hockey Association is proud to recognize their achievement.

Angus, Blaine: Burchell, Darcy; Ball, Norm; Bannerman, Ken; Brown, Tom, Carroll, Ryan; Constant, Guy; Dawe, Al; Dawson, Darryl; Emerson, Dan; Ferguson, Scott; Foster, Tim; Foster, T.J; Gauthier, Cliff; Gauthier, Dave; Graham, Blair; Hawthorne, Jim; Hobor, Terry; Holdsworth, Brent; Houston, Jim; Hutchinson, Scott; Kimmerly, Greg; Kostyk, Peter; LeBlanc, Jim; Lever, Jim; Lewis, Dave; Lucas, Mike; Lynch, Dave; Luxmore, TJ; Marley, Mike; McQuigge, Sean; Miller, Ken; Morley, Bob; Morphew, Rick; Nadin, Bob; Nicholson, Kendrick; Oakman, Scott; Ogilvie, Dave; Park, Joe; Pearce, Mike; Peel, Tim; Pollock, Clarke, Proctor, Sandy; Reid, Sean; Regan, Dave; Robb, Doug; Schaly, Rick; Singleton, Rick; Spada, Craig; Sparks, Ralph; Stephenson, John; Van Massenhoven, Don; Walkom, Stephen; Warren, Dean; Wiffen, Steve; Willsie, John; Winter, Justin; Wright, Dave.

IIHF World Championship Assignments

The following is a list of current and former OHA officials who were selected to officiate at IIHF World Championships. Note: Hugh MacLean was a NHL/OHA referee, the CAHA Referee-in-Chief and later the OHA President 1976-1978. Also Dinty Moore was the OHA President from 1942-1945. Lou Marsh was an OHA/NHL Referee and the Outstanding Canadian Athletic of the Year is currently awarded in his name. Lou Marsh officiated every game in the 1932 Olympics.

LAST FIRST	YEAR	EVENT	POSITION	GAMES
AMELL, Derek	2004	WCH	Linesman	4
ANGUS, Blaine	1991	WM20	Referee	5
BELL, Bob	1990	WM	Linesman	8
BROWN, Tom	1975	WM	Referee	9
BURCHELL, Darcy	2009	WM18	Referee	6
BURCHELL, Darcy	2010	WM20	Referee	6
BURCHELL, Darcy	2011	WM	Referee	9
CAMERON, Lonnie	1994	OG-M	Linesman	7
CARMAN, Jim	1992	OG-M	Linesman	9
D'AMICO, John	1981	CC	Linesman	5
D'AMICO, John	1984	CC	Linesman	7
D'AMICO John	1987	CC	Linesman	8
DEVORSKI, Greg	2004	WCH	Linesman	6
DEVORSKI, Paul	2004	WCH	Referee	6
DEVORSKI, Paul	2006	OG-M	Referee	5
DEVORSKI, Paul	2010	OG-M	Referee	5
DRISCOLL, Scott	1996	WCH	Linesman	4
EMERSON, Dan	1986	WM20	Linesman	7
FINN, Ron	1981	CC	Linesman	3
FINN, Ron	1984	CC	Linesman	4
FINN, Ron	1987	CC	Linesman	6
FRASER, Kerry	1996	WCH	Referee	5
FRASER, Kerry	1998	OG-M	Referee	6

FRIDAY, Bill	1976	CC	Referee	2
GRAHAM, Blair	1977	WM20	Referee	5
GREGSON, Terry	1982	WM	Referee	6
GREGSON, Terry	1996	WCH	Referee	5
HOBOR, Terry	2004	WM18	Referee	4
HOOD, Bruce	1976	CC	Referee	3
HOOD, Bruce	1981	CC	Referee	4
HOOD, Bruce	1985	WM	Referee	6
HUTCHINSON, Scott	2002	WM	Referee	7
KOHARSKI, Don	1987	CC	Referee	6
KOHARSKI, Don	1991	CC	Referee	5
KOHARSKI, Don	2004	WCH	Referee	5
KOVACHIK, Brad	2004	WCH	Linesman	4
LEVER, Jim	1981	WM20	Referee	4
LEVER, Jim	1984	OG-M	Referee	6
LEWIS, Bryan	1984	CC	Referee	6
LEWIS, Dave	2012	WM	Referee	7
LYNCH, Dave	1988	WM20	Referee	4
LYNCH, Dave	1991	WM	Referee	6
MACLEAN, Hugh	1960	OG-M	Referee	9
MACLEAN, Hugh	1961	WM	Referee	4
MADILL, Greg	1979	WM	Referee	6
MARSH, Lou	1932	OG-M	Referee	12
MCCREARY, Bill	1991	CC	Referee	3
MCCREARY, Bill	1998	OG-M	Referee	6
MCCREARY, Bill	2002	OG-M	Referee	7
MCCREARY, Bill	2010	OG-M	Referee	5
MASCHIO, Lou	1962	WM	Referee	9
MASCHIO, Lou	1964	OG-M	Referee	10
MILLER, Steve	1999	WM20	Linesman	7
MILLER, Steve	2006	OG-M	Linesman	6
MOORE, Dinty	1949	WM	Referee	6
MORLEY, Bob	1989	WM	Referee	5
NADIN, Bob	1972	OG-M	Referee	7
O'HALLORAN, Dan	2010	OG-M	Referee	6
POLLOCK, Kevin	2004	WCH	Referee	4
PROCTOR, Sandy	1983	WM20	Referee	6
ROBB, Doug	1978	WM20	Referee	5
SCAPINELLO, Ray	1981	CC	Linesman	5
SCAPINELLO, Ray	1991	CC	Linesman	6

SCAPINELLO, Ray	1996	WCH	Linesman	7
SCAPINELLO, Ray	1998	OG-M	Linesman	5
STICKLE, Leon	1981	CC	Linesman	5
STICKLE, Leon	1984	CC	Linesman	5
VANMASSENHOVEN, Don	2004	WCH	Referee	4
VANMASSENHOVEN, Don	2006	OG-M	Referee	5
VINES, Mark	1991	CC	Linesman	4
WALKOM, Stephen	2002	OG-M	Referee	5
WALKOM, Stephen	2004	WCH	Referee	6
WATSON, Harry	1933	WM	Referee	5
WICKS, Ron	1984	CC	Referee	4
WILSIE, John	1986	WM20	Referee	3
WILLMOT, Jessie	2011	WM20	Linesman	7
WILLMOT, Jessie	2012	WM	Linesman	9
WRIGHT, Dave	2000	WM18	Referee	5
WRIGHT, Dave	2001	WM	Referee	7

WHERE ARE THEY NOW?
Ivan Locke

OHA Referee-in-Chief, Gary Moroney announced the retirement of OHA Referee Supervisor, Ivan Locke effective December 31st, 2011.

Appointed by Hugh McLean and Cliffe Phillips in 1971, Ivan has been an active supervisor in the Ontario Hockey Association for 41 years and is presently in his 64th year of being involved with hockey officiating including his involvement in minor hockey.

At one time Ivan had looked after the Kingston area as well as his involvement in the Oshawa and surrounding areas. Some of his graduates to the OHL and NHL include Alan Glaspell, Greg Madill, Derek Amell, Dean Morton, Dave Lewis, Mike Pryde and others. An instructor with minor hockey as well as the Ontario Hockey Association, Ivan has been a positive influence on officials at all levels as they move forward with their development.

Among Ivan's many rewards and recognitions for his service to hockey, he received an award from Hockey Ontario in 1984, followed by the coveted OHA Gold Stick in 1994 and the OHF Bill Richmond Award in 1998. He was inducted into the Oshawa Sports Hall of Fame in 2001 and most recently, the OMHA Honour Award in 2009. The most telling recognition of Ivan's work with young officials was the naming in 1990 of the "Ivan Locke Award", an OHA award that is presented annually to the official deemed to be the "Most Improved Official" in the OHA.

Oshawa referees Dave Lewis and Mike Pryde organized a get-to-together of 40 officials and supervisors to wish Ivan well in his retirement. They presented Ivan with a framed OHA sweater for his recreation room. NHL officials Derek Amell and Dean Morton each had their NHL sweater autographed and sent to him.

Remember When With... Ivan Locke

CL: Looking back, how did you get involved in officiating?

IL: I finished playing Juvenile but I still loved the game. The next season I applied to referee as a lot of games only had one referee. I was accepted and it has been full speed ahead from then until now.

CL: In your officiating career, are there any games that stand out as highlights?

IL: Two come to mind. In the spring of 1955, there was a sold out game at Maple Leaf Gardens between Toronto and St Catharines for the OHA Junior A Championship. Hugh McLean was the Referee and Loring Doolittle and I were the Linesmen. Billy "Hinky" Harris of Toronto went end to end in the second period to score a goal to put Toronto ahead 2-1. That's the way the game ended and Toronto went on to win the Memorial Cup. Many of those players went on to play in the NHL.

The second game was in 1990 in Ottawa at the Womens' First World Championship at the Ottawa Civic Auditorium. There were about 10,000 fans on hand for the Sunday game to see Canada defeat the USA to win the Championship. I was there all week helping supervise the officials including the final game.

CL: What was the toughest game you ever refereed?

IL: It was an Intermediate game in Cobourg with Lakefield as the visiting team. It was a one referee, one linesman system of officiating. The game was rough right from the start with a lot of stick work. In the first period, there were 16 minors, 3 majors and one misconduct penalty. The second period was much the same until with about four minutes left in the second, the Lakefield bench emptied, strangely the Cobourg did not. There were several fights and several players were injured. I sent both teams to their dressing rooms. Both team Managers said they could not guarantee me they could control their players. There was an on duty Police Sergeant who said the same thing about the fans. The Major of Cobourg was there and said if I didn't call the game, he would read the riot act to both teams and the game would be over. So at that point, I had to call the game.

CL: What was your toughest call?

IL: Having to decide when an official had to be released from the OHA Officiating staff.

CL: You were always available to help out at the OHA Referees' Schools.

IL: I always enjoyed the Referee Schools and meeting all the young officials because they loved hockey and officiating. Being able to hopefully help them improve and learn was a bright spot for us as well as for them. It gave some of the experience officials at the schools the opportunity to make the

OHA staff and later some caught on with the OHL and others in later years made it to the NHL.

Working closely with OHA coordinators Charlie Lennox and Will Norris over the years at the schools was an honour. Working with Sam Sisco and Ken Miller was always something I looked forward to as well as renewing our friendship. In later years when the NHL officials conducted the schools for the OHA, it was always a pleasure to meet and work with them. I have great memories of all of them who were involved with the Referee Schools.

CL: I understand you had a problem with an upset parent?

IL: It was a Junior C game, Pt Perry at Bowmanville and an upset parent came up behind me and grabbed my clipboard and threw it over the boards. I went down to the glass and his son skated over and picked up the clipboard and handed it to me over the glass. I went back to where I was standing and two Bowmanville Directors were already there. One was an off duty police officer and he escorted the parent to the front door and removed him from the arena. The Directors asked me if I was ok and I ensured them I was. <u>Case Closed.</u>

CL: You were part of an interesting experiment with Gerry Cheevers.

IL: Yes, Gerry Cheevers, the great Boston Hall of Fame goalie, once gave it up as a junior with the OHA St Mikes Majors. He played a forward position for three games and earned an assist in the first game. I was a Linesman in that game.

CL: You have a good story about referee Loring Doolittle.

IL: In Lindsay, referee Loring Doolittle was handing off the puck to me for a corner face-off in a two-man referee system. Long time fan, Ma Clayton was giving her usual abuse to the referees. As he started to skate out of the end zone, he passed by her and said, "What are you doing tonight Ma?" Her reply was, "You wouldn't be any good at that either Doolittle."

CL: Do you have any other Ma Clayton stories?

IL: Several years later, during an OMHA Juvenile final series, a fan was giving it to me pretty good. At the end of the first period, I asked the other referee, Bill Crowley, if he knew who the fan was giving me the hard time. He told me it was Ma Clayton from Lindsay. I told him I thought she was dead. As we were skating around to start the second period, sure enough it was Ma Clayton. So I gave her a little wave with my hand. "Don't wave to me Locke," she yelled, "you're no friend of mine."

I met Ma a few years later at a game. She was in a wheelchair with both legs amputated just above the knees. We shook hands, had a nice chat and a few laughs and parted friends.

CL: Who were the best officials you ever worked with?

IL: Hugh McLean, Bob Nadin and Jim Boddy. They all had great game control, respect of the players and coaches and were completely focused on the game.

CL: In your opinion what determines a good official?

IL: A good official is determined by his skating skills, his hustle, his rule knowledge and his application of the rules on and off the ice. He must have respect for the game, the participants and his fellow officials.

CL: Do you have any advice for young officials?

IL: You must have 100% concentration at all times (even at play stoppages). Be aware of what is happening and what has the potential to happen and never, tell a hockey player a lie.

Totally dedicated, committed and always positive, Ivan will be remembered as a true gentleman and a man of integrity and class.

Ivan and Irene are enjoying their retirement in Oshawa with their dog, Brady.

Rules Quiz #11 *(answers on page 138)*
Questions from Hockey Canada Rule Book

1. If the puck is shot by the attacking team and deflects off a defenseman, then off the referee into the goal, does it count?

    A. Yes
    B. No

2. What penalty is assessed a team who request a stick measurement and the stick is found to be legal?

    A. No penalty
    B. Bench minor
    C. Game ejection to coach
    D. Penalty shot

3. What penalty is assessed to an opposing player who distracts a player taking a penalty shot?

    A. Awarded goal
    B. Gross misconduct
    C. Ten minute misconduct plus repeat shot if it failed

4. What penalty is assessed a defenseman who is checking an opponent in front of the net and deliberately steps on his stick, breaking it?

    A. Minor for interference
    B. Gross misconduct
    C. Ten minute misconduct penalty
    D. Game misconduct

"Hey Ref, how can you guys be asleep with all these lights on?"

Chapter 12

WHY DID YOU HANG THEM UP?

This has always been a question that every Hockey Organization struggles to understand. Most officials start when they are young because they love the game. It is better than pumping gas or stocking shelves and it gives them some exercise and a little money. But as they progress up the officiating ladder, the pressure increases. The parents and the fans are not laughing anymore, and some are out of control with tunnel vision. In the Ontario Hockey Association, we would lose about 50 oficials a year out of 400. Age, travel, and injuries, are some of the reasons. In one of our surveys we asked "WHY?" Here are a few of their answers:

Ron Asselstine: "My heart said, GO; but my knees said NO."

Bob Spence: "It wasn't fun out there anymore."

Will Norris: "There comes a time when you know, you can feel it, you can sense it."

George Wilson: "No dinner, no sleep, no time."

Sam Sisco: "My feet sent a message to my brain."

Jim Lever: "One look in the mirror."

Ivan Locke: "When the arena clock started running slower."

Jeff Caplan: "I was burnt out and needed to get away for awhile for a bit but never came back."

Jim King: "I explained to Bill Hanley that I had been giving out a great number of misconduct penalties lately and I was listening too closely to the players' beefs. Bill mentioned, Jim I think your time is up."

John Callaghan: "A family comes along and your life goes in a different direction plus the lack of respect shown by the players, coaches and fans."

Bill Devorski: "My age and skating legs gave out."

Mike Lucas: "I moved to WARM, beautiful British Columbia."

Mike Lucas

WHERE ARE THEY NOW?
Bob Morley

After 30 years with the OHA and almost 2500 Amateur, Professional and International hockey games, referee Bob Morley hung up his skates. Born in England, the Hamilton resident worked his last game (Sr AAA), at Dundas, Ontario, March 05, 2005.

Bob was a referee in the OHA, OHL AHL, the UHL and the NHL. He obtained his Hockey Canada Level 6 Certification in 1986. He was awarded the OHA John Blackwell Award as their Most Deserving Official in 1992 and he was awarded the Jack Clancy Award in 1999 as the Most Dedicated Official in the OHA. In 2005 he was inducted onto the OHA Referees' Honour Roll. He also worked many International Games including the 1987 Ivestia Cup in Moscow, the 1989 World A Pool Championships in Sweden, the 1991 Canada Cup and the 1999 World University games.

Remember When With... Bob Morley

CL: Looking back, how did you get involved in hockey officiating?

BM: I played a little hockey but got crushed at a JR B tryout camp. While at the arena I saw a sign that said 'Referees Wanted'. So I thought I would give it a try and I signed up.

CL: You had a very long career as an official, did you ever think you would last that long?

BM: I wasn't sure I would last a week. It wasn't until I was standing at centre ice in the Luznicki Ice Palace in Moscow, the same arena where Paul Henderson scored that famous goal and I was refereeing the Soviets versus the Czechs during the days of communism, that I realized that something special was happening. The first stoppage of play, I touched the net at the end of the arena, and said to myself, "Wow – I am in the Soviet Union."

CL: That Czech/ Russia game had to be super special, how did you get selected to do that game?

BM: I was selected by Hockey Canada to work the Izvestia Tournament from a pool of Level 6 officials from across Canada. I was a candidate for the '88 Calgary Olympics and HC wanted to see how I did in an IIHF Tournament. I didn't get Calgary, but I was assigned the '89 Worlds in Stockholm.

CL: In all those games that you officiated, were there any that stood out as special moments?

BM: There were many, but being selected to referee in 26 Sutherland Cups for the OHA was special as was my first NHL game, my first AHL game, my first OHL game and even when I flew to a game. I consider all were special moments.

CL: What is the tough part of being an official?

BM: The travel, and the time away from home. I am a home body (hard to believe), and used to look at lights in homes coming from games and they appeared to be warm and inviting, and I wished I was home. I spent a month in Sweden, and couldn't wait to get back to Hamilton.

CL: There are always weird things that happen in games, can you give us any examples?

BM: There was an enraged lady in Kingston that leaned over the glass and strangled me with her purse straps as I skated by. She actually took my feet out from under me. Then there was another lady in Cambridge that reached over the glass and slapped me on the side of the head. There was even a puck that got stuck in the rafters, only to wiggle out later in the game, and hit me on the top of the head – any of these would count as some of my weird game happenings.

CL: What will you miss most about not being on the ice?

BM: I think working with the guys and being in the dressing room. That's what I am going to miss and some of the interaction with the teams. But really, I'd had enough. That's why I appreciate all that I did.

CL: Your son, Rob, worked as an OHA linesmen before he went out west to University. Did you get a chance to work with him on the ice?

BM: I did, and it was a thrill and very special event for both of us.

CL: Tell us about your favourite fan in Stratford?

BM: A fan used to lean over the glass at the penalty box and yell at me wearing a minor hockey Referee's sweater. One night, I skated out at the start of a playoff game, and threw him one of my old OHA sweaters to wear. If he was going to yell at me, he might as well be in an OHA sweater with my name on the back. I think he still wears it!

CL: How did you handle all the abuse from the spectators?

BM: As far as fans go, I didn't mind the abuse as long as it was not vulgar. I didn't like the fans yelling obscenities when there were kids in the crowd. Mostly, I simply didn't listen to them.

CL: Tell us about the Buffalo phone call.

BM: A couple of years ago, I was sitting at home watching Monday Night Football when the phone rang. I could hear a lot of noise in the background. "Is that you Bob?" a voice said." "Yes, who is this?" I said, "It is a referee. Can you tell me the penalty for shooting the puck over the glass?" he said. I asked, "Was it after the whistle?" "Yes, into the crowd," said the referee, "It is a ten minute misconduct, isn't it?" "No, it is a Gross Misconduct," I said.

Just a minute he said and I could hear him say, "No, no it is a Gross now get him out of here." Who are you talking to?" I asked. "The captain," said the referee. "Where are you?" I asked. "<u>I'm in the penalty box</u>," he replied.

CL: You worked with a lot of different referees when you were a linesman. Who would you consider the best?

BM: Bob Nadin, Jim Lever, John Willsie and Doug Robb all had earned the respect of the teams. But I am sure the respect their peers had for them meant a lot more. Boy, they made it fun!

CL: Do you have advice for the referees?

BM: You must recognize and react to any tempo or standard change immediately.

Bob has been a Supervisor of Officials for 23 years in the Hamilton area. He started in 1990 while he was still refereeing games. He also helped supervise the Niagara and Delhi area officials at various times until a permanent supervisor could be assigned.

Bob retired from the City of Hamilton in June 2011 and after a short vacation, became the full time OHA Referee Assignor in September, 2011. Bob is now the Director of Officiating and is responsible for the implementation of the new "state-of-the-art" assigning system for the OHA Officials. His many years of experience in the officiating world and his years with Parks and Recreation for the City of Hamilton made him the ideal candidate for the job.

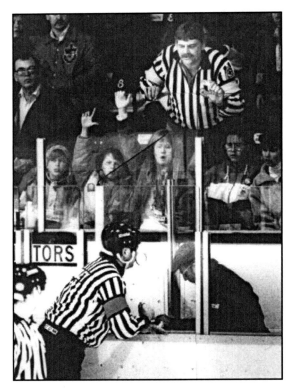

Bob Morley and his Favourite Fan

Rules Quiz #12 *(answers on page 138)*
Questions from Hockey Canada Rule Book

1. A stick is thrown to a player on the ice by a teammate who is also on the ice who picks up the stick. What is the referee's decision?
    A. Minor to player throwing the stick
    B. Major to player picking up stick
    C. Minor penalty to the player throwing the stick plus minor to player who picks up the stick
    D. No penalties, play continue

2. Is it possible for a player being assessed a minor penalty for being the Instigator and another minor penalty for being the Aggressor in the same fight?
    A. Yes
    B. No

3. What happens if a goalkeeper throws his stick at the puck during the course of a penalty shot?
    A. The penalty shot would be repeated
    B. Goalkeeper is removed and the shot is repeated with another goalie
    C. Award a goal

4. What penalty shall be assessed a player in the penalty box who grabs or molests a timekeeper?
    A. Additional minor penalty
    B. Additional major penalty
    C. Game misconduct
    D. Match penalty

Rules Quiz Answers
Answers from Hockey Canada Rule Book

Quiz #1
1. D
2. C
3. C
4. A

Quiz #2
1. C
2. D
3. A
4. A

Quiz #3
1. B
2. B
3. A
4. A

Quiz #4
1. C
2. A
3. A
4. C

Quiz #5
1. A
2. B
3. C
4. A

Quiz #6
1. B
2. B
3. A
4. A

Quiz #7
1. B
2. B
3. A
4. B

Quiz #8
1. B
2. B
3. A
4. B

Quiz #9
1. D
2. B
3. D
4. C

Quiz #10
1. C
2. D
3. B
4. C

Quiz #11
1. B
2. B
3. C
4. A

Quiz #12
1. C
2. A
3. C
4. D

Lest We Forget

Mark Clark

Darrell Ellwood

Briant Duncan

Dave Whaley

John Ashley, John McCauley, John D'Amico

Cam Rundle, Rob Waddell, Lou Maschio,

Hugh McLean, Frank Slota, Gregg Madill,

John Blackwell, Jack Clancy, George Hayes,

Gord Fevreau, George Graham, Blair Graham,

George Gravelle, Jim Hickey, John May.

"Hey Ref, next time you cross the road, don't look."

Chapter 13

Remembering Hugh McLean

Hugh Mclean did it all in Officiating. He refereed everything from Minor hockey to World Championships including the Olympics. He spent twenty-nine years in Amateur hockey and ten years in the NHL He retired from officiating in 1971 to become the C.A.H.A (now Hockey Canada) Referee-in-Chief. After five years, he was elected President of the Ontario Hockey Association and resigned his C.A.H.A. Referee-in-Chief position due to the added responsibilities of his new appointment. The C.A.H.A. then offered the job to Bob Nadin. Hugh was awarded the OHA Gold Stick 1980 and in 1988 was made a Life Member of the Ontario Hockey Association.

In his officiating career, He refereed the Stanley Cup finals, the Calder Cup, the Hardy Cup, and the Allan Cup. He refereed 9 games in the Winter Olympics in Squaw Valley, U.S.A. in 1960 and refereed the World Championships in Geneva, Switzerland in 1961. The only major championship he did not get to work was the Memorial Cup.

As the C.A.H.A. Referee-in-Chief, he was responsible for the officials for the 1974 World Hockey Association Canada-Russia series and the World Junior Championship in Winnipeg in the same year.

There are many different reports about Hughie's famous incident involving Montreal Canadiens star,

Rocket Richard in 1951. The following in his version of what happened:

"The play was coming out of the end zone and Richard thought the Detroit goalie had tripped him. I was skating up the ice and Richard put his stick in the small of my back. I gave him a penalty. Elmer Lach and Detroit's Leo Reese were already in the penalty box. Richard didn't go in right away. I told him, "Get in the box or you'll get more." Canadiens' captain, Butch Bouchard, told Richard to get in the box. As Richard entered the box, Reese stood up and before you knew it they were both swinging their sticks at each other. Eddie Mepham, my Linesman, jumped into the penalty box and Richard picked him up and threw him out. I then gave Richard a Game Misconduct."

The next night in New York, McLean was at the Piccadilly Hotel when the Canadiens came through the lobby. Richard grabbed McLean by the tie after he thought McLean had made a passing remark. Linesman, Jim Primeau came to his rescue. Considerable profanity filled the air but cooler heads separated the trio. NHL President, Clarence Campbell, fined Richard $500.00 for conduct prejudicial to the welfare of the game of hockey.

In 1987, Hugh Mclean thought he had been awarded the Order of Canada from Governor-General Jeanne Sauve. He received many phone calls and telegrams from friends congratulating him on his award. It turned it was another Hugh McLean who was a musician and a Professor at the University of Western Ontario. Hugh was deeply disappointed by the turn of events.

Hugh was not without a sense of humour. Former OHA President, Brent Ladds tells about going to a

Hockey Canada meeting in Montreal with Hugh and several colleagues. We said that we'd be able to call some of Hughie's old girlfriends when we got there. Hughie replied "That was thirty years ago, you'd have to dig them all up!"

Hugh McLean was a stickler on an official's appearance and in particular the length of his hair. He was famous for saying, "We don't tell you how long to wear your hair but then again we are the ones handing out the assignments."

In 1965, Referee Hugh McLean kept a tight rein on a Senior AAA game between Kingston and Oakville much to the dismay of the 1200 fans on hand. Later watching players receive awards for hat tricks he remarked, "These guys get all the rewards while all a referee gets is abuse."

Hugh McLean was a tough minded referee who stood for no nonsense on the ice. He was tough but fair and well respected by the players. Hugh once told a meeting of referees, "There are three kinds of referees; the bookworm, who calls everything exactly by the book. The referee who waits until the game is out of control before he starts making calls and then there is the referee who depends on good common sense. You should all strive to be the latter."

Hugh McLean had a significant impact on the game; He was honest and hard working. His word was always good.

Hugh passed away April 24, 1997 at the age of 84.

Remembering Gord Fevreau

Gord was a character guy who had returned from the NHL to officiate many important games for the OHA. In the summer, he was a top level umpire with his friends Archie French and Lou Visconti. They worked the Men Fastball League at Kew Beach Gardens for many years. He also was an umpire in the AAA International League and worked games at the old Maple Leaf Stadium.

I remember Gord was the referee in my first game as an OHA linesman at the old Dixie arena. There was a big fight in the corner and the other linesman and I got in there as quickly as we could and tried to break it up. Out of the corner of my eye, I could see Gord leaning on his elbow on the top of the net. When we finally got them apart, he said, "Two each for Roughing." I remember thinking, what have I got myself into.

Gord wore old skates with no tendon guards and he only got them sharpened once a year. I remember a game at the old Weston arena. There was no glass or screening around the boards in those days. He put on a delayed penalty and he hopped up on the boards to get out of the way as the play came around to his side. The players crashed into the boards and knocked him over into the seating area completely out of sight. There was a moment's pause, and the first thing you saw was his arm coming up, still with the delayed penalty signal, then, the rest of him all covered with dirt.

Gord had been an NHL referee and he knew the rules. If he thought the play was offside as he was coming down the ice, he wouldn't hesitate to blow his whistle even though you were right there looking at it. It was his game.

He had the respect of all the players and coaches. He was reluctant to call fringe or marginal penalties but sometimes he would let a little too much go and I remember a lady in Barrie leaned over the boards and hit him with her purse as he skated by. He stopped the play and just pointed at her as she ran down the aisle and right out the emergency exit door.

Gord had an old car and it seemed whenever there was a game in Kingston, his old car was in the garage being fixed. One of the linesmen always ended up driving to the Kingston games.

Larry Clark tells a great story about a SRAAA game in Collingwood in 1963 when a donnybrook broke out in the first 10 seconds of the game. Gord called the captains together after calm was restored (it took about a half hour). Then he reset the clock to zero and restarted the game with no penalties. It was a terrific game taking less than two hours to play.

Gord had a certain style of officiating that no other official could duplicate, although many tried.

Gord loved the Senior AAA hockey and the fans. He always had a crowd of people visit him in the dressing room between periods. You had to get in quick just to get a seat and then just sit there quietly because you didn't know who those people were. I remember one night we went out to start the game after the flood and we (the two Linesmen) went onto the ice thinking Gord was right behind us. After circling the ice a couple of times there was still no Gord. We finally spotted him up in the stands sitting in a seat talking with the spectators.

He used to like to go to the team Booster Clubs after the games and everyone wanted to buy him a beer. He would have the whole table full of beer. He also stashed some under the table. I think they finally put in a rule that the officials were not allowed to go to team Booster clubs.

We liked to play practical jokes on the referees but they never seemed to work on Gord. One night in Cambridge, the linesman, Larry Regan, put a mannequin's hand up the sleeve of his sweater with the puck stuffed in the fingers. After the National Anthem, Larry skated to centre and gave Gord the puck and he ended up with the whole hand. Larry skated away leaving Gord at centre with the hand. Gord just looked at it and swung it around his head and threw it into the stands. The whole arena erupted, especially the Cambridge bench who were aware of what was going to happen.

Gord was inducted onto the OHA's Referee Honour Roll in 1980.

When Gord died his friend Archie French gave the eulogy and it was filled with humourous stories of their good times and friendship over the years.

Remembering Blair Graham

Blair "Bugsy" Graham was a Level 6 OHA Referee from 1955 to 1977. He was a stock broker by trade and retired in August of 1999 after 44 years in the business. He and his wife, Joan, moved to their beautiful, renovated home in the Picton area. He spent his winters at his condo in Puerto Vallarta, Mexico and his summers on the Picton golf course. He was selected to work the World Juniors in 1977 in Czechoslovakia and was inducted onto the OHA's Referee Honour Roll in 1980. Here are some of his game experiences from an earlier interview.

CL: Tell us how you got the name "Bugsy"?

BG: There was some problems in an exhibition game in Hamilton and for the return match, Bill Hanley sent in three senior officials to referee one period and line the other two. While I was a Linesman, I assessed a ten minute misconduct penalty. The other two referees started to kid me about having "Rabbit Ears". It didn't take long for the word to spread around the League.

CL: Why, what happened?

BG: One night in Peterborough, I signaled the Goal Judges and was about to signal the Timekeeper, when Bob Gainey, the Peterborough captain, came over to me and said, "Roger (Coach Neilson) wants to know if you will need this?" And, he handed me a wad of cotton batten. I looked over at the Peterborough bench and every player had his hands up to his ears making like rabbits.

CL: What was your reaction?

BG: I put my hands near my hips and very quickly all the hands on the Peterborough bench came down.

CL: What happen in Guelph?

BG: When we came into the dressing room at the end of the first period, there were live rabbits all over the place and little baskets of Easter eggs everywhere compliments of Lou Maschio and Hugh McLean.

CL: I hear you really like carrots?

BG: One night after a game as I was driving down my street, I noticed there were signs on hockey sticks stuck in my neighbours' lawns. Signs like "Welcome Home Bugs". When I got to my house, my whole front lawn was covered with carrots. Someone had backed a truck up on the lawn and dumped a whole load of carrots. The next day after I cleared off the carrots, there were tire tracks a foot deep on my newly soded lawn. Never did find out who did it.

CL: You had an interesting call when 2 goals were scored in the same stoppage in a Toronto Marlie JrA game at Maple Leaf Gardens.

BG: Yes, Toronto was leading 3-2 with less than 2 minutes remaining and Peterborough was getting ready to remove their goaltender. Peterborough was breaking up the ice and a Peterborough defenseman, Rick Cunningham, clearly hooked down a Toronto player to keep him from getting back into the play. I assessed him a minor penalty. Toronto quickly scored on the power play to go ahead 4-2. It took a while for the rink attendants to clear the ice of debris. When I looked over at the Peterborough bench no one was on the ice. I was waiting at centre ice to drop the puck but no one moved from the bench. Finally, I gave them a delay of game penalty shot. The goalie went back in to take the shot. When the Toronto player, Dave Gardner, skated in to take the shot, the Peterborough goalie threw off his mask and came skating out. Gardner looked at me and said, "What should I do?" I said, "Shoot it in the net." I think Roger got into some hot water over that one.

CL: What about the goalie with the glass jaw?

BG: It was a SrA game, Barrie in Collingwood and I remember late in the game Barrie scored a disputed goal. The Collingwood goalie chased me all the way to the blue line. I stopped and went nose to nose with him. All of a sudden he flinched and I thought he was going to throw a punch. My reaction was to flick a quick right, which caught him right on the point of his chin and he went down like a bag of rocks. The fans and his teammates went nuts. When the game ended, the Barrie coach, Bep Guidolin, sent out his two tough guys, Rick McLoughlin and Johnny MacMillan to escort us off the ice. We needed a police escort to get out of town that night.

CL: Any advice for young officials?

BG: When you are bringing the whistle up or raising your arm for a delayed penalty, just pinch or hit your pants which gives you a slight delay before you commit (i.e. a trip and the player doesn't go down).

Blair passed away December 23, 2012 in Mexico.

Remembering Frank Slota

Frank will be remembered best as one of the most colourful referees of the OHA in the 1950's. He refereed hockey all across Ontario when players such as Bobby Hull, Stan Makita and Bobby Orr were in their prime playing junior hockey. He was selected to referee the Memorial Cup and Allan Cup during his long career which lasted from 1950 to 1979. He was an old school referee with a style that was uniquely his own. He would let the teams play and cracked down when he had to. Frank was awarded the OHA's Gold Stick in 1977 and was inducted onto the OHA's Referee Honour Roll in 1982.

CL: You saw Bobby Orr make a terrific play to save a goal in Oshawa.

FS: Yes, It was the last minute of play and Oshawa was down by a goal with their goalie out of the net. The face-off was in the Toronto end. They won the draw and a Toronto player broke out skating towards the empty Oshawa net. Bobby skating backwards got himself in front of the Toronto player. He slipped and skidded into the net. The Toronto player shot the puck and Bobby caught it in mid-air in the goal crease. I blew the whistle and leaned over Bobby telling him it was a terrific play but that it was a penalty shot. Bobby's coach gave me a bad time so I ejected him. Then Bobby came over to me to say his coach had told him to say a few things. I then ejected him. Toronto didn't score on the penalty shot but it was probably the best play I ever saw by a player.

CL: How about the fan heckling Stan Mikita in St Catharines?

FS: I saw Stan skating to the end boards where a fan had been giving him a bad time. Stan was ready to go into the crowd after him. I said, "Stan that will cost you $25.00." Stan turned around and said, "Thanks Frank, I can't afford $25.00."

CL: Gordie Howe is a nice guy?

FS: In a game in which Gordie Howe played, I had my two young children with me. When we got off the ice I asked Gordie if I could get a picture of him with my two children. Gordie came into the dressing room and I took the picture of him with my two children, one on each of his knees. Great guy!

CL: How about the player who was upset with you?

FS: A Kitchener player threw his stick up in the air in disgust. I said to him if that stick comes down and lands on the ice you're out of this game. He jumped into the air and caught the stick.

CL: Did they recognize you with your hairpiece?

FS: The first year I had my hairpiece, I did a game in Stratford. While I was standing in the corner of the rink, I heard a fan ask another fan,"Who is that referee?" The man answered, "That's Slota." The reply he got was, "I know Slota." When I came back into that end for a face-off, the man leaned over the boards and yelled, "Hey Slota, you're no better than your old man."

Frank passed away at age 86 on July 27, 2008.

Remembering Roger Neilson

No, Roger was not a referee but he was a challenge to any referee who worked his games. Roger knew the Rule Book and constantly scanned the Rules looking for loopholes he could use to his advantage. And he found them. During the pre-season, Roger always asked the OHA to send a senior referee out to talk to his players. This idea eventually caught on with other teams as they began to realize the importance of their players knowing the rules. Here are some of the stories from his days of coaching the JrA Peterborough Petes in the OHA.

One night in Hamilton, his team had a one goal lead late in the game with under a minute remaining when they received a penalty. When the puck was dropped he put another player over the boards to make them even on the ice. The referee put up his arm on a delayed penalty and when Peterborough gained possession of the puck (and they didn't try very hard to get possession), he gave them a "too many men on the ice" penalty. Meanwhile precious seconds came off the clock. They were now two players short and when the puck was dropped this time, he put two players over the boards and again they were even on the ice. More time was ticking off the clock. When play was stopped, they received an additional "too many men penalty." A team cannot be shorthanded more than two players on the ice so he did it again for the third time. Finally the game ended and the Hamilton coach, Eddie Bush, went crazy and threw all his team's sticks on the ice, but there was nothing in the Rule Book that said you couldn't do this. The next year, a new rule (now Hockey Canada Rule 2.5 f) was added that called for a penalty shot for 'deliberate illegal substitution" with less than two minutes remaining in a game.

Another of Roger's rule challenges was to put a defenseman in goal to take a penalty shot against his team. He chose Ron Stackhouse and he would rush out at the player and take him out. Again there was nothing in the Rules that said this was not allowed. Next year another new rule (now Hockey Canada Rule 4.9b note) was added that no player other than a goaltender was permitted to tend goal during a penalty shot.

Roger had another trick up his sleeve when a penalty shot was called against him. As the opposing player started to skate in and crossed the blue line, he would have his goalie throw off his mask and skate out of the goal and say "Hold it, hold it". In most cases, the opposing player would think the shot was going to be taken over and he would just give up or shoot the puck in the corner. If he did that the penalty shot <u>was over</u>.

One night Roger's team arrived late for a game and the referee would not allow his team a warm-up. So on the first shift of the game when the play went into the opposing team's end zone, a Peterborough player went down in severe agony after being knocked into the boards. He moaned and rolled around on the ice. The Peterborough trainer came out and quickly called for a stretcher. Meanwhile, two Peterborough defensemen were down at the other end warming up their goalie. The injured player was taken off the ice but miraculously recovered and returned to action shortly after play resumed.

I was at a coach's clinic one year giving a session on rules and between my talks I would listen in on Roger's sessions to the coaches. He said he had a crucial face-off late in a game and he had a winger take the face-off against the other team's centre. The winger would wack the other player's stick and the centre would wack him back. He said nine out of ten times the Linesmen would throw both players out of the face-off and then he would come in with his centre against one of their wingers. He said what have you got to lose? If he only throws out your player you bring in your centre anyway.

Roger had a "Sleeper Play" that he used successfully several times in games and is worth mentioning here. He used it in the second period when his bench was at the other team's blue line. When they were on a power play and the other team iced the puck, a forward would come off the ice but no one would go on for him. The Peterborough defenseman would stop behind his net to setup a rush. The other team's defensemen would move up over the centre red line. The Peterborough defenseman would make one pass up to a forward at the blue line that was kitty-corner to the bench. He would then fire the puck at his bench's door. The trainer would open the door and the player who went off would come out and take the pass behind the opposing team's defenseman and have a clear breakaway. I saw it work many times leaving the opposing defensemen wondering "Where did he come from?" Boy, wouldn't Roger like it now with the offside pass rule no longer in effect.

Roger had a dog named Jacques and he used him in practices. He would put him on the ice in front of the goal and he would not go behind the goal to chase a player. It was deemed a good lesson for his players.

He also used Jacques to get through any crowds of irate fans after games, although someone would have to hold his tail so it wouldn't wag.

He had a good sense of humour and respected the senior referees and rarely tried any of his tricks on the younger referees.

Games were always interesting with Roger because you never knew what to expect. He made us better officials by keeping us all on our toes and got us back into the Rule Book especially before any of his games.

Roger succumbed to cancer on June21, 2003.

Brent Holdsworth and Darcy Burchell

Mike Pearce   Terry Hobor

First Provincial JrA All-Star Game -1973
Blair Graham, Bob Nadin, Jim Lever

Timeout- Jaromir Jagr and Scott Dricoll

Bob Morley and Wayne Gretzky

Canada (World Hockey Assoc) vs Russia-1974
Jim LeBlanc, Tom Brown

Mario Lemieux and Scott Driscoll

Sean McQuigge   **Scott Oakman**

Bill Devorski

Paul Devorski   **Greg Devorski**

Ryan Wilson   **Ben Wilson**

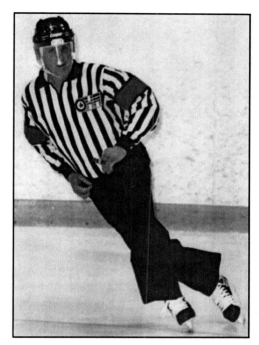

Ken Bannerman

Korey Bannerman   **Kevin Bannerman**

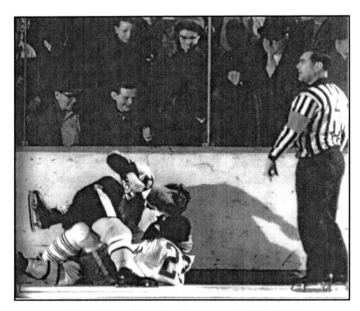

Bobby Orr, Pat Quinn and Bill Friday

NHL 4 on 4 Lockout Tournament- 1994
Dean Morton, Kevin Pollock, Steve Miller, Brad Kovachik with Ron Hoggarth and Gordie Howe.

Referee John Coburn punched in face in JrA
Player got a ten year suspension

Dave Koziel, Scott Hutchinson, Brett Punchard
First ever OSHL game Sep17, 2004 in Barrie.
(Their sweaters are yellow and black)

Scott Hutchinson   Rob Palm

 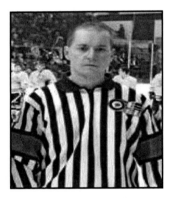

Steve Baker   Pete Kostyk

T.J. Luxmore   Dave Lewis

John Brown

John Willsie

Brain Coles, Garey Wilson, Joe Lafranco, Ed Butler and Ralph Sparks

Sean Reid

Ken Bodendistel

OHL Referee-in-Chief
Conrad Hache

Glenn Sherwood

"Hey Ref, I found a cell phone, it must be yours, it has four missed calls."

Chapter 14
OHA SUPERVISORS' TIPS...

The objectives of good supervision are to assist the development of officials through meaningful feedback. It is the job of the supervisors to develop consistency in the assessment of officials with reference to rule interpretations, rule enforcement, positioning, and procedural techniques. It is to provide instructional follow-up, which will reinforce the Hockey Canada Officiating program.

This section consists of over 1200 tips for referees and linesmen **right off the evaluation sheets** filled out by the supervisors of the OHA, The Supervisors all give assessments of what they observe and what they consider sincere, honest feedback to help each official reach their potential.

We feel strongly that this will be a great benefit to all officials. They will be able to pick up invaluable information from the evaluation tips which will help them become better officials.

It will also be an eye opener for the fans as to what the Supervisors are looking for in an official.

Supervisors' Tips

BRYAN LEWIS

Former: OMHA Referee; OHA Referee; NHL Referee; NHL Development Co-Ordinator; NHL Director of Officiating; ECHL Referee-in-Chief; Central Hockey league Supervisor.

Current: CHL Referee-in-Chief; OUA Referee in Chief; OHA Supervisor (Toronto West).

Bryan Lewis
on *Referees:*

When player goes down it does not mean the referee's arm automatically goes up.

When there is a disputed goal, re the net came off, give a washout signal, then consult with your linesmen and have it announced.

You are too laid back going into end zone; "go to the whip."

Be sure to watch the entire rink, not just puck.

Don't get to a point in your game where "nothing looks bad."

Require tighter standard for actions at net and in the crease area.

Go to the coach only when it is beneficial to you and don't stay too long.

Face the timekeeper to start game and face benches for all other face-offs.

Can't wait too long to blow whistle when goalie injured.

Move in on scrambles to see loose pucks.

Keep hands off players, there is a perception problem with that.

Be aware of the free hand on opposing player's body or stick.

Maintain a firm standard on scrums. Let them know the referee is running this part of the game.

Be alert to stick use via a cheap shot manner, especially behind the play.

Start line change procedure a little sooner, if nothing going on.

Use your legs in your skating stride and less arm movement to save energy.

There is no need to hand signal a goal so long.

Don't bend over an injured player, stand back and look.

Try not to get out into mid rink so far, you get in the road.

Do not stay on ice talking to coach at end of periods. It is much better to talk to them in the hallway, if necessary.

I would encourage you to speak to / verbally advise players behind the play to stop the nonsense of any potential penalty actions. Let them know you are there and watching.

When skating into the defensive zone, go as deep as the deepest forechecker.

Caution re a throwing puck to a fan. It is not your puck(s).

Make the penalty fit the crime.

Bryan Lewis
on *Linesmen:*

Don't put an icing signal on when it would take a tornado to get the puck down the ice.

Face-offs - one minor move by center and out he went....not sure if appropriate as game importance intensifies, especially in defensive zones.

Be sure to blow whistle to start face-off when referee's arm goes down.

Covered for referee okay but need more hustle back to the blueline.

When there is an altercation, get penalized player out of area then let go of him.

When player gets penalty and there is broken stick on ice, get player to penalty box before you pick up the broken stick.

On face-offs, get encroachment earlier before the puck is dropped and don't point with left hand while setting up, keep it still.

On icing, don't wait until puck crosses goal line before washing it out.

It is not necessary to point at player when you call an offside.

Caution when signaling with head down; watch out!

Stay alert and ready to go if there is trouble.

Hit often: give players the boards.

When there is icing from mid-rink, think "face-off location" to keep the referee away from benches.

Supervisors' Tips

LANCE ROBERTS

Former: WHL Referee; IHL Referee; AHL Referee; NHL Referee; Hockey Canada Supervisor.

Current: NHL Development Manager; OHA Supervisor (Guelph/Kitchener).

Lance Roberts
on *Referees:*

Do not sacrifice rule standard for game flow.

Your judgment must be clear with a strong understanding of what is a battle versus what is a penalty.

Establish a clear standard with interference and rough play after the whistle.

Keep working on skating mobility to be quick with play action. You may want to cut down on stops and starts and do more turns with the play.

Read and react quicker to play action coming into the zone and get your feet moving.

Be careful you don't get caught in the corner, anticipate play and use your mobility.

Need a strong standard with restraining fouls and stick infractions.

Watch distance travelled for potential charging calls.

Slow down when calling penalties and be in control for stronger on-ice presence.

Attack the puck to get to a power position with a full vision of players and ice.

Keep focused on clear penalties, maintain composure and show authority with confident calls.

Watch tunneling on the puck; get your sight line up.

Don't cross behind play or end up in middle of ice coming into end zone.

You must watch stopping high up in the zone. Move deeper into end zone and focus on getting to the goal line to be in a stronger position.

Go to the net hard for better sightline on covered puck or to blow play down quicker when needed.

Warn goalie of delay of game penalty for coming out of net to freeze puck.

When setting up in the end zone to come out with play, go as deep as the forechecker, then curl in behind and come out with play.

Need to work on edges for crossovers and power turns to help with play pursuit and for mobility with play action down low. You were caught at times well behind play.

Lance Roberts
on *Linesmen:*

Watch and be aware of coincidental penalties expiring and always watch players leaving the penalty box.

Read play and anticipate on stoppages for quick movement to problems.

Need to work on skating with power stride and mobility to develop your natural skating ability.

Must improve awareness and read game action to anticipate problem situations and get a quick reaction on whistle.

Make signals strong with authority and at shoulder height for wave-offs.

Take the players right off the ice after a fight situation.

Work hard on face-offs, drop puck with authority and get back to your position with speed to release your partner.

Read and react on face-offs when moving to the line, always know where the puck is off the draw.

Check back on icings prior to blowing whistle.

Keep yourself between the player and the box after a fight.

Must be focused and see play clearly at your line for strong judgment on offsides.

After a fight situation keep your awareness up around the bench area.

On face-offs, watch you don't move into puck drop; be set before dropping puck.

You must work on communication and awareness with partner and referee. You must not shy away from making thoughts or decisions known. Need better concentration while play is stopped.

Supervisors' Tips

GUS BAMBRIDGE

Former: OMHA Referee; OHA Referee.

Current: OMHA Supervisor; OMHA Instructor; OHA Supervisor (Oshawa).

Gus Bambridge
on *Referees:*

On your positioning up and down the ice, stay closer to the boards so you don't end up in the play or run into players. Move back to within an arm length of the linesman.

When puck is in player's feet on opposite side of ice, don't go behind net and tell them to move it, blow play down.

Move into stoppage location using good verbal commands to players stopping any problems.

On line changes make sure you make eye contact with the benches. You sometimes appear to just raise your arm with no eye contact.

If you go to the bench and cut conversation off quickly, don't go back in same stoppage.

Always turn towards the centre of the ice. Never turn your back on players.

Keep skating end to end, you appear to be slowing down through the neutral zone. When there are shots on goal, you are only at blueline.

When you talk to a captain, there is no need to go and explain to the coach unless it is a complicated set of penalties.

When puck goes to net, you have to go there also. You are standing back flat- footed.

On stoppage, just don't skate by. Stop and make sure no problems and players are moving to face-off location.

A Goaltender going to bench for equipment repairs must be replaced or a delay of game penalty would be assessed.

Don't get too far ahead of play leaving the end zone. Let play pass you and follow it up ice.

Make sure when the puck is high sticked, the offending team does not gain an advantage when play blown down.

You should go in as far as attacking player so if puck is turned over you are in position to go with play.

Gus Bambridge
on *Linesmen:*

If you are going to wave off icing, wave it off. Don't change your mind on look back to partner.

If your partner is moved off his line, you have to anticipate and move up faster. It is not the referee's responsibility to make this call.

Make sure centres are square and sticks in white area on face-offs, so they are fair for both teams. Don't let them coast into face-off. Your partner should be calling any encroachment behind your back.

You have to anticipate stoppages and move in quickly, player first, then puck.

Stay on ice at end of warm-up to make sure only two players left to pickup pucks or a penalty must be assessed.

You should use more verbal commands at blueline and on icings.

On face-offs, drop puck, hesitate, see where puck goes and then move out.

If referee is caught, you must go all the way into the goal line to cover for him.

When referee moves to top of circle for line change, make sure he is back in position before dropping puck.

In a possible fight situation, if you can get in before it starts, then get in if it is safe to do so.

When at your blueline position, stay back at boards. You appear to like moving towards centre of ice as puck crosses line.

Icings should only be waved off if the player could have played the puck or should have played the puck.

On face-offs, make sure players are in position and your partner is back near blue line before dropping puck.

On icings, skate hard all the way to goal line, you start coasting inside blueline.

Always watch line changes making sure you are between the teams. If something happens you will be able to get in.

Supervisors' Tips

RICK MORPHEW

Former: OMHA Referee; OHA Level VI Referee; IHL Referee; OMHA Supervisor; CHA Standards Committee.

Current: OMHA Referee-in-Chief; Ontario Hockey Federation Referee-in-Chief; OHA Supervisor (Oshawa).

Rick Morphew
on *Referees:*

Setting up in the end zone does not always mean go to end boards and watch play. You got caught not moving your feet.

You need to work whole ice surface and not just from the top of the circle in. You have the skating ability to do this but not always used.

Occasionally you would stop outside the end zone when the puck shot deep and one attacker, but you stopped on red line side of linesman. You should stop on the side closer to end zone in case you are required to move quickly to the net.

I need you to be more active controlling benches at end of periods and game.

Consider the number of times you go below goal line when you may be able to simply bump and pivot.

Remember on scrums/fights to position yourself so you can see the benches.

You use good penalty signals 95% of the time with proper execution as per procedures. I need to you to do this all of the time.

You need to adjust your end zone positioning when play is on your side. The end boards are not the best position to set up.

Do not point with one finger on penalty calls.

I would have liked you to be more vocal at certain times when teams do not want to play.

Consider handling player coming from bench to talk to you by turning away or putting up the "stop sign."

When altercations start, consider where you stand and what limitations does this positioning have for you.

Rick Morphew
on *Linesmen:*

You have a tendency to want to stay on the line even if it means taking a body check from a player. You need to release and let play push you in or bump down.

When working the blueline your reaction to quickness of play sometimes resulted in your getting to line after the play crossed. I need you to be there 100% of the time.

You seem to be giving the impression that you may be a bit laid back and I know you have the size and skating ability to do this level of hockey.

Make teams work to gain an icing call as most of the time the player goes to the attacking player and leaves the puck.

I would suggest that you skate backward to lead play to your blueline allowing you to track play at all time as you are facing it.

Would like to see you develop a presence that would see your calls are sold with strength and decisiveness.

I would like to see you work on your arm signal. Occasionally your arm is bent and hand is turned out.

When you enter an altercation do not take player from behind. Use your body size to get in from the side instead of collaring the player to move him.

Supervisors' Tips

BOB MORLEY

Former: OHA Level VI Referee; OHL Referee; CHL Referee; AHL Referee; NHL Referee; OHA Supervisor (Hamilton).

Current: OHA Director of Officiating.

Bob Morley
on *Referees:*

You must ensure that high-risk penalties are seen and called. This can be best accomplished by not just focusing on the puck but by having a broader view of entire ice surface.

Not to be discussed in front of your peers, BUT your fitness level appears to have deteriorated. It is showing up in the stands and I believe it is affecting your skating and pursuit of the play.

Put yourself in a position to view all the players all of the time.

Don't be in too much of a hurry to get the box, slow it down. Stay in the vicinity of the infraction and take your time. It gives your call credibility and rarely draws questions.

Use your strong skating to your advantage by a stronger pursuit of the play.

As you go into the end zone direct yourself toward the net and try to get a little closer.

You took way too long to resolve some minor penalties and allowed the players to control your explanation.

A penalty differential in a scrum always pays dividends.

It is not necessary to explain all penalties to the players; it creates a situation you don't need.

At the end of the period you must focus on players, not goals and assists.

Stay in the area of an injured player before you make your call. Do not rush to get to the penalty box.

You must recognize/react to any tempo or standard change immediately.

On an infraction when a stick is involved, the stick infraction is best called.

In the two-referee system, you must communicate with your partner when you both put up your arm at the same time on a penalty; it is important to get together and solidify the call.

A slight delay on your penalty calls might give you a little latitude to adjust, if required.

It's good to watch for retaliation but you must ensure an immediate whistle to the offending team.

In the two referee system, stay out of the middle of the ice as the back man and spend a little less time behind net when front man.

Stay away from the benches at the end of a period when they want to discuss penalties.

If your style is to keep the play moving than apply that to the goalkeepers as well.

Keep in mind obvious high-risk infractions will not interrupt the flow of a good hockey game.

You would be better to curl in behind the play and follow it out as opposed to waiting for it to come to you.

When you wash out a goal, make sure you have the reason announced.

Your fitness level is suspect based on your on ice appearance. You need to lose some weight.

Rule of thumb is to make contact with the referee's crease on your penalty calls; do not make them at centre ice.

It is best to give the "animated" coach a bench minor penalty right off the bat; that is his warning.

Think about shifting your concentration from the puck to the "troubled player."

Stay away from "multiple whistles"; it can become a bad/hard habit to break.

Work hard to make sure you are where you should be in each zone.

Try to keep your "position" on your hand signals consistent.

Turn your head to glance back, not your body. Otherwise you will lose sight of most of the play/players.

You should work on being more receptive of advice and/or observations being given to you as opposed to argumentative. You give the appearance to your peers, and even more importantly to the Supervisor, that you may not be coachable, a trait that will end up costing you the ability to advance.

Suggest that you might be more aggressive at times "attacking" the net. You are at times hesitant to get at the goalkeeper.

Bob Morley
on *Linesmen:*

Try to put yourself in an area of player activity at end of the period. The dressing room key and the puck are not important.

Suggest you keep your comments to yourself regarding a referee's call. If you are asked, speak, if not keep quiet.

You must be aware of who is being penalized and where they are after the whistle.

Don't forget to cover for referee if he gets tied up at start of period or after a goal.

Keep in mind that the puck must go down 5 seconds after the whistle.

If there are issues at the timekeeper's box, you must advise the referee and let him handle the situation.

It is either icing or no icing when the puck leaves the stick; you can't defer the call until the puck hits centre.

Make sure you do a quick count of players on ice prior to face-offs.

You really need to work on your weight as it detracts from your steady work.

On offsides, do not anticipate, wait for the action, then signal or blow your whistle.

You must always stay with your partner during multiple fight situations.

Do not allow a penalized player to cross the ice unattended after a fight.

You must anticipate the referee's whistle to get into the "action" on stoppages.

Try not to be to "animated" when you remove players from the face-off.

Try to have a little less "Jump" when you back out of the face-offs; be calm, calculated and methodical.

Use your pre-game time to communicate your pre-game "Plan of Attack" with your partner relating to icing procedures and after the whistle action.

Make sure you and your partner go off the ice after the first team to leave at a mutual exit. It puts you there to deter/view any problems.

On face-offs, make sure you maintain your Hockey Canada face-off stance, no crouch.

Make sure if you are covering deep, that you continue with the coverage. Once you are caught in the zone you must surrender your line to your partner and he must stay at your line until you take it back from him.

Supervisors' Tips

BOB NADIN

Former: THL Referee; Level VI OHA Referee; CAHA Referee-in-Chief; NHL Supervisor.

Current: IIHF Rules Committee; IIHF Supervisor; Olympic Supervisor; OUA Supervisor; OHA Supervisor (Toronto East).

Bob Nadin
on *Referees:*

When there is an injured player (and trainer comes out), the referee should remain in the area of the injured player.

When the referee does not observe an incident when a player has been injured, do not hesitate to check with linesmen.

When following the play up ice with play on far side, move further out from boards to get a better angle.

Do not make any comments on the length of or possible suspensions on any penalty.

It is most important to move quick and close to the net, as it is very difficult to make a close decision when you are back in the corner.

Start early with a strict standard on the interference to and protection of the goalie.

When play goes behind net, don't wait at hash marks, skate in curl and go.

You need to get quicker and deeper into the end zones.

When assessing a penalty, don't wait around and discuss with players but don't leave the troubled area until all is clear.

In the end zone, turn your body so you can watch play along boards and front of net, and stand up straight. What more can you see by bending over?

Come in closer when reporting penalties to penalty timekeeper.

Don't turn away too quickly from the point shot when the defending player is charging out at him.

The player never threw a punch, he just pushed the other player away, maybe a roughing call but no way was it 5 + Game for fighting.

When there is a scrum, move over quickly and make your presence felt to let people know that you are in charge.

Watch your body language in tough situations.

Start you line change procedure a little quicker. The home team players are coming over at the last minute. It is the same procedure as linesmen on face-offs, make sure all players are off and linesmen are in position.

You are leaving the end zone too quick and in the way of players especially around the hash marks. When it is obvious play will stay in the end zone, why move out?

Use your voice to show authority and take control and be more forceful in assessing penalties.

When following play up ice, don't let a player's body block your view from getting a good angle on the play.

Go to bench quicker, don't wait for coach to get too animated.

Show more authority and be a little "meaner" with players at times and not so much of a "gentleman".

You must take the checking from behind hit and not substitute it with boarding. In this type of hit, you must check with partner to see who had the best angle. Make the discussion quick.

Bob Nadin
on *Linesmen:*

The back linesman must be aware of the player/goalkeeper exchange on a delayed penalty or a goalie coming out near end of the game.

Move in quickly on stoppages of play when there is a gathering of players.

When a player slaps the opponent's stick before the puck goes down, he should be removed.

Skate hard all the time and show more hustle retrieving the puck.

On icings, as the front man, wave it off before it gets to or over the goal line.

You must have good signal co-ordination with your partner.

When the play comes at you at the blue line, move inside instead of stopping before the blue line.

You must show consistent judgment on icing the puck situations and handling delayed offsides.

When centres are late coming into the face-off, make them stop and set up straight.

On face-offs, try to "consul" the players to avoid having to remove one or having any encroachment. Check behind <u>before</u> blowing whistle.

Why skate and wait at penalty box with player when there is no problem.

Signals should be confident but not intimidating or demonstrative.

On face-offs don't drop puck until partner in position.

Caution re use of voice or signal (washout) on obvious non-offside.

Don't go in too deep to cover the net when referee is not that far behind.

You must have consistent judgement standard on icing the puck situations.

Watch your "body language", it is too casual and lacks enthusiasm.

As back linesman, leave your position as soon as defending team gains position to be at your blue line before play gets to the line. At times you wait too long up near center ice.

Supervisors' Tips

RICK SINGLETON

Former: OMHA Referee; OHA Level I Referee; OMHA Supervisor.

Current: OMHA Clinic Instructor; OHA Recertification Clinic Co-Ordinator; OHA Supervisor (London).

Rick Singleton
on *Referees:*

Leaning on the goal is not the type of image you should cultivate.

When you send a player to the bench, watch until completion.

You have a tendency to move into mid ice in the end zone causing the potential for interference with play. Try to move less, your vision of play will be just as good if not better.

On interference calls, if it is something specific, i.e. a trip, call it that.

When an altercation happens at the end of a period your focus should move to the benches.

The face-off must come outside when all players have moved into the zone during an altercation.

There were a lot of gloves in the face (washes) after the whistle. I'd like to see you move in on that sort of thing.

Remember the value of a single minor only after whistle gatherings. Get the odd man differential whenever possible. This can be a valuable game control device.

I thought you spent too much time and energy explaining your calls.

I thought that had you reacted to some quite obvious infractions early in the game, your overall position would have been much stronger.

You seem to be skating too hard and as a result going beyond the play.

During a fight situation you must take control; allowing players to remain in area is perilous.

You react too slowly and leniently to the wrestling type stuff. You need to make the control presence calls more consistently.

On a disputed goal it is to your advantage to be seen as clearly engaging the linesmen.

The no goal call was a good call but you would have benefited from a more emphatic sale of the call.

When assessing a penalty or have one on delay, stay aware of total ice activity, don't over focus on the call.

I thought you were a little too generous and patient on some of the early gatherings and a little easy on elbow high hits.

As players are working for puck in corner, don't wait too long on the whistle; you must be aware of players' focus.

Conversations at the bench should be used carefully; don't let coach take advantage.

You allowed the goalie to go to his bench without consequences. Why? This diminishes your role in the game and makes the next guy who handles it properly, look bad.

Be careful that your verbal interventions don't suggest an "excitement". I know you are in total control but others might perceive things differently.

Keep your head on a swivel and do several random checks over your shoulder as you go up the ice. Pay attention to off puck players and trailers out of the zone.

Your handling of gathering type situations might be enhanced by more obvious involvement. A sharp whistle and a growly bark are often helpful.

While verbal intervention is a good thing, don't use it in place of penalties.

On gatherings, while a second whistle can often be a good device, I'm not sure it's as effective when used on all occasions.

Rick Singleton
on *Linesmen:*

Occasionally, you are a little late getting to your line as play moves through the neutral zone.

Consider a slightly more upright position when dropping the puck.

Be aware of your partner's position and move quickly to cover when necessary.

I would like to see you clearly inside the line when play enters the zone.

You might consider not pulling away from your partner's end as quickly as you are.

I would like to see decisions on icings made by the hash marks.

I don't like to see a linesman climb the glass unless it's the only way out.

You performance is hindered by what appears to be a lack of energy, enthusiasm and crispness. You seem to be a little slow to react to changes in game flow and direction.

One concern is your movement away from the boards to allow traffic behind you.

As necessary, allow play to push you through rather than try to hold the line taking the chance of either getting in the play or injured.

When dealing with a "hot" player, be sure you don't lose your focus and let him get away from you.

When you enter an altercation, be sure you do not grab a player from the back. Your identity is not evident to him and you are in a poor location to see the player's position.

I would like to see a little more crispness in your signals and a little more hustle between whistles.

Don't go into altercations alone, wait for your partner and wait for the sticks to come down.

On delayed offside situations, I'd prefer the words "offside" or "OK" to be used. These are unambiguous while "clear" lacks precision in the situation.

Supervisors' Tips

JIM MAITLAND

Former: Bluewater Referee; OMHA Referee; OHA Referee; OMHA Supervisor.

Current: OHA Supervisor (Sarnia).

Jim Maitland
on *Referees:*

When explaining your penalties to the players, use less hand gestures, it looks threatening sometimes.

You need to set the tone early on the stuff after the whistle otherwise you are going to be in for a long game.

When calling multiple penalties, make sure you give the signals, so the teams know what was called.

You need to go to the net. You are skating back towards the boards when you should be moving up to at least the face-off dot.

Make sure the players wearing mouth-guards are wearing them properly.

When disallowing a goal, make sure you have it announced as to why it was not allowed.

When going to the penalty box to give a penalty, make sure you skate backwards keeping all the players in your sight.

You need to focus more on the free hand.

You give the benches too much of your time.

In the two-referee system, after an altercation, get together with your partner so it doesn't look like he is making all the calls.

You are skating with the play and you need to be at least one zone back and checking behind once in awhile.

Use your voice to keep players focused on the play.

Skate hard through the neutral zone and don't coast.

On altercations, you need to back out and get in position so you can watch the scrum and the benches.

You need to consistently call the punches after a check and after the whistle.

After a controversial goal, go to the bench if you feel it is necessary to talk to the coach but don't stay 10 feet away.

On end zone positioning, you are going too deep and getting caught in the play; need to bump up the boards.

Jim Maitland
on *Linesmen:*

Don't go into an altercation when the players have their sticks up. "Your safety is more important."

You are holding your signals too long. Drop your arm down as soon as your partner waves off an icing.

On any end zone face-off, after dropping the puck, hold your position and let the play go around you then backup to boards and leave the zone.

On altercations, let up on manhandling the players.

On line changes and after whistles get between players and try to be at the benches when a change is made to prevent any potential problems.

You have a good standard on end zone face-offs but, you need to have the same standard for neutral ice face-offs; they are just as important.

Need to be stricter on encroachment, your partner is removing players and you are allowing them to cheat on the face-offs.

When going into an altercation, get between the players and don't come over the back of a player.

Neutral ice face-offs need to be treated the same as end zone face-offs. Square up the centres. If you do remove a centre, don't go to a quick face-off, the same rules still apply.

When there is an injury and you are the back linesman, get between the benches. Don't stand around and discuss with partner.

You need to pay more attention to the benches on line changes and don't be too focused on the puck.

You should be skating backwards to your line 95% of the time to keep the play in front of you.

The standard for dropping the puck is from an upright position and puck coming out from the belt.

When you are the back linesman, you need to be stricter on encroachment; You need to protect your partner's back.

Supervisors' Tips

KEN HARRIS

Former: OMHA Referee; OHA Referee.

Current: OHA Supervisor (Kingston).

Ken Harris
on *Referees:*

Avoid getting too far out from boards into players' lanes.

When positioned along boards you have a tendency to rest your arm along the top of the boards, it gives an impression of being tired.

During a fight, remember to move non-combatants to neutral zone and watch for coaches dumping the next line out prematurely causing an uneven number of players on the ice. You should be in a position to "halt" that line change.

Be aware when there is a gathering at net and all attacking players are standing at net, face-off should be outside line.

With a noisy crowd, at times the whistle could not be heard. It is necessary to blow whistle sharper and louder.

Remember to control the starting 5 players at the beginning of each period. Make sure these duties are assigned prior to start of game.

Tighten up on push, rough, high sticks after the whistle. Get a discipline rough call to be able to set an early standard. It would help with quicker times between face-offs.

On the 3man system on line changes, I would like you to come out from the corner more, look at the benches and give a clear visible signal. Try to avoid leaving your arm up too long allowing teams to take their time making the change.

Would like to see an early jump to follow play, then continue behind play deep into zone. You are giving impression you are too casual.

Make sure you signal penalty infractions every time, once at whistle and again at penalty box.

Avoid long conversations at the bench; make them short and sweet, especially since he was talking about a past penalty.

Get into the practice of having the reason for no goal announced over P.A system.

You need to tighten up on infractions where player takes his hand off his stick and grabs opponent with free hand.

When play coming at you in the dot area, move your feet to get back to the boards in a safe position, rather then being blown over.

Penalty arm signals need to be straighter, your arm, wrist and hand are bent over your head rather than vertical.

Don't get trapped behind net looking through at goal line rather than looking in from dot area.

On stoppages, especially in net area, give a quick, sharp whistle avoiding other players getting involved.

You could save energy by not stopping completely at blueline to watch play develop but instead curl down inside blueline doing crossovers to change direction.

Remember if all officials have gathered for a chat, who's watching the players?

Ken Harris
on *Linesmen:*

Make sure players are following pre-game polices including goalies' masks. You still have to enforce chinstraps. Rather than chase individual players, report numbers to captain in pre-game warm-up.

When slipping over blueline to allow play to continue, avoid turning your back to players on way back to line position, keep play in front of you by skating backwards.

When you are conducting face-offs in the end zone, give time for partner to get back to his line before dropping puck. Give a quick look in his direction.

When icing is initiated close to red line, a hard shoot in, be vocal to let your partner know he must continue into zone.

When calling icing as the front man, make sure the defenseman makes an attempt at puck. Washout or vocal call early as possible, it is not automatic, get deeper into zone.

During face-offs, puck should be going directly down. Your hand is coming up, sometimes in chest area.

On face-offs after blowing your whistle, get puck dropped quickly. It seems like you are forcing puck down causing you to rock on your skates, try bending you knees slightly.

When attacking player coming down your side of the ice, bump down the boards so you can still make the offside call without getting involved in the play.

Don't be afraid to yell at a player shooting the puck deep into the zone. Let him know you are there, protect yourself.

After initiating icing, follow the play right up to your partner's blueline. If you peel back too soon to your end zone, you're leaving your partner with little protection.

Be strict with skate placement of centres; make sure they are behind the "T" line. If they cheat, quickly remove them.

On face-offs, don't allow centre man to come in late carrying his momentum through dot area. Stop him early or replace him.

When puck is deep in your partner's zone, you should be closer to his blueline for a quick jump into zone if problems or stoppages.

Patrol bench area while players are coming or going in close contact, you must be alert and ready to react.

When making an encroachment call from the back position, it is not necessary to skate all the way to dot, just signal attacking/defensive player.

You need to get a jump to be at your blueline before play crosses line; the players were beating you to the line.

At your blueline, you are going too deep off the line. Don't go more than 2 steps.

Supervisors' Tips

KEN BANNERMAN

Former: OMHA Referee; OMHA Supervisor; OHA Level VI Referee.

Current: OHA Supervisor (Barrie).

Ken Bannerman
on *Referees:*

Don't allow play in corner to keep you up high along boards, you are too far from net, bump down.

Be careful to not assess penalties for intensity.

Stay away from players at penalty box.

Some early verbal communication in scrums may have stopped the "stuff" later in the game.

Get players to bench during a fight.

Don't allow your penalty procedure to become aggressive. Slow down your penalty signals.

You must protect goalies even if contact is minor, as it will escalate.

It appeared by your body language that your emotions got to you. Do not let your emotions elevate with the game.

You must move with the play as it breaks, you can't hang back.

On a penalty call, you must get arm straight up in the air and a bit more firmness on the signal will give you a stronger ice presence.

Allow the play to dictate penalties not the score and make all penalties 100% a penalty.

Do not showboat your penalty signal; it does nothing for your image.

In a game where the puck is sticking on ice after flooding, stop play for a few minutes and give it a chance to freeze.

You might want to try using the word "Relax" to the players after a whistle.

When you see a scoring opportunity, get to the best position possible to observe the action.

You tend to overskate the play at times and missed some cheap shots behind you.

As the referee, you can take charge of face-offs; they must be fair.

I would like to see quicker whistles along boards when a player is down.

Ken Bannerman 2 x 2 System
on *Referees:*

After an icing and the front man is skating from one end to the other, I see it as good practice to point to where the face-off is going to be as he usually beats the liner to the other end and the other two officials are watching the benches and line change.

The high referee must be aware of the man coming out of the penalty box who goes to the bench as we have the opportunity for a premature substitution at the bench as well.

When you each have a penalty at the same time only one should report it as someone must watch the players and line change.

On a Fight in the end zone I believe it is the job of the back referee to be aggressive telling the players to go to the bench. The other referee whose end it is should watch the fight (we finally get to watch some of them now).

When I asses your skating now, be aware I will be focusing more on your backward skating and end zone AGILITY as it is important we continue to be at the net and stay out of the way without ALWAYS going behind the net. I feel going behind the net should only be as a last resort.

As we all know ice presence is important and now that we have two of you out there together it is easy to compare separately both the good and the bad. To try to blend different personalities and game styles is an area we should try to work on to make sure that one referee does not look better than the other. What I am talking about is the way we skate during or after whistles and communicating with players. The teams are more apt to talk to an official who is approachable or who they understand better, so as much as this is a major task we should try to at least show the same body language and skating intensity as your partner. I ask all of you to think about this as you work with different partners.

Ken Bannerman
on *Linesmen:*

In the pre-game warm-up, more attention to detail is required; keep your eyes on the players.

Don't let teams time your face-offs.

On icings, players are not expected to knock puck from the air as it goes past them.

On a delayed offside continue with the verbal "Offside".

On a fight, be careful not to grab a player from behind.

Do not do NHL/OHL puck drops.

You must look back after blowing whistle as front man on icings to look for problems.

Always escort a hot player off the ice especially if he has to go past the visiting goalie.

Puck drop is a downward motion not out and down. It should drop flat and not bounce. After you drop the puck just drift back a bit to avoid to action area of the puck away from your skates.

A bit more zip required after whistles. Anticipate whistles and don't get caught flat-footed.

Do not like to see a linesman up sitting on the boards.

Keep washout signal at shoulder height.

Don't release your line too early, it might cause confusion.

If a player is defenceless in a fight, you must get in.

Always be aware when trouble players are on the ice.

Take charge early on face-offs and slow down as game intensifies.

Be careful on your face-off exit. It is too fast and you are getting involved in play.

Use verbal so players will hear and understand without looking at you.

Do not cross the ice as front man during play.

Back man must watch the benches on a penalty shot or shoot-out.

Do not drop too far inside the blueline; try to hold the line longer.

You should collapse with clock at end of period.

Caution on a close offside; you immediately bolt across blueline; pause and take a look.

Check net after a player goes skate first into netting.

After icing, do not let players get behind you; things can happen.

Always keep heart to puck; it is easier to move out of the way.

Slow down your face-offs. You have 5 seconds so make them stop and set up right.

Be careful not to leave players who were the reason play was stopped and they are still jawing at each other after things had been broken up.

Supervisors' Tips

JOHN MCCUTCHEON

Former: OMHA Referee; OHA Referee; OHL Linesman; NHL Official.

Current: OMHA Supervisor; OMHA Instructor; OHA Supervisor (North-West).

John McCutcheon
on *Referees:*

Awareness, anticipation and keep skating, it will help your positioning.

When a team is down one player, you seem to let up on the standard. You can't let this happen.

You didn't react to what was going on as the game got tougher.

You are cheating on your positioning by waiting between blueline and centre for the team to bring puck out. Get in there, curl and come out with play.

You called interference but a better call would have been hooking.

Watch you don't get too deep in the end zone. I would rather see you move to the top of the circle than go below the goal line.

I was disappointed in your lackluster approach. You need to step it up, hustle and show everyone who is running the game.

Your positioning is terrible; you look like you are puck shy.

You need to be proactive to the play instead you are reacting and are always a step behind.

When a team is in a delayed penalty situation, you must be aware of what player will be coming out of box and when he will come out of the box.

John McCutcheon
on *Linesmen:*

When a team is late getting a player out on a line change, you can't drop puck when a player is in an offside position.

Make sure you are further off the boards; you are getting hit a lot.

When your partner gets pushed off his line, you need to quickly react and cover his line.

Wave-off signals are too high and it is not necessary to point to where the puck was touched after a wave-off.

You can be a big help to referee if you make him aware of time left on clock as you get near the end of a period.

As the back official, watch for goalkeeper substitutions on delayed penalties.

Try to anticipate the play so that you are at your line before the play crosses. Try to be just slightly inside the line for a better view of play crossing line.

Anticipate stoppages so that you can get in faster when whistle blows to help separate players and prevent problems.

Follow play when calling an offside. Don't go directly to face-off dot.

Your line work is effective but you need to bring your level up a couple of notches if you want to be assigned to a higher level of hockey.

You may be using unnecessary signals when a player is crossing blueline with puck and there is no teammate around. Is there a need to wave it okay?

Be aware of player coming out of penalty box on a delayed minor penalty.

Stand tall on face-offs; being bent over means you could be wearing a stick.

On a delayed offside signal, bring arm straight down, not out.

You don't hustle at certain times to be in the best position. Back linesman on stoppages, hustle in from centre line; on icing, hustle harder; covering for your partner, hustle up to his line.

On face-offs, worry about players in front of you, your partner will look after players behind you. Also you should try standing up a little straighter when dropping puck.

Try to always skate backwards to your line from the centre line, it enables you to view the whole play.

When there is a face-off in your partner's end zone, try to hold his line until he releases you or you need to move.

On player changes, the back linesman should skate between the two teams.

Supervisors' Tips

DOUG ROBB

Former: OMHA Referee; OHA Level 6 Referee;

Current: OHA Supervisor (Brantford).

Doug Robb
on *Referees:*

Start earlier calling penalties to take control, it makes life easier.

When skating into end zone, look over your shoulder at the neutral zone. A quick look may catch any nonsense behind play.

You give the appearance of being uptight and very stiff and you have an intimidating style, which indicates a lack of confidence. Try relaxing your shoulders.

Check with injured player before assessing penalty. Shows you care and a progressional move (hit, injury and call). It also gives you time to think.

Move in closer quicker when puck is around the net.

No matter what, call the stick infractions very close, this helps to control the game.

Take a quick look back at point after shot to ensure sticks are down and no one is running at the point man.

Too timid at times, move in and be more vocal.

Don't allow so many conversations during game; warn them to keep away.

Stop inside blueline to prevent linesman from blocking your movement and view of end zone.

You must be calm and cool while presenting signals at the infraction location as well as at the penalty box area. Remember at the stoppages to stop, take a deep breath and relax to give yourself that relaxed look versus a stiff appearance.

Supervisors' Tips

MIKE BILJETINA

Former: OMHA Referee; OHA Referee

Current: OHA Supervisor (Hamilton).

Mike Biljetina
on *Referees:*

Try to keep your eye on the goalie slashing, especially when short-handed.

You must blow your whistle and point at the net when a goal is scored.

Don't stand too close to the players during a gathering, stand back. You will have a better view.

After assessing a penalty, keep the penalized player in view for further infractions.

You are standing on the goal line or behind it much too long, once you bump down and the boards are clear return to home base or half piston if required.

Anticipate the play to avoid starts and stops.

Raise arm that does not block your view on line changes.

Be sure not to position yourself behind net when puck is there.

Be aware of the players behind you to avoid problems.

After discussion last game regarding making penalty signals while in motion you continue to do so. This is a bad habit that you are going to have to break. You are also doing your line change procedure in motion.

Watch for players leaving their feet on checks and keep an eye on sticks in the danger zone (can opener).

On close no goal situations, make sure you give the washout signal.

When you request a coach to place a player inthe penalty box, make sure he does not delay the game making his selection.

Ensure players have the zippers done up on their pants or send them off.

At the end of a period, be aware of players leaving the bench without being waved on.

Remember only the starting five are allowed on ice at the start of a period.

Watch for encroachment on face-offs and call it early.

When a player is injured from a major penalty, position yourself closer to him to examine the extent of the injury.

As a referee we accept criticism to a point but once it becomes verbal abuse, we must react.

Teams were waiting at the start of the second period to go on the ice but had to wait for the officials. Whose responsibility is it? "Be Ready".

You must stay within 1 line of the play when it is breaking out. You have a tendency to be too far back from the play, as was evident when signalling a goal from centre ice.

When player is injured on a penalty there is no urgency for you to report the penalty immediately. Assess the situation (injury) in a composed demeanor to determine whether a major should be called. This will prevent you from having to change your call as you did this game.

When a player is guilty of starting a fight, the call is 5 for fighting + GM + 2 for INS. Do not replace the INS with RO. This is the wrong application of the rules.

Mike Biljetina
on *Linesmen:*

Who's running the face-offs? There is too much hesitation. Blow your whistle when the referee drops his arm, not when the teams get set.

More hustle is needed after the goalie freezes the puck.

When there are multiple fights be sure to escort players right off the ice before returning to intervene in another fight.

After an altercation, one linesman is required to escort player to box. The other linesman should be keeping all players in view.

After a goal is scored, try to position yourself at the benches for the after goal celebration.

I would like to see you position yourself closer to your partner's blue line, especially when he goes in deep.

Be aware of the goalie crossing paths with the opposition at the end of a period as well as the start of the period.

Don't be in a hurry to pick up puck after a whistle, observe the situation with the players first.

Do not turn your back on the benches until a line change has been completed.

When the puck is in your end, you should be standing outside the blueline, not on it. This is basic positioning.

You should skate with the players on a line change; not ahead of them.

Do not wait until the last second to wave off an icings, you must anticipate the play.

I would like to see a quicker reaction on gatherings so you can get a jump on them.

Blow your whistle louder and sharper but not so drawn out.

Take a couple of strides then skate backwards when leaving your partner's end.

As the intensity slowed down, so did you. Keep skating until the final buzzer.

Skating hard after every whistle will help prevent problems. Try to stay focused for the entire game.

When teams exit the same gate at the end of a period, follow the home team off the ice to be a "buffer" between the teams.

Supervisors' Tips

CHARLIE LENNOX

Former: THL Referee; OHA Referee; NYHL Referee-in-Chief; MOHA Referee-in-Chief; OHA Supervision Co-Ordinator; OHA Referee Co-Ordinator.

Current: OHA Supervisor (Toronto West).

Charlie Lennox
On *Referees*

On the line change, don't let the visiting team change after you put your arm down.

When the puck is high sticked and the other team picks it up, you could give a washout signal.

You sometimes take a long time getting started after multiple penalties.

If the net comes off, or a pane of glass comes out or a player is hurt, why not give a double blow on the whistle instead of the same old one toot. It just lets everyone know it is something different.

When an attacking player is hurt and down and the defending player gets control of the puck, blow it down when they get into the neutral zone.

Watch out for the defenseman's free hand grabbing onto a player's sweater or his stick.

When you have a gathering, don't leave the area too soon to assess penalties.

You need to move up quicker to centre ice when the play goes into your partner's end zone in the 2 referee system.

Like to see you try closing your fingers when you are skating, it might save you a broken finger if you get wacked.

It would be beneficial if you were more forceful verbally when you have a gathering.

On the line change procedure, try to be in the vicinity of centre ice so both teams can see you rather than way across the ice on the far side. It is tough to have any eye contact with the bench from that far away.

In the 2 x 2 officiating system, when you are the back referee during a scrum in your partner's end, I would like you to come over the blueline and position yourself so you can keep the defensemen back, watch the benches and still see the scrum.

There was a lot of stuff after the whistles that might have been prevented by calling some early penalties with a differential. As the old saying goes, "A penalty differential always pays dividends".

When you explain something to one coach, make sure you let the other team's coach know what it was all about.

Caution; when the play is coming at you out of the offensive zone, don't drift into the centre ice area, try to stay in the lane between the hash marks and the boards.

We talked about the shot that hit the goalie in the facemask and I felt you could have blown the play dead at that point. He seemed ok and I could see you were watching him as play left the zone but why take the chance.

For the positioning for a penalty shot or a shootout, we put a referee and one linesman on the goal line. When the shootout was in your partner's end, and you were the back referee, you curled in behind the shooter and came down behind him on same side as the referee on the goal line. It would be better if you came down on the other side (linesman's side) so you get a different angle on the shot.

Charlie Lennox
On Linesmen

As the front linesman, you need to be ready to get in fast to the net on the whistle. The back Linesman should not beat you in there.

In a 3 man system you have to be ready to cover for the referee on a quick break or cover your partner's line when he covers for the referee on a quick break.

On a penalty shot or shootout if you are the back linesman, your job is to watch the benches especially the team who had the shot called against them. To do that, you have to come off the boards about ten feet and face the benches and concentrate. Keep in mind if someone did distract the shooter by throwing a stick or a glove, could you advise the referee who did it?

Don't come off the boards to sell the wave-off. You sometimes are dodging players when you do this. Don't overdo your calls.

You can't come out in pre-game warm-up or at the start of a period with your chin strap UNDONE. The players can't do it and neither can you.

You display strong, crisp signals with good line calls. I like the fact that you don't wave every offside but are always in position to make the call.

On face-offs, you need to get square to the players. You are standing half turned 'like a baseball player at the plate with his foot in the bucket'.

You are a big guy so there is no need nor is there any advantage to going into a crouch as the play crosses your blueline. Stand Tall.

The icing the puck procedure was well handled but don't make it too easy for them. The defenseman has to make an effort to get the puck and not just turn away and several I thought could have been waved off.

You have a bad habit of holding onto the boards with one hand as play comes at you. Please don't do this. Instead bump down. To avoid contact.

Don't leave your line to go into the corner to pick up a broken stick. You got caught at the top of the circle when the play crossed your line.

Your face-offs were fair puck drops but after you drop the puck, back to the side boards and then go back towards your blue-line rather than backing into the corner.

I did not feel you had a good game and did many things that need correction. To be specific: mentally get into the game, skate faster, don't lean on the boards, don't talk to benches and work on your face-offs.

There is no presentation of puck for face-offs in the OHA. It is to be dropped from the waist.

The face-offs were fair but I would like you stand a little taller, you are in a 3/4 crouch and the puck comes down from your knee giving a slight advantage to the centre on that side.

Like the way you positioned yourself to watch the goalie coming out on a delayed penalty.

You must anticipate the play and get to the net quicker after a whistle.

Sometimes when you are back linesman and there is encroachment on your partner's corner face-off, you skate in to point out the offender...it is not necessary to do this...just signal which team was encroaching.

Supervisors' Tips

LEON STICKLE

Former: OMHA Referee; OHA Official; NHL Linesman; NHL Supervisor.

Current: CHL Senior Supervisor of Officals; OHA Supervisor (Guelph/Kitchener).

Leon Stickle
On Referees

I would like to see you NOT turn your back to the front of the net when watching the play at the boards on your side of the rink. This would be the time to use 'a pivot' and 'c' cut to be able to see both areas of concern.

Adheres to all expected standards and procedures and not afraid to deal with the benches when trying to squash any 'trash talking' taking place.

Avoid the congested areas in the end zones by not standing still and making good selections to move to safe locations.

You must be especially tuned into the fouls that can lead to major problems if not 'nicked in the bud'.

Use your skating strengths when caught in any kind of traffic and/or congested areas in the end zone to get to 'safe' areas with good sightlines. Don't be afraid to 'bump' up the half wall when necessary to avoid being pinned, and return to expected home base area immediately when the opening arises.

Please come to a stop in front of the penalty box (when possible) when reporting penalties so the penalty timekeeper has no excuse for reporting the wrong call.

DON'T forget to move the players away from the immediate vicinity of a fighting situation instead of letting them hang around and act as cheerleaders.

When the play is in your end zone, try to consistently acquire the best sightlines available by moving in and out of the preferred areas of the 'home' base.

With play at the net you must exhibit a strong presence without becoming directly involved in the play. This will enable you to make the proper decision on whether the puck frozen or not.

In this chippy game, I felt that if you had not 'stayed' focused, we may still be in the building!

In the end zone, I would like to see you be a little more active along the goal line with the thought in mind that you have to go to the net during scrums, and close-in plays at the net.

Whenever you have a 'disallowed' goal, be sure you follow the necessary procedure of reporting it to the Penalty Bench and have an announcement made explaining the reason for not counting the goal.

Sometimes you do get positioned too deep in the corners with play in close proximity, but because you are such a strong skater, you can usually get yourself out of any predicaments. My best advice would be to NOT get that deep in the first place as it does take its toll on sightlines when you are scrambling to find a 'safe' area from which to operate.

It is necessary to work very hard in all zones to establish and maintain the best positioning possible while keeping adequate sightlines to your immediate surroundings and the goal area.

Don't forget to make sure that a player penalized for the warm-up violation DOES start the game in the Penalty Box.

You handled the line change procedure well but would like to see you be more visible to both benches by conducting this procedure from a more open part of the ice (this just negates any complaints by Coaches that they did not see your arm up).

Remember that 'boarding' when from behind and hitting into the boards is better termed 'checking from behind' when it is a hit to the numbers.

When you have the close in scrambles at the net, don't hesitate to move closer to the goal area. This also sells any critical calls that you have to make as the players see your presence there.

Make sure early in the game to set a clear standard with play battles that warrant penalties.

Move closer to your partner's end zone when working as the 'high' referee. Somewhere between the red line and blue line is acceptable. Always keep in mind that maintaining open sightlines to the play will prove to be your 'best friend'. You can be a little more active when you are the 'high' man and always give yourself the benefit of those sightlines.

I feel that both you and your partner could have reacted earlier in the game to the scrums that (at the net) were happening at almost every stoppage. It's easier to get your point across early with differential penalties than by waiting too deep into the game. All that does is send a message of inconsistency!

I would like to see less explaining to coaches (at the benches) over your calls. They are NOT going to change your decision, so pick your spots and make it seem like you are in full control and quit entertaining ALL of their concerns.

One thing that I did notice was when you are using a strong pivot to avoid the players in a congested area; you tend to only half pivot and end up actually in a vulnerable position between the play and the net. If you complete the 'cut' it will get you out of harm's way, prevent you from having your back to the net, and still give you complete sightlines of all players.

Leon Stickle
On Linesmen

When you are the front man on icings, use your speed when returning to the far end zone for the faceoff (this is your turn to shine and let everyone know that you are a good skater!).

It is important to ALWAYS give a good 'release' signal to your partner when taking back responsibility of your blue line.

You must have good backwards mobility and lots of awareness pertaining to any after whistle scrums.

Be careful not to drift in so far over your line when making your line calls as it distorts the position of the puck to the line.

You have a good rapport with the players just don't be overly close with them as your friend today could become your enemy tomorrow!

As mentioned following the game, your encroachment standard needs some improvement. Please focus more attention on players not being outside of the face-off circle. One encroachment now will be three next week if not nipped now.

Please blow the whistle harder and with authority as on at least 3 occasions it was hard to hear and play continued a little longer than it should have.

Don't forget to always give your partner the release signal when taking back your line...I realize that sometimes you feel that using that signal means nothing, but from my viewing area, it makes everything look very 'professional' and should become habit.

Supervisors' Tips

JERRY PATEMAN

No Picture Available

Former: OMHA Referee; IHL Official; NHL Linesman.

Current: ECHL Supervisor; OHA Supervisor (Windsor).

Jerry Pateman
On Referees

Felt that you didn't react to the chippiness early and that led to a chippy second period that was getting a bit out of hand. You being the senior ref, I thought you would have clamped down on them and helped your partner out, or at least communicated to him to get a hold of it.

Be ready to go on the ice quicker than 30 seconds left on clock. Designate someone to check the time on clock.

Thought at times you were too far back when the play was in your partners end. You called a penalty (good call) but you called it from two zones back. Not good.

Please refrain from crossing your arms as you skate away from the penalty box or the bench area as it conveys a look of "hurry up, I don't want to be here all night." Don't give the teams a reason to get Po'd.

I would like to see you get closer to the net, especially when play is in and around the goalie. A couple of times you had quick whistles when the puck was still loose.

Make good use of your "C" cuts. At times you were stopping and getting caught flat footed and it burns too much energy trying to get back up to speed.

Be aware of whole ice surface when you are in a three man system. At times you were looking at the puck area and forgetting about the other players.

You are getting caught on fast breaks out of the zone. I would like to see you anticipate the play breaking the other way quicker so that you are not caught flat footed.

In the 2 x 2 system, as the back referee, when sustained play is in the end zone, get closer to blue-line for a better look.

When play is around the net, get close, and be present when it ends, players less likely to start a scrum with you there.

When players are going hard along boards in end zone, keep in motion and pivot off the boards to let them go by.

Don't get caught too far in the corner when play is in tight to the net. Easier to say you saw it, if you are there, rather than back so far. Get in closer.

I would like to see you not stop as often. I want you to continue to skate by using the figure eight as much as possible so that you don't waste energy by stopping and starting.

When two guys are fighting for position in front of the net and its getting a little chippy, just don't stand there: be vocal and give them a warning (keep sticks down, etc.) that way they know you are there and aware of what they are doing.

Make sure when you assess penalties, (even with a partner) you don't lose sight of the other players on the ice.

While letting players throw hard body checks, be vigilant to them finishing hits with high sticks.

Stay alert to players delivering body-checks after skating a long way, or too long after player getting hit has gotten rid of the puck.

Try not to POINT at the penalized player. Use your whole hand, (it makes it less personal).

As the neutral zone official when the play is in your partner's end zone don't wander out too far towards centre. Stay closer to the boards - maybe an arm's length or two from the linesman (or where the linesman would be if not on that side).

Jerry Pateman
On Linesmen

I didn't like that icing that you and partner called in the first period. You waved it off (partner did) when no one could have gotten it. It was a perfect time to establish your icing standard as it was very early in the game.

You initiated an icing in OT that was close but nonetheless it WAS icing and the fact that your calls WERE consistent all game, the offending team complained, but, not nearly as much had you and your partner not been as tight on icings all game.

Face-offs were well handled: just don't lose sight of the guys in front. Make sure the centers are ready, but, don't allow wingers in front of you to sneak in.

As a team during the fights, I thought you and partner were either not communicating well or you just weren't getting the upper hand in breaking them up. Want you to anticipate more and quicker. If you see a potential scrum is going to break out as you are the back man: move up so that you aren't going to get there much later than partner, especially if the play is in the opposite corner.

Don't worry about retrieving the puck after a whistle, when play is chippy.

Be aware of players when they are jawing at each other as they go by the benches. This is where a good linesman can separate himself from a mediocre one. It also helps the referees.

I believe you are in good shape but I have noticed that perhaps you are lacking a jump in your step. Your anticipation of a potential scrum may be going through your mind but your feet aren't moving at the same pace.

Be aware of ALL the players that may be in zone when puck enters or re-enters the zone.

Be ready to come up to partner's line when the short-handed team is clearing the puck out on partner's side of ice.

When your partner calls an offside in his zone on a play that originated in your end of the rink: point to the spot where the faceoff will take place so you give players coaches, and everyone else knowledge of where the faceoff will take place.

You skate well, but your anticipation of play breaking towards you is not consistent. At times you get caught leaving your line early as well.

Want you to anticipate when play will be blown dead in your zone so that you are there to prevent potential scrums from erupting.

Don't go into fights alone! Communicate with your partner. Look at the first fight and stick with it. Break it up and get them to penalty box. Do the same for the next fight etc.

Be careful not to get caught not anticipating play. At times you were getting to the blue-line the same time as the play. Be sure you are there first.

On an icing, when you are the back linesman and you are going to wave off the play because the puck was at the centerline, (a close call), make sure you give a washout signal and not just yell. It is not only for your partners but also for coaches and fans alike.

Supervisors' Tips

MIKE PEARCE

Former: OMHA Referee; OHA Level 6 Referee; AHL Linesman; OHL Referee; GTHL Manager of Officiating; OHA Supervisor (Sarnia).

Current: OHA Supervisor Alumni

Mike Pearce
On Referees

Here is a tip for you. When there is an altercation in the end zone & your partner is watching it & the linesman are involved breaking things up, move closer to the benches. There was chirping going on from players on each bench & you were focused on the altercation.

As discussed in the post game supervision, ensure penalties are reported RAW and not RO penalties when the infraction occurs after the whistle. This is an important distinction.

I particularly liked when you worked the piston to perfection during back-to-back goal mouth scrambles. The play began with a goal mouth scramble. You moved to half piston, then to the net briefly to see the puck on the opposite side of the net. The play suddenly moved towards you. You backed up to home base then had to rapidly return to the net to get a look at second goal mouth scramble.

There was an immediate scrum after a check and the following five minutes of play was rough resulting in additional penalties. This likely could have been de-escalated with the assessment of the CFB. Please ensure you do not substitute penalties for a CFB.

Good positioning to see goal mouth scrambles and scoring opportunities. You got caught once and had to spin 360 degrees to avoid contact with players. Remember to bump and pivot.

A couple of times tonight, you "sold" calls through assertiveness. Although the appropriate penalty was called, the extra "umph" demonstrated control and de-escalated potential scrums.

You had no issues with sight lines and overall end zone positioning, but stricter adherence to piston is required as per Hockey Canada standards.

As the neutral zone official when the play is in your partner's end zone don't wander out too far towards centre. Stay closer to the boards - maybe an arm's length or two from the linesman (or where the linesman would be if not on that side).

Mike Pearce
On Linesmen

You displaced great work as the front official hustling into the zone to be close to the puck as it crossed the goal line. I particularly liked this at 12:49 of the 1st period when there was a foot chase to the puck and you were right there with the players. It looked awesome.

You showed sound judgment especially when washing out potential icings when players neglect to play playable pucks.

Be more aware of line change attempts after icings. In the 1st period, the referee caught a player sneaking onto the ice. In this instance your body position remained in the same direction that it was prior to the stoppage. With both benches on the same side of the ice and the on-ice players in the far end, turn to face the benches.

In the 1st period, your partner held his blue line under pressure. You immediately recognized the potential that he may need help and got to his line quickly to cover. It became apparent that he could make the line call and you immediately returned to normal positioning. Great work!

Supervisors' Tips

JOE PAOLINI

Former: OMHA Referee; OHA Referee.

Current: OHA Supervisor (Toronto West).

Joe Paolini
On Referees

One thing to keep in mind as the back referee, don't get involved in the scrums in front of the net and keep an eye on the benches.

It is important to be visible to both benches when operating the line change procedures and also be very aware of the on-ice players when icing has been called.

Try to consistently acquire the best sight lines available by moving in and out of the preferred areas of the 'home' base.

No issues with sight lines and overall end zone positioning, but try to be a little deeper as play comes into the zone. This will allow better reaction time and allow you to see the play develop.

Try to stay a little closer to the boards when moving up and down the nice and not get caught behind the goal line.

After you make the signal at the penalty box you turned and skated directly in the path of the penalized player. Try to turn away from the penalized player so he has to go out of his way to verbally dispute the call and everyone will see it. Then if an additional minor or misconduct penalty is assessed everyone in the rink can see the player chasing you around to dispute the call.

Supervisors' Tips

MARK PARE

Former: OHA Official; IHL Linesman; NHL Linesman, Ron Foxcroft Award-2010.

Current: OHA Supervisor (Windsor).

Mark Pare
On Referees

Give yourself some room in end-zone; hang back a little so you are not too close to the action. You are a good enough skater to catch up through the neutral zone.

Keep play in front of you and stay on the perimeter so you don't get in the way.

Overall your penalty selections were well executed. However, be careful that you don't focus on the puck and forget the front of the net.

You skate very well, but would like to see you anticipate or read the play breaking towards you better.

Position yourself around net when play gets close, and present when it ends, players less likely to start a scrum with you there.

CONFIDENCE: After you made the first penalty call of the game, your partner had the rest, but you didn't force yourself on the game, as someone with less confidence in themselves may be prone to do.

When sustained play is in end zone, as back referee get closer to blue-line for a better look.

When play is on far boards, get closer to net to have a better view of players, if the play reverses, stay along goal-line and back out.

When players are going hard along boards in end zone, keep in motion and pivot off the boards to let them go by.

When you are high man when play is in end-zone, be ready to step up and make call that partner can't see.

Stay above goal-line for best look at goal mouth area, if play comes at you in circle, get back to boards or go down low to stay out of traffic.

Stay alert to players delivering body-checks after skating a long way, or too long after player getting hit has gotten rid of the puck.

Be ready to penalize player who, having been beaten to the outside, uses a free hand to slow down opponent.

Try to make your penalty signals in a controlled manner, not hurried or over-officious.

Mark Pare
On Linesmen

Work with partner to move off blue-line when defending team about to clear puck, he can move up and you can stay out of harm's way.

Be patient when exiting end-zone after face-off when play is on the same side.

During a delayed penalty call, if you are back linesman, watch for goaltender coming to bench to change for an extra attacker.

Once play crosses your blue-line, keep facing play and back out of zone, don't turn your back to the play. To avoid contact along boards, face play, rather than turn away from it.

After ejecting a centre from face-off; take a little time to get next player in set and stopped.

When play is going up partners' side of ice to his blue-line, get moving through the neutral zone to his line in case he is moved off the blue-line. Stay in closer to his line on power plays in his end, in case the short-hand team clears puck out of zone at him.

Stay on line until partner gets back in position from end-zone face offs. Come off boards a little so puck won't hit you and stay behind D-man trying to keep puck in.

Good exits on face-offs. Stay in corner if puck on same side, let partner cover line until it's clear to exit.

Make signals more emphatic, wave close plays to sell the call. Signal first; then give reason for wave-off.

If defending player turns away from puck without trying to play it, wave off icing.

Supervisors' Tips

CRAIG SPADA

Former: OMHA Referee; OHA Level VI Referee; OHL Referee; AHL Referee; NHL Referee.

Current: OHA Supervisor (Niagara).

Craig Spada
on *Referees:*

It is to your advantage as back referee to move up away from the red line and closer to the blue line. This is important when having to make a penalty call. This is easier to control while one team is on the power play.

You seem to skate forward then adjust to backwards as play breaks out. You are therefore turning your back to the play too much.

Just one concern and that was the late slash to the goalie early in the game, in this play you ended up taking the player who retaliated and no penalty the player who really started the scrum. Just be aware of the first action.

Please do not jump forward and lose your consistent position just because of a delayed penalty on your arm. Stay focused and keep the game in front at all times.

I believe a HC was the call not holding, the point was you knew it was a penalty so take your time with the signal. You can even wait until you get to the box in this case.

You can improve on your sightlines by a simple move right or left to give you the view needed to see the penalty. Create the angles in the game and avoid the straight on views where you get blocked out.

On puck control when the puck changes hands, you must react. This will avoid you standing a lot and create movement outside the line and in the end zone. Your sightlines will improve.

You need to carry a more relaxed nature. Avoid always bending your hands to your knees when PRESSURED, stand straight, calm and relaxed and your overall PRESENCE will improve.

When bumping remember to get back to where the entire game is in front of you, thus leaving no chance for a missed hit.

When a coach is upset, get away from the bench, out near to center ice, make him yell so all can hear, not just you. Make him look bad and deserving of the penalty.

Good standard throughout, good job not letting up on the high risk infractions especially on the numerous CFB and HC. Did not fold continued to call penalties right to the end in a game where teams were not being controlled by their benches.

Remember to avoid meeting up with the coach as he exits the ice between periods. This will only be trouble.

Craig Spada
on *Linesmen:*

Please remember to avoid head movements and jesters during the face off. Simply use your voice to get players into position.

On face-offs just make sure you are not bent over each and every faceoff as discussed, be ready in an upright position as to not throw off centers and wingers prior to the draw.

On a delayed offside call when a player has no interest of retreat, blow the whistle and stop play.

Please make sure you take the player all the way to the penalty box after an altercation before you turn your back on him.

Remember to be action-reaction, player on line change someone gives a guy a shot, slash etc... Maybe not a penalty but let him know you saw it, verbally or penalty whatever warrants the situation. Just never ever do nothing.

Supervisors' Tips

BRENT HOLDSWORTH

Former: OHA Level VI Referee; OHL Referee.

Current: OHA Supervisor (Hamilton).

Brent Holdsworth
on *Referees:*

Try to utilize the "CONE" in the end to allow you to created good sight lines for infractions and loose pucks around the net.

During a fighting altercation, be sure to position yourself where the fight and the rest of the players on the ice are in plain view. When you are the back man, make sure you support the back side of the scrum that your partner might not be able to see.

In the 2 man ref system, you need better awareness on what penalties are being called and ones that are being served, this allows better game management and prevents over calling infractions that you may not need.

You are spending too much time behind the goal line or deep in the corner during your end zone positioning. Make sure to utilize the "CONE" positioning, this will allow better sightlines for infractions and loose pucks around the net. Any position behind the goal line or deep in the corner will make you vulnerable to interfere with the play.

Need to anticipate better around the net after the whistle, especially when there is a gathering. Once the whistle has gone, you can make your presence felt by getting to the net and then communicating with the players. This shows the players you're still involved and may prevent any further infractions.

Brent Holdsworth
on *Linesmen:*

As the back man be sure to stay along the boards, tonight you spent too much time floating out towards the middle of the ice. Always keep yourself away from the play.

During a potential icing, communicate better with the players and the benches that are trying to substitute prior to the stoppage of play.

You should never find yourself climbing the boards to avoid the play. Bump out and back into position.

Reaction must be a lot faster when the goalie leaves the crease during a potential icing call.

Supervisors' Tips

RALPH SPARKS

Former: THL Referee; THL Supervisor; THL Ref-in-Chief; OHA Referee; OHA Supervisor (Toronto/Barrie).

Current: OHA Supervisor Alumni.

Ralph Sparks
on *Referees:*

After calling a penalty, don't be in a hurry to get to get to the penalty box.

Faster whistles along the boards would stop a lot of nonsense that leads to fights.

Not forceful enough on mouth-guards and helmets tilted back.

When a team is killing a penalty, you should skate deeper into the zone as far as the first forechecker.

Do not take your eyes off the puck to pick up a broken stick; kick it to the side.

When a confrontation starts, try skating toward them while you are talking.

Suggest you move in closer to a penalized player to save your lungs.

You are following the puck too close (tunnel vision) and it is causing you to miss too many fouls.

Avoid coasting when puck is deep and you have just crossed the centre line.

When puck is around net but no scoring chance, take quick look back if you know there are opposing players back at the blueline.

Everything you want on the scoresheet must be told to the timekeeper.

Don't let players delay game by carrying on a prolong conversation.

You are spending way too much time behind the goal line when you should be out in front and in position to work the "piston". Avoid going behind goal line when play does not force you there.

Don't be too anxious on calling a penalty. Give yourself that split second before making the call but, once you put your arm in the air, it can't come down without a penalty call.

Suggest you be more forceful with benches at the end of the periods, don't be too lax.

Ralph Sparks
on *Linesmen:*

Make sure your partner is in proper position before dropping the puck on end zone face-offs.

Suggest you move up closer to partner's line on icing calls.

When a fight breaks out, wait for your partner before entering.

When covering for referee on a fast break avoid making a signal for a goal or no goal.

Following stoppages of play when there is a confrontation between players, instead of skating around perimeter, try to get in between them quickly to help referee control situations.

Keep your hands out of your pockets and show more hustle on every whistle.

Don't get into the habit of placing your hands on a penalized player on his way to the penalty box.

On icings, make the player play the puck, do not automatically call the icing.

You must react a little faster to cover your partner's line when he is covering for the referee on a breakaway.

Supervisors' Tips

WAYNE MCDONALD

Former: OMHA Referee; OHA Referee; OHA Supervisor (North-Central).

Current: OHA Supervisor Alumni

Wayne McDonald
on *Referees:*

Try being a little more vocal with players and move in closer to scrums after the whistle. But don't get so close that you lose your prospective with the benches and the rest of the ice surface. Get the differential if possible.

Watch those quick line changes especially during scrums after the whistle. Keep them back.

During those after whistle scrums, you have got to get the players, who are hanging around, out of there. Blow your whistle and caution them back.

You have a tendency to fade right in behind the goal line, too often, instead of going to home base or half piston.

When a player was injured and the coach was upset, I don't think it was a good idea to go over to the bench. It just upset him more and you had to throw him out.

I find you really lagging behind the play and I think you are coasting too much through the neutral zone when you should be still skating hard.

On end zone positioning, don't go so deep that you get caught on quick breaks and have to skate hard to catch up. Anticipate the play and move quicker.

On the line change signal try moving out or near top of the circle especially when you are on same side as the benches.

Try to avoid moving in too close to players during after whistle scrums; you lose sight of things going on behind you.

Try to maintain that zero tolerance consistency on stick infractions throughout game.

Watch those player hits when they jump and their skates are off the ice.

You are far too officious and centre of attention. You need to tone it down. You are supposed to be invisible out there.

Try not to focus on the puck all the time; you are missing the other infractions.

I find you spend too much time explaining your penalty calls to the players and the benches.

It is nice to be a good guy but don't forget you have responsibilities to both teams.

You can holler until you are blue in the face and you can give them co-incidental penalties all night. It doesn't stop the problem. Deal with it early and try to get the initial infraction. It might help eliminate some of the problems.

Remember when you are skating around prior to the game you're supposed to have your chinstrap done up. Set the example.

Try to avoid skating in the middle of the ice rather than skating in your lane. Try to reduce the amount of time in "no man's land".

Supervisors' Tips

RON ASSELSTINE

Former: Guelph Minor Association; OHA Official; World Hockey Association Official; NHL Linesman; Fox40 Sports Award Winner; OHA Supervisor. (Guelph area)

Current: OHA Supervisor Alumni.

Ron Asselstine
on *Referees:*

When making the line change signal during player changes, move out into open ice so the coaches can see you.

When calling a penalty that could be interpreted as either holding, or roughing, interference or hooking call the most obvious rather than calling interference.

Remember when assessing a penalty, you identify the player by number and colour of sweater with your voice plus signal then repeat it at the penalty box. Do it for every penalty, every time.

Don't be afraid to get close to the action and use your skating skills to accelerate through the neutral zone. A few times you got caught behind the play because you were coasting through the neutral zone.

Come to a full stop in front of the penalty timekeeper when giving the penalty signal.

Remember to keep a close watch on the benches at the end of a long shift so the teams don't cheat on the changes waiting for the tired player to leave the ice.

Ron Asselstine
on *Linesmen:*

Remember not to cross in front of the net on icings, stay in your lane. If you had to wave it off, you would be way out of position.

Work on your signals, especially the "washout". Fingers should be closed arms straight out and stand erect.

Do not try to make the call "in heavy traffic". If you feel pressure, go with it and allow your partner to move up and make the call.

Remember to back out of the end zone after face-offs.

Don't over anticipate the whistle in your partner's end and move in too quickly. Let him cheat towards the scrum, you cover his line, then when the whistle blows, you can move in.

Supervisors' Tips

BOB SPENCE

Former: OMHA Referee; OHA Official; OHA Supervisor (Sarnia).

Current: OHA Supervisor Alumni.

Bob Spence
on *Linesmen:*

Square up centres on face-offs, they were able to draw puck on their forehand.

When the referee called a Gross Misconduct and you knew it was a Match, you should have reported it to him.

You are very inconsistent on icings. You waved off the icings when nobody could have played the puck.

You are responsible for the players behind your partner on end zone face-offs.

You waved out the centremen, rather than tell them to get out when the players in front of you entered the circle on an end zone face-off.

Don't leave your partner's blueline too early, as it will be left uncovered until he gets back to his position.

Be sure to blow your whistle every time after the referee drops his arm.

When it is obvious on a delayed offside that they're not going to clear the zone, blow your whistle sooner.

Try to show some enthusiasm for the whole game instead of only 50 minutes. It looked at the start of the game like you didn't want to be there.

On icing when your partner goes deep after stopping play to pick up puck, move up to his blueline in case anything happens after the whistle.

When you are pushed off your blueline towards centre and your partner covers, you take his blueline and then switch back when it is safe to do so.

You focus on puck too much after the whistle, which forced the referee to call penalties because you weren't there to prevent the pushing and shoving.

Make up your mind sooner on icings; you are waiting too long to wave them off and go with puck down the ice instead of waiting for it to cross the icing line.

Supervisors' Tips

SAM SISCO

Former: OHA Referee; IHLReferee; NHL Supervisor; OHA Supervisor (Windsor); OHL Supervisor; IHL VP Hockey Operations.

Current: OHA Supervisor Alumni.

Sam Sisco
on *Referees:*

When you are assessing penalties, always skate backward to penalty box keeping all players in view.

Over signalling, you are making too many wave-offs at net and make goalkeepers move the puck.

In the 3 man system, do not proceed the play out of the zone; let the play develop in front of you.

When assessing multiple penalties, allow only one player from each team near penalty box for the explanation.

You have a tendency to stay in corner, move to net when puck is in the crease area.

When you have gatherings at every stoppage, send a message and tighten up your standard.

Do not leave scene of an altercation too soon.

Maintain enforcement on stick and rough play infractions from beginning to end of game.

Sam Sisco
on *Linesmen:*

You must be quick to react and move in to prevent any possible altercations.

Don't give an advantage to team icing the puck by being too lenient with too many wave-offs.

Be less physical when separating players during a potential altercation. During a fight and all players are still standing, come in from the side; do not grab a player from behind.

On stoppages, move to players rather than to puck and a little more anticipation is needed as you are late getting into gatherings at the net.

When the play is coming over your blueline, setup inside to better see the puck as it crosses and don't washout obvious non-offsides. Blow whistle immediately on carryover offsides. On face-offs, do not telegraph release of puck with an upward motion.

Supervisors' Tips

MIKE DUGGAN

Former: Maple Ridge B.C. Referee; Etobicoke Hockey Association Referee; OHA Referee; Oha Supervisor (Brampton).

Current: Streetsville Referee-in-Chief; OHA Supervisor Alumni.

Mike Duggan
on *Referees:*

Be consistent with the line change procedure, head up and make eye contact with coaches.

Make sure you clear the zone (including goalie) during a fight, get the numbers and get the game going.

Always take the stuff after the whistle with a differential when possible.

You are still too far behind play especially crossing the blueline. Skate harder over the blueline in pursuit of play.

Speed up your penalty procedure; don't stand around with your hand in the air.

Get closer to the net in the end zones and anticipate the play for better positioning so you can see the whole situation.

When you have players behind you as you break with the play, look back every other stride.

Don't cross the ice in front of the play.

You were too deep too often when there was no need, bump UP the boards.

Lengthen your skating strides and get closer in pursuit and tighten your end zone turns inside the dot.

If you have to go the bench to explain something, make sure you take a linesman with you EVERY TIME.

Your whistles at stoppages of play need to be louder and longer, you could have a problem in a noisy rink.

Try to anticipate play and you will have less skating and more energy.

On a penalty, you are too far away from penalty box when reporting to scorekeeper. Try to give the signal in the referee's crease instead of centre ice.

During altercations, keep the players and benches in front of you; you can hold a line change if there's potential trouble at the time.

Use the Captain or Assistant rather than going to the bench so often and don't go when coach calls you over unless it is prudent.

When calling a penalty point with your hand and don't point in the player's face.

You're behind the goal line too often. You're skating much more than you have to and you get caught behind the play. Don't go so deep in the end zone.

Don't leave a gathering until you are sure nothing else is going on.

Call RAW (Rough after Whistle) rather than RO (Rough).

Try to look a little more "Alive", not quite so laid back.

Mike Duggan
on *Linesmen:*

Make your wave off signal so your arms are parallel to the boards and straight out from your shoulders.

Don't turn your back on face-off exits, keep the play in front of you at all times.

Sit-ups will improved your on ice image along with a new sweater.

Don't enter a fight by yourself unless there is a valid reason to do it.

Do not lean on the boards at any time, it looks bad.

Make sure your face-off drop is straight down from the top of your jock.

Do not leave a player after a fight until he is all the way off the ice.

On goalie substitutions, the back linesman takes numbers and watches the goalie off and the player on.

Don't go so far over the blueline as play crosses, one metre over is enough.

Work on your backward crossovers for face-off exits.

On offsides, be ready, anticipate the play and be prompt with your whistle. Don't hesitate or wave it then blow it.

No hand signal when you return to your blueline after a face-off.

If two players are "jawing", stay with them until they are both off the ice.

Try to look a little more relaxed on the ice; calm and in control.

You must cover for your partner if he has to bail out.

Supervisors' Tips

DAVID MONTGOMERY

Former: GTHL Referee; OHA Referee; OHA Supervisor.

Current: GTHL Supervisor; OHA Supervisor Alumni.

David Montgomery
on *Referees:*

Early overreaction to play is affecting your positioning in the neutral zone.

You must have a good after the whistle penalty awareness of all player activity.

When play is deep, don't move up the boards and comprise your coverage and movement to the net.

When your game pacing settles down, don't drift, "focus".

When play in corner, don't let players behind you; give them clearance but don't turn your back to slot play.

When you signal a penalty, don't leave too soon.

General impression is you have a very relaxed demeanor, maybe too relaxed.

Post whistle visits to benches and group discussions have a double-edged perception.

Try not to over skate the play coming out of the defending zone.

David Montgomery
on *Linesmen:*

Don't leave your partner's blueline in transition until he is back/close to his line.

When your partner is caught mid-ice behind the play, cover his line.

You must have good anticipation and conflict coverage with solid hustle and teamwork.

On face-off set-up, give a balanced puck drop and exit and don't rush into traffic.

You must have good awareness to anticipate the play and react to post whistle player movement.

The back man on an icing must move up to cover his partner's line when he is deep in the zone.

Minimize movement on face-offs to avoid ejecting the players and don't rush the puck drop.

Supervisors' Tips

MEL HUCTWITH

Former: OHA Referee; OHA Supervisor (London); OHA Referees' Honour Roll 1990.

Current: OHA Supervisor Alumni.

Mel Huctwith
on *Referees:*

On several occasions you have a tendency to skate against the flow. When the defending team gains clear possession, stop skating toward that end.

When you assess penalties it seems to me that you are being overly deliberate before you move toward the penalty box. This extra attention delay draws more attention than you really want.

As you know I encourage referees to talk to players but you would look better if you were to limit the number of players in the huddle.

I am seeing a tendency on the part of referees to get too close to skirmishes. You really reduce the information you might want by getting in too tight. I think you would be better to stand back 15 to 20 feet and use your voice to settle the players involved and to let the coaches know what you are thinking at that exact instant.

Prolonged stoppages along the boards draw more attention to you. They tend to cause puzzlement. A quicker whistle would be a useful practice.

You would do well to control the tendency to participate in multiple player conversations.

You should use your "voice" signal louder and longer more often. It helps the aggressive player make better decisions and it helps the "victim" to understand the difference between a non-call and a missed call.

On corner face-offs you are coming too far out of the end zone to deliver the line change signal.

When assessing penalties, you can extend your presence with a stronger more authoritative stride; this helps to sell your call.

You would improve your role on skirmishes by being seen and heard to be directing players away.

The only change I would offer would be to limit/reduce your consultations with players. They add to slowing of pace, well intention but not perceptibly useful.

Not sure why you wouldn't take a position on the goalie sitting on the bench without a helmet. Your butt is the one most directly on the line, followed closely by mine then the OHA.

It looks to me like you would be safer, happier and prettier if you were to reduce the number of times you skate into the corner on top of the puck.

Stopping short at the hash marks when the puck is on your side gives you just as good a view as the other way.

I suggest that it would be to your advantage to soften your signals. Whatever you can do to enhance your matter-of-fact businesslike position in the game works to your advantage.

We would like to have to call fewer penalties at this time of the year but it seems to be the only way to keep the <u>kids from criminal behaviour.</u>

Mel Huctwith
on *Linesmen:*

Some night you will wish that you had not used your judgment wave-off when your partner is covering your line. We should never see two linesmen waving off the same call at the blueline.

As the back linesman, when the shorthanded team shoots the puck, I think you should give your partner the wave-off signal to remind him of the non-icing situation.

You have a tendency to drive out of the end zone after a face-off, for everyone sake, slow it down.

When the play is at your partner's blueline on his side of the rink, I would like to see you slide down toward his line for double coverage.

At your blueline, when play is in the neutral zone, you would be better to stand inside instead of on or outside the line. This mindset would reduce the chances of keeping the puck from entering the end zone.

You could add to your strong presence if you were to open up the "burners" on icings.

When you break with the play on a fast break be careful that you do not pull off your line too early as you go in.

On an icing watch when the defenseman turns away, you should consider washing out the icing.

You would look better if you slowed your judgement wave-offs at your blueline.

Your acceleration is choppy; it appears to me that you are bending your knees more than is necessary to get full use of your ankle extension.

Supervisors' Tips

AL DAWE

Former: THL Referee; OHA Level 6 Referee; OHA Supervisor (North-Central); OHA BD of Directors; Video Goal Judge (MLG); OHA Jack Clancy Award winner 1986.

Current: OHA Supervisor Alumni.

Al Dawe
on *Referees:*

Do not turn your back on things going on behind you. Take a quick look back.

Your penalty selection was inconsistent and you never seemed to "get in your groove".

Don't turn away and head for the penalty box until you are certain nothing is happening.

Move closer to net on scrambles.

Don't call penalties from opposite side of ice; move in closer to the penalized player before giving signal.

Talk a little more to players during stoppages and gatherings; it will relax you and give the impression of confidence.

Get penalties recorded quicker and play resumed as soon as possible after a skirmish. You are taking too long a delay.

Don't be in a hurry to leave gatherings to go to penalty box. Send the offenders there but you stay until the threat is over.

Check on injured player before giving length of penalty to timekeeper.

Hustle to problem areas after blowing your whistle.

Al Dawe
on *Linesmen:*

Stay with original fighter until he's off the playing surface.

Try to be a little more vocal to partner on close plays.

On face-offs, it appeared you were throwing puck down too hard.

Keep track of shorthanded situations for icing and for players returning from penalty box.

Once trainer arrives at an injured player, get away from scene, you only invite abuse.

Supervisors' Tips

IVAN LOCKE

Former: OMHA referee; OHA referee; THL referee; OMHA Supervisor/Instructor; OHA Supervisor (Oshawa); OWHA Referee-in-Chief; OHA Gold Stick; OHF Bill Richmond Award, OMHA Honour Award, Oshawa Hall of Fame

Current: OHA Supervisor Alumni.

Ivan Locke
on *Referees:*

When play moving up ice, keep checking behind you more than once or twice.

When changing direction, try to make shorter turns instead of starts and stops.

After assessing a penalty, keep an eye on the penalized player for possible trouble.

When assessing penalties after a gathering, try to get any players who came a distance to be involved and were not involved originally.

When a player takes one hand off his stick, watch to see if he holds the attacking player with his free hand.

Your positioning leaves a bit to be desired at times.

Try to anticipate the play moving out of the end zone and follow-up closer behind the play and keep skating right through the neutral zone.

When the play comes towards you in the end zone, try not to move too far. Let it pass you and be ready for a quick change of play back to the net.

Move right to the net if there is a scramble or fight and position yourself to be able to see the players and the benches.

It's okay to be on the goal line in the end zone if it puts you in a better position to view the play, but stay off the end boards.

Try to watch the play behind and the play away from the puck a bit closer. Some liberties are being taken when you are looking the other way.

Don't let players come into the referee crease at any time and don't take so long explaining your calls.

Keep skating to well inside the blueline. Don't coast into the end zone and go as deep as the deepest attacking player.

When giving penalty signals, be sure to stop. Don't skate on by.

Make eye contact with the benches to control the line changes.

If you are out of position on the goal line, don't try to compensate too soon. Keep your eye on play.

Try to keep any discussions short with players or coaches.

When there is a fight, send all other players to their benches.

Have any disallowed goals, when puck goes into net, announced over the P.A giving reason for no goal.

After a shot or pass, try to take a quick look back to watch the follow through.

Ivan Locke
on *Linesmen:*

Try not to go too far inside your blueline, unless forced in, one stride is enough.

On an end zone face-off, move straight back to the boards and then out to the blueline. Try not to stay too long in the end zone, get back to your line as quick as safely possible.

Don't let players coast into your face-off and make sure their sticks are lined up correctly and off the spot. If they won't move their sticks, remove the players from the face-off.

Make sure penalty times are on the clock before dropping the puck on a face-off.

After a whistle, your first priority is to concentrate on the players, then the puck.

On face-offs, both linesmen should be counting the number of players on the ice.

Work on your skating and hustle a bit more.

You should be at your blueline before the puck gets there. Don't let it pass you in the neutral zone.

Try to use your peripheral vision up and down to watch the far side of the blueline when the puck is near you.

When you are returning the puck after icing, slow down and watch the players on a line change.

Supervisors' Tips

JOHN MAY

Former: THL Referee; OHA Referee; Metro JrA Supervisor; OHA Supervisor (Toronto).

Current: OHA Supervisor Alumni.

John May
on *Referees:*

Face-off standard should be same as linesmen.

Be sure to move to net on scrambles or close plays but avoid swinging out to watch play as this has potential for screening goalie.

You must establish a strong penalty standard by emphasizing stick and restraining fouls.

When a goal is scored illegally, disallow it and have it announced.

Stick standard could have been applied earlier making some late period calls less essential.

Try for more consistency, I had difficulty defining and assessing your penalty standard.

Avoid pointing to penalty box after giving player a penalty.

Suggest more use of peripheral vision for activity beside and behind you.

Avoid too many rapid gestures as well as the "come along" signal when calling a penalty.

Be aware that Hockey Canada guidelines want at least a foot in referee's crease when reporting a penalty.

Use your communication skills effectively to prevent penalty situations and maintain control.

John May
on *Linesmen:*

You must be alert for encroachment in partner's end zone face-offs.

Avoid keeping signal on when you are forced off the line.

Good clear signals but make them complete, especially on delayed offsides.

Washout signals should be more emphatic, appearing decisive; sell the call.

Be sure to check behind you as part of setup routine on face-offs.

You must appear confident and energetic in your positioning, signals and late calls.

Avoid over-anticipating and wait for puck to cross the line before delaying an offside.

OHA Past and Present Officials

Ken Miller

Sandy Proctor

Blaine Angus

Mike Marley

Tom Lundy

Scott Oakman

Don Van Massenhoven   **Wes McCauley**

Ron MacLean

Ron Hoggarth   Ron Finn

Bill McCreary   Tim Peel

Scott Driscoll, Stephen Walkom, Greg Devorski

Matt Pavelich   George Hayes

Red Storey and Hugh McLean

Kevin Pollock   Clarke Pollock

Don Van Massenhoven, Justin Winter,
Deb Maybury and Stephen Walkom at
Level VI Clinic, Charlottetown, P.E.I. 1990

Brad Beer

Steve Miller   Al Kimmel

Will Norris

Derek Amell

Brad Kovachik

Greg Kimmerly   Mark Shewchyk

Dan O'Halloran   Dean Morton

George Ashley   Scott Cherrey

Brad Fagan   Bob Beatty

Jerry Olinski   George Wilson

Dave, Ivan and Eric with their father Ken Bryce

Bob Hodges Ron Asselstine

Canada/Russia, Hamilton-1989
Al Kimmel, Stephen Walkom, Brian Marshall

Scott Hoberg

Mike Hoberg

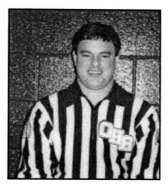
Bob Bell

Dave Lynch

Dave Ogilvie

Dean Warren

World U20 Championship, Russia, 2013
Matt Traub

Provincial JrA All-Star Game, Jan21, 2004
Toby Beam, Mike Anderson, Mike Neill

Gary Moroney

Tony Steyaert

Bill Brethauer

Bill Howes

Lou Maschio

Bert Kea

 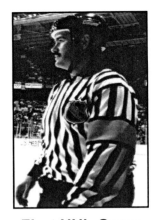

Terry Gregson

First NHL Game
Nov 11, 1993 - Boston
Don Van Massenhoven

Scott Driscoll   Ray Scapinello

Bob Langdon   Steve Miller

"Hey Ref, if you need the money that bad, why don't you sell your *&#@ skates."

Chapter 15

PAST AND PRESENT OFFICIALS

Due to large number of officials that worked the OHA over the years, we have not attempted to list them in the index. The OHA year by year lists (2013-1912) are missing the following years: 1949-57, 59-75 and 77-78. We have put extensive research in attempting to locate these missing years but so far we have not been successful.

Ontario Hockey Association

OHA Season 2012-2013
BARRIE: SUPERVISOR: Ken Bannerman; OFFICIALS: Dave Angus; Chris Arts; Korey Bannerman; Joshua Battiston; Ryan Beaulieu; Ed Black; Joe Dewar; Louie Dewar; Thomas Dewar; Ryan Dolmage; Ryan Elbers; Jeff Lees; Paul McQuillan; Josef Park; Jeff Pratt; Jonathan Rose; Kyle Smith; **GTA WEST (formerly Brampton):** SUPERVISORS: Charlie Lennox & Joe Paolini; OFFICIALS: Walter Araujo; Antonio Cacciacarro; Paul Callon; Paul Dadd; Scott Ferguson; Matthew Fullan; Brian Grant; Ryan Holmstead; Kyle Kennery; Craig Kipling; Jeff McVean; Brennan Mercer; Ryan Moniz; Adam Morell; Mike Neill; Ryan Park; Corey Piche; Jimmy Presant; Jason Rabjohn; Gilles Richard; Niall Smith; David Thiffault; Ryan White; Matthew Wilson; Michael Zujko; **BRANTFORD (formerly DELHI):** SUPERVISOR: Doug Robb; OFFICIALS: Mark Beenackers; Jim Brudz; Ryan Calbeck; Josh Ion; Dan Moore; Sean Morrow; Kevin Morton; Braden Murray; Tyler Stefan; Cameron

Stone; Marshall Stone; Adam Wojtkowiak; **GUELPH:** SUPERVISORS: Leon Stickle & Lance Roberts; OFFICIALS: Douglas Adlam; Bob Beatty; Chris Blake; Travis Bondy; James Bradshaw; Derek Bridgman; Hugh Budziarek; Nick Burke; Joel Campbell; Jeff Chambers; Eric Chute; Chad Drown; Jason Faist; Seth Ferguson; TJ Foster; Brett Frede; Jimmy Gagnon; Matt Gervais; Ben Gingerich; Matthew Gregory; Michael Guardiero; Chad Hepburn; Brendan Higgins; Steve Kelly; Dustin McCrank; Kevin McKinnon; Jean-Francois Menard; Steve Percy; Garrett Rank; Kyle Rank; Phil Rawn; Emil Sabo; William Smith; Steve Tsandelis; Fraser Williams; Ben Wilson; Ryan Wilson; **HAMILTON**: SUPERVISOR: Brent Holdsworth; OFFICIALS: Trevor Atkinson; Kyle Barclay; Steven Black; Scott Brown; Richard Craven; Joseph Goguen; Michael Harrington; Adam Harris; David Jaskula; Wes Kindree; Denis Kudryavtsev; Geoff Lawson; Brenden McGillivray; Kyle Melko; Dale Murphy; Eric Pienkosz; Darren Purnell; Scott Ransom; Steve Stasiuk; Alton Stead; Jesse Wilmot; Darryl Wolfe; Michael Wortel; **KINGSTON:** SUPERVISORS: Ken Harris & Al Detlor; OFFICIALS: Eric Asselstine; Thomas Baker; Ian Brooks; Andrew Brown; Chris Buxton; Nicholas Cooke; Ryan DeKairelle; Rick Finn; Chris Galway; Justin Kuipers; Sean MacDonald; James McGuey; Dan McKeown; Christopher McLean; Marco McRae; Brad Moore; Stephen O'Reilly; Duane Parliament; Cory Piche; Kevin Pons; Stephen Prinzen; Jonathan Rouillard-Lamy; Darren Sloboda; Ron Stakes; Ryan Thompson; Shane Wannamaker; Andrew Willmetts; **LONDON:** SUPERVISOR: Rick Singleton; OFFICIALS: Josh Ackworth; Brent Atkinson; Brandon Baltazar; Marc Berthiaume; Matthew Bossence; Matt Clark; Simon Coutu; Chris Faulkner; Chris Fraumeni; David Gardner; Andrew Gartly; Stephen Gould; Andrew Jackson; Ryan Langmuir; Scott Lealess; Raymond McManus; Chad Murray; Luke Murray; Mike Noble; Duane Nutt; Jeremy Parking; Chad Petrie; Alex Ross; Scott Schlegel; Brent R Thompson; Chris Thornton; Kevin Umansky; Ryan VanHeeswyk; Jamie VanKasteren; Bill Waye; Jarren Anger; Joel Archambault; Mike Bolibruck; Jeff Campbell; Justin Creamer; Trevor Donaldson; Quincy Evans;

Darcyustin Webb; Bob Wright; Don Yeoman; James Yeoman; **NIAGARA:** SUPERVISOR: Mike Biljetina; OFFICIALS: Dan Adie; D Hemauer; Cory Hopper; Colton Hrcak; Peter Kostyk; Tyler Lawson; Mitch MacPherson; Patrick Myers; Eric Robertson; James Steers; Kristopher Tessarolo; Joshua Wall; Drew Williams; **NORTH CENTRAL:** SUPERVISOR: Gary Moroney; OFFICIALS: Jonathan Andress; Mike Arnold; David Black; Chris Carnegie; Sean Chatland; Sean Eden; Travis Ford; Justin Herrington; Steven Ley; Michael Marley; Rob Palm; Brian Potvin; Daniel Ransom; Daniel Sepe; Daniel Szypka; Matthew Traub; Ben Venditti; Joey Wilson; **NORTH WEST:** SUPERVISOR: John McCutcheon; OFFICIALS: Chad Adamson; Shandor Alphonso; Michael Daltrey; Jason Fischer; Matt Fischer; Colin Graham; Dean Grahame; Curtis Harding; Brandon Hillis; Ryan Hollister; Josh Keil; Jamie Lang; Jordan Lang; Luc Lang; Todd Long; Doug MacNeil; Greg McArthur; Andy McNaughton; Joshua Morrison; Steve Morrison; Brett Nichol; Kendrick Nicholson; Andy O'Leary; Patrick Rozendal; Gavin Stewart; Matt Stirling; Ryan Styles; Jason Torry; Scott Walls; Dennis Watson; Blake Wilson; Andrew Zippel; **OSHAWA:** SUPERVISORS: Rick Morphew & Gus Bambridge; OFFICIALS: Matthew Arbour; Sheldon Berezowski; Steve Brown; Jordan Browne; Jeff Clarkson; Sean Coles; Ken Cornelius; John Czerniawski; Paul Drummond; Steven Gallagher; Scott Gray; Darryll Hancock; Tyler Kirkland; Ben Kirkwood; Justin Knaggs; Andrew Markew; Evan McCrory; Brad McCutcheon; Ryan Middaugh; Kyle Neadles; William Neadles; Brian Park; Dwayne Phillips; Paul Reid; Mike Ricica; David Sankey; Andrew Thompson; Paul Wade; Ryan Watson; Andrew West; Michael Williams-Bell; **SARNIA:** SUPERVISORS: Jim Maitland & Mike Pearce; OFFICIALS: Glenn Anderson; Cheyenne Batten; Justin Belanger; Pete Bowen; Tyler Callander; Clint Campbell; Tim Cox; Craig Dease; Dan Dolson; Sean Geene; Christopher Harwood; Sean McLoughlin; Kyle Mellor; Brandon Palmer; Jeff Parney; Brian Pearson; Scott Prangley; Cody Simpson; Brian Somes; Mike Taylor; Robert Veccia; Darcy Vink; Kyle Vink; Craig Williams; **TORONTO:** SUPERVISOR: Bob Nadin; OFFICIALS:

Jordan Banfield; Ross Bain; Joel Barron; JeanCarlo Cedrone; Jeffrey Crawford; Steven Dunlop; Joe Fenech; Matthew Fergenbaum; Chris Ferreira; Matt Filodoro; David Gauthier; Jason Goldenberg; Don Haag; Andrew Hubbard; Michael Manson; Jonathan Meilach; Nick Mintsopoulos; Elias Mitoulas; Ed Munroe; Aaron Neely; Tyson Orlie; Steven Picco; Josh Schein; Ben Smith; Blair Surette; Jonathan Wallace; **WINDSOR:** SUPERVISORS: Jerry Pateman & Mare Pare; OFFICIALS: Andy Anthony; Kevin Blundell; Greg Campbell; Christian Cortese; AJ DeSantis; Kyle Flood; Jonathan Forbes; Shawn Hamelin; Ryan Lachine; Chris Long; Nick Long; Joe Monette; Jacob Morassut; Wayde Peltier; Brad Potter; Allan Provost; Jason Rauth; Ryan Renaud; Sean Sampson; John Thompson; Kyle Vermast

OHA Season 2011-2012
BARRIE: Supervisor Ken Bannerman; OFFICIALS: Chris Arts, Korey Bannerman, Kevin Bannerman, Josh Battiston, Ryan Beaulieu, Ed Black, Patrick Cavanagh, Louie Dewar, Tom Dewar, Joe Dewar, Ryan Dolmage, Anders Hagman, Jeff Lees, Todd Lewis, Dan MacDonald, Paul McQuillan, Joe Park, Jeff Pratt, Jonathan Rose, Kyle A. Smith, Chris Whalen, Scott Wilson. **BRAMPTON:** Supervisors Mike Duggan & John May, OFFICIALS: Ken Armstrong, Walter Araujo, Brent Atkinson, Antonio Cacciacarro, Paul Callon, Jeff Campbell, Todd Clark, Paul Dadd, Scott Ferguson, Matt Fullan, Christopher Gomes, Brian Grant, Ryan Holmstead, Kyle Kennery, Jeff McVean, Brennan Mercer, Ryan Moniz, Mike Neill, Jon Nestorovic, Joe Paolini, Ryan Park, Jimmy Presant, Jason Rabjohn, Gilles Richard, Niall Smith, Eric Sutton, Dave Thiffault, Ryan White, Matt Wilson, Mike Zujko. **DELHI:** Supervisor Doug Robb OFFICIALS: Mark Beenackers, Darrin Bronizewski, Jim Brudz, Jason Hicks, Josh Ion, Jordan McIntyre, Dan Moore, Kevin Morton, Braden Murray, Brent Stefan, Tyler Stefan, Cameron Stone, Marshall Stone, Adam Wojtkowiak. **GUELPH:** Supervisors Lance Roberts & Leon Stickle OFFICIALS; Doug Adlam, Bob Beatty, Brent Bloch, James Bradshaw, Derek Bridgman, Hugh Budziarek, Nick Burke, Joel Campbell, Jeff Chambers, Eric Chute, Chad Drown,

Jason Faist, Seth Ferguson, T.J.Foster, Brett Frede, Jimmy Gagnon, Ben Gingerick, Matt Gregory, Mike Guardiero, Chad Hepburn, Brendan Higgins, Steve Kelly, Scott Keys, Stephen Mackie, Dustin McCrank, Steven Percy, Jake Radcliffe, Garrett Rank, Kyle Rank, Phil Rawn, Emil Sabo, Bill Smith, Steve Tsandelis, Fraser Williams, Ben Wilson, Ryan Wilson. **HAMILTON:** Supervisors, Bob Morley & Mike Biljetina, OFFICIALS: Trevor Atkinson, Kyle Barclay, Steve Black, Scott Brown, Richard Craven, Trevor Donaldson, Michael Harrington, Adam Harris, David Jaskula, Wes Kindree, Denis Kudryavtsev, Geoff Lawson, Brenden McGillivray, Kyle Melko, Dale Murphy, Eric Pienkosz, Darren Purnell, Scott Ransom, Steve Stasiuk, Alton Stead, Kris Tessarolo, Jesse Wilmot, Darryl Wolfe, Mike Wortel. **KINGSTON:** Supervisor Ken Harris & Scott Lavendor OFFICIALS: Tom Baker, Steve Berry, Ian Brooks, Andrew Brown, Ben Buxton, Chris Buxton, Nick Cooke, Ryan DeKairelle, Mark Doornbos, Rick Finn, Chris Galway, Rob Garden, Justin Kuipers, Daniel Luxmore, Dan McKeown, Chris McLean, Marco McRae, Brad Moore, Stephen O'Reilly, Ben Palmer, Duane Parliament, Kevin Pons, Stephen Prinzen, Darren Sloboda, Ron Stakes, Shane Wannamker. **LONDON:** Supervisor Rick Singleton, Mentors: Ray McManus, Bill Waye, OFFICIALS: Josh Ackworth, Steve Baker, Brandon Baltazar, Mark Berthiaume, Terry Bonter, Matt Bossence, Matt Clark, Simon Coutu, Chris Faulkner, Chris Fraumeni, Dave Gardner, Curtis Gartly, Steve Gould, Andrew Jackson, Dave Landers, Ryan Langmuir, Scott Lealess, Scott McEwen, Ray McManus, Luke Murray, Mike Noble, Duane Nutt, Jeremy Parking, Chad Petrie, Mike Sangster, Scott Schlegel, Brent R. Thompson, Chris Thornton, Kevin Umansky, Ryan Van Heeswyk, Jamie Van Kasteren, Bill Waye, Justin Webb, Bob Wright, Don Yeoman. **NIAGARA:** Supervisors Bob Morley & Mike Biljetina, OFFICIALS: Joel Archambult, Daniel Adie, Darren Anger, Mike Bolibruck, Tom Boese, Justin Creamer, Ryan Elbers, Darcy Hemauer, Peter Kostyk, Tyler Lawson, Patrick Myers, Mitch McPherson, Eric Robertson, Kyle Smith, James Steers, Josh Wall, Drew Williams. **NORTH-CENTRAL:** Supervisor Gary Moroney & Bryan

Lewis, OFFICIALS: Jonathan Andress, Mike Arnold, David Black, Chris Carnegie, Sean Chatland, Sean Eden, Matt Fergenbaum, Louie Gabriele, Stephen Ley, Mike Marley, Sean McQuigge, Rob Palm, Brain Potvin, Dan Ransom, Frankie Rocca, Daniel Sepe, Dan Szypka, Matt Fischer, Matthew Traub, Ben Venditti, Jonathan Wallace, **NORTH-WEST:** Supervisor John McCutcheon, OFFICIALS: Chad Adamson, Shandor Alphonso, Jason Fischer, Dean Grahame, Ryan Hollister, Craig Kipling, Jamie Lang, Jordan Lang, Todd Long, Doug Macneil, Greg McArthur, Josh Morrison, Steve Morrison, Brett Nichol, Kendrick Nicholson, Patrick Rozendal, Gavin Stewart, Ryan Styles, Jason Torry, Scott Walls, Dennis Watson, Blake Wilson, Andrew Willmetts. **OSHAWA:** Supervisors: Ivan Locke, Gus Bambridge & Rick Morphew, OFFICIALS: Matt Arbour, Sheldon Berezowski, Matthew Black, Steve Brown, Jordan Browne, Ryan Carmichael, Jeff Clarkson, Sean Coles, Ken Cornelius, John Czerniawski, Paul Drummond, Steve Gallagher, Scott Gray, Darryl Hancock, Craig Harness, Tyler Kirkland, Ben Kirkwood, Justin Knaggs, David Lichacz, Andrew Markew, Evan McCrory, Brad McCutcheon, Ryan Middaugh, Gord Miles, Sean Morrow, Kyle Needles, William Needles, Brain Park, Dwayne Phillips, Mike Pryde, Paul Renaud, Mike Ricica, David Sankey, Andrew Thompson, Paul Wade, Ryan Watson, Andrew West, Michael Williams-Bell. **SARNIA:** Supervisor: Jim Maitland & Mentor Mike Pearce. OFFICIALS: Glenn Anderson, Justin Belanger, Pete Bowen, Tyler Callender, Clint Campbell, Tim Cox, Craig Dease, Dan Dolson, Sean Geene, Chris Harwood, Jim Hawthorne, Sean McLaughlin, Kyle Mellor, Brandon Palmer, Jeff Parney, Mike Pearce, Brain Pearson, Ryan Presley, Brain Somes, Rob Veccia, Darcy Vink, Kyle Vink. **TORONTO:** Supervisors: Bob Nadin & David Montgomery, OFFICIALS: Ross Bain, Jordan Banfield, Joel Barron, Michael Cairns, Jeff Crawford, Jean Carlo Cedrone, Steve Dunlop, Joe Fenech, Matt Filodoro, Dave Gauthier, Jason Goldenberg, Don Haag, Tyler Hawthorne, Andrew Hubbard, Jared Mackey, Michael Manson, Jonathan Meilach, Nick Mintsopoulos, Ed Munroe, Aaron Neely, Tyson Orlie, Steven Picco, Josh Schein, Ben Smith, Blair

Surette. **WINDSOR:** Supervisors: Matt Pavelich & Jerry Pateman, OFFICIALS: Andy Anthony, Chey Batten, Kevin Blundell, Greg Campbell, Christian Cortese, A.J.Desantis, Chris Ferreira, Jonathan Forbes, Kyle Flood, Shawn Hamelin, Ryan Hutchinson, Ryan Lachine, Chris Long, Nick Long, Joe Monette, Jake Morassut, Walter Peltier, Brad Potter, Allan Provost, Jason Rauth, Ryan Renaud, Sean Sampson, Mike Scanlan, John Thompson, Kyle Vermast.

OHA Season 2010-2011
BARRIE: Supervisor Ken Barnerman; OFFICIALS: Chris Arts, Chris Baetz, Korey Bannerman, Kevin Bannerman, Josh Battiston, Ed Black, Patrick Cavanagh, Louie Dewar, Joe Dewar, Ryan Dolmage, Anders Hagman, Mike James, Ben Kirkwood, Jeff Lees, Todd Lewis, Allan Madil, Paul McQuillan, Joe Park, Jeff Pratt, Jonathan Rose, Scott Sefton, Kyle A. Smith, Chris Whalen. **BRAMPTON:** Supervisors Mike Duggan & John May, OFFICIALS: Walter Araujo, Antonio Cacciacarro, Paul Callon, Todd Clark, Pau Dadd, Scott Ferguson, Christopher Gomes, Brandon Grant, Brian Grant, Ryan Holmstead, Rick Janco, Kyle Kennery, Jeff McVean, Brennan Mercer, Ryan Miehm, Ryan Moniz, Mike Neill, Jon Nestorovic, Dave Newsome, Robert Padt, Joe Paolini, Ryan Park, Jimmy Presant, Jason Rabjohn, Gilles Richard, Niall Smith, Chris Smyk, Eric Sutton, Dave Thiffault, Ryan White, Matt Wilson, Mike Zujko. **DELHI:** Supervisor Doug Robb OFFICIALS: Dave Blum, Darrin Bronizewski, Jim Brudz, Jesse Buchan, Jason Hicks, Josh Ion, Jordan McIntyre, Dan Moore, Sean Morrow, Kevin Morton, Braden Murray, Brent Stefan, Tyler Stefan, Cameron Stone, Colin Town, Adam Wojtkowiak. **GUELPH:** Supervisors Lance Roberts & leon Stickle OFFICIALS; Doug Adlam, Bob Beatty, Brent Bloch, James Bradshaw, Derek Bridgman, Hugh Budziarek, Nick Burke, Joel Campbell, Eric Chute, Chad Drown, Jason Faist, Matt Fergenbaum, Seth Ferguson, T.J.Foster, Brett Frede, Lanny Fuller, Jimmy Gagnon, Matt Gregory, Mike Guardiero, Chad Hepburn, Brendan Higgins, Brandon Hillis, James Johnston, Steve Kelly, Scott Keys, Stephen Mackie, Dustin McCrank, Steven

Percy, Lee Poteck, Garrett Rank, Phil Rawn, Emil Sabo, Graham Shantz, Bill Smith, Tim Steen, Fraser Williams, Ben Wilson, Ryan Wilson. **HAMILTON:** Supervisors, Bob Morley & Mike Biljetina, OFFICIALS: Kyle Barclay, Steve Black, Scott Brown, Darcy Burchell, Richard Craven, Matt Fullan, Michael Harrington, Adam Harris, Matt Higson, Brent Holdsworth, Jason Jackson, David Jaskula, Wes Kindree, Denis Kudryavtsev, Geoff Lawson, Brenden McGillivray, Dale Murphy, Darren Purnell, Scott Ransom, Steve Stasiuk, Alton Stead, Jesse Wilmot, Darryl Wolfe, Mike Wortel. **KINGSTON:** Supervisor Ken Harris, OFFICIALS: Ian Brooks, Andrew Brown, Ben Buxton, Chris Buxton, Tyler Conner, Nick Cooke, Mike Cranley, Ryan DeKairelle, Mark Doornbos, Rick Finn, Chris Galway, Rob Garden, Justin Kuipers, Scott Lavendor, Daniel Luxmore, Dan McKeown, Chris McLean, Marco McRae, Brad Moore, Stephen O'Reilly, Ben Palmer, Duane Parliament, Kevin Pons, Chris Ryan, Darren Sloboda. **LONDON:** Supervisor Rick Singleton, Mentors: Ray McManus, Bill Waye, OFFICIALS: Jason Arsenault, Brent Atkinson, Steve Baker, Brandon Baltazar, Mark Berthiaume, Terry Bonter, Matt Bossence, Dan Boyd, Matt Clark, Simon Coutu, Chris Faulkner, Chris Fraumeni, Dave Gardner, Curtis Gartly, Steve Gould, Andrew Jackson, Dave Landers, Scott Lealess, Mike Logan, Dan MacDonald, Scott McEwen, Ray McManus, Luke Murray, Mike Noble, Duane Nutt, Connor OBrien, Jeremy Parking, Mike Sangster, Scott Schlegel, Derek Skinner, Brent R. Thompson, Chris Thornton, Kevin Umansky, Ryan Van Heeswyk, Jamie Van Kasteren, Bill Waye, Bob Wright, Don Yeoman. **NIAGARA:** Supervisors Bob Morley & Mike Biljetina, OFFICIALS: Daniel Adie, Darren Anger, Mike Bolibruck, Jeff Campbell, Justin Creamer, Ryan Elbers, Mike Gage, Jeff Hanna, Darcy Hemauer, Mark Isherwood, Mike Kostyk, Peter Kostyk, Tyler Lawson, Patrick Myers, Mitch McPherson, Eric Robertson, Kyle Smith, Steven St Angelo, Josh Wall, Drew Williams. **NORTH-CENTRAL:** Supervisor Gary Moroney & Bryan Lewis, OFFICIALS: Carlo Aletto, Mike Allen, Jonathan Andress, Mike Arnold, David Black, Chris Carnegie, Sean Chatland, Ryan Dupuis, Sean Eden, Louie Gabriele, Jason Hann, Dean

Herzberg, Shane korman, Dave Koziel, Stephen Ley, Mike Marley, Sean McQuigge, Rob Palm, Brain Potvin, Dan Ransom, Frankie Rocca, David Santi, Daniel Sepe, Dan Szypka, Matt Fischer, Matthew Traub, Ben Venditti, Jonathan Wallace, **NORTH-WEST:** Supervisor John McCutcheon, OFFICIALS: Chad Adamson, Jason Barlow, Jason Fischer, John Fischer, Dean Grahame, Ryan Hollister, Craig Kipling, Layne Lavis, Scott Lawson, Dave Lisk, Todd Long, Doug Macneil, Greg McArthur, Josh Morrison, Steve Morrison, Brett Nichol, Kendrick Nicholson, Patrick Rozendal, Dave Shropshall, Derek Skinner, Gavin Stewart, Ryan Styles, Jason Torry, Dave Van **Kooten, Scott Walls, Dennis Watson, Blake Wilson. OSHAWA:** Supervisors: Ivan Locke, Gus Bambridge & Rick Morphew, OFFICIALS: Matt Arbour, Sheldon Berezowski, Matthew Black, Steve Brown, Jordan Browne, Ryan Carmichael, Jeff Clarkson, Sean Coles, Ken Cornelius, John Czerniawski, Paul Drummond, Steve Gallagher, Scott Gray, Darryl Hancock, Craig Harness, Tyler Kirkland, Ben kirkwood, Justin Knaggs, Dave Lewis, David Lichacz, Andrew Markew, Evan McCrory, Brad McCutcheon, Ryan Middaugh, Gord Miles, Kyle Neadles, William Neadles, Brain Park, Dwayne Phillips, Mike Pryde, Paul Renaud, Mike Ricica, David Sankey, Andrew Thompson, Paul Wade, Ryan Watson, Andrew West, Michael Williams-Bell. **SARNIA:** Supervisor: Jim Maitland, OFFICIALS: Glenn Anderson, Pete Bowen, Tyler Callender, Clint Campbell, Tim Cox, Rob Dalgetty, Craig Dease, Dan Dolson, Sean Geene, Chris Harwood, Jim Hawthorne, George Langstaff, Jake Langstaff, Sean McLaughlin, Kyle Mellor, Brandon Palmer, Jeff Parney, Mike Pearce, Brain Pearson, Ryan Presley, Brain Somes, Rob Veccia, Darcy Vink, Kyle Vink. **TORONTO:** Supervisors: Bob Nadin & David Montgomery, OFFICIALS: Ross Bain, Jordan Banfield, Joel Barron, Sean Bernard, Michael Cairns, Ryan Carroll, Jeff Crawford, Jean Carlo Cedrone, Steve Dunlop, Joe Fenech, Matt Filodoro, Dave Gauthier, Jason Goldenberg, Mike Gordon, Don Haag, Andrew Hubbard, Darryl James, Jared Mackey, Michael Manson, Jonathan Meilach, Nick Mintsopoulos, Ed Munroe, Tyson Orlie, Steven Picco, Sean Pindar, Joshua Roberts, Josh Schein,

Ben Smith, Blair Surette. **WINDSOR:** Supervisors: Matt Pavelich & Jerry Pateman, OFFICIALS: Chey Batten, Ryan Beaulieu, Kevin Blundell, Mike Boucher, Greg Campbell, Christian Cortese, A.J.Desantis, Chris Ferreira, Jonathan Forbes, Kyle Flood, Shawn Hamelin, Ryan Hutchinson, Ryan Lachine, Nick Long, Jeff Mayea, Joe Monette, Jake Morassut, Brad Potter, Allan Provost, Jason Rauth, Ryan Renaud, Sean Sampson, Mike Scanlan, John Thompson, Kyle Vermast.

OHA Season 2009-2010
BARRIE: Supervisor Ken Bannerman; OFFICIALS: Chris Arts, Chris Baetz, Korey Bannerman, Kevin Bannerman, Ed Black, Ken Cook, Louie Dewar, Ryan Dolmage, Chris Kelly, Ben Kirkwood, Jeff Lees, Todd Lewis, Allan Madil, Joe Park, Jeff Pratt, Jonathan Rose, Scott Sefton, Kyle A. Smith, Chris Whalen, Scott Wilson. **BRAMPTON:** Supervisors Mike Duggan & John May, OFFICIALS: Walter Araujo, Ken Armstrong, PAntonio Cacciacarro, Paul Callon, Todd Clark, Paul Dadd, Scott Ferguson, Shawn Garrett, Christopher Gomes, Brandon Grant, Brian Grant, Ryan Holmstead, Rick Janco, Tom Jukes, Kyle Kennery, Tom Lough, Justin Maguire, Glen McBryde, Jeff McVean, Brennan Mercer, Ryan Miehm, Ryan Moniz, Mike Neill, Jon Nestorovic, Dave Newsome, Robert Padt, Joe Paolini, Jimmy Presant, Jason Rabjohn, Gilles Richard, Niall Smith, Chris Smyk, Eric Sutton, Dave Thiffault, Ryan White, Matt Wilson, Mike Zujko. **DELHI:** Supervisor Bob Morley, Mentor John Searle, OFFICIALS: Dave Blum, Darrin Bronizewski, Jim Brudz, Chris Dewachter, Jason Hicks, Josh Ion, Mark MacKenzie, Dan Moore, Sean Morrow, Kevin Morton, Mark Nemeth, Dan Schmidt, John Searle, Brent Stefan, Tyler Stefan, Cameron Stone, Colin Town, Adam Wojtkowiak. **GUELPH:** Supervisors Lance Roberts OFFICIALS; Doug Adlam, Bob Beatty, Brent Bloch, James Bradshaw, Derek Bridgman, Nick Burke, Joel Campbell, Eric Chute, Ben Connelly, Dan Dietrich, Chad Drown, Jaren Eydt, Brad Fagan, Jason Faist, Seth Ferguson, John Fischer, Brett Frede, Lanny Fuller, Jimmy Gagnon, Adam Good, Matt Gregory, Mike Guardiero, Chad Hepburn, Brendan Higgins, Brandon Hillis, Sean

Hutton, Steve Kelly, Scott Keys, T.J. Luxmore, Dustin McCrank, Blake Moggy, Steven Percy, Lee Poteck, Garrett Rank, Emil Sabo, Graham Shantz, Bill Smith, Tim Steen, Adam Taylor, Ben Wilson, Ryan Wilson. **HAMILTON:** Supervisors, Bob Morley & Mike Biljetina, OFFICIALS: Kyle Barclay, Steve Black, Scott Brown, Darcy Burchell, Craig Colett, Richard Craven, Matt Fullan, Michael Harrington, Adam Harris, Matt Higson, Brent Holdsworth, Jason Jackson, Wes Kindree, Denis Kudryavtsev, Geoff Lawson, Brenden McGillivray, Kyle Melko, Dale Murphy, Mike Ostaszewicz, Darren Purnell Steve Stasiuk, Alton Stead, Jesse Wilmot, Darryl Wolfe, Matt Wolfe, Mike Wortel. **KINGSTON:** Supervisor Ken Harris, OFFICIALS: Dave Baker, Bob Bell, Steven Berry, Ian Brooks, Ben Buxton, Chris Buxton, Tyler Conner, Nick Cooke, Mike Cranley, Ryan DeKairelle, Mark Doornbos, Rick Finn, Chris Galway, Justin Kuipers, Scott Lavendor, Daniel Luxmore, Dan McKeown, Chris McLean, Marco McRae, Brad Moore, Bill Newman, Stephen O'Reilly, Duane Parliament, Kevin Pons, Chris Ryan, Darren Sloboda, Ron Stakes, Shane Wannamaker. **LONDON:** Supervisor Rick Singleton, Mentors: Ray McManus, Bill Waye, OFFICIALS: Jason Arsenault, Mike Assaf, Brent Atkinson, Brain Bailkowski, Steve Baker, Mark Berthiaume, Terry Bonter, Matt Bossence, Dan Boyd, Jason Brady, Kevin Brown, Bruce Byers, Stepan Chwaluk, Matt Clark, Chris Faulkner, Chris Fraumeni, Dave Gardner, Curtis Gartly, Steve Gould, Andrew Jackson, Dave Landers, Mike Logan, Scott McEwen, Ray McManus, Luke Murray, Duane Nutt, Jeremy Parking, Scott Rasenberg, Sean Reid, Patrick Rozendal, Mike Sangster, Scott Schlegel, Mike Speziale, Brent R. Thompson, Chris Thornton, Kevin Umansky, Ryan Van Heeswyk, Jamie Van Kasteren, Bill Waye, Bob Wright, Don Yeoman, James Yeoman. **NIAGARA:** Supervisors Bob Morley & Mike Biljetina, OFFICIALS: Daniel Adie, Darren Anger, Mike Bolibruck, Jeff Campbell, Justin Creamer, Mike Gage, Geoff Gamble, Jeff Hanna, Darcy Hemauer, Mark Isherwood, Mike Kostyk, Peter Kostyk, Tyler Lawson, Patrick Myers, Eric Robertson, Kyle Smith, Josh Wall, Drew Williams. **NORTH-CENTRAL:** Supervisor Gary Moroney & Bryan Lewis, OFFICIALS:

Carlo Aletto, Mike Allen, Jonathan Andress, Mike Arnold, David Black, Chris Carnegie, Sean Chatland, Ryan Dupuis, John Eminger, Matt Fergenbaum, Louie Gabriele, Jason Hann, Dean Herzberg, Shane korman, Dave Koziel, Mike Marley, Sean McQuigge, Rob Palm, Brain Potvin, Dan Ransom, Frankie Rocca, David Santi, Daniel Sepe, Matthew Traub, Ben Venditti, Jonathan Wallace, **NORTH-WEST:** Supervisor John McCutcheon, OFFICIALS: Chad Adamson, Jason Barlow, Jason Fischer, Dean Grahame, Craig Kipling, Jordan Lang, Layne Lavis, Scott Lawson, Dave Lisk, Todd Long, Doug Macneil, Greg McArthur, Josh Morrison, Steve Morrison, Kendrick Nicholson, Dave Shropshall, Derek Skinner, Gavin Stewart, Ryan Styles, Dave Van Kooten, Scott Walls, Dennis Watson, Craig Williams, Blake Wilson. **OSHAWA:** Supervisors Ivan Locke, Gus Bambridge & Rick Morphew, OFFICIALS: Matt Arbour, Steve Armitage, Sheldon Berezowski, Matthew Black, Steve Brown, Jordan Browne, Ryan Carmichael, ord Coggins, Sean Coles, Ken Cornelius, John Czerniawski, Darryl Dawson, Paul Drummond, Steve Gallagher, Darryl Hancock, Craig Harness, Brent Hewlett, Padraig Kelly, Tyler Kirkland, Justin Knaggs, Dave Lewis, David Lichacz, Rob Macgregor, Andrew Markew, Evan McCrory, Brad McCutcheon, Ryan Middaugh, Gord Miles, Kyle Neadles, William Neadles, Brain Park, Dwayne Phillips, Mike Pryde, Paul Renaud, Mike Ricica, David Sankey, Andrew Thompson, Paul Wade, Ryan Watson. Michael Williams-Bell. **SARNIA:** Supervisor Jim Maitland, OFFICIALS: Glenn Anderson, Pete Bowen, Clint Campbell, Tim Cox, Rob Dalgetty, Dan Dolson, Sean Geene, Chris Harwood, Jim Hawthorne, Rob Hawthorne, Tyler Hawthorne, George Langstaff, Sean McLaughlin, Brandon Palmer, Jeff Parney, Mike Pearce, Brain Pearson, Ryan Pressley, Brain Somes, Rob Veccia, Darcy Vink, Kyle Vink. **TORONTO:** Supervisors Bob Nadin & David Montgomery, OFFICIALS: Ross Bain, Jordan Banfield, Joel Barron, Sean Bernard, Michael Cairns, Ryan Carroll, Jeff Crawford, Steve Dunlop, Joe Fenech, Matt Filodoro, Dave Gauthier, Jason Goldenberg, Mike Gordon, Don Haag, Andrew Hubbard, Darryl James, Jamie Lang, Jared Mackey, Michael Manson, Jonathan Meilach, Nick

Mintsopoulos, Ed Munroe, Tyson Orlie, Ryan Park, Steven Picco, Sean Pindar, Joshua Roberts, Ben Smith, Mat Stiver-Balla, Blair Surette, Anthony Tersigni, Sotaro Yamaguchi. **WINDSOR:** Supervisors Matt Pavelich & Jerry Pateman, OFFICIALS: Mike Aubin, Joshua Battiston, Ryan Beaulieu, Kevin Blundell, Mike Boucher, Tyler Callender, Grag Campbell, Christian Cortese, A.J.Desantis, Jonathan Forbes, Shawn Hamelin, Ryan Hutchinson, Ryan Lachine, Nick Long, Jeff Mayea, Joe Monette, Jake Morassut, Brad Potter, Allan Provost, Jason Rauth, Ryan Renaud, Sean Sampson, Mike Scanlan, John Thompson, Kyle Vermast.

OHA Season 2008-2009
BARRIE: Supervisor Ken Bannerman; OFFICIALS: Chris Arts, Chris Baetz, Korey Bannerman, Kevin Bannerman, Ed Black, Ken Cook, Louie Dewar, Joe Fenech, Grant Fournier, Anders Hagman, Michael Kelly, Jeff Lees, Todd Lewis, Allan Madil, Jonathan Martin, Joe Park, Jeff Pratt, Richard Rider, Scott Sefton, Kyle A. Smith, Chris Whalen, Scott Wilson. **BRAMPTON:** Supervisors Mike Duggan & John May, OFFICIALS: Walter Araujo, Ken Armstrong, Paul Callon, Todd Clark, Scott Ferguson, Shawn Garrett, Brandon Grant, Brian Grant, Ryan Holmstead, Tom Jukes, Tom Lough, Justin Maguire, Glen McBryde, Brennan Mercer, Mike Neill, Jon Nestorovic, Dave Newsome, Robert Padt, Joe Paolini, Jason Rabjohn, Gilles Richard, Andy Rozalowsky, Niall Smith, Chris Smyk, Eric Sutton, Dave Thiffault, Ryan White, Matt Wilson. **DELHI:** Supervisor Bob Morley, Mentor John Searle, OFFICIALS: Darrin Bronizewski, Jim Brudz, Ryan Elliott, Josh Ion, Alan Hafferty, Mark MacKenzie, Dan Moore, Sean Morrow, Kevin Morton, Mark Nemeth, Dan Schmidt, John Searle, Brent Stefan, Tyler Stefan, Cameron Stone, Colin Town, Adam Wojtkowiak. **GUELPH:** Supervisors Lance Roberts & Greg Devorski, OFFICIALS: Doug Adlam, Bob Beatty, Brent Bloch, James Bradshaw, Derek Bridgman, Matt Brophy, Joel Campbell, Eric Chute, Ben Connelly, Dan Dietrich, Chad Drown, Brad Fagan, Jason Faist, John Fischer, Brett Frede, Lanny Fuller, Mark Galloway, Adam Good, Matt Gregory, Mike Guardiero, Chad Hepburn, Brandon Hillis,

Sean Hutton, Steve Kelly, Chris Kelly, Scott Keys, T.J. Luxmore, Dustin McCrank, Ryan Miehm, Blake Moggy, Steven Percy, Graham Shantz, Bill Smith, Tim Steen, Adam Taylor, Ben Wilson, Ryan Wilson. **HAMILTON:** Supervisors, Bob Morley & Mike Biljetina, OFFICIALS: Kyle Barclay, Steve Black, Scott Brown, Darcy Burchell, Richard Craven, Matt Fullan, Michael Harrington, Adam Harris, Matt Higson, Brent Holdsworth, Jason Jackson, Wes Kindree, Geoff Lawson, Kevin McKnight, Dale Murphy, Mike Ostaszewicz, Darren Purnell Steve Stasiuk, Alton Stead, Jesse Wilmot, Darryl Wolfe, Matt Wolfe, Mike Wortel. **KINGSTON:** Supervisor Ken Harris, OFFICIALS: Dave Baker, Bob Bell, Steven Berry, Ian Brooks, Chris Buxton, Mike Cranley, Bryan Detlor, Rick Finn, Rob Garden, Rod Hall, Sean Jenkins, Justin Kuipers, Scott Lavendor, Adam Lough, Daniel Luxmore, Chris McLean, Marco McRae, Brad Moore, Bill Newman, Stephen O'Reilly, Duane Parliament, Kevin Pons, Dave Regan, Chri sRyan, Darren Sloboda, Ron Stakes, Shane Wannamaker, Grant White. **LONDON:** Supervisor Rick Singleton, Mentors: Ray McManus, Bill Waye, OFFICIALS: Mike Assaf, Brain Bailkowski, Steve Baker, Mark Berthiaume, Terry Bonter, Matt Bossence, Dan Boyd, Kevin Brown, Bruce Byers, Matt Clark, Chris Dewachter, Dan Dolson, Chris Faulkner, Chris Fraumeni, Dave Gardner, Curtis Gartly, Steve Gould, Andrew Jackson, Dave Landers, Mike Logan, Scott McEwen, Ray McManus, Luke Murray, Duane Nutt, Jeremy Parking, Lee Poteck, Scott Rasenberg, Sean Reid, Scott Roode, Patrick Rozendal, Mike Sangster, Mike Speziale, Brent R. Thompson, Chris Thornton, Kevin Umansky, Ryan Van Heeswyk, Jamie Van Kasteren, Bill Waye, Bob Wright, Don Yeoman, James Yeoman. **NIAGARA:** Supervisors Bob Morley & Mike Biljetina, OFFICIALS: Daniel Adie, Darren Anger, Mike Bolibruck, Jeff Campbell, Justin Creamer, Mike Gage, Geoff Gamble, Jeff Hanna, Darcy Hemauer, Mark Isherwood, Chris Kereluk, Mike Kostyk, Peter Kostyk, Tyler Lawson, Patrick Myers, Payl Quaranta, Kyle Smith, Drew Williams. **NORTH-CENTRAL:** Supervisor Scott Hutchinson, OFFICIALS: Carlo Aletto, Mike Allen, Mike Arnold, David Black, Chris Carnegie, Sean Chatland, Nick Cooke, Ryan Dupuis,

John Eminger, Louie Gabriele, Jason Hann, Dean Herzberg, Terry Hobor, Shane korman, Dave Koziel, Mike Marley, Sean McQuigge, Nick Ouwroules, Rob Palm, Frankie Rocca, David santi, Paul Santi, Matthew Traub, Ben Venditti, Ted Voinou, Jonathan Wallace, Michael Williams-Bell. **NORTH-WEST**: Supervisor John McCutcheon, OFFICIALS: Chad Adamson, Jason Barlow, Dave Blum, Jason Gallagher, Dean Grahame, Craig Kipling, Jordan Lang, Layne Lavis, Dave Lisk, Todd long, Doug Macneil, Steve Morrison, Kendrick Nicholson, Chris Proctor, Derek Skinner, Kevin Snieder, Ryan Styles, Ken Stubbs, Dave Van Kooten, Scoyy Walls, Dennis Watson, Ryan Whitney, Craig Williams, Blake Wilson. **OSHAWA**: Supervisors Ivan Locke, Gus Bambridge & Rick Morphew, OFFICIALS: Matt Arbour, Matthew Black, Steve Brown, Jordan Browne, Ben Buxton, Ryan Carmichael, Sean Coles, Ken Cornelius, John Czerniawski, Darryl Dawson, Paul Drummond, Steve Gallagher, Scott Gray, Darryl Hancock, Craig Harness, Brent Hewlett, Mike Jank, Padraig Kelly, Tyler Kirkland, Ben Kirkwood, Dave Lewis, David Lichacz, Rob Macgregor, Andrew Markew, Evan McCrory, Brad McCutcheon, Dan McKeown, Gord Miles, William Neadles, Brain Park, Dwayne Phillips, Mike Pryde, Paul Renaud, Mike Ricica, David Sankey, Andrew Thompson, Christian Vesnaver, Paul Wade, Ryan Watson. **SARNIA**: Supervisor Jim Maitland, OFFICIALS: Glenn Anderson, Pete Bowen, Clint Campbell, Tim Cox, Rob Dalgetty, Sean Geene, Chris Harwood, Jim Hawthorne, Rob Hawthorne, Tyler Hawthorne, George Langstaff, Sean McLaughlin, Brandon Palmer, Jeff Parney, Mike Pearce, Brain Pearson, Brain Somes, Marty Swan, Rob Veccia, Darcy Vink. **TORONTO**: Supervisors Bob Nadin & David Montgomery, OFFICIALS: Ross Bain, Jordan Banfield, Joel Barron, Sean Bernard, Ryan Carroll, Brain Colaiezzi, Jeff Crawford, Steve Dunlop, Dave Gauthier, Jason Goldenberg, Mike Gordon, Don Haag, Andrew Hubbard, Darryl James, Jamie Lang, Michael Manson, Jonathan Meilach, Nick Mintsopoulos, Ed Munroe, Tyson Orlie, Ryan Park, Steven Picco, Sean Pindar, Brad Potter, Joshua Roberts, Ben Smith, Mat Stiver-Balla, Blair Surette, Anthony Tersigni, Sotaro Yamaguchi.

WINDSOR: Supervisors Matt Pavelich & Jerry Pateman, OFFICIALS: Mike Aubin, Kevin Blundell, Mike Boucher, Jason Brady, Tyler Callender, Grag Campbell, Christian Cortese, A.J.Desantis, Jonathan Forbes, Shawn Hamelin, Ryan Hutchinson, Ryan Lachine, Jeff mayea, Jim McGinlay, Joe Monette, Jake Morassut, Doug Prince, Allan Provost, Jason Rauth, Ryan Renaud, Sean Sampson, Mike Scanlan, John Thompson, Kyle Vermast.

OHA Season 2007-2008
BARRIE: Supervisor Ken Bannerman OFFICIALS: Chris Arts, Korey Bannerman, Ed Black, Dave Bly, Louie Dewar, Grant Fournier, Anders Hagman, Mike Kelly, Jeff Lees, Todd Lewis, Al Madill, Jonathan Martin, Joe Park, Jeff Pratt, Richard Rider, Scott Sefton, Chris Whalen.
BRAMPTON: Supervisors Mike Duggan & John May, OFFICIALS: Walter Araujo, Ken Armstrong, Paul Callon, Sean Chatland, Todd Clark, Chris Cucoch, Shawn Garrett, Brian Grant, Brandon Grant, Rick Janco, Tom Jukes, Tom Lough, Justin Maguire, Glen McBryde, Mike Neill, Dave Newson, Micheal Nomi, Rob Padt, Joe Paolini, Jason Rabjohn, Niall Smith, Chris Smyk, Eric Sutton, Dave Thiffault, Ryan White.
DELHI: Supervisor Bob Morley, OFFICIALs: Darren Bronizewski, Jim Brudz, Troy Charlton, Ryan Elliott, Jason Hicks, Josh Ion, Paul Jones, Mark MacKenzie, Sean Morrow, Kevin Morton, Mark Nemeth, Jamie Nunn, Dan Schmidt, John Searle, Trevor Stevens, Cameron Stone, Colin Town. **GUELPH:** Supervisor Lance Roberts OFFICIALS: Doug Adlam, Bob Beaty, Brent Bloch, Derek Bridgman, Jordan Browne, Joel Campbell, Eric Chute, Dan Dietrich, Chad Drown, Brad Fagan, Jason Faist, Seth Ferguson, John Fischer, Lanny Fuller, Mark Galloway, Adam Good, Matt Gregory, Mike Guardiero, Brandon Hillis, Scott Keys, Todd Long, Thomas Luxmore, Dustin McCrank, Blake Moggy, Steven Percy, Graham Shantz, Bill Smith, Tim Steen, Adam Taylor, Rob Tilt, Jeremy Weber, Michael Williams-Bell, Ben Wilson Ryan Wilson. **HAMILTON:** Supervisors Bob Morley & Mike Biljetina, OFFICIALS: Daniel Adie, Kyle Barclay, Scott Brown, Darcy Burchell, Richard Craven, Matt Fullan, Jason Jackson, Brent Holdsworth, Wes Kindree, Geoff

Lawson, Kevin McKnight, Dale Murphy, Mike Ostaszewicz, Darren Purnell, Stuart Ryerson, Steve Stasiuk, Alton Stead, Jesse Wilmot, Darryl Wolfe, Mike Wortel, Michael Zbucki. **KINGSTON:** Supervisor Ken Harris, OFFICIALS: Dave Baker, Bob Bell, Ian Brooks, Mike Cranley, Al Detlor, Rick Finn, Rob Garden, Sean Jenkins, Rod Hall, Scott Lavender, Justin Kuipers, Tyler Lawson, Adam Lough, Tony McCambridge, Dan McKeown, Chris McLean, Marco McRae, Brad Moore, Nick Myers, Stephen OReilly, Duane Parliament, Kevin Pons, Dave Regan, Chris Ryan, Darren Sloboda Shane Wannamaker. **LONDON:** Supervisor Rick Singleton, OFFICIALS: Mike Assaf, Steve Baker, Brain Bailkowski, Terry Bonter, Matt Bossence, Dan Boyd, Ryan Bradshaw, Kevin Brown, Bruce Byers, Matt Clark, Chris Dewachter, Chris Faulkner, Chris Fraumeni, Dave Gardner, Curtis Gartly, Steve Gould, Mike Logan, Andrew Jackson, Dave Landers, Scott McEwen, Ray McManus, Duane Nutt, Jeremy Parking, Lee Poteck, Scott Rasenberg, Sean Reid, Scott Roode, Patrick Rozendal, Mike Sangster, Mike Spezaiale, Brent Thompson, Dave Thompson, Chris Thornton, Kevin Umansky, Jamie Van Kasteren, Jason Van Massenhoven, Darrell Vitello, Bill Waye, Bob Wright, Don Yeoman, James Yeoman. **NIAGARA:** Supervisors Bob Morley, Mike Biljetina & Craig Spada. Officials: John Adamek, Daniel Adie, Darren Anger, Mike Bolibruck, Justin Creamer, Mark Drennan, Michael Fowler, Mike Gage, Steve Gallagher, Geoff Gamble, Jeff Hanna, Darcy Hemauer, Mark Isherwood, Chris Kereluk, Mike Kostyk, Pete Kostyk, Patrick Myers, Paul Quaranta, Kyle Smith, Rod West, Drew Williams. **NORTH-CENTRAL:** Supervisors Bryan Lewis OFFICIALS: Carlo Aletto, Mike Allen, Chris Carneigie, Nick Cooke, Ryan Dupius, John Eminger, Jason Hann, Dean Herzberg, Shane Korman, Dave Koziel, Nick Lacroce, Mike Marley, Sean McQuigge, Rob Moore, Scott Oakman, Nick Ouwroules, Rob Palm, Aaron Pourmand, Frankie Rocca, Dave Santi, Paul Santi Jonathan Wallace. **NORTH-WEST:** Supervisor John McCutcheon & Jeff Smith, OFFICIALS: Chad Adamson, Jason Barlow, Dave Blum, Jason Gallagher, Dean Grahame, Craig Kipling, Jamie Lang, Jordan Lang, Layne Lavis, Dave Lisk, Doug MacNeil, Brad McCutcheon, Steve

Morrison, Larry Murphy, Kenderick Nicholson, Chris Proctor, Lee Rodgers, Kevin Sneider, Ken Stubbs, Ryan Styles, Dave Van Kooten, Scott Walls, Dennis Watson, Ryan Whitney, Craig Williams, Blake Wilson. **OSHAWA:** Supervisors Ivan Locke, Gus Bambridge & Rick Morphew, OFFICIALS: Matt Black, Steve Brown, Ben Buxton, Ryan Carmichael, Sean Coles, Ken Cornelius, John Czerniawski, Paul Drummond, Scott Gray, Darryl Hancock, Craig Harness, Brent Hewlett, Mike Jank, Padraig Kelly, Tyler Kirkland, Ben Kirkwood, Dave Lewis, Dave Lichacz, Rob Macgregor, Geoff Matthews, Andrew Markew, Evan McCrory, Gord Miles, Will Neadles, Brian Park, Dwayne Phillips, Mike Pryde, Paul Renaud, Mike Ricica, Dave Sankey, Mark Sliwowicz, Andrew Thompson, Christian Vesnaver, Paul Wade. **SARNIA:** Supervisors Bob Spence & Jim Maitland, OFFICIALS: Glen Anderson, Pete Bowen, Tim Cox, Rob Dalgetty Jr, Dan Dolson, Sean Geene, Chris Harwood, Jim Hawthorne, Rob Hawthorne, Tyler Hawthorne, George Langstaff, Kyle Mellor, Sean McLaughlin, Brandon Palmer, Jeff Parney, Mike Pearce, Brain Pearson, Brian Somes, Adam Swan, Bill Swan, Marty Swan, Darcy Vink, Rob Veccia. **TORONTO:** Supervisors Bob Nadin & David Montgomery, OFFICIALS: Mike Arnold, Ross Bain, Joel Barron, Sean Bernard, David Black, Ryan Carroll, Chris Clow, Brain Colaiezzi, Steve Dunlop, Joe Fenech, Dave Gauthier, Jason Goldenberg, Mike Gordon, Don Haag, Duane Hayes, Andrew Hubbard, Darryl James, Jonathan Meilach, Nick Mintsopoulos, Ed Munroe, Tyson Orlie, Ryan Park, Steve Picco, Sean Pindar, Brad Potter, Josh Roberts, Ben Smith, Anthony Tersigni, Nick Spiro. **WINDSOR**: Supervisor Matt Pavelich, OFFICIALS: Mike Aubin, Kevin Blundell, Mike Boucher, Jason Brady, Tyler Callender, Greg Campbell, Christian Cortese, Jonathan Forbes, Shawn Hamelin, Ryan Hutchinson, Jeff Mayea, Jim McGinlay, Joe Monette, Doug Prince, Allan Provost, Jason Rauth, Ryan Renaud, Sean Sampson, Pat Scarlett, John Thompson, Kyle Vermast.

OHA Season 2006-2007
BARRIE: Supervisor Ralph Sparks OFFICIALS: Chris Arts, Kevin Bannerman, Korey Bannerman, Chris Beiers,

Ed Black, Steve Black, Joe Conway, Louie Dewar, Grant Fournier, Anders Hagman, Mike Kelly, Todd Lewis, Al Madill, Jim McFarlin, Joe Park, Jeff Pratt, Scott Sefton, Steve Skolny, Chris Whalen. **BRAMPTON**: Supervisors Mike Duggan & John May, OFFICIALS: Walter Araujo, Ken Armstrong, Paul Callon, Todd Clark, Chris Cucoch, Matt Fullan, Brian Grant, Brandon Grant, Tom Jukes, Tom Lough, Justin Maguire, Glen McBryde, Mike Neill, Micheal Nomi, Rob Padt, Joe Paolini, Jason Rabjohn, Scott Schlegel, Niall Smith, Chris Smyk, Eric Sutton, Dave Thiffault, Ryan White. **DELHI:** Supervisor Bob Morley, OFFICIALs: Darren Bronizewski, Jim Brudz, Troy Charlton, Brent Elbers, Josh Ion, Paul Jones, Mark MacKenzie, Kevin Morton, Mark Nemeth, Jamie Nunn, Dan Schmidt, John Searle, Trevor Stevens, Cameron Stone, Colin Town. **GUELPH:** Supervisor Lance Roberts & Rick Morphew OFFICIALS: Doug Adlam, Bob Beaty, Brent Bloch, Derek Bridgman, Jordan Browne, Eric Chute, Curtis Darling, Dan Dietrich, Brad Fagan, Jason Faist, Setth Ferguson, John Fischer, Lanny Fuller, Mark Galloway, Adam Good, Matt Gregory, Mike Guardiero, Kelly Ingalls, Scott keys, Marty Kirwan, Jeff Lees, Todd Long, Thomas Luxmore, Dustin McCrank, Scott McEwen, Steven Percy, Graham Shantz, Bill Smith, Tim Steen, Adam Taylor, Rob Tilt, Darrell Vitello, Jeremy Weber, Michael Williams-Bell, Ben Wilson. **HAMILTON:** Supervisors Bob Morley & Mike Biljetina, OFFICIALS: Daniel Adie, Kyle Barclay, Scott Brown, Darcy Burchell, Richard Craven, John Crowe, Jason Jackson, Brent Holdsworth, Wes Kindree, Geoff lawson, Kevin McKnight, Dale Murphy, Mike Ostaszewicz, Darren Purnell, Steve Stasiuk, Alton Stead, Jesse Wilmot, Darryl Wolfe, Mike Woretl, Michael Zbucki. **KINGSTON:** Supervisor Ken Harris, OFFICIALS: Dave Baker, Bob Bell, Ian Brooks, Josh Conner, Mike Cranley, Al Detlor, Rick Finn, Rob Garden, Sean Jenkins, Scott Lavender, Tyler Lawson, Adam Lough, Tony McCambridge, Dan McKeown, Chris McLean, Marco McRae, Brad Moore, Dave Mullins, Nick Myers, Stephen OReilly, Duane Parliament, Kevin Pons, Dave Regan, Chris Ryan, Darren Sloboda. **LONDON:** Supervisor Rick Singleton, OFFICIALS: Mike Assaf, Steve Baker, Brain Bailkowski, Terry Bonter, Matt Bossence,

Ryan Bradshaw, Kevin Brown, Bruce Byers, AAron Chadwick, Matt Clark, Jim Clements, Chris Dewachter, Chris Faulkner, Chris Fraumeni, Dave Gardner, Curtis Gartly, Steve Gould, Andrew Jackson, Dave Landers, Ray McManus, Andrew Michalski, Michael Michalski, Duane Nutt, Robert Perrier, Lee Poteck, Scott Rasenberg, Sean Reid, Scott Roode, Patrick Rozendal, Mike Sangster, James Sinfield, Mike Spezaiale, Brent Thompson, Dave Thompson, Chris Thornton, Kevin Umansky, Jamie Van Kasteren, Jason Van Massenhoven, Bill Waye, Bob Wright, Don Yeoman, Mike Yeoman. **NIAGARA:** Supervisors Bob Morley & Mike Biljetina. Officials: John Adamek, Darren Anger, Mike Bolibruck, Mark Drennan, Michael Fowler, Mike Gage, Cary Gagnon, Steve Gallagher, Geoff Gamble, Jeff Hanna, Darcy hemauer, Mark Isherwood, Chris kereluk, Mike Kostyk, Pete Kostyk, Paul Quaranta, Kyle Smith, Rod West, Drew Williams. **NORTH-CENTRAL:** Supervisors Bryan Lewis & Ken Bannerman, OFFICIALS: Carlo Aletto, Mike Allen, Chris Carneigie, John Eminger, Jason Hann, Brian Hoffman, Shane Korman, Dave Koziel, Nick Lacroce, Mike Marley, Sean McQuigge, Geoff Miller, Sean Morrow, Rob Moore, Ryan Oneill, Nick Ouwroules, Rob Palm, Frankie Rocca, Paul Santi, Wayne Timbers, Matthew Traub, Ted Voinou. **NORTH-WEST:** Supervisor John McCutcheon, OFFICIALS: Chad Adamson, Dave Blum, Jason Gallagher, Dean Grahame, Richard Judges, Craig Kipling, Jamie Lang, Layne Lavis, Dave Lisk, Doug MacNeil, Brad McCutcheon, Steve Morrison, Larry Murphy, Glen Murray, Kenderick Nicholson, Chris Proctor, Chris Reed, Lee Rodgers, Kevin Sneider, Ken Stubbs, Dave Van Kooten, Scott Walls, Dennis Watson, Ryan Whitney, Craig Williams, Blake Wilson. **OSHAWA:** Supervisors Ivan Locke & Gus bambridge, OFFICIALS: Matt Black, Steve Brown, Ryan Bruce, Ben Buxton, Ryan Carmichael, Sean Coles, Ken Cornelius, Darryl Dawson, Paul Drummond, Dave Gauthier, Darryl Hancock, Craig Harness, Brent Hewlett, Mike Jank, Padraig Kelly, Tyler Kirkland, Ben Kirkwood, Dave Lewis, Dave Lichacz, Rob Macgregor, Geoff Matthews, Andrew Markew, Evan McCrory, Gord Miles, Brian Park, Dwayne Phillips, Mike Pryde, Paul Reid, Paul Renaud, Mike Ricica, Dave

Sankey, Mark Sliwowicz, Andrew Thompson, Brad Upton, Christian Vesnaver, Paul Wade. **SARNIA:** Supervisors Bob Spence & Jim Maitland, OFFICIALS: Glen Anderson, Pete Bowen, Chad Cox, Tim Cox, Rob Dalgetty Jr, Sean Geene, Chris Harwood, Jim Hawthorne, Rob Hawthorne, Tyler Hawthorne, Georrge Langstaff, Kyle Mellor, Sean McLaughlin, Brandon Palmer, Jeff Parney, Brain Pearson, Brian Somes, Bill Swan, Marty Swan, Rob Veccia. **TORONTO:** Supervisors Bob Nadin & Garey Wilson, OFFICIALS: Mike Arnold, Ross Bain, Joel Barron, Sean Bernard, David Black, Ryan Carroll, Kris Chraba, Chris Clow, Matt Davie, Joe Fenech, Jason Goldenberg, Mike Gordon, Don Haag, Terry Hobor, Darryl James, Jonatthan Meilach, Nick mintsopoulos, Ed Munroe, Tyson Orlie, Ryan Park, Steve Picco, Sean Pindar, Brad Potter, Josh Roberts, Nick Spiro, Dave Vince, Jonathan Wallace. **WINDSOR:** Supervisor Matt Pavelich, OFFICIALS: Mike Aubin, Kevin Blundell, Mike Boucher, Jason Brady, Tyler Callender, Greg Campbell, Christian Cortese, Jonathan Forbes, Stephen hadfield, Shawn Hamelin, Ryan Hutchinson, Jeff Mayea, Jim McGinlay, Joe Monette, Doug Prince, Allan Provost, Jason Rauth, Ryan Renaud, Sean Sampson, Pat Scarlett, John Thompson, Kyle Vermast, Jeff Weglarz, Mark Wuerch.

OHA Season 2005-2006
BARRIE: Supervisor Ralph Sparks Officials: Korey Bannerman, Kevin Bannerman, Chris Beiers, Ed Black, Steve Black, Joe Conway, Louie Dewar, Grant Fournier, Anders Hagman, Tim Hasenack, Jay Hutton, Todd Lewis, Allan Madill, Jonathan Martin, Jim McFarlin, Josef Park, Jeff Pratt, Jonathan Rose, Scott Sefton, Steve Skolony.
BRAMPTON: Supervisors; Mike Duggan & John May. Officials: Walter Araujo, Ken Armstrong, Paul Callon, Ryan Carroll, Todd Clark, Chris Cucoch, Matt Fullan, Shawn Garrett, Brian Grant, Tom Lough, Thomas Jukes, Glen McBryde, Mike Neill, Michael Nomi, Robert Padt, Joe Paolini, Ryan Park, Darren Price, Jason Rabjohn, Joshua Roberts, Niall Smith, Chris Smyk, Eric Sutton, Dave Thiffault. **DELHI:** Supervisor: Bob Morley. Officials: Jeff Beech, Darrin Bronizewski, Jim Brudz,

Jamie Carman, Troy Charlton, Brent Elbers, Josh Ion, Paul Jones, Mark MacKenzie, Sean Morrow, Mark Nemeth, Jamie Nunn, Rob Reid, John Searle, Tyler Stefan, Trevor Stevens, Colin Town. **GUELPH:** Supervisors: Lance Roberts & Rick Morphew. Officials: Doug Adlam, Bob Beatty, Brent Bloch, Derek Bridgmsn, Arron Chadwick, Scott Cherrey, Brad Fagan, Jason Faist, Seth Ferguson, John Fischer, Lanny Fuller, Adam Good, Matt Gregory, Mark Galloway, Mike Guardiero, Kelly Ingalls, Marty Kirwan, Todd Long, Tom Luxmore, Mike Malott, Scott McEwen, Blake Moggy, Dan Schmidt, Graham Shantz, Dave Shepley, Bill Smith, Ian Smith, Tim Steen, Ralph Urbanke, Paul Wade, Jeremy Weber, Michael Williams-Bell, Ben Wilson. **HAMILTON:** Supervisors: Bob Morley & Mike Biljetina. Officials: Scott Brown, Darcy Burchell, John Crowe, Brent Holdsworth, Wes Kindree, Geoff Lawson, Kevin McKnight, Dale Murphy, Mike Ostaszewicz, Darren Purnell, Steve Stasiuk, Alton Stead, Darryl Wolfe, Mike Wortel, Mike Zbucki. **KINGSTON:** Supervisor: Ken Harris. Officials: Dave Baker, Bob Bell, Ian Brooks, Jamie Carr, Mike Cranley, Al Detlor, Bryan Detlor, Rick Finn, Rob Hillier, Sean Jenkins, Scott Lavendor, Tyler Lawson, Adam Lough, Chris McLean, Marco McRae, Brad Moore, David Mullins, Nick Myers, Stephen O'Reilly, Duane Parliament, Kevin Pons, Dave Regan, Darren Sloboda, Ron Stakes, Shane Wannamaker, Brian Wareham. **LONDON:** Supervisors: Mel Huctwith & Rick Singleton. Officials: Mike Assaf, Steve Baker, Terry Bonter, Ryan Bradshaw, Kevin Brown, Bruce byers, Matt Clark, Jim Clements, Paul Colbran, Jeff Cosman, Chris Dewachter, Chris Faulkner, Chris Fraumeni, Dave Gardner, Steve Gould, Chad Houben, Richard Hume, Dave Landers, Ray McManus, Michael Michalski, Andrew Michalski Robert Perrier, Scott Rasenberg, Sean Reid, Scott Roode, Mike Sangster, James Sinfield, Dave Thompson, Brent R. Thompson, Chris Thornton, Kevin Umansky, Jason Van Massenhoven, Doug Vandyk, Jamie Vankasteren, Bill Waye, Bob Wright, Don Yeoman, Mike Yeoman. **NIAGARA:** Supervisors: Mike Biljetina & Bob Morley. Officials: John Adamek, Darren Anger, Mike Bolibruck, Brent Coulombe, Michael Fowler, Mike Gage, Cary

Gagnon, Steve Gallagher, Geoff Gamble, Jeff Hanna, Darcy Hemauer, Mark Isherwood, Chris Kereluk, Pete Kostyk, Mike Kostyk, Andrew Markew, Paul Quaranta, Kyle Smith, Rod West, Drew Williams. **NORTH-CENTRAL:** Supervisor: Bryan Lewis. Officials: Carlo Aletto, Mike Allen, Chris Carneige, Aaron Draper, Jason Hann, Brian Hoffman, Scott Hutchinson, Dave Koziel, Nick Lacroce, Mike Marley, Sean McQuigge, Geoff Miller, Rob Moore, Aaron Pourmand, Ryan O'Neill, Scott Oakman, Nick Ouwroules, Rob Palm, Frankie Rocca, Paul Santi, Wayne Timbers, Matthew Traub, Ted Voinou. **NORTH-WEST:** Supervisor: John McCutcheon. Officials: Chad Adamson, Jason Barlow, Dave Blum, Lionel "Doug" Crawford, Jason Gallagher, Dean Grahame, Richard Judges, Dave Lisk, Doug MacNeil, Brad McCutcheon, Steve Morrison, Larry Murphy, Glen Murray, Kenderick Nicholson, Chris Proctor, Chris Reed, Lee Roberts, Patrick Rozendal, Kevin Smith, Gavin Stewart, Ken Stubbs, Dave Van Kooten, Dean Vincent, Dennis Watson, Ryan Whitney, Scott Walls. **OSHAWA:** Supervisors: Ivan Locke & Gus Bambridge. Officials: Matthew Black, Steve Brown, Ryan Bruce, Ben Buxton, Ryan Carmichael, Sean Coles, Ken Cornelius, Darryl Dawson, Paul Drummond, Dave Gauthier, Mike Hamilton, Darryl Hancock, Craig Harness, Brian Hoard, Mike Jank, Dave Lichacz, Dave Lewis, Rob MacGregor, Geoff Matthews, Gord Miles, Mike Pearce, Dwayne Phillips, Mike Pryde, Paul Renaud, Mike Ricica, David Sankey, Mark Sliwowicz, Andrew Thompson, Adam Taylor, Brent Thompson, Brad Upton, Christian Vesnaver, Robert Welsh. **SARNIA:** Supervisors: Bob Spence & Jim Maitland. Officials: Glenn Anderson, Robert Anderson, Peter Bowen, Tyler Callender, Chad Cox, Tim Cox, Sean Geene, Chris Harwood, Jim Hawthorne, Rob Hawthorne, Tyler Hawthorne, George Langstaff, Mike Mathieson, Seam McLaughlin, Kevin Morton, Brandon Palmer, Jeff Parney, Steven Percy, Brian Pearson, Brian Somes, Bill Swan, Marty Swan, Mark Vangriendt, Rob Veccia, Craig Williams. **TORONTO:** Supervisors: Bob Nadin & Garey Wilson. Officials: Ross Bain, Joel Barron, Sean Bernard, David Black, Kris Chraba, Chris Clcw, Matt Davie, Paul Gallant,

Mike Gordon, Don Haag, Terry Hobor, Chris Hodgins, Darryl James, Jonathan Meilach, Nick Mintsopoulos, Ed Munroe, Chris Nyers, Tyson Orlie, Sean Pindar, Brett Punchard, Nick Spiro, Dave Vince, Jonathan Wallace. **WINDSOR:** Supervisor: Matt Pavelich. Officials: Mike Aubin, Kevin Blundell, Greg Campbell, Christian Cortese, Jonathan Forbes, Steve Hadfield, Andrew Jackson, Ryan Lachine, Jim McGinlay, Allan Provost, Jason Rauth, Ryan Renaud, Sean Sampson, Pat Scarlett, John Thompson, Mark Wuerch, Kyle Vermast, Jeff Weglarz.

OHA Season 2004-2005
BARRIE: Supervisor: Ralph Sparks. Officials: Korrey Bannerman, Chris Beiers, Ed Black, Steve Black, Joe Conway, Louie Dewar, Briant Duncan, Grant Fournier, Anders Hagman, Tim Hasenack, Devon Hutton, Jay Hutton, Todd Lewis, Allan Madill, Jim McFarlin, Josef Park, Jeff Pratt, Jonathan Rose, Scott Sefton, Steve Skolony. **BRAMPTON:** Supervisors: Mike Duggan & John May. Officials: Walter Araujo, Toby Beam, Paul Callon, Ryan Carroll, Todd Clark, Sean Coles, Chris Cucoch, Matt Fullan, Paul Gallant, Shawn Garrett, Michael Goumas, Brian Grant, Thomas Jukes, Brian Harasymchuk, Tom Lough, Mike Neill, Glen McBryde, Michael Nomi, Robert Padt, Joe Paolini, Ryan Park, Darren Price, Jason Rabjohn, Joshua Roberts, Niall Smith, Chris Smyk Eric Sutton. **DELHI:** Supervisors: Bob Morley & Mike Biljetina. Officials: Jeff Beech, James Bradshaw, Jim Brudz, Jamie Carman, Chris Dewachter, Brent Elbers, Richard Enlund, Josh Ion, Paul Jones, Mark MacKenzie, D.J. McQueen, Jamie Nunn, Rob Reid, John Searle, Brent Stefan, Tyler Stefan, Colin Town. **GUELPH:** Supervisors: Lance Roberts, Ray Scapinello & Bill Devorski. Officials: Bob Beatty, Brent Bloch, Derek Bridgmsn, Richard Carrer, Arron Chadwick, Scott Cherrey, Neil Christopher, Brad Fagan, Jason Faist, Josh Fraser, Lanny Fuller, Matt Gregory, Mark Galloway, Jason Guardiero, Mike Guardiero, Ryan Hutchinson, Kelly Ingalls, Garry Johnson, Marty Kirwan, Tom Luxmore, Jim MacEachern, Mike Malott, Mike McCreary, Scott McEwen, Blake Moggy, Aran Myers, Jason Pettapiece, Dan Schmidt, Graham Shantz, Dave Shepley, Ian Smith, Tim

Steen, Rob Tilt, Ralph Urbanke. **HAMILTON**: Supervisors: Bob Morley & Mike Biljetina. Officials: Scott Brown, Darcy Burchell, John Crowe, Brent Holdsworth, Darryl James, Wes Kindree, Geoff Lawson, Kevin McKnight, Bob Morley, Dale Murphy, Mike Ostaszewicz, Darren Purnell, Travis Riggin, Steve Stasiuk, Alton Stead, Darryl Wolfe, Mike Wortel Gord Zaroski. **KINGSTON:** Supervisor: Ken Harris. Officials: Dave Baker, Bob Bell, Ian Brooks, Ryan Bruce, Mike Cranley, Al Detlor, Bryan Detlor, Rick Finn, Chris French, Rob Hillier, Sean Jenkins, Scott Lavendor, Robert Longfield, Chris McLean, Marco McRae, Rob Mills, Brad Moore, David Mullins, Nick Myers, Stephen O'Reilly, Duane Parliament, Dave Regan, Mike Reid, Darren Sloboda, Ron Stakes, Shane Wannamaker, Brian Wareham. **LONDON:** Supervisors: Mel Huctwith & Rick Singleton. Officials: Mike Assaf, Steve Baker, Mark Bennett, Terry Bonter, Ryan Bradshaw, Kevin Brown, Matt Clark, Jim Clements, Paul Colbran, Chris Faulkner, Chris Fraumeni, Dave Gardner, Steve Gould, Chad Houben, Andrew Jackson, Dave Landers, Jeremy Lee, Mike Logan, Mike Madersbacher, Ray McManus, Michael Michalski, Andrew Michalski Dave Page, Robert Perrier, Scott Rasenberg, Sean Reid, Mike Sangster, James Sinfield, Shaun Taylor, Dave Thompson, Brent R. Thompson, Chris Thornton, Kevin Umansky, Jason Van Massenhoven, Doug Vandyk, Jamie Vankasteren, Bill Waye, Bob Wright, Mike Yeoman. **NIAGARA:** Supervisors: Craig Spada, Bob Morley & Mike Biljetina. Officials: Darren Anger, Mike Arnold, Mike Bolibruck, Brent Coulombe, Michael Fowler, Mike Gage, Steve Gallagher, Geoff Gamble, Jeff Hanna, Darcy Hemauer, Chris Kereluk, Pete Kostyk, Mike Kostyk, Andrew Markew, Don McArthur, Dave Stortz, Paul Quaranta, Rod West, Drew Williams. **NORTH-CENTRAL:** Supervisor: Bryan Lewis. Officials: Carlo Aletto, Mike Allen, Chris Carneige, Paolo Carretta, Pete Gardner, Jason Hann, Brian Hoffman, Scott Hutchinson, Dave Koziel, Nick Lacroce, Mike Marley, Sean McQuigge, Geoff Miller, Rob Moore, Ryan O'Neill, Scott Oakman, Nick Ouwroules, Rob Palm, Frankie Rocca, Paul Santi, Wayne Timbers, Matthew Traub, Ted Voinou. **NORTH-WEST:** Supervisor: John McCutcheon. Officials: Chad

Adamson, Trevor Alexander, Jason Barlow, Dave Blum, Lionel "Doug" Crawford, John Fischer, Dean Grahame, Dave Hornsby, Dave Lisk, Doug MacNeil, Brad McCutcheon, Steve Morrison, Larry Murphy, Glen Murray, Kenderick Nicholson, Chris Proctor, Lee Roberts, Patrick Rozendal, Kevin Smith, Ken Stubbs, Dave Van Kooten, Dennis Watson, Ryan Whitney, Scott Walls. **OSHAWA:** Supervisors: Ivan Locke & Gus Bambridge. Officials: Matthew Black, Steve Brown, Ben Buxton, Ryan Carmichael, Jamie Carr, John Coburn, Ken Cornelius, Dave Crowley, Darryl Dawson, Paul Drummond, Adam Good, Mike Hamilton, Darryl Hancock, Craig Harness, Brian Hoard, Mike Jank, Dean Jenkins, Dave Lewis, Rob MacGregor, Geoff Matthews, Gord Miles, Dwayne Phillips, Mike Pryde, Paul Renaud, David Sankey, Mark Sliwowicz, Shawn Szorady, Adam Taylor, Brent Thompson, Brad Upton, Christian Vesnaver, Dave Wedlake, Robert Welsh. **SARNIA:** Supervisors: Bob Spence & Jim Maitland. Officials: Glenn Anderson, Robert Anderson, Dave Belling, Eric Bryce, Lloyd Cottel, Chad Cox, Tim Cox, Sean Geene, Jim Hawtthorne, George Langstaff, Mike Mathieson, Seam McLaughlin, Kevin Morton, Brandon Palmer, Jeff Parney, Steven Percy, Brian Pearson, Brian Somes, Bill Swan, Marty Swan, Beau Taylor, Mark Vangriendt, Rob Veccia, Craig Williams. **TORONTO:** Supervisors: Bob Nadin & Garey Wilson. Officials: Ross Bain, Joel Barron, Sean Bernard, David Black, Jason Blundon, Kris Chraba, Chris Clow, Matt Davie, Jason Goldenberg, Mike Gordon, Don Haag, Terry Hoboer, Chris Hodgins, Pete Kourtis, David Lichacz, Nick Mintsopoulos, Ian Munro, Ed Munroe, Chris Nyers, Tyson Orlie, Bill Smith, Nick Spiro, Dave Vince, Jonathan Wallace. **WINDSOR:** Supervisor: Matt Pavelich. Officials: Mike Aubin, Kevin Blundell, Greg Campbell, Bob Clifford, Christian Cortese, P.J. Dupuis, Jonathan Forbes, Steve hadfield, Ryan Lachine, Dennis Lennox, Jim McGinlay, Allan Provost, Jason Rauth, Ryan Renaud, Sean Sampson, Pat Scarlett, John Thompson, Mark Wuerch, Kyle Vermast.

OHA Season 2003-2004
BARRIE: Supervisor: Ralph Sparks. Officials: Korey Bannerman, Chris Beiers, Ed Black, Steve Black, Joe Conway, Briant Duncan, Bent Elbers, Kevin Frew, Anders Hagman, Tim Hasenack, Devon Hutton, Jay Hutton, Todd Lewis, Allan Madill, Jim McFarlin, Josef Park, Jeff Pratt, Jonathan Rose, Todd Wand, Gavin Watson. **BRAMPTON:** Supervisprs" Mike Duggan & John May. Officials: Mike Anderson, Walter Araujo, Toby Beam, Ryan Carroll, Todd Clark, Sean Coles, Chris Cucoch, Paul Gallant, Shawn Garrett, Michael Goumas, Brain Grant, Brian Harasymuck, Thomas Jukes, Glen McBryde, Mike Neill, Michael Nomi, Robert Padt, Joe Paolini, Darren Price, Roger Proulx, Jason Rabjohn, Joshua Roberts, Niall Smith, Chris Smyk. **DELHI:** Supervisor: Bob Hodges. Officials: Jeff Beech, James Bradshaw, Jim Brudz, Chris Dewachter, Richard Enlund, Josh Ion, Paul Jones, Mark MacKenzie, Dave McRae, Mark Nemeth, Jamie Nunn, Rob Reid, John Searle, Brett Smith, Brent Stefan, Colin Town. **GUELPH:** Supervisors: Bill Devorksi, Lance Roberts & Al Kimmel. Officials: Bob Beatty, Brent Bloch, Derek Bridgman, Deny Brulotte, Richard Carrer, Scott Cherrey, Neil Christopher, Brad Fagan, Jason Faist, Josh Fraser, Lanny Fuler, Mark Galloway, Jason Guardiero, Mike Guardiero, Kelly Ingalls, Gary Johnston, Mike Mallot, Chris McCracken, Mike McCreary, Blake Moggy, Kenderick, Nicholson, Michael Patterson, Jason Pettapiece, Sean Reid, Michael Roberts, Steve Routenburg, Dan Schmidt, Graham Shantz, Dave Shepley, Ian Smith, Adam Taylor, Rob Tilt, Ralph Urbanke. **HAMILTON:** Supervisors: Bob Morley & Mike biljetina. Officials: Darcy Birchell, Scott Brown, John Crowe, Jeff Hanna, Brent Holcsworth, Geoff Lawson, Bill McKnight, Kevin McKnight, Bob Morley, Rob Morley, Dale Murphy, Mike Ostaszewicz, Darren Purnell, Travis Riggin, Steve Stasiuk, Chris Stevenson, Darryl Wolfe, Mike Wortel. **KINGSTON:** Supervisor: Ken Harris. Officials: Dave Baker, Bob Bell, Ian Brooks, Greg Brown, Al Detlor, Bryan Detlor, Rick Finn, Chris French, Rob Hillier, Sean Jenkins, Tim Kelly, Scott Lavendor, Robert Longfield, Brad Moore, David Mullins, Nick Myers, Stephen O'Reilly, Ted Padley, Duane Parliament, Dave

Regan, Jack Renshaw, Darren Slobada, Ron Stakes, Shane Wannamaker, Brain Wareham. **LONDON:** Supervisors: Rick Singleton & Mel Huctwith. Officials: Mike Assaf, Steve Baker, Mark Bennett, Terry Bonter, Ryan Bradshaw, Kevin Brown, Matt Clark, Jim Clements, Paul Colbran, Chris Faulkner, Chris Fraumeni, Steve Gould, Jeremy Lee, Mike Logan, Ray McManus, Michael Michalski, Dave Page, Robert Perrier, Scott Rasenburg, Chris Reed, Mike Sangster, Jay Simpson, James Sinfield, Stephen Skolny, Chris Thornton, Dave Thompson, Nathan Troyer, Kevin Umansky, Jason Van Massenhoven, Carl Vink, Scott Walls, Bill Waye, Bob Wright, Mike Yeoman. **NIAGARA:** Supervisor: Craig Spada. Officials: Darren Anger, Mike Arnold, Mike Bolibruck, Gary Corsi, Mark Drennan, Michael Fowler, Mike gage, Steve gallagher, Geoff gamble, Darcy hemauer, Chris kereluk, Mike Kostyk, Pete Kostyk, Don McArthur, Mitch Osborne, Paul Quaranta, Dave Stortz, Rod West. **NORTH-CENTRAL:** Supervisor: Bryan Lewis. Officials: Carlo Aletto, Mike Allen, Jamie Carman, Paolo Carretta, Jeff Carter, Chris Clow, Bill Cober, Pete Gardner, Brian Hoffman, Scott Hutchinson, Marty Kirwan, Dave Koziel, Nick Lacroce, Tom Lough, Mike Marley, Sean McQuigge, Geoff Miller, Rob Moore, Ryan O'Neill, Scott Oakman, Nick Ouwroules, Rob Palm, Frankie Rocca, Paul Santi, Wayne Timbers, Matthew Traub, Ted Voinou. **NORTH-WEST:** Supervisor: John McCutcheon. Officials: Chad Adamson, Trevor Alexander, Jason Barlow, Nigel Black, Dave Blum, Lionel Crawford, Dean Grahame, Dave Hornsby, Dave Lisk, Doug McNeil, Brad McCutcheon, Steve Morrison, Larry Murphy, Glen Murray, Chris Proctor, Lee Rodgers, Patrick Rozendal, Kevin Smith, Ken Stubbs, Dave Van Kotten, Dennis Watson, Ryan Whitney. **OSHAWA:** Supervisors: Ivan Locke & Gus bambridge. Officials: Matthew Black, Steve Brown, Chris Cairns, Ryan Carmichael, Jamie Carr, John Coburn, Ken Cornelius, Dave Crowley, Darryl Dawson, Paul Drummond, Adam Good, Tony Goulah, Mike Hamilton, Darryl Hancock, Craig Harness, Brian Hoard, Darryl James, Mike Jank, Dean Jenkins, Dave Lewis, Rob MacGregor, Geoff Matthews, Gord Miles, Dwayne Phillips, Mike Pryde, Paul

Renaud, David Sankey, Mark Sliwowicz, Shawn Szorady, Brent Thompson, Brad Upton, Christian Vesnaver, Dave Wedlake, Robert Welsh. **SARNIA:** Supervisor: Bob Spence. Officials: Glenn Anderson, Robert Anderson, Dave Belling, Eric Bryce, Lloyd Cottel, Chad Cox, Tim Cox, Robert Dalgety, Tim Dolbear, Sean Geene, Jim Hawthorne, Chad Houben, George Langstaff, Bill MacAlpine, Mike Mathieson, Kevin McAlpine, Kevin Morton, Jeff Parney, Steven Percy, Brian Somes, Bill Swan, Marty Swan, Beau Taylor, Mark Vandergriendt, Rob Veccia, Craig Williams. **TORONTO:** Supervisors: Bob Nadin & Garey Wilson. Officials: Ross Bain, Jordan Banfield, Sean Bernard, David Black, Jason Blundon, Ben Buxton, Kris Chraba, Jeffrey Crawford, Matt Davie, Jason Goldenberg, Mike Gordon, Don Haag, Terry Hobor, Chris Hodgins, Cris Kalangis, Pete Kourtis, David Lichacz, Matthew Manor, Nick Mintsopoulos, Ian Munro, Ed Munroe, Chris Nyers, Mike Pearce, Brett Punchard, Scott Sefton, Bill Smith, Nick Spiro, Robert Sylvester. **WINDSOR:** Supervisor: Matt Pavelich. Officials: Mike Aubin, Kevin Blundell, Greg Campbell, Bob Clifford, Christian Cortese, Jonathan Forbes, Steve Hadfield, Ryan Hutchinson, Ryan Lachine, Jim McGinlay, Allan Provost, Jason Rauth, Ryan Renaud, Sean Sampson, Pat Scarlett, Lee Simpson, John Thompson.

OHA Season 2002-2003
BARRIE: Supervisor: Ralph Sparks. Officials: Ken Bannerman, Korey Bannerman, Chris Beiers, Ed Black, Steve Black, Joe Conway, Louie Dewar, Briant Duncan, Brent Elbers, Kevin Frew, Morris Gervais, Anders Hagman, Mike Hamilton, Tim Hasenack, Devon Hutton, Jay Hutton, Todd Lewis, Allan Madill, Jim McFarlin, Josef Park, Jeff Pratt, Scott Sefton, Gavin Watson.
BRAMPTON: Supervisors: Mike Duggan & Bryan Lewis. Officials: Mike Anderson, Walter Araujo, Toby Beam, Ryan Carroll, Todd Clark, Sean Coles, Chris Cucoch, Paul Gallant, Shawn Garrett, Michael Goumas, Brian Grant, Brad Hamilton, Brian Harasymchuk, Thomas Jukes, Glen McBryde, Mike Neill, Michael Nomi, Robert Padt, Joe Paolini, Darren Price, Roger Proulx, Joshua Roberts, Niall Smith, Greg Sorrell, Shane Wannamaker. **DELHI:**

Supervisor: Bob Hodges. Officials: Jeff Beech, Jim Brudz, Chris Dewachter, Richard Enlund, Josh Ion, Paul Jones, Mark MacKenzie, Dave McRae, Jeremy Morrison, Mark Nemeth, Jamie Nunn, Rob Reid, John Searle, Brett Smith, Brent Stefan, Colin Town. **GUELPH:** Supervisors: Bill Devorski, Lance Roberts & Al kimmel. Officials: Bob Beatty, Dana Bennett, Brent Bloch, Derek Bridgman, Deny Brulotte, Scott Cherrey, Neil Christopher, Jeff Cox, Ryan Darrall, Brad Fagan, Jason Faist, Josh Fraser, Lanny Fuller, Mark Galloway, Jason Guardiero, Mike Guardiero, Kelly Ingalls, Gary Johnston, Mike Malott, Chris McCracken, Mike McCreary, Jason Meyer, Blake Moggy, Michael Patterson, Jason Pettapiece, Mike Roadknight, Michael Roberts, Steve Routenberg, Dan Schmidt, Graham Shantz, Dave Shepley, Ian Smith, Tim Steen, Rob Tilt, Ralph Urbanke. **HAMILTON:** Supervisor: Bob Morley. Officials: Mike Biljetina, Darcy Burchell, Shawn Brenn, Scott Brown, John Crowe, Jeff Hanna, Brent Holdsworth, Geoff Lawson, Paul MacDonald, Bill McKnight, Kevin McKnight, Bob Morely, Rob Morley, Mike Ostaszewicz, Darren Purnell, Travis Riggin, Steve Stasiuk, Chris Stevenson, Darryl Wolfe, Mike Wortel **KINGSTON:** Supervisor: Ken Harris. Officals: Aaron Amey, Dave Baker, Bob Bell, Ian Brooks, Chris Clow, Mike Cranley, Al Detlor, Bryan Detlor, Chris French, Rob Hillier, Sean Jenkins, Scott Lavender, Robert Mills, Brad Moore, Nick Myers, Stephen O'Reilly, Ted Padley, Duane Parliament, Dave Regan Jack Renshaw, Darren Sloboda, Ron Stakes. **LONDON:** Supervisors: Rick Singleton & Mel Huctwith. Officials: Mike Arts, Mike Assaf, Steve Baker, Mark Bennett, Terry Bonter, Kevin Brown, Ian Clark, Matt Clark, Jim Clements, Jamie Dekraauw, Jeff Edwards, Chris Faulkner, Steve Gould, Jim Kean, Tim Lane, Mike Logan, Ray McManus, Andrew Michalski, Michael Michalski, Dave Page, Robert Perrier, Scott Rasenberg, Chris Reed, Mike Sangster, Jay Simpson, James Sinfield, Stephen Skolny, Shaun Taylor, Dave Thompson, Chris Thornton, Nathan Troyer, Kevin Umansky, Carl Vink, Bill Waye, Bob Wright, Mike Yeoman. **NIAGARA:** Supervisor: Craig Spada. Officials: Daren Anger, Mike Bolibruck, Gary Corsi, Todd Dawdy, Mark Drennan, Michael Fowler, Mike

Gage, Geoff Gamble, Darcy Hemauer, Robert Judd, Chris Kereluk, Mike Kostyk, Pete Kostyk, Don McArthur, Larry Moore, Mitch Osborne, Paul Quaranta, Dave Stortz, Rod West, Dennis Winger. **NORTH-CENTRAL:** Supervisor: Gary moroney. Officials: Carlo Aletto, Mike Allen, Jamie Carman, Paolo Carretta, Jeff Carter, Bill Cober, Pete Gardner, Jason Hann, Terry Hobor, Scott Hutchinson, Mart Kirwan, Dave Koziel, Nick Lacroce, Tom Lough, Mike Marley, Sean McQuigge, Geoff Miller, Ryan O'Neill, Scott Oakman, Nick Ouwroules, Rob Palm, Mike Pearce, Frankie Rocca, Jonathan Rose, Paul Santi, Wayne Timbers, Ted Voinou. **NORTH-WEST:** Supervisor: John McCutcheon. Officials: Chad Adamson, Trevor Alexander, Jason Barlow, Dave Blum, Kris Chraba, Lionel "Doug" Crawford, Dean Grahame, Lance Holmes, Dave Hornsby, Brent Huras, Dave Lisk, Doug MacNeil, Ryan Marshall, Brad McCutcheon, Steve Morrison, Larry Murphy, Glen Murray, Chris Proctor, Lee Rodgers, Kevin Smith, Ken Stubbs, Dave Van Kooten, Scott Walls, Dennis Watson, Ryan Whitney. **OSHAWA:** Supervisors: Ivan locke & Gus bambridge. Officials: Matthew Black, Steve Brown, Chris Cairns, Ryan Carmichael, Jamie Carr, Ken Cornelius, Dave Crowley, Darryl Dawson, Paul Drummond, Tony Goulah, Darryl Hancock, Craig Harness, Brian Hoard, Mike Jank, Dean Jenkins, John Kalar, Dave Lewis, Rob MacGregor, Geoff Matthews, Gord Miles, David Mullins, Dwayne Phillips, Mike Pryde, Paul Renaud, Ryan Robinson, David Sankey, Mark Sliwowicz, Mark Smail, Corey Strand, Shawn Szorady, Brent Thompson, Brad Upton, Christian Vesnaver, Dave Wedlake, Robert Welsh. **SARNIA:** Supervisor: Bob Spence. Officials: Glenn Anderson, Robert Anderson, Dave Belling, Eric Bryce, Lloyd Cottel, Chad Cox, Tim Cox, Robert Dalgety, Tim Dolbear, Sean Geene, Jim Hawthorne, Chad Houben, George Langstaff, Bill MacAlpine, Jim Maitland, Mike Mathieson, Kevin McAlpine, Kevin Morton, Jeff Parney, Steven Percy, Brian Somes, Bill Swan, Marty Swan, Beau Taylor, Barry Vale, Mark Vandergriendt, Rob Veccia, Craig Williams, Bill Yurchuk. **TORONTO**: Supervisors: Bob Nadin & john May. Officials: Ross Bain, Sean Bernard, David Black, Jason Blundon, Ben Buxton, Jeffrey Crawford, Matt

Davie, Jason Goldenberg, Mike Gordon, Don Haag, Chris Hodgins, Cris Kalangis, Pete Kourtis, David Lichacz, Matthew Manor, Rob Moore, Ian Munro, Ed Munroe, Chris Nyers, Bill Smith, Nick Spiro, Garey Wilson. **WINDSOR:** Supervisor: Matt Pavelich. Officials: Mike Aubin, Kevin Blundell, Greg Campbell, Bob Clifford, Christian Cortese, Jonathan Forbes, Steve Hadfield, Ryan Hutchinson, Ryan Lachine, Jim McGinlay, Paul McKinney, Allan Provost, Jason Rauth, Ryan Renaud, Sean Sampson, Pat Scarlett, Lee Simpson, Robert Sylvester, John Thompson.

OHA Season 2001-2002
BARRIE: Supervisor: Ralph Sparks. Officials: Ken Bannerman, Korey Bannerman, Chris Beiers, Ed Black, Stevew Black, Joe Conway, Kelly Draycott, Briant Duncan, Kevin Frew, Morris Gervais, Tim Hasenack, Devon Hutton, Jay Hutton, Todd Lewis, Allan Madill, Jim McFarlin, Jason Meyer, Martin O'Grady, Josef Park, Jeff Pratt, Scott Sefton, Rob Veccia, Gavin Watson. **BRAMPTON:** Supervisors: Mike duggan & Bryan Lewis. Officials: Mike Anderson, Walter Araujo, Toby Beam, Todd Clark, Sean Coles, Shawn Garrett, Brad Hamilton, Brian Harasymchuk, Thomas Jukes, Glen Mcbryde, Mike Neill, Stuart O'Reilly, Robert Padt, Joe Paolini, Terry Pierce, Darren Price, Roger Proulx, Joshua Roberts, Niall Smith, Greg Sorrell, Scott Topping. **DELHI:** Supervisor: Bob Hodges. Officials: Jeff Beech, Mike Bessagato, Chris Dewachter, Ken Gallagher, Josh Ion, Paul Jones, Mark Mackenzie, Bill Mcknight, Dave Mcrae, Jeremy Morrison, Mark Nemeth, Jamie Nunn, Walter Olivieri, Rob Reid, John Searle, Brent Stefan, Colin Town. **GUELPH:** Supervisors: Bill Devorski, Tom LaFrance & Al Kimmel. Officials: Bob Beatty, Dana Bennett, Dave Bertrand, Brent Bloch, Derek Bridgman, Deny Brulotte, Neil Christopher, Jeff Cox, Ryan Darrall, Brad Fagan, Jason Faist, Tom Farr, Jason Finley, Lanny Fuller, Mark Galloway, Jason Guardiero, Mike Guardiero, Darryl Hancock, Kevin Hastings, Brent Hughes, Kelly Ingalls, Gary Johnston, Mike Malott, Chris Mccracken, Mike Mccreary, Scott Mclean, Blake Moggy, Michael Patterson, Mike Roadknight, Michael Roberts, Steve Routenburg,

Dan Schmidt, Graham Shantz, Dave Shepley, Mark Shewchyk, Ian Smith, Tim Steen, Perry Stone, Kris Taggart, Rob Tilt, Ralph Ubanke. **HAMILTON:** Supervisor: Bob Morley. Officials: Mike Biljetina, Darcy Burchell, Shawn Brenn, Scott Brown, John Crowe, Jeff Hanna, Brent Holdsworth, Geoff Lawson, Paul Macdonald, Kevin Mcknight, Bob Morley, Rob Morley, Mike Ostaszewicz, Chris Stevenson, Darryl Wolfe, Mike Wortel. **KINGSTON:** Supervisor: Ken Harris. Officials: Aaron Amey, Dave Baker, Bob Bell, Terry Bonter, Greg Brown, Chris Clow, Mike Cranley, Al Detlor, Bryan Detlor, Chris French, Rob Hillier, Sean Jenkins, Tim Kelly, Scott Lavendor, Rob Mills, Brad More, Nick Myers, Stephen O'Reilly, Ted Padley, Duane Parliament, Dave Regan, Ron Stakes, Shane Wannamaker. **LONDON:** Rick Singleton & Mel Huctwith. Officials: Mike Arts, Steve Baker, Mark Bennett, Matt Clark, Jamie Dekraauw, Jeff Edwards, Brent Edwards, Chris Faulkner, Steve Gould, Bob Graham, Jim Kean, Tim Lane, Mike Logan, Mike Mcleod, Ray Mcmanus, Andrew Michalski, Michael Michalski, Dave Page, Robert Perrier, Chris Reed, Jay Simpson, James Sinfield, Stephen Skolny, Shaun Taylor, Dave Thompson, Kevin Towers, Nathan Troyer, Kevin Umansky, Carl Vink, Bill Waye, Dave Whaley, Mike Yeoman. **NIAGARA:** Supervisor: Craig Spada. Officials: Darren Anger, Mike Bolibruck, Gary Corsi, Todd Dawdy, Darren Flagg, Mike Gage, Geoff Gamble, Michael Gordon, Darcy Hemauer, Robert Judd, Chris Kereluk, Pete Kostyk, Don Mcarthur, Larry Moore, Paul Quaranta, Dave Stortz, Steve Webb, Rod West, Dennis Winger. **NORTH-CENTRAL:** Supervisor: Wayne McDonald. Officials: Carlo Aletto, Mike Allen, Paolo Carretta, Jeff Carter, Tim Clute, Bill Cober, Pete Gardner, Jason Hann, Terry Hobor, Scott Hutchinson, Dave Koziel, Nick Lacroce, Tim Lough, Mike Marley, Sean Mcquigge, Ryan O'Neill, Scott Oakman, Nick Ouwroules, Rob Palm, Mike Pearce, Jonathan Rose, Paul Santi, Wayne Timbers, Ted Voinou. **NORTH-WEST:** Supervisor: John McCutcheon. Officials: Chad Adamson, Trevor Alexander, Jason Barlow, Dave Blum, Fred Clendenning, Lionel Crawford, Dean Grahame, Lance Holmes, Dave Hornsby, Brent Huras, Dave Lisk, Doug Macneill, Taylor Mali, Ryan

Marshall, Steve Morrison, Larry Murphy, Glen Murray, Chris Proctor, Lee Rodgers, Kevin Smith, Ken Stubbs, Dave Van Kooten, Dennis Watson, Ryan Whitney. **OSHAWA:** Supervisors: Ivan locke & Gus Bambridge. Officials: Brad Ashby, Matthew Black, Mike Brown, Steve Brown, Chris Cairns, Ryan Carmichael, Jamie Carr, John Coburn, Ken Cornelius, Dave Crowley, Darryl Dawson, Paul Drummond, Craig Harmess, Mike Jank, Dean Jenkins, John Kalar, Rob Macgregor, Geoff Matthews, Gord Miles, David Mullins, Dwayne Phillips, Mike Pryde, Paul Renaud, Ryan Robinson, David Sankey, Mark Sliwowicz, Mark Smail, Brian St Thomas, Corey Strand, Shawn Szorady, Brent Thompson, Brad Upton, Christian Vesnaver, Dave Wedlake, Robert Welsh. **SARNIA:** Supervisor: bob Spence. Officials: Glenn Anderson, Robert Anderson, Dave Belling, Eric Bryce, Lloyd Cottel, Chad Cox, Tim Cox, Robert Dalgety, Tim Dolbear, Sean Geene, Jimhawthorne, George Langstaff, Bill Macalpine, Jim Maitland, Mike Mathieson, Kevin Mcalpine, Jeff Parney, Steven Percy, Brian Somes, Bill Swan, Marty Swan, Beau Taylor, Barry Vale, Mark Vandergriendt, Bill Yurchuk. **TORONTO:** Supervisors: Bob Nadin & John May. Officials: Ross Bain, Sean Bernard, David Black, Jason Blundon, Jamie Carman, Ryan Carroll, Kris Chrabe, Ian Culbert, Matt Davie, Paul Gallant, Jason Goldenberg, Don Haag, Cris Kalangis, Pete Kourtis, David Lichacz, Jason Macchesney, Matthew Manor, Rob Moore, Ian Munro, Ed Munroe, Chris Nyers, Bill Smith, Nick Spiro, Garey Wilson. **WINDSOR:** Supervisor: Matt Pavelich. Officials: Mike Aubin, Kevin Blundell, Greg Campbell, Bob Clifford, Darrell Ellwood, Jonathan Forbes, Steve Hadfield, Matt Henderson, Ryan Hutchinson, Ryan Lachine, James Mcginlay, Paul Mckinney, Allan Provost, Ryan Renaud, Geoff Rutherford, Sean Sampson, Pat Scarlett, Lee Simpson, Robert Sylvester, John Thompson, Jeff Weglarz.

OHA Season 2000-2001
BARRIE: Supervisors: Ken Bannerman & Ralph Sparks. Officials: Ken Bannerman, Korey Bannerman Chris Beiers, Ed Black, Steve Black, Kelly Draycott, Briant Duncan, Kevin Frew, Morris Gervais, Tim Hasenack,

Devon Hutton, Jay Hutton, Todd Lewis, Allan Madill, Jason Meyer, Josef Park, Martin O'Grady, Jeff Pratt, Scott Sefton, Rob Veccia, Gavin Watson. **BRAMPTON:** Supervisor: Mike Duggan. Officials: Mike Anderson, Walter Araujo, Toby Beam, Todd Clark, Sean Coles, Shawn Garrett, Brad Hamilton, Brian Harasymchuk, Thomas Jukes, Glen Mcbryde, Mike Neill, Stuart O'Reilly, Robert Padt, Joe Paolini, Terry Pierce, Darren Price, Roger Proulx, Joshua Roberts, Niall Smith, Greg Sorrell, Scott Topping. **DELHI:** Supervisor: Bob Hodges. Officials: Jeff Beech, Mike Bessagato, Jamie Carman, Dave Davey, Chris Dewachter, Mike Edmiston, Ken Gallagher, Josh Ion, Paul Jones, Trevor Lamb, Mark Mackenzie, Dave Mcrae, Mark Nemeth, Jamie Nunn, Walter Olivieri, Rob Reid, John Searle, Brent Stefan. **GUELPH:** Supervisors: Bill Devorski, Tom LaFrance & Ron Asselstine. Officials: Bob Beatty, Dave Bertrand, Brent Bloch, Deny Brulotte, Neil Christopher, Jeff Cox, Ryan Darrall, Brad Fagan, Tom Farr, Jason Finley, Lanny Fuller, Mike Guardiero, Jason Guardiero, Darryl Hancock, Brent Hughes, Kelly Ingalls, Gary John Ston, Jason Lawrence, Chris Mccracken, Mike Mccreary, Bill Mcknight, Scott Mclean, Blake Moggy, Larry Murphy, Jeff Nazzer, Phil Olinski, Michael Roberts, Steve Robinson, Steve Routenburg, Dan Schmidt, Graham Shantz, Tim Steen, Kris Taggart, Rob Tilt, Ralph Urbanke. **HAMILTON:** Supervisor: Bob Morley. Officials: Mike Biljetina, Darcy Burchell, John Crowe, Brent Holdsworth, Geoff Lawson, Paul Macdonald, Kevin Mcknight, Bob Morley, Rob Morley, Scott Moreton, Mike Ostaszewicz, Michael Patterson, Matt Putos, Mark Shewchyk, Steve Stasiuk, Chris Stevenson, Mike Wortel. **KINGSTON:** Supervisor: Ken Harris. Officials: Aaron Amey, Dave Baker, Bob Bell, Terry Bonter, Jamie Carr, Chris Clow, Mike Cranley, Al Detlor, Sean Jenkins, Chris French, Dave Hamrick, Rob Hillier, Tim Kelly, Scott Lavendor, Dan Maloney, Rob Mills, Brad Moore, Nick Myers, Stephen O'Reilly, Ted Padley, Duane Parliament, Kevin Postma, Dave Regan, Ian Sant, Ron Stakes, Shane Wannamaker. **LONDON:** Supervisors: Mel Huctwith & Rick Singleton. Officials: Mike Arts, Steve Baker, Terry Barton, Tim Barton, Mark Bennett, Dan Boyd, Greg

Brown, Joe Celestin, Jamie Dekraauw, Jeff Edwards, Brent Elbers, Chris Faulkner, Steve Gould, Bob Graham, Mike Hildenbrand, Jim Kean, Tim Lane, Mike Logan, Dan Mathieson, Mike Mcleod, Ray Mcmanus, Scott Morrison, Rob Neable, Dave Page, Robert Perrier, Dave Shepley, Jay Simpson, James Sinfield, Shaun Taylor, Dave Thompson, Scott Topping, Kevin Towers, Nathan Troyer, Kevin Umansky, Carl Vink, Bill Waye, Dave Whaley, Mike Yeoman. **NIAGARA:** Supervisor: Bob Morley. Officials: Darren Anger, Mike Bolibruck, Gary Corsi, Darren Flag, Mike Gage, Geoff Gamble, Mike Gordon, Jeff Hanna, Richard Hedden, Darcy Hemauer, Robert Judd, Chris Kereluk, Pete Kostyk, Don Mcarthur, Larry Moore, Paul Quaranta, Craig Spada, Dave Stortz, Mike Soucie, Steve Webb, Rod West, Dennis Winger. **NORTH-CENTRAL:** Supervisor: Wayne McDonald. Officials: Mike Allen, Paolo Carretta, Jeff Carter, Tim Clute, Bill Cober, Adam Fiorillo, Pete Gardner, Kevin Hastings, Terry Hobor, Scott Hutchinson, Dave Koziel, Nick Lacroce, Tom Lough, Scott Manor, Mike Marley, Scott Oakman, Ryan O'Oeill, Nick Ouwroules, Rob Palm, Mike Pearce, Jonathan Rose, Scott Taylor, Wayne Timbers, Ted Voinou. **NORTH-WEST:** Supervisors: George Wilson & John McCutcheon. Officials: Chad Adamson, Trevor Alexander, Jason Barlow, Dave Blum, Fred Clendenning, Lionel Crawford, Dean Grahame, Ian Hargrave, Lance Holmes, Dave Hornsby, Brent Huras, Dave Lisk, Taylor Mali, Ryan Marshall, Steve Morrison, Glen Murray, Chris Proctor, Lee Rodgers, Kevin Smith, Ken Stubbs, Jim Torrie, Dave Van Kooten, Dennis Watson. **OSHAWA:** Supervisors: Ivan Locke & Gus Bambridge. Officials: Brad Ashby, Matthew Black, Mike Brown, Steve Brown, Chris Cairns, Ryan Carmichael, Ryan Carroll, John Coburn, Ken Cornelius, Dave Crowley, Darryl Dawson, Paul Drummond, Anthony Goulah, Mike Jank, Dean Jenkins, Chris Hodgins, Rob Macgregor, Geoff Matthews, Gord Miles, Dwayne Phillips, Paul Renaud, Ryan Robinson, David Sankey, Mark Sliwowicz, Mark Smail, Ian Smith, Corey Strand, Brian St Thomas, Shawn Szorady, Trevor Parker, Christian Vesnaver, Dave Wedlake, Robert Welsh, Scott Wright. **SARNIA:** Supervisor: Bob Spence. Officials: Glenn Anderson,

Robert Anderson, Bill Beveridge, Pete Bowen, Eric Bryce, Lloyd Cottel, Chad Cox, Tim Cox, Robert Dalgety, Tim Dolbear, Sean Geene, Dave Hanstein, Jim Hawthorne, George Langstaff, Jim Maitland, Mike Mathieson, Bill Macalpine, Kevin Mcalpine, Steve Miller, Jeff Parney, Steve Percy, Owen Shelton, Brian Somes, Bill Swan, Marty Swan, Beau Taylor, Barry Vale, Mark Vandergriendt, Bill Yurchuk. **TORONTO;** Supervisors: Bob Nadin & John May. Officials: Ross Bain, Sean Bernard, David Black, Jason Blundon, James Brooks, Kris Chraba, Gilles Couturier, Matt Davie, Aaron Ferguson, Paul Gallant, Don Haag, Cris Kalangis, Pete Kourtis, David Lichacz, Matthew Manor, Rob Moore, Ian Munro, Ed Munroe, Chris Nyers, Bill Smith, Nick Spiro, Garey Wilson. **WINDSOR;** Supervisor: Matt Pavelich. Officials: Mike Aubin, Kevin Blundell, Greg Campbell, Todd Clark, Bob Clifford, Christian Cortese, Darrell Ellwood, Jonathan Forbes, Pat Germanese, Steve Hadfield, Matt Henderson, Ryan Hutchinson, Ryan Lachine, James Mcginlay, Paul Mckinney, Allan Provost, Ryan Renaud, Geoff Rutherford, Pat Scarlett, Lee Simpson, Robert Sylvester, John Thompson, Jeff Weglarz.

OHA Season 1999-2000
BARRIE: Supervisors: Ken Bannerman & Ralph Sparks. Officials: Ken Bannerman, Chris Beiers, Ed Black, Steve Black, Briant Duncan, Brent Elbers, Kevin Frew, Morris Gervais, Anders Hagman, Tim Hasenack, Jay Hutton, Scot Keller, Todd Lewis, Jason Meyer, Martin O'Grady, Josef Park, Jeff Pratt, Tim Russell, Scott Sefton, Gavin Watson. **BRAMPTON:** Supervisor: Mike Duggan. Officials: Mike Anderson, Darren Anger, Walter Araujo, Dave Banfield, Jeff Campbell, Sean Coles, Jamie Cosgriffe, Angelo D'Amico, Shawn Garrett, Dan Kordic, Kevin Lynch, Ron Maclean, Glen Mcbryde, Bob Mckellar, Brian Millman, Mike Neill, Stuart O'Reilly, Dave O'Oullivan, Rob Padt, Joe Paolini, Terry Pierce, Roger Proulx, Adam Reid, Joshua Roberts, Greg Sorrell, Zach Stewart, Dave Wright. **DELHI:** Supervisor: Bob Hodges. Officials: Jeff Beech, Mike Bessagato, Jamie Carman, Dave Davey, Chris Dewachter, Mike Edmiston, Robert

Harrison, Josh Ion, Paul Jones, Trevor Lamb, Mark Mackenzie, Dave Mcrae, Mark Nemeth, Jamie Nunn, Walyy Olivieri, Rob Reid, John Searle, Brent Stefan. **GUELPH:** Supervisors: Bill Devorski, Ron Asselstine & Tom LaFrance. Officials: Bob Beatty, Dave Bertrand, Brent Bloch, Deny Brulotte, Neil Christopher, Jeff Cox, Darren Crocker, Brad Fagan, Tom Farr, Lanny Fuller, Jason Guardiero, Mike Guardiero, Brent Hughes, Kelly Ingalls, Gary Johnston, Al Kimmel, Jason Lawrence, Bill Mcknight, Scott Mclean, Adam Meyer, Blake Moggy, Larry Murphy, Jeff Nazzer, Phil Olinski, Dave Pfohl, Steve Robinson, Steve Routenburg, Dan Schmidt, Graham Shantz, Perry Stone, Mike Stowe, Kris Taggart, Ralph Urbanke. **HAMILTON:** Supervisor: Bob Morley. Officials: Mike Biljetina, Darcy Burchell, Kevin Cruickshanks, John Crowe, Ryan Darrall, Brent Holdsworth, Bob Hooper, Geoff Lawson, Paul Macdonald, Bob Morley, Scott Moreton, Mike Ostaszewicz, Wade Perniac, Matt Putos, Mark Shewchyk, Steve Stasiuk, Chris Stevenson, Mike Wortel. **KINGSTON:** Supervisor: Ken Harris. Officials: Aaron Amey, Dave Baker, Bob Bell, Terry Bonter, Jamie Carr, Chris Clow, Al Detlor, Chris French, Don Haag, Dave Hamrick, Rob Hillier, Shawn Jenkins, Tim Kelly, Scott Lavender, Rob Longfield, Dan Maloney, Matt Manor, Rob Mills, Brad Moore, Stephen O'Reilly, Ted Padley, Duane Parliament, Kevin Postma, Dave Regan, Ian Sant. **LONDON:** Supervisors: Mel Huctwith & Rick Singleton. Officials: Mike Arts, Steve Baker, Terry Barton, Tim Barton Dan Boyd, Greg Brown, Joe Celestin, Chad Cox, Jamie Dekraauw, Jeff Edwards, Chris Faulkner, Steve Gould, Bob Graham, Mike Hildenbrand, Jim Kean, Tim Lane, Bob Langdon, Mike Logan, Dan Mathieson, Mike Mcleod, Ray Mcmanus, Scott Morrison, Rob Neable, Dave Page, Robert Perrier, Mike Robinson, Rick Singleton, James Sinfield, Jay Simpson, Lee Simpson, Dave Thompson, Scott Topping, Marc Toth, Kevin Towers, Kevin Umansky, Bill Waye, Dave Whaley, Mike Yeoman. **NIAGARA:** Supervisor: Bob Morley. Officials: Mike Bolibruck, Brent Bistrisky, Todd Coopman, Gary Corsi, David Corvers, Darren Flagg, Mike Gage, Mike Gordon, Richard Hedden, Darcy Hemauer, Robert Judd, Peter Kostyk, Don Mcarthur, Larry Moore,

Paul Robertson, Miie Soucie, Craig Spada, Dave Stortz, Jay Warren, Dennis Winger. **NORTH-CENTRAL:** Supervisor: Wayne McDonald. Officials: David Black, Paul Bourgard, Paolo Carretta, Jeff Carter, Tim Clute, Bill Cober, Craig Coletti, Hugh Currie, Sean Doyle, Paul Bourgard, Paolo Carretta, Jeff Carter, Tim Clute, Bill Cober, Craig Coletti, Hugh Currie, Sean Doyle, Scott Ellis, Murray Evans, Adam Fiorillo, Tom Foote, Kevin Hastings, Terry Hobor, Scott Hutchinson, David Koziel, Nick Lacroce, Tom Lough, Scott Manor, Michael Marley, Sean Mcquigge, Scott Oakman, Ryan O'Oeill, Nick Ouwroules, Rob Palm, Matt Parlette, Dan Paquette, Mike Pearce, Darren Price, Jonathan Rose, Scott Taylor, Wayne Timbers, Ted Vionou, Delton Zehr. **NORTH-WEST**: Supervisors: George Wilson & John McCutcheon. Officials: Chad Adamson, Trevor Alexander, Dave Blum, Linel Crawford, Richard Goring, Dean Grahame, Ian Hargrave, Lance Holmes, Brent Huras, Reg Illman, Murray Kaye, Dave Lisk, Allan Madill, Steve Morrison, Glenn Murray, Trevor Parker, Darrin Potts, Chris Proctor, Lee Rodgers, Kevin Smith, Ken Stubbs, Rob Veccia, Steve Wallace, Tim Walter, Dennis Watson. **OSHAWA:** Supervisors: Ivan Locke & Gus Bambridge. Officials: Brad Ashby, Matthew Black, Steve Brown, Ryan Carmichael, Ryan Carroll, John Coburn, Ken Cornelius, Mike Cranley, Dave Crowley, Darryl Dawson, Paul Drummond, Mike Feeley, Tony Goulah, Chris Hall, Chris Hodgins, Mike Jank, Rob Mcgregor, Geoff Matthews, Gord Miles, Dwayne Phillips, Paul Renaud, Ryan Robinson, Dave Sankey, Mark Sliwowicz, Mark Smail, Iam Smith, Brian St Thomas, Corey Strand, Shawn Szorady, Brent Thompson, Brad Upton, Christian Vesnaver, Dave Wedlake, Rob Welsh, Scott Wright. **SARNIA:** Supervisor: Bob Spence. Officials: Glenn Anderson, Robert Anderson, Bill Beveridge, Eric Bryce, Lloyd Cottel, Tim Cox, Robert Dalgety, Tim Dolbear, Sean Geene, Dave Hanstein, Jim Hawthorne, Sean Lalonde, George Langstaff, Bill Macalpine, Jim Maitland, Mike Mathieson, Kevin Mcalpine, Mark Mccabe, Chris Mccracken, Dean Mceachern, Steve Miller, Jeff Parney, Steve Percy, Owen Shelton, Bill Swan, Marty Swan, Barry Vale, Mark Vandergreindt. **TORONTO:**

Supervisors: Bob Nadin & John May. Officials: James Brooks, Mike Cairns, Kris Chraba, Paul Gallant, Cris Kalangis, Pete Kourtis, Alex Ivan, Dave Lichacz, Rob Moore, Ian Munro, Ed Munroe, Chris Nyers, Bill Smith, Nick Spiro, Phil Switzer, Garey Wilson. **WINDSOR:** Supervisor: Matt Pavelich. Officials: Mike Aubin, Mark Bennett, Kevin Blundell, Greg Campbell, Todd Clark, Bob Clifford, Christian Cortese, Kevin Douglas, Darrell Ellwood, Jonathan Forbes, Pat Germanese, Stephen Hadfield, Matt Henderson, Ryan Hutchinson, James Mcginlay, Al Provost, Ryan Renaud, Geoff Rutherford, Sean Sampson, Pat Scarlett, John Thompson, Jeff Weglarz.

OHA Season 1998-1999
BARRIE: Supervisors: Ken Bannerman & Ralph Sparks. Officials: Ken Bannerman, Chris Beiers, Steve Black, Brent Elbers, Kevin Frew, Morris Gervais, Mike Hales, Tim Hasenack, Ryan Jackson, Todd Lewis, Justin Murdock, Martin O'Grady, Josef Park, Jeff Pratt, Scott Sefton, Dave Slingerland, Gavin Watson. **BRAMPTON:** Supervisor: Mike Duggan. Officials: Mike Anderson, Darren Anger, Walter Araujo, Toby Beam, Sean Coles, Jamie Cosgriffe, Angelo D'Amico, Shawn Garrett, Tom Lough, Kevin Lynch, Ron Maclean, Glen Mcbryde, Bob Mckellar, Mike Neill, Stuart O'Reilly, Dave O'Oullivan, Rob Padt, Joe Paolini, Terry Pierce, Roger Proulx, Matt Putos, Adam Reid, David Shaw, Greg Sorrell, Scott Taylor, Dave Wright. **DELHI:** Supervisor: Bob Hodges. Officials: Mike Bessagato, Dave Davey, Mark Dumesnil, Josh Ion, Dean Jenkins, Bob Harrison, Mike Kipp, Trevor Lamb, Mark Mackenzie, Dave Mcrae, Pat Meahan, Kevin Mighton, Mark Nemeth, Jamie Nunn, Wally Olivieri, Rob Reid, Bryan Richards, Jeff Spoelstra, Brent Stefan. **GUELPH:** Supervisors: Bill Devorski & Ron Asselstine. Officials: Bob Beatty, Dave Bertrand, Deny Brulotte, Neil Christopher, Jeff Cox, Brad Fagan, Lanny Fuller, Ken Gallagher, Scott Grein, Mike Guardiero, Brent Hughes, Kelly Ingalls, Gary Johnston, Bill Mcknight, Scott Mclean, Adam Meyer, Jason Meyer, Blake Moggy, Larry Murphy, Jeff Nazzer, Phil Olinski, Cal Pergolas, Dave Pfohl, Steve Robinson, Steve Routenburg, Dan Schmidt, Graham

Shantz, Perry Stone, Mike Stowe, Kris Taggart, Ralph Urbanke, Joel Washkurak. **HAMILTON:** Supervisor: Bob Morley. Officials: Keith Beaudin, Mike Biljetina, Darcy Burchell, John Crowe, Kevin Cruickshanks, Ryan Darrall, Brent Holdsworth, Bob Hooper, Geoff Lawson, Mike Leblanc, Paul Macdonald, Bob Morley, Wade Perniac, John Searle, Mark Shewchyk, Jeff Smith, Steve Stasiuk, Chris Stevenson, Mike Wortel. **KINGSTON:** Supervisor: Ken Harris. Officials: Aaron Amey, Dave Baker, Bob Bell, Terry Bonter, Jamie Carr, Chris Clow, Al Detlor, Chris French, Jeff Geen, Tony Goulah, Don Haag, Dave Hamrick, Shawn Jenkins, Tim Kelly, Scott Lavendor, Lyle Lloyd, Rob Longfield, Dan Maloney, Matt Manor, Ray Mcguinness, Rob Mills, Stephen O'Reilly, Ted Padley, Duane Parliament, Dave Regan, Ian Sant, Murray Smith. **LONDON:** Supervisors: Mel Huctwith & Rick Singleton. Officials: Terry Barton, Tim Barton, Dan Boyd, Greg Brown, Joe Celestin, Chad Cox, Briant Duncan, Jeff Edwards, Jim Kean, Brad Gibb, Stephen Gould, Bob Graham, Andrew Kerr, Tim Lane, Bob Langdon, Jason Lawrence, Mike Logan, Dan Mathieson, Ray Mcmanus, Rob Moore, Rob Neable, Robert Perrier, Mike Robinson, Lee Simpson, Rick Singleton, Dave Thompson, Scott Topping, Kevin Umansky, Bill Waye, Dave Whaley, Mike Yeoman. **NIAGARA:** Supervisor: Bob Morley. Officials: Brent Bistrisky, Mike Bolibruck, Todd Coopman, Gary Corsi, Dave Corvers, Aaron Ferguson, Darren Flagg, Mike Gage, Mike Gordon, Richard Hedden, Robert Judd, Peter Kostyk, Don Mcarthur, Larry Moore, Mike Ostaszewicz, Paul Robertson, Mike Soucie, Craig Spada, Dave Stortz, Jay Warren, Steve Webb. **NORTH-CENTRAL:** Supervisor: Wayne McDonald. Officials: Chad Adamson, David Black, Paul Bourgard, Paolo Carretta, Jeff Carter, Hugh Currie, Sean Doyle, Scott Ellis, Murray Evans, Adam Fiorillo, Tom Foote, Richard Goring, Kevin Hastings, Terry Hobor, Scott Hutchinson, David Koziel, Scott Manor, Michael Marley, Sean Mcquigge, Scott Oakman, Ryan O'Neill, Nick Ouwroules, Rob Palm, Mike Pearce, Chris Proctor, Darren Price, Lee Rodgers, Jonathan Rose, Tom Rigatti, Shane Sinyard, Ken Stubbs, Wayne Timbers, Ted Vionou, Delton Zehr. **NORTH-WEST:** Supervisors: George Wilson & Tom LaFrance.

Officials: Trevor Alexander, Dave Blum, Fred Clendenning, Lionel Crawford, Robin Cubitt, Dean Grahame, Patrick Haefling, Brent Huras, Reg Illman, Murray Kaye, Allan Madill, Steve Morrison, Trevor Parker, Darrin Potts, Kevin Smith, Steve Wallace, Tim Walter, Dennis Watson, Rob Veccia. **OSHAWA:** Supervisors: Ivan Locke & Gus bambridge. Officials: Mike Brown, Steve Brown, Ryan Carmichael, John Coburn, Ken Cornelius, Mike Cranley, Dave Crowley, Darryl Dawson, Chris Hall, Jim Houston, Mike Jank, Rob Macgregor, Geoff Matthews, Gord Miles, Dean Morton, Dwayne Phillips, Paul Renaud, Ryan Robinson, Dave Sankey, Mark Sliwowicz, Ian Smith, Brian St Thomas, Corey Strand, Steve Surcon, Shawn Szorady, Brent Thompson, Brad Upton, Christian Vesnaver, Dave Wedlake, Scott Wright. **SARNIA:** Supervisor: Bob Spence. Officials: Glenn Anderson, Robert Anderson, Bill Beveridge, Eric Bryce, Lloyd Cottel, Robert Dalgety, Tim Dolbear, Sean Geene, Dave Hanstein, Jim Hawthorne, Sean Lalonde, George Langstaff, Bill Macalpine, Jim Maitland, Mike Mathieson, Kevin Mcalpine, Mark Mccabe, Chris Mccracken, Dean Mceachern, Steve Miller, Jeff Parney, Steve Percy, Owen Shelton, Bill Swan Marty Swan, Barry Vale. **TORONTO:** Supervisors: Bob Nadin & John May. Officials: James Brook, Mike Cairns, Paul Gallant, Alex Ivan, Cris Kalangis, Peter Kourtis, Nick Lacroce, Dave Lichacz, Warren Magnus, Brian Millman, Ed Moffatt, Ian Munro, Ed Munroe, Chris, Nyers Matt Parlette, Tim Peel, Dan Rideout, Bill Smith, Nick Spiro, Phil Switzer, Scott Whittemore, Garey Wilson. **WINDSOR:** Supervisor: Matt Pavelich. Officials: Mike Aubin, Mark Bennett, David Bohdal, Greg Campbell, Bob Clifford, Christian Cortese, Kevin Douglas, Darrell Ellwood, Jonathan Forbes, Jay Frederick, Pat Germanese, Stephen Hadfield, Matt Henderson, Ryan Hutchinson, James Mcginlay, Al Provost, Ryan Renaud, Geoff Rutherford, Sean Sampson, Pat Scarlett, John Thompson Jeff Weglarz.

OHA Season 1997-1998
BARRIE: Supervisors: Ken Bannerman & Ralph Sparks. Officials: Ken Bannerman, Chris Beiers, Michael Black,

Steve Black, Scott Ellis, Kevin Frew, Morris Gervais, Mike Hales, Brian Harasymchuk, Scott Hutchinson, Justin Murdock, Martin O'Grady, Josef Park, Tim Russell, Scott Sefton, Dave Slingerland, Jeff Pratt, Gavin Watson. **BRAMPTON:** Supervisor: Mike Duggan. Officials: Mike Anderson, Darren Anger, Toby Beam, Walter Araujo, Sean Coles, Jamie Cosgriffe, Angelo D'Amico, Kevin Ferguson, Shawn Garett, Ron Maclean, Glen Mcbryde, Wes Mccauley, Bob Mckellar, Mike Neill, Dave O'Oullivan, Rob Padt, Joe Paolini, Terry Pierce, Roger Proulx, Adam Reid, Matt Putos, Greg Sorrell, Dave Shaw, John Stephenson, Andy Wigley, Dave Wright. **DELHI**: Supervisors: doug Robb & Bob Hodges. Officials: Tim Christo, Dave Davey, Mark Dumesnil, Mike Kipp, Trevor Lamb, Pat Meahan, Kevin Mighton, Mark Nemeth, Rob Nixon, Jamie Nunn, Wally Olivieri, Rob Reid, Bryan Richards, Jeff Spoelstra, Brent Stefan. **GUELPH**: Supeervisors: Bil Devorski & Ron Asselstine: Officals: Paul Ariss, Bob Beatty, Dave Bertrand, Joe Celestin, Neil Christopher, Brad Fagan, Tom Farr, Lanny Fuller, Scott Grein, Mike Guardiero, Robert Harrison, Brent Hughes, Kelly Ingalls, Gary Johnston, Adam Meyer, Bill Mcknight, Scott Mclean, Blake Moggy, Larry Murphy, Jeff Nazzer, Jeff Noble, Phil Olinski, Cal Pergolas, Steve Robinson, Steve Routenburg, Dan Schmidt, Perry Stone, Mike Stowe, Kris Taggart, Greg Troyer, Ralph Urbanke, Joel Washkurak. **HAMILTON:** Supervisor: Bob Morley. Officials: Darcy Burchell, Steve Cheeseman, John Crowe, Kevin Cruickshanks, Ryan Darrall, Brent Holdsworth, Bob Hooper, Sean Lalonde, Geoff Lawson, Mike Leblanc, Paul Macdonald, Bob Morley, Wade Perniac, John Searle, Jeff Smith, Steve Stasiuk, Kyle Woods, Mike Wortel. **KINGSTON:** Supervisor: Ken Harris. Officials: Aaron Amey, Dave Baker, Terry Bonter, Bob Bell, Chris Clow, Al Detlor, Chris French, Dave Hamrick, Scott Lavendor, Lyle Lloyd, Ray Mcguinness, Matt Manor, Scott Manor, Rob Mills, Stephen O'Reilly, Mark Phillips, Dave Regan, Brad Reid, Cam Rundle, Erik Sant, Ian Sant, Rick Searle, Kevin Smith, Murray Smith. **LONDON:** Supervisors: Mel Huctwith & Rick Singleton. Officials: Dan Boyd, Darren Crocker, Lawrence Cole, Chad Cox, James Degraw, Briant Duncan, Kevin Ferguson, Steve Gould, Bob

Graham, Paul Hess, Jim Kean, Tim Lane, Bob Langdon, Jason Lawrence, Mike Logan, Dan Mathieson, Mike Mcleod, Ray Mcmanus, Steve Miller, Rob Moore, Mark Morissette, Robert Perrier, Mike Robinson, Rick Singleton, Dave Thompson, Scott Topping, Kevin Umansky, Bill Waye, Dave Whaley, Bill Yurchuk, Jason Zehr, JP Zubec. **NIAGARA:** Supervisor: Kalvin Forrest. Officials: Brent Bistrisky, Mike Bolibruck, Todd Coopman, Gary Corsi, Darren Flagg, Kalvin Forrest, Mike Gage, Richard Hedden, Brian Iafrate, Robert Judd, Peter Kostyk, Larry Moore, Mike Ostaszewicz, Derek Rickard, Paul Robertson, Craig Spada, Dave Stortz, Mike Soucie, Jay Warren, Steve Webb. **NORTH-CENTRAL:** Supervisors: Al Dawe & Wayne Mcdonald. Officials: Chad Adamson, Dave Blum, Paul Bourgard, Paolo Carretta, Jeff Carter, Hugh Currie, Murray Evans, Bruce Fallis, Greg Fantino, Adam Fiorillo, Tom Foote, Richard Goring, Kevin Hastings, Terry Hobor, David Koziel, Sean Mcquigge, Kevin Leaman, Scott Oakman, Ryan O'Neill, Nick Ouwroules, Rob Palm, Mike Pearce, Darren Price, Chris Proctor, Jim Reeves, Tom Rigatti, Lee Rodgers, Shane Sinyard, Ken Stubbs, Scott Tatlor, Wayne Timbers, Ted Voinou. **NORTH-WEST:** Supervisors: George Wilson & Tom LaFrance. Officials: Trevor Alexander, Lionel Crawford, Robin Cubitt, Steve Elliott, Craig Foley, Dean Grahame, Brent Huras, Murray Kaye, Allan Madill, Steve Morrison, Paul Robson, Rob Veccia, Steve Wallace, Tim Walter, Dennis Watson, Delton Zehr. **OSHAWA:** Supervisors: Ivan Locke & Gus Bambridge. Officials: Gus Bambridge, Mike Brown, Steve Brown, John Coburn, Mike Collinson, Ken Cornelius, Dave Crowley, Darryl Dawson, Steve Dick, Mike Feeley, Chris Hall, Jim Houston, Mike Jank, Rob Macgregor, Geoff Matthews, Gord Miles, Dean Morton, Mark Palmer, Dwayne Phillips, Paul Renaud, Ryan Robinson, Dave Sankey, Mark Smail, Ian Smith, Corey Strand, Steve Surcon, Brent Thompson, Brian St Thomas, Brad Upton, Christian Vesnaver, Dave Wedlake, Scott Whittemore, Scott Wright. **SARNIA:** Supervisor: Bob Spence. Officials: Glenn Anderson, Robert Anderson, Bill Beveridge, Eric Bryce, Ivan Bryce, Dave Corvers, Lloyd

Cottel, Robert Dalgety, Tim Dolbear, Sean Geene, Dave Hanstein, Jim Hawthorne, George Langstaff, Bill Macalpine, Jim Maitland, Mike Mathieson, Kevin Mcalpine, Chris Mccracken, Dean Mceachern, Gregg Mceachern, Steve Miller, Jeff Parney, Steve Percy, Owen Shelton, Bill Swan, Marty Swan, Barry Vale. **TORONTO:** Supervisors: Bob Nadin & John May. Officials: Steve Cathcart, Richard Dutton, Paul Gallant, Dale Glynn, Jim Harwood, Alex Ivan Cris Kalangis, Pete Kourtis, David Lichacz, Tom Lough, Warren Magnus, Brian Millman, Ed Moffatt, Ian Munro, Ed Munroe, Tim Peel, Dan Rideout, Bill Smith, Sandy Stenhouse, Mick Spiro, Phil Switzer, Garey Wilson. **WINDSOR:** Supervisor: Matt Pavelich. Officials: Mike Aubin, Phil Bellaire, Mark Bennett, David Bohdal, Joe Bouzide, Deny Brulotte, Greg Campbell, Bob Clifford, Christian Cortese, Kevin Douglas, Jonathan Forbes, Jay Frederick, Steve Hadfield, James Mcginlay, Al Provost, Brent Pye, Ryan Renaud, Geoff Rutherford, Sean Sampson, Pat Scarlett, John Thompson Jeff Weglarz.

OHA Season 1996-1997
BARRIE: Supervisor: Ken Bannerman: Officials: Rick Ahern, Wayne Aresenault, Ken Bannerman, Scott Ellis, Morris Gervais, Brian Harasymchuk, Scott Hutchinson, Todd Lewis, Justin Murdock, Josef Park, Jeff Pratt, Rick Redwood, Tim Russell, Scott Sefton, Gavin Watson, Tim Yorke. **BRAMPTON:** Supervisor: Mike Duggan. Officials: Mike Anderson, Toby Beam, Angelo D'Aamico, Dan Emerson, Shawn Garrett, Ron Maclean, Glen Mcbryde, Bob Mckellar, Mike Neill, Joe Paolini, Adam Reid, Greg Sorrell, John Stephenson, Dan Walker, Andy Wigley, Dave Wright, Scott Wright. **DELHI:** Supervisors: Doug Robb & Tony Steyaert. Officials; John Anderson, Tim Christo, Steve Cruickshank, Dave Davey, Mark Dumesnil, Brian Fitzpatrick, Gary Furler, Ken Gallagher, Mike Kipp, Trevor Lamb, Pat Meahan, Kevin Mighton, Mark Nemeth, Rob Nixon, Jamie Nunn, Wally Olivieri, Rob Reid, Jeff Spoelstra, Brent Stefan. **GUELPH:** Supervisors: Bill Devorski, Rick Morphew & Lance Roberts. Officials: Paul Ariss, Steve Barton, Bob Beatty, Neil Christopher, Brad Fagan, Tom Farr, Lanny Fuller,

Mike Guardiero, Scott Grein, Brent Hughes, Gary Johnston, Robert Judd, Bill Mcknight, Scott Mclean, Blake Moggy, Larry Murphy, Jeff Noble, Phil Olinski, Cal Pergolas, Kevin Pollock, Bryan Richards, Steve Robinson, Steve Routenburg, Dan Schmidt, Shane Sinyard, Perry Stone, Mike Stowe, Kris Taggart, Ralph Urbanke, Terry Wicklum, Pat Widmeyer, Joel Washkurak. **HAMILTON:** Supervisor: Bob Morley. Officials: Mike Biljetina, Darcy Burchell, Ian Boyter, Steve Cheeseman, John Crowe, Kevin Cruickshanks, Ryan Darrall, Brent Holdsworth, Bob Hooper, Geoff Lawson, Mike Leblanc, Paul Macdonald, Bob Morley, John Searle, Jeff Smith, Steve Stasiuk, Lee Willson, Mike Wortel. **KINGSTON:** Supervisor: Cam Rundle. Officials: Aaron Amey, Bob Bell, Terry Bonter, Al Detlor, Chris French, Tom Greenwood, Dave Hamrick, Scott Lavendor, Lyle Lloyd, Dan Maloney, Matt Manor, Ray Mcguinness, Rob Mills, Sean Ogston, Dave Regan, Cam Rundle, Erik Sant, Ian Sant, Rick Searle, Kevin Smith, Murray Smith. **LONDON:** Supervisors: Mel Huctwith & Rick Singleton. Officials: Brennan Beattie, Brad Beer, Dan Boyd, Joe Celestin, Chad Cowan, Darren Crocker, Briant Duncan, Kevin Ferguson, Steve Gould, Paul Hess, Jim Kean, Bob Langdon, Jason Lawrence, Mike Logan, John Martin, Dan Mathieson, Mike Mcmahon, Ray Mcmanus, Steve Miller, Haven Minor, Rob Moore, Mark Morissette, Robert Perrier, Mike Robinson, Rick Singleton, Kevin Umansky, Bill Waye, Dave Whaley, Bill Yurchuk, Jason Zehr, JP Zubec. **NIAGARA:** Supervisor: Kalvin Forrest. Officials: Brent Bistrisky, Darren Flagg, Kalvin Forrest, Mike Gage, Frank Girhiny, Richard Hedden, Brian Iafrate, Al Isherwood, Peter Kostyk, Dave Mikolasek, Larry Moore, Terry Pizzacalla, Derek Rickard, Paul Robertson, Dan Simoneau, Mike Soucie, Craig Spada, Dave Stortz, Jay Warren, Steve Webb. **NORTH-CENTRAL:** Supervisor: Al Dawe. Officials: Dave Bertrand, Dave Blum, Paul Bourgard, Scott Camerson, Paolo Carretta, Jeff Carter, Bruce Fallis, Greg Fantino, Adam Fiorillo, Tom Foote, Terry Hobor, David Koziel, Kevin Leaman, John Martini, Sean Mcquigge, Scott Oakman, Ryan O'Neill, Mike Pearce, Darren Price, Chris Proctor, Jim Reeves, Lee

Rodgers, Dave Slingerland, Ken Stubbs, Wayne Timbers, Greg Troyer, Martin Yeager. **NORTH-WEST:** Supervisors: George Wilson & Tom LaFrance. Officials: Trevor Alexander, Lionel Crawford, Robin Cubitt, Steve Elliott, Mike Freeman, Dean Grahame, Rob Harrison, Brent Huras, Allan Madill, Steve Morrison, Paul Robson, Robert Stone, Jim Torrie, Sylvester Urbshott, Rob Veccia, Dennis Watson, Delton Zehr. **Oshawa:** Supervisors: Ivan Locke & dave Lynch. Officials: Derek Amell, Steve Brown, John Coburn, Mike Collinson, Ken Cornelius, Dave Crowley, Darryl Dawson, Steve Dick, Stewart Emerson, John Gerelus, Chris Hall, Jim Houston, Mike Jank, Rob Macgregor, Geoff Matthews, Gord Miles, Dean Morton, Mark Palmer, Dwayne Phillips, Paul Renaud, Dave Sankey, Ian Smith, Corey Strand, Brian St Thomas, Christian Vesnaver, Paul Weatherbee. **SARNIA:** Supervisors: Bob Spence & Don van Massenhoven. Officials: Glenn Anderson, Robert Anderson, Bill Beveridge, Eric Bryce, Ivan Bryce, Dave Corvers, Lloyd Cottel, Robert Dalgety, Tim Dolbear, Sean Geene, Jason Hanscn, Dave Hanstein, Jim Hawthorne, George Langstaff, Bill Macalpine, Jim Maitland, Kevin Mcalpine, Dean Mceachern, Gregg Mceachern, Steve Miller, Jeff Parney, Brian Patterson, Owen Shelton, Bill Swan, Beau Taylor, Jeff Vandermeersch. **TORONTO:** Supervisors: Bob Nadin & Ralph Sparks. Officials: Darren Berehowsky, Steve Cathcart, Chris Edwards, Paul Gallant, Dale Glynn, Alex Ivan, Warren Magnus, Brian Millman, Ed Munroe, Tim Peel, Ralph Sparks, Phil Switzer, Scott Whittemore, Bill Wiles, Garey Wilson. **WINDSOR:** Supervissor: Matt pavelich. Officials: Mike Aubin, Jim Batke, Phil Bellaire, Mark Bennett, David Bohdal, Joe Bouzide, Deny Brulotte, Mike Burton, Greg Campbell, Bob Clifford, Christian Cortese, Darrell Ellwood, Jonathan Forbes, Jay Frederick, Mike Huczel, James Mcginlay, Al Provost, Brent Pye, Ryan Renaud, Shannon Sampson, Pat Scarlett, John Thompson, Jeff Weglarz, Mark Wuerch.

OHA Season 1995-1996
BARRIE: Supervisor: Ken Bannerman. Officials: Rick Ahern, Wayne Aresenault, Ken Bannerman, Dave

Bertrand, Scott Ellis, Morris Gervais, Brian Harasymchuk, Scott Hutchinson, Doug Hyde, Todd Lewis, Darren Morrison, Justin Murdock, Dave Ogilvie, Josef Park, Dave Power, Jeff Pratt, Rick Redwood, Tim Russell, Scott Sefton, Gavin Watson, Tim Yorke. **BRAMPTON:** Supervisors: Mike Duggan & Peter Balsdom. Officials: James Allen, Mike Anderson, Toby Beam, Bill Carson, Angelo D'Amico, Dan Emerson, Jason Filey, Jay Lewis, Ron Maclean, Glen Mcbryde, Bob Mckellar, Steve Miller, Mike Neill, Joe Paolini, Adam Reid, Frank Rossi, Chris Schweitzer, Greg Sorrell, John Stephenson, Andy Wigley, Dave Wright, Scott Wright. **DELHI:** Supervisors: Doug Robb & Tony Steyaert. Officials: John Anderson, Larry Boden, Henry Catry, Tim Christo, Steve Cruickshank, Dave Davey, Mark Dumesnil, Brian Fitzpatrick, Gary Furler, Ken Gallagher, Mike Kipp, Trevor Lamb, Pat Meahan, Kevin Mighton, Mark Nemeth, Rob Nixon, Jamie Nunn, Wally Olivieri, Rob Reid, Jim Ryan, Jeff Spoelstra, Brent Stefan. **GUELPH:** Supervisors: Bill Devorski, Rick Morphew & Lance Roberts. Officials: Steve Barton, Bob Beatty, Neil Christopher, Mark Dalbello, Domenic Dotto, Brad Fagan, Tom Farr, Lanny Fuller, Mike Galloway, Scott Grein, Gary Johnston, Robert Judd, Bill Mcknight, Scott Mclean, Blake Moggy, Phil Olinski, Cal Pergolas, Kevin Pollock, Steve Robinson, Doug Richard, Bryan Richards, Steve Routenburg, Dan Schimdt, Shane Sinyard, Perry Stone, Mike Stowe, Ralph Urbanke, Gord Young, Joel Washkurak, Pat Widmeyer. **HAMILTON:** Supervisors: Bob Morley & Larry Baxter. Officials: Mike Biljetina, Darcy Burchell, Steve Cheeseman, John Crowe, Kevin Cruickshanks, Brent Holdsworth, Bob Hooper, Mike Leblanc, Geoff Lawson, Paul Macdonald, Scott Moreton, Bob Morley, John Searle, Jeff Smith, Steve Stasiuk, Keith Walker, Lee Willson, Mike Wortel. **KINGSTON:** Supervisor: Cam Rundle. Officials: Aaron Amey, Bob Bell, Terry Bonter, Al Detlor, Chris French, Tom Greenwood, Dave Hamrick, Scott Lavendor, Lyle Lloyd, Dan Maloney, Matt Manor, Ray Mcguinness, Rob Mills, Sean Ogston, Dave Regan, Cam Rundle, Erik Sant, Ian Sant, Rick Searle, Kevin Smith, Murray Smith. **LONDON:** Supervisor: Rick Singleton. Officials: Brennan Beattie,

Brad Beer, Mike Carter, Joe Celestin, Chad Cowan, Darren Crocker, Tim Dolbear, Brian Donaher, Briant Duncan, Steve Gould, Paul Hess, Jim Kean, Brad Kovachik, Bob Langdon, Jason Lawrence, Jim Lewis, Mike Logan, John Martin, Dan Mathieson, Ray Mcmanus, Kelly Mehlenbacher, Steve Miller, Haven Minor, Rob Moore, Mark Morissette, Robert Perrier, Paul Petrie, Jeff Smith, Rick Singleton, Trevor Vincent, Bill Waye, Dave Whaley, Jason Zehr, Jp Zubec. **NIAGARA:** Supervisor: Kalvin Forrest. Officials: Darren Flagg, Kalvin Forrest, Mike Gage, Frank Girhiny, Pete Guarasci, Richard Hedden, Brian Iafrate, Al Isherwood, Pete Kostyk, Mike Macgillivray, Dave Mikolasek, Larry Moore, Terry Pizzacalla, Pete Prophet, Paul Robertson, Dan Simoneau, Craig Spada, Mike Soucie, Dave Stortz, Steve Webb. **NORTH-CENTRAL:** Supervisor: Al Dawe. Officials: Dave Blum, Paul Bourgard, Scott Cameron, Paolo Carretta, Jeff Carter, Bruce Fallis, Greg Fantino, Tom Foote, Terry Hobor, Brock Kelly, David Koziel, Kevin Leaman, John Martini, Scott Oakman, Mike Pearce, Martin Porteous, Darren Price, Chris Proctor, Lee Rodgers, Dave Slingerland, Ken Stubbs, Wayne Timbers, Greg Troyer, Richard Wand. **NORTH-WEST:** Supervisors: George Wilson & Tom LaFrance. Officials: Trevor Alexander, Lionel Crawford, Robin Cubitt, Tom Gillespie, Dale Glynn, Dean Grahame, Terry Hall, Robert Harrison, Brent Huras, Paul Kitchen, Mike Freeman, Steve Macmillan, Steve Morrison, Paul Robson, Robert Stone, John Thompson, Jim Torrie, Sylvester Urbshott, Rob Veccia, Kevin Williamson, Jim Wright, Delton Zehr. **OSHAWA:** Supervisor: Ivan Locke. Officials; Derk Amell, Bob Bell, John Coburn, Mike Collinson, Ken Cornelius, Dave Crowley, Darryl Dawson, Steve Dick, Stewart Emerson, Kevin Ferguson, Pat Gooley, John Gerelus, Chris Hall, Jim Houston, Mike Jank, Rob Macgregor, Geoff Matthews, Gord Miles, Dean Morton, Mark Palmer, Dwayne Phillips, Ian Smith, Corey Strand, Brian St Thomas, Dan Walker, Paul Weatherbee, Dave Wedlake, Scott Whittemore. **SARNIA:** Supervisor: Bob Spence. Officials: Glenn Anderson, Robert Anderson, Bill Beveridge, Eric Bryce, Ivan Bryce, Jim Clements, Lloyd Cottel, Dave Corvers, Robert Dalgety, Derek Edwards,

Sean Geene, Jason Hanson, Dave Hanstein, George Langstaff, Bill Macalpine, Jim Maitland, Kevin Mcalpine, Dean Mceachern, Gregg Mceachern, Jeff Parney, Brian Patterson, Robert Patterson, Owen Shelton, Bill Swan, Beau Taylor, John Vandendries, Jeff Vandermeersch. **TORONTO:** Supervisor: Bob Nadin & Ralph Sparks. Officials: Darren Berehowsky, Steve Cathcart, Derek Cox, Chris Edwards, Paul Gallant, Jim Harwood, Alex Ivan, Warren Magnus, Sean Mcquigge, Brian Millman, Ed Munroe, Tim Peel, Ralph Sparks, Phil Switzer, Bill Wiles, Garey Wilson. **Windsor:** Supervisor: Matt Pavelich. Officials: Jim Batke, Mark Bennett, Joe Bouzide, Deny Brulotte, Mike Burton, Greg Campbell, Bob Clifford, Christian Cortese, Darrell Ellwood, Jonathan Forbes, Jay Frederick, Mike Huczel, James Mcginlay, Chris Muzzin, Al Provost, Brent Pye, Ryan Renaud, Shannon Sampson, Pat Scarlett, John Thompson, Terry Turner, Mark Wuerch.

OHA Season 1994-1995
BARRIE: Supervisor: Bill Howes. Officials: Rick Ahern, Ken Bannerman, Dave Bertrand, Briant Duncan, Scott Ellis, Morris Gervais, Brian Harasymchuk, Doug Hyde, Scott Hutchinson, Brock Kelly, Todd Lewis, Darren Morrison, Dave Ogilvie, Josef Park, Dave Power, Rick Redwood, Tim Russell, Gavin Watson. **BRAMPTON:** Supervisor: Mike Duggan & Peter Balsdom. Officials: James Allen, Mike Anderson, Toby Beam, Bill Carson, Sean Coles, Angelo D'Amico, Dan Emerson, Jason Filey, Jay Lewis, Ron Maclean, Glen Mcbryde, Mike Neill, Terry Pierce, John Stephenson, Andy Wigley, Dave Wright. **DELHI:** Supervisors: Tony Steyaert & Doug Robb. Officials: Larry Boden, Henry Catry, Steve Cruickshank, Dave Davey, Mark Dumesnil, Brian Fitzpatrick, Gary Furler, Ken Gallagher, Mike Kipp, Bill Kusch, Pat Meahan, Kevin Mighton, Mark Nemeth, Rob Nixon, Jamie Nunn, Rob Reid, Jim Ryan, Brent Stefan. **GUELPH:** Supervisors: Bill Devorski, Rick Morphew & Lance Roberts. Officials: Paul Ariss, Bob Beatty, Dave Blum, Neil Christopher, Mark Dalbello, Domenic Dotto, Brad Fagan, Tom Farr, Lanny Fuller, Mike Galloway, Gary Johnston, Robert Judd, Bob Mckellar, Bill Mcknight, Scott

Mclean, Phil Olinski, Cal Pergolas, Kevin Pollock, Doug Richard, Bryan Richards, Steve Robinson, Steve Routenburg, Pat Scarlett, Dan Schmidt, Shane Sinyard, Perry Stone, Mike Stowe, Ralph Urbanke, Mick Wicklum, Gord Young, **HAMILTON:** Supervisors: Bob Morley & Larry Baxter. Officials: Larry Baxter, Mike Biljetina, Steve Cheeseman, John Crowe, Kevin Cruickshanks, Chris Duckworth, George Harrison, Joe Heslop, Bob Hooper, Paul Macdonald, Brian Marshall, Bill Mcginnes, Bob Morley, Scott Moreton, Bll Searle, John Searle, Jeff Smith, Steve Stasiuk, Dave Thompson, Keith Walker, Lee Willson, Mike Wortel. **KINGSTON:** Supervisor: Ivan Locke. Officials: John Anderson, Mike Couchran, Chris French, Tom Greenwood, Ken Harris, Mike Hill, Lyle Lloyd, Dan Maloney, Ray Mcguinness, Rob Mills, Sean Ogston, Dave Regan, Ken Reid, Cam Rundle, Erik Sant, Ian Sant, Rick Searle, Kevin Smith, Murray Smith, Mike Stewart, Dan Walker. **LONDON:** Supervisor: Rick Singleton. Officials: Darren Anger, Brennan Beattie, Brad Beer, Dave Belling, Mike Carter, Joe Celestin, Guy Constant, Chet Couture, Chad Cowan, Tim Dolbear, Brian Donaher, Brian Grasby, Steve Gould, Joe Haughian, Paul Hess, Brad Kovachik, Bob Langdon, Jason Lawrence, Jim Lewis, David Marsh, Derrick Martin, Dan Mathieson, Ray Mcmanus, Kelly Mehlenbacher, Steve Miller, Haven Minor, Mark Morissette, Paul Petrie, Rick Singleton, Jeff Smith, Jeff Tyers, Bill Waye, Dave Whaley, Jason Zehr, Jp Zubec. **NIAGARA:** Supervisors: Mike Macgillivray & Kalvin Forrest. Officials: Dave Anderson, Frank Beres, Scott Christopher, Chuck Farkas, Darren Flagg, Kalvin Forrest, Mike Gage, Frank Girhiny, Pete Guarasci, Richard Hedden, Al Isherwood, Mike Macgillivray, Dave Mikolasek, Terry Pizzacalla, Bill Prophet, Pete Prophet, Paul Robertson, Dan Simoneau, Mike Soucie, Craig Spada, Dave Stortz, Jim Walters, Steve Webb. **NORTH-CENTRAL:** Supervisor: Al Dawe. Officials: Paul Bourgard, Paolo Carretta, Bruce Fallis, Tom Foote, Terry Hobor, Kevin Leaman, Kevin Maguire, John Martini, Scott Oakman, Martin Porteous, Darren Price, Chris Proctor, Lee Rodgers, Frank Rossi, Dave Slingerland, Ken Stubbs, Wayne Timbers, Richard Wand. **NORTH-WEST:** Supervisors: George Wilson & Tom

LaFrance. Officials: Trevor Alexander, Pete Chisholm, Lionel Crawford, Robin Cubitt, Dave Currie, Brian Deitner, Tom Gillespie, Dean Grahame, Robert Harrison, Ken Higgins, Dave Hornsby, Graham Humphrey, Brent Huras, Paul Kitchen, Jim Macleod, Steve Macmillan, Blake Moggy, Steve Morrison, Paul Robson, John Stanley, Rob Stone, Jim Torrie, Rob Veccia, Kevin Williamson, George Wilson, Jim Wright. **OSHAWA:** Supervisors: Ivan Locke & Jim Houston. Officials: Derek Amell, Brad Bob Bell, Bruce Brownhill, John Coburn, Mike Collinson, Ken Cornelius, Dave Crowley, Darryl Dawson, Steve Dick, John Gerelus, Pat Gooley, Pat Gaudet, Chris Hall, Jim Houston, Mike Jank, Rob Macgregor, Geoff Matthews, Dean Morton, Mark Palmer, Dwayne Phillips, Ian Smith, Corey Strand, Brent Thompson, Paul Waetherbee Ashby, Dave Wedlake, Scott Whittemore. **SARNIA:** Supervisor: Hugh Devin. Officials: Glenn Anderson, Robert Anderson, Bill Beveridge, Ryan Brady, Dave Bryce, Eric Bryce, Ivan Bryce, Jim Clements, Lloyd Cottel, Joe Cowley, Robert Dalgety, Derek Edwards, Sean Geene, Jason Hanson, Dave Hanstein, Jim Hawthorne, Scott Hughson, George Langstaff, Bill Macalpine, Jim Maitland, Kevin Mcalpine, Greg Mceachern, Dean Mceachern, Brian Patterson, Mark Routley, Owen Shelton, Bill Swan, Beau Taylor, John Vandendries, Jeff Vandermeersch, Delton Zehr. **Toronto:** Supervisor: Ralph Sparks. Officials: Darren Berehowsky, Jeff Caplan, Steve Cathcart, Chris Edwards, Paul Gallant, Jim Harwood, Alex Ivan, Warren Magnus, Brian Millman, Ed Munroe, Matt Parlette, Tim Peel, Ralph Sparks, Phil Switzer, Bill Wiles, Garey Wilson. **Windsor:** Supervisor: Matt Pavelich. Officials: Jim Batke, Mark Bennett, Joe Bouzide, Deny Brulotte, Greg Campbell, Stewart Cambpell, Bob Clifford, Christian Cortese, Dave Corvers, Darell Ellwood, Scott Emmerton, Thomas Faubert, Jonathan Forbes, Jay Frederick, Scott Hoberg, Harry Hodgson, Mike Huczel, Chris Muzzin, Al Provost, Ryan Reanud, Sean Sampson, Terry Turner, Mark Wuerch.

OHA Season 1993-1994
BARRIE: Supervisors: Bill Howes & Ken Bannerman. Officials: Rick Ahern, Ken Bannerman, Briant Duncan, Scott Ellis, Morris Gervais, Brian Harasymchuk, Scott Hutchinson, Doug Hyde, Brock Kelly, Todd Lewis, Darren Morrison, Dave Ogilvie, Josef Park, Dave Power, Bill Rawn, Tim Russell, Rick Schaly, Gavin Watson. **BRAMPTON:** Supervisor: Mike Duggan. Officials: James Allen, Mike Anderson, Peter Balsdon, Toby Beam, Bill Carson, Chris Dickson, Dan Emerson, Andre Fauteux, Jason Filey, Jay Lewis, Ron Maclean, Richard Mclean, Glen Mcbryde, Andy Mayhew, Mike Neill, Terry Pierce, John Stephenson, Dave Wright. **DELHI:** Supervisors: Tony Steyaert & Doug Robb. Officials: John Anderson, Scott Belair, Larry Boden, Henry Catry, Tim Christo, Steve Cruickshank, Mark Dumesnil, Brian Fitzpatrick, Gary Furler, Jack Harris, Scott Kemp, Mike Kipp, Bill Kusch, Darryl Lee, Pat Meahan, Kevin Mighton, Mark Nemeth, Jamie Nunn, Rob Reid, Jim Ryan. **GUELPH:** Supervisors: Bill Devorski & Rick Morphew. Officials: Paul Ariss, Bob Beatty, Dave Blum, Scott Craig, Mark Dalbello, Domenic Dotto, Andrew Drinkwalter, Brad Fagan, Tom Farr, Lanny Fuller, Mike Galloway, Gary Johnston, Al Kimmel, Tom Lewis, Darryl Matthews, John Mckelvie, Bill Mcknight, Scott Mclean, Rick Morphew, Rob Nixon, Phil Olinski, Geoff Pasher, Cal Pergolas, Kevin Pollock, Mark Riffer, Doug Richard, Bryan Richards, Steve Robinson, Steve Routenburg, Pat Scarlett, Dan Schmidt, Ralph Urbanke, Mike Wicklum, Gord Young. **HAMILTON:** Supervisor: Bob Morley. Officials: Larry Baxter, Mike Biljetina, Steve Cheeseman, John Crowe, Kevin Cruickshanks, Chris Duckworth, George Harrison, Joe Heslop, Bob Hooper, Steve Iljanic, Corey Leonard, Paul Macdonald, Brian Marshall, Bob Morley, Barry^Oara, Bill Searle, John Searle, Steve Stasiuk, Dave Thompson, Rick Tonkovitch, Keith Walker, Lee Willson, Mike Wortel. **KINGSTON:** Supervisor: Ivan locke. Officials: Al Detlor, Chris French, Jeff Geen, Tom Greenwood, Ken Harris, Jim Henderson, Mike Hill, Lyle Lloyd, Dan Maloney, Geoff Matthews, Ray Mcguinness, Paul Murphy, Sean Ogston, Ken Reid, Cam Rundle, Ian Sant, Rick Searle, Murray Smith, Mike Stewart, Mike

Stowe, Dan Walker, Bruce Wright. **LONDON:** Supervisor: John Willsie. Officials: Robert Anderson, Steve Baker, Brad Beer, Dave Belling, Mike Carter, Joe Celestin, Guy Constant, Chet Couture, Chad Cowan, Brian Donaher, Steve Gould, Brian Grasby, Paul Hess, Brad Kovachik, Bob Langdon, Jason Lawrence, Jim Lewis, Brad Longfield, David Marsh, Derrick Martin, Dan Mathieson, Kelly Mehlenbacher, Ray Mcmanus, Steve Miller, Haven Minor, Mark Morissette, Paul Petrie, Rick Singleton, Jeff Smith, Bill Waye, Dave Whaley. **NIAGARA:** Supervisors: Mike MacGillvray & Kalvin Forrest. Officials: Dave Anderson, KGlvin Forrest, Frank Beres, Scott Christopher, Chuck Farkas, Darren Flagg, Mike Gage, Frank Girhiny, Pete Guarasci, Richard Hedden, Al Isherwood, Mike Macgillivray, Dave Mikolasek, Terry Pizzacalla, Bill Prophet, Pete Prophet, Paul Robertson, Dan Simoneau, Mike Soucie, Dave Stortz, Jim Walters. **NORTH-CENTRA:** Supervisors: Al Dawe & Don Hopkins. Officials: Don Abel, Paul Bourgard, Paolo Carretta, Tom Foote, Jay Gilbert, Frank Giroux, Guy Govis, Terry Hobor, Kevin Leaman, Kevin Maguire, John Martini, Martin Porteous, Darren Price, Lee Rodgers, Frank Rossi, Shane Sinyard, Dave Slingerland, Perry Stone, Ken Stubbs, Wayne Timbers, Richard Wand. **NORTH-WEST:** Supervisors: George Wilson & Tom LaFrance. Officals: Pete Chisholm, Lionel Crawford, Robin Cubitt, Dave Hornsby, Graham Humphrey, Paul Kitchen, Tom Lafrance, Jim Macleod, Steve Macmillan, Blake Moggy, Steve Morrison, Paul Robson, Miles Shiels, Jeff Smith, Marty Souch, Jim Torrie, Greg Troyer, Rob Veccia, Steve Wilkins, Kevin Williamson, George Wilson. **Oshawa:** Supervisors: Ivan Locke & Jim Houston. Officials; Derek Amell, Brad Ashby, Gus Bambridge, Bob Bell, Bruce Brownhill, John Cane, John Coburn, Mike Collinson, Ken Cornelius, Dave Crowley, Don Daigle, Darryl Dawson, Steve Dick, Stewart Emerson, Pat Gaudet, John Gerelus, Jim Houston, Mike Jank, Rob Macgregor, Chuck Macmillan, Al Mazerall, Brian Mcdermott, Paul Mcgriskin, Dean Morton, Mark Palmer, Dwayne Phillips, Greg Rennie, Ian Smith, Brent Thompson, Brad Upton, Paul Weatherbee, Dave Wedlake. **SARNIA:** Supervisors: Hugh Devin & Bob

Spence. Officials: Glenn Anderson, Larry Beaton, Bill Beveridge, Ryan Brady, Dave Bryce, Eric Bryce, Ivan Bryce, Jim Clements, Lloyd Cottel, Joe Cowley, Robert Dalgety, Tim Dolbear, Derek Edwards, Sean Geene, Jim Hawthorne, George Langstaff, Jim Maitland, Bill Macalpine, Kevin Mcalpine, Dean Mceachern, Brian Patterson, Robert Patterson, Mark Routley, Owen Shelton, Bill Swan, Beau Taylor, John Vanderdries, Jason Zehr. **TORONTO:** Supervisor: Ralph Sparks. Officials: Jeff Caplan, Steve Cathcart, Jim Harwood, Alex Ivan, Brian Millman, Ed Munroe, Dave Purdon, Phil Sherwood, Ralph Sparks, Sandy Stenhouse, Phil Switzer, Dean Warren, Bill Wiles, Garey Wilson. **WINDSOR:** Supervisors: Sam Sisco & Vic McMurren. Officials: Jim Batke, Mark Bennett, Joe Bouzide, Greg Cmpbell, Stewart Campbell, Bob Clifford, Christian Cortese, Dave Corvers, Darrell Ellwood, Scott Emmerton, Thomas Faubert, Jonathan Forbes, Jay Frederick, Scott Hobert, Harry Hodgson, Chris Muzzin, Terry Paradie, Matt Parlette, Al Provost, Ryan Renaud, Sean Sampson, Shannon Sampson, Terry Turner, Mark Wuerch.

OHA Season 1992-1993
BARRIE: Supervisors: Bill Howes & Ken Bannerman. Officials: Rick Ahern, Brad Ayres, Ken Bannerman, Briant Duncan, Morris Gervais, Brian Harasymchuk, Scott Hutchinson, James Mcginlay, Brock Kelly, Todd Lewis, Darren Morrison, Dave Ogilvie, Josef Park, Dave Power, Dave Purdon, Bill Rawn, Tim Russell, Rick Schaly, Joe Taibi, Gavin Watson. **BRAMPTON:** Supervisor: Mike Duggan. Officials: James Allen, Mike Anderson, Peter Balsdon, Toby Beam, Bill Carson, Chris Dickson, Eric Douglas, Andre Fauteux, Stephen Giles, Matt Gregory, Garry Kipfer, Jay Lewis, Andy Mayhew, Richard Mccauley, Mike Neill, Jim Pollock, Evan Steed, John Stephenson, Alex Stobo, Andy Wigley, Dave Wright. **DELHI:** Supervisors: Tony Steyaert & Doug Robb. Officials: John Anderson, Larry Boden, Henry Catry, Tim Christo, Steve Cruickshank, Mark Dumesnil, Brian Fitzpatrick, Gary Furler, Wilf Gurney, Scott Kemp, Bill Kusch, Pat Meahan, Mark Nemeth, Ian Nichols, Jamie Nunn, Rob Reid, Jim Ryan. **GUELPH:** Supervisors: Bill

Devorski & Rick Morphew. Officials: Paul Ariss, Bob Beatty, Neil Christopher, Scott Craig, Mark Dalbello, Daw Claude, Greg Dvorski, Domenic Dotto, Andrew Drinkwalter, Brad Fagan, Tom Farr, Mike Galloway, Gary Johnston, Don Mackinnon, Darryl Matthews, Glen Mcbryde, John Mckelvie, Rick Morphew, Rob Nixon, Phil Olinski, GeogFf Pasher, Cal Pergolas, Kevon Pollock, Doug Richard, Mark Riffer, Steve Routenburg, Pat Scarlett, Dan Schmidt, Pat Smola, Ralph Urbanke, Mike Wicklum, Gord Young. **HAMILTON:** Supervisors: Bob Morley & Cliff Gauthier. Officials: Larry Baxter, Mike Biljetina, Steve Cheeseman, John Crowe, Chris Duckworth, Cliff Gauthier, George Harrison, Joe Heslop, Bob Hooper, Steve Ilijanic, Paul Macdonald, Ron Maclean, Brian Marshall, Bob Morley, Barry O'Hara, John Searle, Steve Stasiuk, Rick Tonkovich, Keith Walker, Lee Willson, Norm Watson, Mike Wortel. **KINGSTON:** Supervisors: Bert Kea. Officials; Al Detlor, Chris French, Jeff Geen, Tom Greenwood, Glenn Grice, Ken Harris, Jim Henderson, Mike Hill, Lyle Lloyd, Dan Maloney, Geoff Matthews, Ray Mcguinness, Rick Mclean, Paul Murphy, Sean Ogston, Ken Reid, Cam Rundle, Ian Sant, Murray Smith, Mike Stewart, Mike Stowe, Dan Walker, Bruce Wright. **LONDON:** Supervisor: John Willsie. Officials: Robert Anderson, Rick Baker, Steve Baker, Brad Beer, Dave Belling, Tom Blake, Joe Celestin, Darren Devries, Brian Donaher, Steve Gould, Brian Grasby, Brad Kovachik, Bob Langdon, Paul Lepine, Jim Lewis, Brad Longfield, David Marsh, Dan Mathieson, Bill Mcknight, Ray Mcmanus, Kelly Mehlenbacher, Steve Miller, Mark Morissette, Paul Petrie, Murray Patterson, Rick Singleton, Bill Waye, Dave Whaley. **NIAGARA:** Supervisors: Mike MacGillivray & Kalvin Forrest. Officials: Dave Anderson, Darren Anger, Scott Christopher, Darren Flagg, Kalvin Forrest, Mike Gage, Frank Girhiny, Pete Guarasci, Richard Hedden, Al Isherwood, Mike Macgillivray, Bob Mclaughlin, Dave Mikolasek, Terry Pizzacalla, Bill Prophet, Pete Prophet, Paul Robertson, Dan Simoneau, Dave Stortz, Mike Soucie, Jim Walters. **NORTH-CENTRAL:** Supervisors: Al Dawe & Don Hopkins. Officials: Don Abel, Paul Bourgard, Paolo Carretta, Tom Foote, Jay Gilbert, Frank Giroux,

Guy Govis, Terry Hobor, Kevin Leaman, Kevin Maguire, John Martini, Martin Porteous, Darren Price, Lee Rodgers, Frank Rossi, Shane Sinyard, Dave Slingerland, Perry Stone, Ken Stubbs, Wayne Timbers, Richard Wand. **NORTH-WEST:** Supervisors: George Wilson & Tom LaFrance. Officials: Pete Chisholm, Lionel Crawford, Ian Hargrave, Dave Hornsby, Graham Humphrey, Jamie Kearns, Len Kohl, Paul Kitchen, Tom Lafrance, Jim Macleod, Steve Macmillan, Blake Moggy, Steve Morrison, Paul Robson, Rick Schaly, Jeff Scott, Miles Shiels, Jeff Sippel, Jim Torrie, Rob Veccia, Steve Wilkins, Kevin Williamson, George Wilson. **OSHAWA:** Supervisors: Ivan Locke & Jim Houston. Officials: Derek Amell, Brad Ashby, Bruce Brownhill, Gus Bambridge, Bob Bell, John Cane, Paul Catney, John Coburn, Mike Collinson, Ken Cornelius, Chad Cowan, Dave Crowley, Darryl Dawson, Don Daigle, Stewart Emerson, Pat Gaudet, John Gerelus, Jim Houston, Mike Jank, Dave Lynch, Rob Macgregor, Chuck Macmillan, Al Mazerall, Paul Mcgriskin, Mark Palmer, Dwayne Phillips, Paul Ravary, Ted Reid, Greg Rennie, Ian Smith, Brent Thompson, Brad Upton, Paul Weatherbee, Dave Wedlake. **SARNIA:** Supervisors: Hugh Devin & Bob Spence. Officials: Larry Beaton, Bill Beveridge, Dave Bryce, Eric Bryce, Ivan Bryce, Jim Clements, Lloyd Cottel, Joe Cowley, Robert Dalgety, Tim Dolbear, Derek Edwards, Sean Geene, Paul Goldhawk, Jim Hawthorne, George Langstaff, Bill Macalpine, Jim Maitland, Sandy Martin, Brian Patterson, Robert Patterson, Mark Routley, Owen Shelton, Bob Spence, Bill Swan, Beau Taylor, John Vanderdries, Jason Zehr. **TORONTO:** Supervisor: Ralph Spark. Officials: Jeff Caplan, Giulio Doria, Chris Edwards, Dan Emerson, Jim Harwood, Alex Ivan, Greg Kimmerly, Brian Millman, Ed Munroe, Rick Redwood, Phil Sherwood, Ralph Sparks, Sandy Stenhouse, Phil Switzer, Dean Warren, Bill Wiles, Garey Wilson, Scott Whittemore. **WINDSOR:** Supervisors: Sam Sisco & Vic McMurren. Officials: Jim Batke, Mark Bennett, Joe Bouzide, Greg Campbell, Stewart Campbell, Bob Clifford, Christian Cortese, Dave Corvers, Darrell Ellwood, Scott Emmerton, Thomas Faubert, Rick Fedak, Jason Filey, Jonathan Forbes, Jay Frederick, Scott Hoberg, Harry Hodgson, Craig

Mcdonald, Vic Mcmurren, Chris Muzzin, Terry Paradie, Matt Parlette, Al Provost, Ryan Renaud, Sean Sampson, Terry Turner, Mark Wuerch.

OHA Season 1991-1992
BARRIE: Supervisors: Bil Howes & Ken Bannerman. Officials: Rick Ahern, Brad Ayres, Ken Bannerman, Briant Duncan, Randy Ellis, Tim Foster, Dave Garagan, Morris Gervais, Brian Harasymchuk, Scott Hutchinson, James Mcginlay, Dave Martin, Ken Miller, Darren Morrison, Dave Ogilvie, Josef Park, Richard Perry, Dave Power, Dave Purdon, Bill Rawn, Lee Rose, Tim Russell, Rick Schaly, Brad Scharf, Joe Taibi, Gavin Watson. **BRAMPTON:** Supervisor: Mike Duggan. Officials: James Allen, Mike Anderson, Peter Balsdon, Toby Beam, Bill Carson, Chris Dickson, Eric Douglas, Andre Fauteux, Steve Giles, Matt Gregory, Garry Kipfer, Jay Lewis, Todd Lewis, Andy Mayhew, Glen Mcbryde, Richard Mccauley, Mike Neill, Jim Pollock, John Stephenson, Stobo, Andy Wigley, Dave Wright. **DELHI:** Supervisor: Tony Steyaert. Officials: John Anderson, Larry Boden, Henry Catry, Tim Christo, Steve Cruickshank, Dave Davey, Mark Dumesnil, Brian Fitzpatrick, Gary Furler, Brian Joiner, Scott Kemp, Bill Kusch, Pat Meahan, Mark Nemeth, Ian Nichols, Rob Nixon, Rob Reid, Jim Ryan. **GUELPH:** Supervisors: Bill Devorski & Rick Morphew. Officials: Don Archibald, Paul Ariss, Bob Beatty, Neil Christopher, Scott Craig, Robert Clyson, Mark Dalbello, Ken Dool, Domenic Dotto, Bryan Elliott, Brad Fagan, Tom Farr, Rob Fleming, Mike Galloway, Tom Goessler, Gary Johnston, Al Kimmel, Tim Loasby, Darryl Matthews, Rick Morphew, Phil Olinski, Geoff Pasher, Cal Pergolas, Don Reford, Doug Richard, Mark Riffer, Steve Routenburg, Pat Scarlett, Dan Schmidt, Owen Shelton, Pat Smola, Ralph Urbanke, Mick Wicklum, Steve Wiffen, Gord Young. **HAMILTON:** Supervisors: Bob Morley & Cliff Gauthier. Officials: Larry Baxter, Mike Biljetina, Steve Cheeseman, John Crowe, Chris Duckworth, Cliff Gauthier, George Harrison, Joe Heslop, Bob Hooper, Steve Ilijanic, Paul Macdonald, Ron Maclean, Brian Marshall, Bob Morley, Barry O'Hara, John Searle, Steve Stasiuk, Rick Tonkovich, Keith Walker, Lee Willson,

Norm Watson, Mike Wortel. **KINGSTON:** Supervisor: Bert Kea. Officials: Peter Carroll, Al Detlor, Chris French, Jeff Geen, Tom Greenwood, Glenn Grice, Ken Harris, Jim Henderson, Bert Kea, Lyle Lloyd, Dan Maloney, Geoff Matthews, Ray Mcguinness, Rick Mclean, Rob Mills, Paul Murphy, Sean Ogston, Ken Reid, Cam Rundle, Ian Sant, Murray Smith, Mike Stewart, Mike Stowe, John Turnbull, Dan Walker, Bruce Wright. **LONDON:** Supervisor: Rick Singleton. Officials: Robert Anderson, Mike Arts, Steve Baker, Brad Beer, Dave Belling, Tom Blake, Steve Breau, Joe Celestin, Larry Cooke, Darren Devries, Brian Donaher, Scott Driscoll, Steve Gould, Brian Grasby, Doug Hyde, Brad Kovachik, Jim Kovachik, Jim Lewis, Brad Longfield, David Marsh, Billmatetich, Dan Mathieson, Craig Mcdonald, Bill Mcknight, Ray Mcmanus, Kelly Mehlenbacher, Mark Morissette, Paul Petrie, Rick Singleton, Jeff Smith, Paul Tobin, Bill Waye, Dave Whaley, John Willsie. **NIAGARA:** Supervisors: Ray Prophet * Mike MacGillivray. Officials: Dave Anderson, Glenn Barnes, Robert Courage, Darren Flagg, Kalvin Flagg, Mike Gage, Richard Hedden, Al Isherwood, Mike Macgillivray, Don Mcknight, Bob Mclaughlin, Dave Mikolasek, Bill Patten, Mike Paul, Terry Pizzacalla, Bill Prophet, Pete Prophet, Dan Simoneau, Mike Soucie, Dave Stortz, Jim Walters. **NORTH-CENTRAL:** Supervisors: Al Dawe & Don Hopkins. Officials: Paul Bourgard, Paolo Carretta, Glen Cheyne, Robert Colley, Paul Cooke, Tom Foote, Jay Gilbert, Gut Govis, Kevin Leaman, John Martini, Martin Porteous, Darren Price, Bryan Richards, Lee Rodgers, Frank Rossi, Dave Slingerland, Perry Stone, Wayne Timbers, Richard Wand. **NORTH-WEST:** Supervisor: Jim Oliver. Officials: Pete Chisholm, Lionel Crawford, Claude Daw, Steven Grant, Ian Hargrave, Mike Hill, Dave Hornsby, Graham Humphrey, Jamie Kearns, Paul Kitchen, Tom Lafrance, Jim Macleod, Blake Moggy, Paul Robson, Jeff Scott, Rick Schaly, Miles Shiels, Jeff Sippel, Marty Souch, Evan Steed, Jim Torrie, Steve Wilkins, George Wilson. **OSHAWA:** Supervisor: Ivan Locke. Officials: Derek Amell, Brad Ashby, Gus Bambridge, Bob Bell, Steve Brown, John Cane, Paul Catney, John Coburn, Mike Collinson, Paul Connor, Ken Cornelius, Don Daigle,

Darryl Dawson, Andrew Drinkwalter, Stewart Emerson, Pat Gaudet, John Gerelus, Jim Houston, Mike Jank, Dale Lebritton, Dave Lynch, Chuck Macmillan, Rob Macgregor, Gary Marino, Al Mazerall, Paul Mcgriskin, Mark Palmer, Dwayne Phillips, Paul Ravary, Ted Reid, Brent Thompson, Brad Upton, Paul Waetherbee, Dave Wedlake. **Sarnia:** Supervisors: Hugh Devin & Bob Spence. Officials: Larry Beaton, Bill Beveridge, Dave Bryce, Eric Bryce, Ivan Bryce, Jim Clements, Dave Corvers, Lloyd Cottel, Joe Cowley, Robert Dalgety, Timdolbear, Derek Edwards, Paul Goldhawk, Matt Haley, Jim Hawthorne, Bill Macalpine, Todd Mackenzie, Jim Maitland, Brian Patterson, Robert Patterson, Mark Routley, Bob Spence, Bill Swan, Beau Taylor, John Vanderdries, Don Van Massenhoven, Dick Wilson, Jason Zehr. **Toronto:** Supervisor: Ralph Sparks. Officials: Bruce Brownhill, Jeff Caplan, Giulio Doria, Chris Edwards, Dan Emerson, Murray Evans, Jim Harwood, Alex Ivan, Greg Kimmerly, Brian Millman, Ed Munroe, Rick Redwood, Phil Sherwood, Ralph Sparks, Sandy Stenhouse, Danny Tramontozzi, Phil Switzer, Dean Warren, Scott Whittemore, Bill Wiles, Garey Wilson. **WINDSOR:** Supervisors: Sam Siiisco & Vic McMurrem. Officials: Jim Batke, Mark Bennett, Joe Bouzide, Greg Campbell, Stewart Campbell, Bob Clifford, Jim Craig, Darrell Ellwood, Scott Emmerton, Rick Fedak, Jason Filey, Jay Frederick, Mark Hicks, Mike Hoberg, Scott Hoberg, Harry Hodgson, Vic Mcmurren, Chris Muzzin, Terry Paradie, Matt Parlette, Al Prenoveau, Al Provost, Ryan Renaud, Sean Sampson, Terry Turner, Mark Wuerch.

OHA Season 1990-1991
BARRIE: Supervisors: Bill Howes & Ken Bannerman. Officials: Rick Ahern, Blaine Angus, Brad Ayres, Ken Bannerman, Bill Deering, Briant Duncan, Rob Durnan, Tim Foster, Dave Garagan, Mike Gervais, Terry Hoffman, Brian Harasymchuk, Scott Hutchinson, Bill Rawn, Lee Rose, Brad Scharf, Rick Schaly, Tim Markham, Dave Martin, Wayne Mcdonald, Ken Miller, Steve Neal, Richard Perry, Dave Power, Dave Purdon.

BRAMPTON: Supervisors: Mike Duggan & Garry Kipfer. Officials: Mike Anderson, Peter Balsdon, Toby Beam, Bill Carson, Chris Dickson, Eric Douglas, Chris Edwards, Andre Fauteux, Steve Giles, Matt Gregory, Jay Lewis, Andy Mayhew, Glen Mcbryde, Richard Mccauley, Jim Mcnally, Kelly Mehlenbacher, Jim Pollock, John Stephenson, Alex Stobo, Mike Stowe, Andy Wigley, Justin Winter, Scott Whittemore, Dave Wright. **DELHI:** Supervisor: Tony Steyaert. Officials: John Anderson, Larry Boden, Keith Cardwell, Mark Clark, Tim Christo, Steve Cruickshank, Dave Davey, Mark Dumesnil, Brian Fitzpatrick, Gary Furler, Marshall Grinton, Wilf Gurney, Scott Kemp, Pat Meahan, Ian Nicholls, Rob Reid, Pat Rowland, Jim Ryan. **GUELPH**: Supervisors: Bill Devorski & Rick Morphew. Officials: Paul Ariss, Bob Beatty, Neil Christopher, Robert Clyson, Scott Craig, Mark Dalbello, Paul Dalbello, Greg Devorski, Ken Dool, Scott Driscoll, Bryan Elliott, Mike Engler, Andrew Drinkwalter, Brad Fagan, Tom Farr, Rob Flemming, Mike Galloway, Kevin Fitzgerald, Gary Johnston, Doug Richard, Mark Riffer, Steve Routenburg, Pat Scarlett, Dan Schmidt, Tim Loasby, Al Kimmel, Darryl Matthews, Phil Olinski, Geoff Pasher, Cal Pergolas, Don Redford, Pat Smola, Joe Taibi, Ralph Urbanke, Mike Wicklum, Steve Wiffen, Paul Witmer, Gord Young. **HAMILTON:** Supervisors: Bob Morley & Cliff Gauthier. Officials: Larry Baxter, Mike Biljetina, Steve Cheeseman, John Crowe, Cliff Gauthier, Bob Hagen, George Harrison, Joe Heslop, Greg Higson, Bob Hooper, Brian Joiner, Paul Macdonald, Ron Maclean, Brian Marshall, Bob Morley, Barry O'Hara, Joh Searle, Steve Stasiuk, Rick Tonkovich Keith Walker, Norm Watson, Lee Willson Mike Wortel. **KINGSTON:** Supervisor: Bert Kea. Officials: John Anderson, Pete Carroll, Al Detlor, Tom Greenwood, Glenn Grice, Ken Harris, Jim Henderson, Tim Keller, Lyle Lloyd, Dan Maloney, Geoff Matthews, Ray Mcguinness, Rick Mclean, Rob Mills, Paul Murphy, Sean Ogston, Ken Reid, Cam Rundle, Ian Sant, Mike Stewart, Dan Walker, Bruce Wright. **LONDON:** Supervisor: Rick Singleton. Officials: Robert Anderson, Mike Arts, Steve Baker, Brad Beer, Dave Belling, Tom Blake, Steve Breau, Chris Brooks, Larry Cooke, Chris Chapman, Les Finch, Darren Devries,

Brian Donaher, Scott Emmerton, Doug Fell, Dave Frizzell, Steve Gould, Brian Grasby, Doug Hyde, Jim Kovachik, Jim Lewis, Brad Longfield, David Marsh, Dan Mathieson, Bill Mcknight, Ray Mcmanus, Mark Morissette, Paul Petrie, Phil Sherwood, Jeff Smith, Bill Waye, Dave Whaley, John Willsie. **NIAGARA:** Supervisors: John Blackwell & Ray Prophet. Officials: Dave Anderson, Glenn Barnes, Robert Courage, Darren Flagg, Kalvin Forrest, Al Isherwood, Mike Macgillivray, Don Mcknight, Bob Mclaughlin, Dave Mikolasek, Bill Patten, Mike Paul, Terry Pizzacalla, Bill Prophet, Pete Prophet, Dan Simoneau, Mike Soucie, Dave Stortz, Jim Walters. **NORTH-CENTRAL:** Supervisors: Al Dawe & Don Hopkins. Officials: Rick Baker, Scott Boland, Pul Bourgard, Glen Cheyne, Tom Foote, Jay Gilbert, Guy Govis, Kevin Leaman, John Martini, Michael Mcnally, Martin Porteous, Bryan Richards, Lee Rodgers, Frank Rossi, Dave Slingerland, Perry Stone, Wayne Timbers. **NORTH-West:** Supervisor: Jim Oliver. Officials: Pete Chisholm, Lionel Crawford, Claude Daw, Mike Freeman, Jeff French, John French, Steve Grant, Dave Hornsby, Paul Kitchen, Tom Lafrance, Jim Macleod, Kevin Meriam, Blake Moggy, Jeff Oliver, Dana Robertson, Paul Robson, Rick Schaly, Dave Schuler, Jeff Sippel, Evan Steed, Jim Torrie, Steve Wilkins, George Wilson. **OSHAWA:** Supervisor: Ivan Locke. Officials: Brad Ashby, Gus Bambridge, Bob Bell, Steve Brown, John Cane, Paul Catney, John Coburn, Mike Collinson, Paul Connor, Ken Cornelius, Don Daigle, Darryl Dawson, Pat Gaudet, John Gerelus, Francois Giroux, Dave Harris, Jim Houston, Dale Lebritton, Dave Lynch, Chuck Macmillan, Gary Marino, Paul Mcgriskin, Gil Nieuwendyk, Dwayne Phillips, Paul Ravary, Ted Reid, Brent Thompson, Brad Upton, Paul Weatherbee, Dave Wedlake. **SARNIA:** Supervisors: Hugh Deviv & Bob Spence. Officials: Larry Beaton, Bill Beveridge, Dave Bryce, Eric Bryce, Ivan Bryce, Jim Clements, Lloyd Cottel, Joe Cowley, Robert Dalgety, Derek Edwards, Mike Freeman, Paul Goldhawk, Jim Hawthorne, Bill Macalpine, Jimmaitland, Chuck Nisbett, Brian Patterson, Mark Routley, Owen Shelton, Beau Taylor, Don Van Massenhoven, Dick Wilson, Jason Zehr, Doug Zonneville **TORONTO:** Supervisors: Bob Nadin &

Ralph Sparks. Officials: Bruce Brownhill, Giulio Doria, Dan Emerson, Murray Evans, Jim Harwood, Alex Ivan, Jamie Kearns, Greg Kimmerly, Al Mazerall, Brian Millman, Matt Moyer, Rick Redwood, Sandy Stenhouse, Phil Switzer, Danny Tramontozzi, Dean Warren, Bill Wiles, Garey Wilson. **WINDSOR:** Supervisors: sam Sisvo & Gord Thompson. Officials: Jim Batke, Joe Bouzide, Greg Campbell, Stewart Campbell, Dave Cassidy, Bob Cliford, Jim Craig, Darrell Ellwood, Rick Fedak, Jason Filey, Jay Frederick, Mark Hicks, Scott Hoberg, Mike Hoberg, Harry Hodgson, Dwayne Lambier, Vic Mcmurran, Chris Muzzin, Terry Paradie, Matt Parlette, Alain Prenoveau, Sean Sampson, Terry Turner, Mark Wuerch.

OHA Season 1989-1990
BARRIE: Supervisor: Bill Howes. Officials: Rick Ahern, Dale Amos, Blaine Angus, Brad Ayres, Ken Bannerman, Bill Deering, Briant Duncan, Tim Foster, Mike Gervais, Steve Grant, Trevor Hains, Brian Harasymchuk, Terry Hoffman, Wayne Mcdonald, Ken Miller, Steve Neal, Richard Perry, Dave Power, Dave Purdon, Bill Rawn, Lee Rose, Dave Saab, Rick Schaly, Brad Scharf. **BRAMPTON:** Supervisors: Mike Duggan & Garry kipfer. Officials: Mike Anderson, Peter Balsdon, Toby Beam, Bill Carson, Chris Dickson, Eric Douglas, Andre Fauteux, Steve Giles, Matt Gregory, Gary Kipfer, Jay Lewis, Andy Mayhew, Richard Mcauley, Jim Mcnally, Kelly Mehlenbacher, Jim Pollock, Larry Skillen, John Stephenson, Alex Stobo, Justin Winter. **DELHI:** Supervisor: Tony Steyaert. Officials: Larry Boden, Keith Cardwell, Mark Clark, Dave Davey, Mark Dumesnil, Brian Fitzpatrick, Gary Furler, Marshall Grinton, Wilf Gurney, Scott Kemp, Pat Meahan, Ian Nichols, Rod Reid, Jim Ryan. **GUELPH:** Supervisors: Bill Devorski & Rick Morphew. Officials: Paul Ariss, Bob Beatty, Jim Campbell, Neil Christopher, Scott Craig, Mark Dalbello, Paul Dalbello, Greg Devorski, Ken Dool, Andrew Drinkwalter, Scott Driscoll, Mike Engler, Brad Fagan, Tom Farr, Paul Fitzpatrick, Rob Fleming, Bob Greene, Scott Hutchinson, Gary Johnston, Al Kimmel, Tim Loasby, Darryl Matthews, Wild Meston, Robert Morley,

Rick Morphew, Phil Olinski, Geoff Pasher, Don Redford, Doug Richard, Mark Riffer, Steve Routenburg, Pat Scarlett, Dan Schmidt, Pat Smola, Ralph Urbanke, Steve Walkom, Mike Wicklum, Steve Wiffen, Doug Wilkinson, Gord Young. **HAMILTON:** Supervisors: Cliff Gauthier & Bob Morley. Officials: Mike Biljetina, Steve Cheeseman, Cliff Gauthier, Bob Hagen, George Harrison, Joe Heslop, Greg Higson, Brian Joiner, Ron Maclean, Brian Marshall, Terry Mcloughlin, Bob Morley, Jeff Morley, Kevin Ryan, Brian Switzer, John Searle, Steve Stasiuk, Dave Thompson, Keith Walker, Norm Watson, Andy Wigley, Lee Willson, Mike Wortel. **KINGSTON:** Supervisor: bert kea. Officials: John Anderson, Jim Bolger, Peter Carroll, Al Detlor, Scott Graham, Glenn Grice, Ken Harris, Jeff Hopkins, Bert Kea, Tim Keller, Lyle Lloyd, Dan Maloney, Geoff Matthews, Rick Mclean, Sean Ogston, Mark Palmer, Cam Rundle, Ian Sant, Mike Stewart, Mike Stowe, Dan Walker, Bruce Wright. **LONDON:** Supervisors: Mel Huctwith & Rick Singleton. Officials: Robert Anderson, Mike Arts, Steve Baker, Brad Beer, Tom Blake, Chris Brooks, Chris Chapman, Mel Chupa, Larry Cooke, Marshall Coop, Brian Donaher, Scott Emmerton, Steve Gould, Trevor Hilpert, Jim Kovachik, Brad Lemaich, Jim Lewis, Brad Longfield, David Marsh, Dan Mathieson, Mark Morissette, Paul Petrie, Mark Routley, Phil Sherwood, Rick Singleton, Jeff Smith, Bill Waye, Dave Whaley, Greg Wright. **NIAGARA:** Supervisor: John Blackwell. Officials: Dave Anderson, Glenn Barnes, Darren Flagg, Kalvin Forrest, Al Isherwood, Mike Macgillivray, Don Mcknight, Bob Mclaughlin, Dave Mikolasek, Mike Paul, Terry Pizzacalla, Bill Prophet, Pete Prophet, Dan Simoneau, Mike Simoneau, Mike Soucie, Dave Stortz, Jim Walters. **NORTH-CENTRAL:** Supervisor: Al Dawe. Officials: Rick Baker, Mike Bigelli, Scott Boland, Paul Bourgard, Glen Cheyne, Al Dawe, Bill Fitzpatrick, Tom Foote, Jay Gilbert, Kevin Leaman, John Martini, Robert Mills, Steve Neal, Martin Porteous, Lee Rodgers, Frank Rossi, Dave Slingerland, Perry Stone, Wayne Timbers. **NORTH-WEST:** Supervisor: Jim Oliver. Officials: Brent Baker, Pete Chisholm, Lionel Crawford, Claude Daw, Mike Freeman, Jeff French, John French, Dave Hornsby,

Trevor Hilpert, Tom Lafrance, Dave Leaist, Jim Macleod, Kevin Merian, Blake Moggy, Dana Robertson, Paul Robson, Jeff Scott, Jeff Sippel, Jim Torrie, Todd Wilkie, Steve Wilkins, George Wilson, Pascal Zaitz. **Oshawa:** Supervisor: Ivan Locke. Officials: Gus Bambridge, Bob Bell, Steve Brown, John Cane, Paul Catney, Dave Chevrier, John Coburn, Paul Connor, Ken Cornelius, Don Daigle, Darryl Dawson, Pat Gaudet, John Gerelus, Jim Houston, Dave Lynch, Chuck Macmillan, Todd March, Paul Mcgriskin, Gil Nieuwenyk, Dwayne Phillips, Paul Ravary, Ted Reid, Frank Robinson, Brent Thompson, Brad Upton, Paul Weatherbee, Dave Wedlake, Dwight Woodward. **SARNIA:** Supervisor: Hugh Devin & Chuck Nisbett. OfficiaLs: Bob Barnes, Larry Beaton, Bill Beveridge, Dave Bryce, Eric Bryce, Ivan Bryce, Greg Campbell, Jim Clements, Lloyd Cottel, Gus Coulombe, Joe Cowley, Derek Edwards, Doug Fell, Paul Goldhawk, Les Finch, Jim Hawthorne, Bill Macalpine, Todd Mackenzie, Jim Maitland, Kevin Mcalpine, Chuck Nisbet, Brian Patterson, Bob Spence, Don Vanmassenhoven, Dick Wilson. **TORONTO:** Supervisor: Bob nadin & Ralph Sparks. Officials: Rick Baker, Bruce Brownhill, Giulio Doria, Chris Edwards, Dan Emerson, Murray Evans, Les Finch, Jim Harwood, Ian Huffman, Alex Ivan, Jamie Kearns, Greg Kimmerly, Al Mazerall, Steve Mignardi, Brian Millman, Matt Moyer, Ian Munro, Rick Redwood, Ralph Sparks, Sandy Stenhouse, Dean Warren, Scott Whittemore, Bill Wiles, Garey Wilson, Dave Wright. **WINDSOR:** Supervisors: Sam Sisco & Gord Thompson. Officials: Jim Batke, Joe Bbouzide, Dave Cassidy, Bob Clifford, Jim Craig, Darryl Ellwood, Rick Fedak, Jason Filey, Jay Frederick, Mark Hicks, Mike Hoberg, Scott Hoberg, Harry Hodgson, Dwayne Lambier, Vic Mcuraan, Chris Muzzin, Dan Ohalloran, Alain Prenoveau, Terry Turner.

OHA Season 1988-1989
BARRIE: Supervisor: Bill Howes. Officials: Rick Ahern, Dale Amos, Ken Bannerman, Briant Duncan, Rob Durnan, Randy Ellis, Randy Ford, Tim Foster, Brian Harasymchuk, Terry Hoffman, Brian Hunt, Scott Hutchinson, Ken Miller, Robert Mills, Steve Neal, Richard

Perry, Dave Power, Dave Purdon, Rick Ramsay, Bill Rawn, Dave Saab, Rick Schaly, Brad Scharf, Ken Stevens, Kevin Yakymovich. **BRAMPTON:** Supervisors: Charlie Lennox & Mike Duggan. Officials: Mike Anderson, Peter Balsdon, Toby Beam, Bill Carson, Kelly Clark, Mike Duggan, Andre Fauteux, Jason Filey, Steve Giles, Garry Kipfer, Jay Lewis, Ron Maclean, Andy Mayhew, Kelly Mehlenbacher, Jim Pollock, Don Redford, Larry Skillen, John Stephenson, Alex Stobo, Andy Wigley, Justin Winter. **DELHI:** Supervisor: Tony Steyaert. Officials: Larry Boden, Mark Brown, Mark Clark, Dave Davey, Mark Dumesnil, Brian Fitzpatrick, Marshall Grinton, Paul Groenveld, Wilf Gurney, Scott Kemp, Al Little, Tim Loasby, Pat Meahan, Ian Mitchell, Ian Nichols, Pat Rowland, Jim Ryan. **GUELPH:** Supervisors: Bill Devorski & Rick Morphew. Officials: Paul Ariss, Bob Beatty, Rob Bonthorn, Jim Campbell, Tony Carvalho, Neil Christopher, Scott Craig, Mark Dalbello, Paul Dalbello, Mike Deabreu, Greg Devorski, Marc Dixon, Mike Engler, Brad Fagan, Tom Farr, Paul Fitzpatrick, John Gravett, Bob Greene, Gary Johnston, Jamie Kearns, Al Kimmel, Bob Laurence, Dale Lebritton, Steve Martin, Darryl Matthews, Rick Morphew, Bruce Murray, Phil Olinski, Geoff Pasher, Dave Power, Doug Richard, Mark Riffer, Steve Routenburg, Mark Sabine, Pat Scarlett, Dan Schmidt, Jeff Scott, Pat Smola, Phil Switzer, Ralph Urbanke, Steve Walkom, Tim Waters, Steve Wiffen, Doug Wilkinson, **HAMILTON:** Supervisors: Bryon Jackson & Cliff Gauthier. Officials: Keith Beaudin, Mike Biljetina, Darcy Burchell, John Crowe, Kevin Cruickshanks, Ryan Darrall, Brent Holdsworth, Bob Hooper, Geoff Lawson, Mike Leblanc, Paul Macdonald, Bob Morley, Wade Perniac, John Searle, Mark Shewchyk, Jeff Smith, Steve Stasiuk, Chris Stevenson, Mike Wortel. **KINGSTON:** Supervisor: Bert Kea. Officials: John Anderson, Norm Ball, Jim Bolger, Don Carr, Peter Carroll, Al Detlor, Scott Graham, Glenn Grice, Trevor Haines, Ken Harris, Jeff Hopkins, Jason Kea, Tim Keller, Lyle Lloyd, Dan Maloney, Geoff Matthews, Cam Rundle, Ian Sant, Mike Stowe, Jim Thorne, Bruce Wright. **LONDON:** Supervisors: Mel Huctwith & Rick Singleton. Officials: Steve Baker, Brad Beer, Tom Blake, Eric Bryce,

Chris Chapman, Mel Chupa, Larry Cooke, Marshall Coop, Brian Donaher, Eric Douglas, Scott Emmerton, Rob Fleming, Steve Gould, Bruce Grasby, Jim Kovachik, Brad Lemaich, Brad Longfield, David Marsh, Dan Mathieson, Steve Miller, Murray Patterson, Paul Petrie, Lee Richards, Steve Ringler, Mark Routley, Ed Senez, Phil Sherwood, Rick Singleton, Bill Waye, Dave Whaley, Greg Wright. **NIAGARA:** Supervisors: John Blackwell & Ray Prophet. Officials: Dave Anderson, Glenn Barnes, Chuck Farkas, Darren Flagg, Kalvin Forrest, Al Isherwood, Mike Macgillivray, Mike Marshall, Don Mcknight, Dave Mikolasek, Mike Paul, Terry Pizzacalla, Pete Prophet, Dan Simoneau, Mike Simoneau, Jeff Smith, Mike Soucie, Dave Stortz, John Vancool. **NORTH-CENTRAL:** Supervisor: Gary Moroney. Officials: Don Abel, Blaine Angus, Mike Bigelli, Scott Boland, Paul Bourgard, Al Dawe, Bill Fitzpatrick, Tom Foote, Jay Gilbert, Warren Hughes, Kevin Leaman, John Martini, Wayne Mcdonald, Martin Porteous, Lee Rodgers, Frank Rossi, Dave Slingerland, Perry Stone, Wayne Timbers. **NORTH-WEST:** Supervisor: Jim Oliver. Officials: Dave Burns, Pete Chisholm, Lionel Crawford, Claude Daw, Ron Elliott, Don Freeman, Jeff French, John French, Garry Gravett, Derek Hammond, Trevor Hilpert, Dave Hornsby, Rick Jacklin, Tom Lafrance, Bruce Lyndon, Larry Macpherson, Kevin Merian, Wilf Meston, Paul Robson, Shawn Rourke, Jeff Sippel, Randy Stoddart, Jim Torrie, Todd Wilkie, Steve Wilkins, George Wilson, Pascal Zaitz. **OSHAWA:** Supervisors: Ivan Locke & A. Dick. Officials: Brad Ashby, John Ashby, Gus Bambridge, Bob Bell, John Cane, Paul Catney, Dave Chevrier, John Coburn, Mike Collins, Paul Connor, Ken Cornelius, Don Daigle, Darryl Dawson, Mike Feeley, Pat Gaudet, John Gerelus, Paul Gordon, Jim Houston, Dave Lynch, Chuck Macmillan, Todd March, Paul Mcgriskin, Mike Mcquade, Gil Nieuwendyk, Dwayne Phillips, Paul Ravary, Marty Recoskie, Ted Reid, Frank Robinson, Brent Thompson, Dave Wedlake. **SARNIA:** Supervisors: Hugh Devin & Chuck Nisbett. Officials: Robert Anderson, Bob Barnes, Larry Beaton, Bill Beveridge, Steve Blair, Chris Brooks, Dave Bryce, Eric Bryce, Ivan Bryce, Greg Campbell, Jim Clements, Lloyd Cottel, Gus Coulombe, Joe Cowley, Derek Edwards,

Doug Fell, Les Finch, Paul Goldhawk, Jim Hawthorne, Bill Macalpine, Todd Mackenzie, Kevin Mcalpine, Barry Mcfadden, Chuck Nisbet, Brian Patterson, Brad Paul, Reid Smith, Bob Spence, Don Vanmassenhoven, Dick Wilson, Dave Yorke. **TORONTO:** Supervisor: Bob Nadin & Ralph Sparks. Officials: Mike Arts, Rick Baker, Bruce Brownhill, Pete Cleary, Don Cromar, Giulio Doria, Chris Edwards, Dan Emerson, Murray Evans, Jim Harwood, Ian Huffman, Alex Ivan, Greg Kimmerly, Terry Koharski, Al Mazerall, Steve Mcallister, Richard Mccauley, Steve Mignardi, Brian Millman, Robert Mills, Matt Moyer, Ian Munro, Rick Redwood, Paul Smart, Ralph Sparks, Sandy Stenhouse, John Thompson, Dean Warren, Scott Whittemore, Bill Wiles, Dave Wright. **WINDSOR:** Supervisor: Sam Sisco & Gord Thompson. Officials: Jim Batke, Steve Bezaire, Dave Cassidy, Bob Clifford, Jim Craig, Darrell Ellwood, Jay Frederick, Mark Hicks, Mike Hoberg, Scott Hoberg, Harry Hodgson, Dwayne Lambier, Vic Mcmurran, Chris Muzzin, Dan O'Halloran, Terry Turner.

OHA Season 1987-1988
BARRIE Supervisor: Bill Howes. Officials: Rick Ahern, Ken Bannerman, Jacques Brunet, Rob Durnan, Randy Ford, Brian Harasymchuk, Terry Hoffman, Brian Hunt, Scott Hutchinson, Ken Miller, Robert Mills, Rob K. Mills, Rick Perry, Dave Purdon, Rick Ramsay, Bill Rawn, Jean-Marc Roy, Dave Saab, Rick Schaly, Tim Shaughnessy, Ken Stevens, Kevin Yakymovich, Bob Zaluski. **BRAMPTON:** Supervisor: Charlie Lennox. Officials: Mike Anderson, Peter Balsdon, Kelly Clark, Dave Cormack, Mike Duggan, Andre Fauteux, Gary Johnston, Garry Kipfer, Jay Lewis, Ron Maclean, Andy Mayhew, Jim Pollock, Brad Scharf, Tony Schlegel, Larry Skillen, Jim Steeves, John Stephenson, Alex Stobo, Andy Wigley, Dave Wright. **DELHI:** Supervisor: Tony Steyaert. Officials: Larry Boden, Mark Clark, Shawn Dailey, Mark Dumesnil, Brian Fitzpatrick, Marshall Grinton, Paul Groeneveld, Wilf Gurney, Al Little, Tim Loasby, Ron Markell, Pat Meahan, Pat Rowland, Jim Ryan. **GUELPH:** Supervisor: Bill Devorski. Officials: Paul Ariss, Rick Baker, Bob Beatty, Jim Campbell, Tony Carvalho, Paul

Dalbello, Mike Deabreu, Greg Devorski, Marc Dixon, Mike Engler, Brad Fagan, Tom Farr, Paul Fitzpatrick, Jon Fleming, John Gravett, Bob Greene, Jeff Hanzlik, Jamie Kearns, Al Kimmel, Bob Laurence, Dale Lebritton, Darryl Matthews, Ron Mckelvie, Rick Morphew, Bruce Murray, Phil Olinski, Geoff Pasher, Cyril Pearce, Harvey Primeau, Laurence Ray, Doug Richard, Mark Riffer, Stev Routenburg, Pat Scarlett, Jeff Scott, Jim Simmons, Pat Smola, Ralph Urbanke, Steve Walkom, Tim Waters, Steve Wiffen, Doug Wilkinson, Bruce Wright. **HAMILTON:** Supervisor: Bryon Jackson. Officials: Steve Cheeseman, Matt Duckworth, Gord Duesbury, Cliff Gauthier, George Harrison, Joe Heslop, Greg Higson, Phil Jones, Terry Koharski, Brian Marshall, Terry Mcloughlin, Bob Morley, Jeff Morley, Greg Parker, Brian Schweitzer, John Searle, Steve Stasiuk, Dave Thompson, Jim Walters, Norm Watson, Lee Willson, Clare Zimmerman. **KINGSTON:** Supervisors: Larry Norton & Bert Kea. Officials: John Anderson, Norm Ball, Jim Bolger, Don Carr, Peter Carroll, Al Detlor, Mike Ferguson, Glenn Grice, Ken Harris, Bert Kea, Tim Keller, Lyle Lloyd, Dan Maloney, Geoff Matthews, Sylvain Milton, Cam Rundle, Ian Sant, Jim Thorne, Barry Yates. **LONDON:** Supervisors: Mel Huctwith & Rick Singleton. Officials: Mike Arts, Steve Baker, Brad Beer, Tom Blake, Pete Brenders, Gary Bruggeman, Mel Chupa, Paul Coleman, Larry Cooke, Marshall Coop, Eric Douglas, Bruce Grasby, Darryl Ireland, Brad Longfield, David Marsh, Kelly Mehlanbacher, Murray Patterson, Paul Petrie, Lee Richards, Steve Ringler, Phil Sherwood, Marv Simpson, Rick Singleton, Bill Waye, Dave Whaley, John Willsie, Pete Wloka, Greg Wright. **NIAGARA:** Supervisor: John Blackwell. Offficials: Chuck Farkas, Kalvin Forrest, Al Isherwood, Scott Kemp, Phil Leboudec, Mike Macgillivray, Mike Marshall, Don Mcknight, Dave Mikolasek, Mike Paul, Terry Pizzacalla, Pete Prophet, Dan Simoneau, Mike Soucie, Dave Stortz, John Vangool. **NORTH-CENTRAL:** Supervisor: Gary Moroney. Officials: Don Abel, Blaine Angus, Scott Boland, Paul Bourgard, Al Dawe, Bill Fitzpatrick, Tom Foote, Jay Gilbert, Paul Grant, Wayne Mcdonald, Steve Moran, Steve Neal, Martin Porteous, Lee Rodgers, Frank Rossi, Dave

Slingerland, Wayne Timbers, Justin Winter. **NORTHWEST:** Supervisor: Jim Oliver. Officials: Dave Black, Dean Burnett, Dave Burns, Pete Chisholm, Pete Cleary, Jim Cooper, Lionel Crawford, Claude Daw, Don Freeman, Jeff French, John French, Gary Gravett, Randy Guay, Trevor Hilpert, Dave Hornsby, Rick Jacklin, Tom Lafrance, Bruce Lyndon, Kevin Meriam, Murray Robertson, Paul Robson, Jeff Smith, Jim Torrie, Todd Wilkie, George Wilson, Pascal Zaitz. **OSHAWA:** Supervisor: Ivan Locke. Officials: Brad Ashby, Gus Bambridge, John Cane, Dave Chevrier, John Coburn, Mike Collins, Paul Connor, Darrell Cowan, Don Daigle, Mike Feeley, Pat Gaudet, Paul Gordon, Carl Hartwig, Jim Houston, Dave Lynch, Chuck Macmillan, Todd March, Paul Mcgriskin, Gil Nieuwendyk, Dwayne Phillips, Paul Ravary, Ted Reid, Frank Robinson, Brent Thompson, Berney Turland, Paul Weber, Dave Wedlake. **SARNIA:** Supervisor: Hugh Devin. Officials: Robert Anderson, Bob Barnes, Larry Beaton, Bill Beveridge, Dave Bryce, Eric Bryce Ivan Bryce, Greg Campbell, Jim Clements, Lloyd Cottel, Joe Cowley, Doug Fell, Mike Freeman, Paul Goldhawk, Jim Hawthorne, Sandy Martin, Kevin Mcalpine, Barry Mcfadden, Chuck Nisbet, Brian Patterson, Brad Paul, Reid Smith, Bob Spence, Don Vanmassenhoven, Dick Wilson, Dave Yorke. **TORONTO:** Supervisors: Bob Nadin & Jim Lever. Officials: Pete Balsdon, Mike Bigelli, Bruce Brownhill, Giulio Doria, Mike Duggan, Chris Edwards, Dan Emerson, Murray Evans, Jim Harwood, Ian Huffman, Alex Ivan, Greg Kimmerly, Jay Lewis, Andy Mayhew, Al Mazerall, Steve Mcallister, Richard Mccauley, Matt Moyer, Rick Redwood, Ralph Sparks, Phil Switzer, John Thompson, Dean Warren, Scott Whittemore, Bill Wiles. **WINDSOR:** Supervisors: Sam Sisco & Gord Thompson. Officials: Jim Batke, Jason Belanger, Dave Cassidy, Bob Clifford, Jim Craig, Brian Donaher, Randy Ellis, Darrell Ellwood, Jay Frederick, Mark Hicks, Mike Hoberg, Harry Hodgson, Dwayne Lambier, Vic Mcmurran, Chris Muzzin, Ian Nichols, Dan O'Halloran, Rob Rivait, Dave Schofield.

OHA SEASON 1986-1987
BARRIE: Supervisor: Bill Howes. Officials: Rick Ahern, Dale Amos, Ken Bannerman, Jacques Brunet, Rob Durnan, Randy Ellis, Brian Harasymchuk, Bill Howes, Brian Hunt, Paul Kitchen, Bruce Kitching, Richard Perry, Dave Purdon, Rick Ramsay, Bill Rawn, Rick Schaly, Tim Shaughnessy, Ken Stevens, Don Stinson, Ernie Warnica, Bob Saluski. **BRAMPTON:** Supervisor: Charlie Lennox. Officials: Don Abel, Blaine Angus, Paul Bourgard, Dave Cormack, Al Dawe, Andre Fauteux, Tom Foote, Gary Johnston, Brian Kelly, Garry Kipfer, Brian Landriault, Tom Lundy, Wayne Mcdonald, Steve Neal, Clint Peacock, Dave Pirie, Jim Pollock, Lee Rodgers, Frank Rossi, Kelly Rutherford, Brad Scharf, Larry Skillen, Dave Slingerland, John Stephenson, Jim Steeves, Wayne Timbers, Justin Winter. **DELHI:** Supervisor: Tony Steyaert. Officials: Larry Boden, Jim Carman, Mark Clark, Mark Dumesnil, Brian Fitzpatrick, Marshall Grinton, Wilf Gurney, Scott Kemp, Tim Loasby, Mike Potts, Jim Ryan. **GUELPH:** Supervisor: Bill Devorski. Officials: Rick Baker, Bob Beatty, Jim Campbell, Tony Carvalho, Paul Dalbello, Paul Davidson, Mike Deabreu, Paul Devorski, Marc Dixon, Mike Engler, Brad Fagan, Tom Farr, Jon Fleming, Rob Good, John Gravett, Bob Greene, Jeff Hanzlik, Jim Hauck, Jamie Kearns, Al Kimmel, Bob Kueber, Bob Laurence, Tom Mace, Doug Martin, Darryl Matthews, Rick Morphew, Bruce Murray, Phil Olinski, Geoff Pasher, Cyril Pearce, Ange Poletto, Harvey Primeau, Laurence Ray, Doug Richard, Ian Sant, Jim Simmons, Pat Smola, Ralph Urbanke, Steve Walkom, Tim Watters, Steve Wiffen, Doug Wilkinson. **HAMILTON:** Supervisor: Bryon Jackson. Officials: Larry Baxter, Mike Biljetina, Deon Pieere, Cliff Gauthier, George Graham, Greg Higson, Phil Jones, Brian Marshall, Mark Mcelroy, Terry Mcloughlin, Darrell Mills, Jeff Morley, Bob Morley, Barry O'Hara, Mark Robertson, Kevin Ryan, Tony Schlegel, Brian Schweitzer, John Searle, Dave Thompson, Norm Watson, Ron Wilkie, Lee Willson, Clare Zimmerman. **KINGSTON:** Supervisor: Larry Norton. Officials: John Anderson, Brad Aulthouse, Norm Ball, Len Batley, Don Carr, Peter Carroll, Al Detlor, Glenn Grice, Ken Harris, Jim Heaphy, Bert Kea, Tim Keller, Lyle Lloyd, Dan Maloney, Geoff

Matthews, Sylvain Milton, Cam Rundle, Ian Sant, Jim Thorpe, Barry Yates. **LONDON:** Supervisors: Mel Huctwith & Rick Singleton. Officials: Mike Arts, Steve Baker, Brad Beer, Tom Blake, Pete Brenders, Gary Bruggeman, Mel Chupa, Paul Coleman, Larry Cooke, Marshall Coop, Eric Douglas, Claude Farrier, Jay Gilbert, Bruce Grasby, Karl Gutcher, Brad Horton, Darryl Ireland, Brad Longfield, Kelly Mehlenbacher, Murray Mugford, Murray Patterson, Paul Petrie, Lee Richards, Ray Richards, Steve Ringler, Marv Simpson, Rick Singleton, Dave Thompson, Don Van Massenhoven, Bill Waye, Dave Whaley, John Willsie, Pete Wloka, Greg Wright. **NIAGARA:** Supervisor: John Blackwell. Officials: Russ Bazylewski, Denis Dignard, Chuck Farkas, Kalvin Forrest, Bob Hanna, Al Isherwood, Owen Kennedy, Ken Kidd, Gene Kusy, Mike Macgillivray, Don Mcknight, Don Mcquaig, Al Mecsei, Dave Mikolasek, Pat Paul, Mike Paul, Yvon Poulin, Pete Prophet, Dan Simoneau, Mike Soucie, Dave Stortz, John Vangool, Jim Walters. **NORTH-WEST:** Supervisor: Jim Oliver. Officials: Gary Baker, Dean Burnet, Dave Burns, Pete Chisholm, Mike Churchill, Lionel Crawford, Claude Daw, Don Freeman, Jeff French, John French, Gary Gravett, Rick Jacklin, Steve Macmillan, John Mccutcheon, Bruce Murray, Clarke Pollock, Murray Robertson, Paul Robson, Eric Schwippl, Jeff Scott, Jeff Smith, George Wilson, Dave Wright, Pascal Zaitz. **OSHAWA:** Supervisor: Ivan Locke. Officials: Gus Bambridge, John Cane, Dave Chevrier, John Coburn, Mike Collins, Paul Connor, Darryl Cowan, Don Daigle, Al Glaspell, Carl Hartwig, Jim Houston, Bob Kennett, Don Kett, Dave Lynch, Paul Mcgee, Paul Mcgriskin, Chuck Macmillan, Mike Mcquade, Ray Meek, Gil Nieuwendyk, Dwayne Phillips, Ted Reid, Frank Robinson, Tim Roy, Mark Smith, Bernie Turland, Dave Wedlake. **SARNIA:** Supervisors: Dan Mathieson & Hugh Devin. Officials:: Leon Arsenault, Bob Barnes, Larry Beaton, Jason Belanger, Dave Bryce, Eric Bryce, Ivan Bryce, Jim Clements, Lloyd Cottel, Joe Cowley, Hugh Devin, Doug Fell, Mike Freeman, Jim Hawthorne, Jim Maitland, Sandy Martin, Kevin Mcalpine, Barry Mcfadden, Chuck Nisbet, Brian Patterson, Pat Scarlet, Reid Smith, Bob Spence, Don Vanmassenhoven, Dick Wilson, Dave

Yorke. **TORONTO:** Supervisors: Bob Nadin & Jim Lever. Officials: Peter Balsdon, Bob Bell, Frank Beres, Mike Bigelli, Bruce Cawker, Giulio Doria, Mike Duggan, Dan Emerson, Murray Evans, Les Finch, Paul Fitzpatrick, Jim Harwood, Ian Huffman, Alex Ivan, Greg Kimmerly, Mike Legros, Jay Lewis, Ron Maclean, Andy Mayhew, Al Mazerall, Richard Mccauley, Matt Moyer, Rick Redwood, Phil Sherwood, Ken Shore, Paul Smart, Ralph Sparks, Phil Switzer, Brent Thompson, Dean Warren, Bill Wiles. **WINDSOR:** Supervisors: Sam Sisco & Gord Thompson. Officials: Ken Anderson, Brian Campbell, Dave Cassidy, Bob Clifford, Jim Craig, Brian Donaher, Darrell Ellwood, Jay Frederick, Mark Hicks, Mike Hoberg, Harry Hodgson, Dwayne Lambier, Vic Mcmurran, Don Mouck, Chris Muzzin, Dan O'Halloran, Dave Schofield, Dave Williscraft.

OHA Season 1985-1986
BARRIE: Supervisor: Jim Oiver. Officials: Rick Ahern, Dale Amos, Ken Bannerman, George Boorman, Rob Durnan, Randy Ellis, Bill Howes, Brian Hunt, Paul King, Paul Kitchen, Bruce Kitchng, Richard Perry, Dave Purdon, Pete Quennell, Rick Ramsay, Doug Renkema, Lee Rodgers, Rick Schaly, Tim Shaughnessy, Steve Smith, Ken Stevens, Don Stinson, Phil Switzer, Ernie Warnica, Bob Zaluski. **BRAMPTON:** Supervisors: Bill Brethauer & Charllie Lennox. Officials: Don Abel, Blaine Angus, Paul Bourgard, Dave Cormack, Al Dawe, Andre Fauteux, Tom Foote, Gary Johnston, Brian Kelly, Gary Kipfer, Brian Landriault, Tom Lundy, Steve Mcallister, Wayne Mcdonald, Steve Neal, Clint Pollock, Dave Pirie, Jim Pollock, Lee Rodgers, Frank Rossi, Kelly Rutherford, Brad Scharf, Larry Skillen, Dave Slingerland, John Stephenson, Jim Steeves, Wayne Timbers, Justin Winter. **DELHI:** Supervisor: Tony Steyaert. Officials: Larry Boden, Jim Carman, Mark Clark, John Emerson, Brian Fitzpatrick, Wilf Gurney, Scott Kemp, Marshall Grinton, John Muir, Kerry Nadalin, Doug Robb, Jim Ryan. **GUELPH:** Supervisor: Bill Devorksi. Officials: Campbell, Tony Carvalho, Mike Deabreu, Paul Devorski, Charlie Dickieson, Marc Dixon, Mike Engler, Brad Fagan, Paul Fitzpatrick, Jon Fleming, Bob Good, John Gravett, Bob

Greene, Ab Henshaw, Bob Kueber, Bob Laurence, Tom Mace, Doug Martin, Darryl Matthews, Don Moffat, Rick Morphew, Chris Olinski, Phil Olinski, Geoff Pasher, Cyril Pearce, Ange Poletto, Jim Prang, Jim Simmons, Pat Smola, Brock Walsh, Steve Wiffen, Doug Wilkinson. **HAMILTON:** Supervisor: Bryon Jackson. Officials: Larry Baxter, Don Clannon, Paul Davidson, Andre Fauteux, Cliff Gauthier, George Graham, Greg Higson, Phil Jones, Brian Kelly, Brian Marshall, Mark Mcelroy, Terry Mcloughlin, Bob Morley, Jeff Morley, Darrell Mills, Barry O'Hara, Ron Preston, Phil Richard, Kevin Ryan, Tony Schlegel, Brian Schweitzer, John Searle, Craig Smith, Jeff Upton, Norm Watson, Clare Zimmerman. **KINGSTON:** Supervisor: Larry Norton. Officials: John Anderson, Norm Ball, Len Batley, Franl Beres, Peter Carroll, Al Currie, Al Detlor, Ken Harris, Jim Heaphy, Bert Kea, Tim Keller, Lyle Lloyd, Dan Maloney, Sylvain Milton, Cam Rundle, Alex Rutherford, Dave Sullivan, Jim Thorpe, Barry Yates. **LONDON:** Supervisor: Mel Huctwith. Officials: Mike Arts, Steve Baker, Brad Beer, Tom Blake, Pete Brenders, Gary Bruggeman, Mel Chupa, Paul Coleman, Larry Cooke, Marshall Coop, Dave Cormack, Eric Douglas, Doug Fell, Rob Fleming, Jay Gilbert, Karl Gutcher, Bruce Grasby, Paul Hinde, Brad Horton, Darryl Ireland, Brad Longfield, David Marsh, Kelly Mehlenbacher, Murray Mugford, Murray Patterson, Wayne Pethick, Paul Petrie, Scott Pifer, Lee Richards, Ray Richards, Steve Ringler, Charlie Roach, Phil Sherwood, Marv Simpson, Mark Simpson, Rick Singleton, Al Skinner, Dave Thompson, Marcel Vandermark, Brad Walsh, Bill Waye, Dave Whaley, John Willsie, Pete Wloka, Greg Wright. **NIAGARA:** Supervisor: John Blackwell. Officials: Russ Bazylewski, Dennis Dignard, Dave Dunsby, Chuck Farkas, Kalvin Forrest, Bob Hanna, Owen Kennedy, Ken Kidd, Steve Kozielski, Gene Kusy, Mike Macgiullivray, John Martin, Don Mcquaig, Don Mcknight, Al Mecsei, Dave Mikolasek, Mike Paul, Pat Paul, Yvon Poulin, Pete Prophet, John Smits, Dan Simoneau, Dave Stortz, John Vangool, Jim Walters. **NORTH-WEST:** Supervisor: Jim Oliver. Officials: Gary Baker, Bob Buckton, Pete Chisholm, Paul Clock, Claude Daw, Don Freeman, Jeff French, Gary

Gravett, Rick Jacklin, Jamie Kearns, Brian Liesemer, Bruce Lyndon, Clarke Pollock, Peter Quennell, Paul Robson, Murray Robertson, Eric Schwippl, Jeff Smith, Dave Wright, Pascal Zaitz. **OSHAWA:** Supervisor: Ivan Locke. Officials: Gus Bambridge, John Cane, Dave Chevrier, Mike Collins, Steve Cunningham, Don Daigle, Gord Daniel, Mike Girard, Al Glaspell, Carl Hartwig, Jim Houston, Bob Kennett, Paul Mcgee, Paul Mcgriskin, Mike Mcquade, Gil Nieuwendyk, Mike Passfield, Ted Reid, Frank Robinson, Ken Rumble, Ken Swales, Brent Thompson, Berney Turland, Dave Wedlake. **SARNIA:** Supervisor: Dan Mathieson. Officials: Leon Arsenault, Bob Barnes, Larry Beaton, Garry Bruggeman, Dave Bryce, Ivan Bryce, Jim Clements, Lloyd Cottel, Joe Cowley, Hugh Devin, Les Finch, Mike Freeman, Steve Freeman, Jim Maitland, Kevin Mcalpine, Barry Mcfadden, Murray Mugford, Chuck Nisbet, Brian Patterson, Bob Spence, Don Vanmassenhoven, Dave Yorke, Dick Wilson. **TORONTO:** Supervisors: Bob Nadin & Gary Moroney. Officials: Peter Balsdon, Bob Bell, Mike Bigelli, Brian Burgoyne, Bruce Cawker, Ken Cox, Giulio Doria, Mike Duggan, Dan Emerson, Murray Evans, Dave Falagario, Mark Flanagan, Jim Harwood, Bill Hermanson, Ian Huffman, Alex Ivan, Greg Kimmerly, Mike Legros, Jay Lewis, Dave Lynch, Andy Mayhew, Al Mazerall, Matt Moyer, John Muir, Laurence Ray, Rick Redwood, Paul Rosato, Phil Sherwood, Paul Smart, Ralph Sparks, John Stephenson, John Sullivan, Brent Thompson, Dean Warren, Mike Whalen. **WINDSOR:** Supervisor: sam Sisco. Officials: Ken Anderson, Brian Campbell, Dave Cassidy, Bob Clifford, Jim Craig, Darrell Ellwood, Jay Frederick, Jim Hawthorne, Mark Hicks, Mike Hoberg, Harry Hodgson, Tom Kirby, Dwayne Lambier, Vic Mcmurran, Don Mouck, Chris Muzzin, Dan O'Halloran, Dave Schofield, Reis Smith, Gord Thompson, Dave Williscraft.

OHA Season 1984-1985
BARRIE: Supervisor: Sandy Proctor. Officials: Rick Ahern, Dale Amos, Ken Bannerman, George Boorman, Bruce Cawker, Dave Coursey, Bill Earl, Randy Ellis, Pekka Emdebrant, Keith Kennedy, Paul Kitchen, Paul

King, Scott Mclean, Barry Mcintyre, Wilf Mcquinn, Don Norris, Richard Perry, Sandy Proctor, Pete Quennell, Rick Ramsay, Doug Renkema, Rick Schaly, Tim Shaughnessy, Ken Stevens, Don Stinson, Phil Switzer, Ernie Warnica, Bob Zaluski. **BRAMPTON:** Supervisor: Bill Brethauer. Officials: Blaine Angus, Bill Barber, Steve Barry, Paul Benton, Dave Blatnick, Paul Bourgard, Troy Briggs, Al Dawe, Stan Fay, Paul Grant, Bill Hanlon, Gary Johnston, Mike Earl, Garry Kipfer, Brian Landriault, Tom Lundy, Wayne Mcdonald, Dave Pirie, Lee Rodgers, Howard Scannell, Brad Scharf, Larry Skillen, Ken Steen, Jim Steeves, Wayne Timbers, Larry Van Wyck, Gary White, Bill Wiles, Paul Wilkins, Justin Winter. **DELHI:** Supervisor: Tony Steyaert. Officials: Pete Albano, Larry Boden, Mark Clark, John Emerson, Brian Fitzpatrick, Pete Gardner, Wilf Gurney, Jack Harris, Barry Hussey, Scott Kemp, Mark Mcelroy, John Muir, Doug Robb, Jim Ryan, Phil Saunders, Brian Silverthorn, Patrick Steele. **GUELPH:** Supervisor: Bill Devorski. Officials: Don Abel, Bob Beatty, Jim Bonham, Jim Campbell, Tony Carvalho, Murray Darroch, Mike Deabreu, Paul Devorski, Charlie Dickieson, Kevin Donovan, John Evans, Brad Fagan, Paul Fitzpatrick, Jon Fleming, Jay Frederick, Bob Good, Bob Greene, Ab Henshaw, Rob Kueber, Scott Krueger, Bob Laurence, Tom Mace, Doug Martin, Andy Mayhew, Sean Mccauley, Don Moffat, Rick Morphew, Kerry Nadalin, Chris Olinski, Phil Olinski, Geoff Pasher, Cyril Pearce, Rob Pearce, Ange Poletto, Jimprang, Dan Schmidt, Jim Simmons, Pat Smola, Jeff Upton, Brock Walsh, Steve Wiffen, Doug Wilkinson. **HAMILTON:** Supervisor: Bryon Jackson. Officials: Larry Baxter, Jeff Brianard, Brian Burgoyne, Don Clannon, Paul Davidson, Andre Fauteux, Cliff Gauthier, George Graham, Greg Higson, Phil Jones, Brian Kelly, Brian Marshall, Terry Mcloughlin, Darrell Mills, Bob Morley, Barry O'Hara, Ron Preston, Phil Richard, Doug Robson, Kevin Ryan, Tony Schlegel, Brian Schweitzer, John Searle, Craig Smith, Dave Stortz, Ron Wilkie, Clare Zimmerman. **KINGSTON:** Supervisor: Larry Norton. Officials: John Anderson, Norm Ball, Frank Beres, Garry Buxton, Peter Carroll, Al Currie, Cecil Cowie, Al Detlor, John Emerson, Glenn Grice, Ken Harris, Wayne Harrison, Jim Heaphy, Paul Hinde, Bert Kea, Tim

Keller, Lyle Lloyd, Frank Robinson, Cam Rundle, Dave Sullivan, Jim Thorpe, Dan Wannamaker, Barry Yates. **LONDON:** Supervisor: Mel Huctwith. Officials: Rick Baker, Steve Baker, Tom Blake, Paul Coleman, Marshall Coop, Rob Fleming, Jay Gilbert, Karl Gutcher, Brad Horton, Paul Hinde, Darryl Ireland, Kelly Mehlenbacher, Murray Patterson, Bill Pethick, Paul Petrie, Scott Pifer, Lee Richards, Ray Richards, Steve Ringler, Charlie Roach, Marv Simpson, Mark Simpson, Rick Singleton, Dave Thompson, Marcel Vandermark, Brad Walsh, Dave Whaley, John Willsie, Greg Wright. **NIAGARA:** Supervisor: John Blackwell. Officials: Ron Bazylewski, Russ Bazylewski, Al Callery, Denis Dignard, Dave Dunsby, Chuck Farkas, Kalvin Forrest, Bob Hanna, Bob Kennedy, Owen Kennedy, Ken Kidd, Steve Kozielski, Gene Kusy, Mike Macgillivray, Don Mcknight, Don Mcquaig, Al Mecsei, John Norris, Mike Paul, Pat Paul, Yvon Poulin, John Smits, John Vangool, Lee Vanhorn. **NORTH-WEST:** Supervisor: Jim Oliver. Officials: Garry Baker, Dan Bannerman, Jeff Beresford, Bob Buckton, Pete Chisholm, Mike Churchill, Fred Clendenning, Paul Clock, Kevin D'Arcy, Claude Daw, Don Freeman, Jeff French, Gary Gravett, John Gravett, Rick Jacklin, Frank Jacobi, Jamie Kearns, Brian Liesemer, Steve Mcallister, Pete Nicholl, Clarke Pollock, Paul Robson, Erc Schwippl, Rod Smith, Norm Therien, Pascal Zaitz. **OSHAWA:** Supervisor: Ivan Locke. Officials: Gus Bambridge, Gerry Blodgett, Bill Buys, John Cane, Dave Chevrier, Mike Collins, Steve Cunningham, Don Daigle, Gord Daniel, Al Dick, Mike Girard, Al Glaspell, Steve Gregerson, Jim Houston, Al Junkin, Bob Kennett, Bob Kroonenberg, Paul Mcgee, Paul Mcgriskin, Mike Mcquade, Gil Nieuwendyk, Mike Passfield, Ted Reid, Ken Rumble, Alex Rutherford, Ron Shackelton, Ken Swales, Bernie Turland, Dave Wedlake, Pat Waters. **SARNIA:** Supervisor: Dan Mathieson. Officials: Leon Arsenault, Larry Beaton, Garry Bruggeman, Dave Bryce, Ivan Bryce, Greg Charpentier, Jim Clements, Lloyd Cottel, Joe Cowley, Hugh Devin, Doug Fell, Mike Freeman, Bill Leclair, Kevin Mcalpine, Barry Mcfadden, Chuck Nisbet, Brian Patterson, Randy Smith, Bob Spence, Don Vanmassenhoven, Dave Yorke. **TORONTO:** Supervisrs: Bob Nadin & Gary Moroney.

Officials: Darryl Abram, Bill Beattie, Pete Balsdon, Bob Bell, Mike Bigelli, Steve Brioux, Paul Cooke, Jim Cottrell, Ken Cox, Giulio Doria, Mike Duggan, Dan Emerson, Murray Evans, Dave Falagario, Tom Graham, Jim Harwood, Brian Haus, Bill Hermanson, John Hitch, Bill Howes, Ian Huffman, Alex Ivan, Greg Kimmerly, Mike Legros, Mike Lesage, Jay Lewis, Al Mazerall, Tim Mcwatters, Matt Moyer, Laurence Ray, Rick Redwood, Phil Sherwood, Ralph Sparks, John Sullivan, Lee Taylor, Bruce Tennant, Brent Thompson, Kent Wallace, Dean Warren, Mike Whalen, Dean Wllers. **WINDSOR:** Supervisor: Sam Sisco. Officials: Doug Calhoun, Brian Campbell, Dave Cassidy, Bob Clifford, Craig Collins, Jim Craig, Darrell Ellwood, Paul Fortier, Jim Hawthorne, Mark Hicks, Mike Hoberg, Harry Hodgson, Tom Kirby, Vic Mcmurran, Don Mouck, Chris Muzzin, Dan O'Halloran, Dave Schofield, Reis Smith, Gord Thompson, Dave Williscraft.

OHA Season 1983-1984
BARRIE: Supervisor: Sandy Proctor. Officials: Rick Ahern, Dale Amos, Dan Bannerman, Ken Bannerman, George Boorman, Jacques Brunet, Alan Caswell, Bill Earl, Mike Feeley, Dave Garner, Terry Gilbert, Bill Heitman, Keith Kennedy, Paul King, Dave Lee, John Mccallum, Scott Mclean, Marc Mercier, Wilf Mcquinn, Don Norris, Richard Perry, Rick Ramsay, Brian Reid, Doug Renkema, Rick Schaly, Tim Shaughnessy, Ken Stevens, Don Stinson, Rick Tonkovich, Ernie Warnica, Bob Zaluski. **BRAMPTON:** Supervisor: Bill Brethauer. Officials: Blaine Angus, Bill Barber, Steven Barry, Paul Benton, Dave Blatnick, Paul Bourgard, Al Dawe, Stan Fay, Ken Gordon, Doug Graham, Paul Grant, Bill Hanlon, Darrell Hellowell, John Holder, Gary Johnston, Bob Jones, Mike Earl, Garry Kipfer, Brian Landriault, Paul Maclean, Wayne Mcdonald, Doug Robson, Lee Rodgers, Brad Scharf, Larry Skillen, Rod Smith, Ken Steen, Wayne Timbers, Larry Van Wyck, Gary White, Bill Wiles, Phil Wilkins, Justin Winter. **DELHI**: Supervisor: Tony Steyaert. Officials: Pete Albano, Randy Allgood, Larry Boden, Mark Clark, Mike Dukes, John Emerson, Brian Fitzpatrick, Wilf Gurney, Dan Hambleton, Jack Harris,

Barry Hussey, Scott Kemp, Kerry Nadalin, Dean Opersko, Doug Robb, Tom Rotchill, Jim Ryan, Phil Saunders, Brian Silverthorn, Pat Steele, Jim Stitt. **GUELPH:** Supervisors: Lou Maschio & Bill Devorski. Officials: Randy Bast, Bob Beatty, Kevin Berry, Jim Bonham, Bill Buys, Angus Campbell, Jim Campbell, Tony Carvalho, Murray Darroch, Paul Davidson, Mike Deabreu, Paul Devorski, Bill Dolson, Kevin Donovan, John Evans, Brad Fagan, Paul Fitzpatrick, Jon Fleming, Rob Good, Bob Greene, Scott Hancock, Brian Haus, Ab Henshaw, Rob Kueber, Bob Laurence, Jay Lewis, Tom Mace, Derek Martin, Doug Martin, Sean Mccauley, Rick Morphew, Chris Olinski, Geoff Pasher, Cyrill Pearce, Ange Poletto, Jim Prang, Jim Simons, Mark Riffer, Paul Rosato, Stan Shantz, Pat Smola, Mark Vines, Brock Walsh, Steve Wiffen, Mike Ziegler. **HAMILTON:** Supervisor: Bryan Jackson. Officials: Gareth Bond, Jeff Brianard, Don Brockie, Don Clannon, Tom Culp, Mike Fedorko, Cliff Gauthier, George Graham, Owen Griffiths, Bryan Grigsby, Dave Harlick, Greg Higson, Phil Jones, Brian Kelly, Brian Marshall, Terry Mcloughlin, Darrell Mils, Peter Moffatt, Bob Morley, Jeff Nicol, Barry O'Hara, Brent Pastor, Ron Preston, Bill Price, Phil Richard, Kevin Ryan, Tony Schlegel, Brian Schwitzer, Craig Smith, Dave Stortz, Ron Wilkie, Don Williams, Clare Zimmerman. **KINGSTON:** Supervisor: Larry Norton. Officials: John Anderson, Norm Ball, Garnet Brant, Garry Buxton, Peter Carroll, Al Currie, Cecil Cowie, Al Detlor, John Emerson, Glenn Grice, Ken Harris, Wayne Harrison, Jim Heaphy, Chris Hegarty, Paul Hinde, John Hitch, Bert Kea, Tim Keller, Lyle Lloyd, John Mcgeown, Steve Rice, Frank Robinson, Cam Rundle, Steven Smith, Sid Sparks, Trevor Tackaberry, John Thompson, Jim Thorpe, Dan Wannamaker. **LONDON:** Supervisor: Mel Huctwitth. Officials: Rick Baker, Steve Baker, Dave Blake, Tom Blake, Jeff Brown, Marshall Coop, Dave Cormack, Larry Dann, David Falagario, Mark Flanagan, Brian Mccutcheon, Kelly Mehlenbacher, Jim Nanni, Murray Patterson, Scott Pifer, Lee Richards, Ray Richards, Earl Rhyno, Keith Rivard, Charlie Roach, Al Skinner, Mark Simpson, Marv Simpson, Rick Singleton, George Tryon, Marcel Vandermark, Bill Walsh, Brad Walsh, Ken Walsh,

Pat Waters, Dave Whaley, John Willsie, Greg Wright. **NIAGARA:** Supervisor: John Blackwell. Officials: Ron Bazylewski, Russ Bazlewski, Frank Beres, Brian Burgoyne, Mel Chupa, Harry Dline, Denis Dignard, Dave Dunsby, Kalvin Forrest, Bob Hanna, Bob Kennedy, Ken Kidd, Steve Kozielski, Gene Kusy, Mike Macgillivray, John Martin, Don Mcknight, Don Mcquaig, Al Mecsei, John Norris, Mike Paul, Pat Paul, Tvon Poulin, Ray Prophet, John Smits, Craig Surridge, Jim Walters, John Vangool, Lee Vanhorn. **NORTH-WEST:** Supervisor: Bob Fryday. Officials: Ron Auger, Garry Baker, Jeff Beresford, Bob Buckton, Dave Burns, Pete Chisholm, Mike Churchill, Fred Clendenning, Paul Clock, Claude Daw, Al Dickson, Kevin D'Arcy, Don Freeman, Jeff French, Gary Gravett, Frank Jacobi, Jamie Kearns, Lonie King, Brian Liesemer, Steve Mcallister, John Mccutcheon, Bob Mitchell, Tom Morgan, Clarke Pollock, Brian Richard, Paul Robson, Eric Schwippl, Graham Shaw, Rodney Smith, Norm Therrien, Doug Wilkinson, Pascal Zaitz. **OSHAWA:** Supervisor: Ivan Locke. Officials: Don Abel, Brad Aulhouse, Gus Bambridge, Gerry Blodgett, Brad Boyd, John Cane, Bruce Cawker, Dave Chevrier, Mike Collins, Steve Cunningham, Don Daigle, Daniel Gotdon, Al Dick, Al Glaspell, Stephen Gregersen, Gord Grunwell, Scott Hay, Jim Houston, Al Junkin, Bob Kennett, Rob Kroonenberg, Paul Mcgriskin, Mike Mcquade, Paul Mcgee, Gil Nieuwendyk, Mike Passfield, Steve Phillips, Ted Reid, Ken Rumble, Alex Rutherford, Dave Scotland, Ron Shackleton, Bill Simpson, Ken Swales, Brent Thompson, Bernie Turland, Jeff Upton, Dave Wedlake, Barry Yates. **SARNIA:** Supervisor: Dan Mathieson. Officials: Leon Arsenault, Bob Barnes, Larry Beaton, Garry Bruggeman, Dave Bryce, Ivan Bryce, Greg Charpentier, Jim Clements, Joe Cowley, Hugh Devin, Clare Dolan, Les Finch, Bill Leclair, Kevin Mcalpine, Barry Mcfadden, Chuck Nisbet, John Smith, Randy Smith, Bob Spence, Don Vanmassenhoven, Arnie Ward, Dave Yorke. **TORONTO:** Supervisors: Bob Nadin & Gary Moroney. Officials: Peter Balsdon, Bob Bell, Mike Bigelli, David Blair, Steve Brioux, Norm Carriere, Steve Cloutier, Paul Cooke, Jim Cottrell, Ken Cox, Giulio Doria, Murray Downs, Mike Duggan, Dan Emerson, Murray Evans,

Andre Fauteux, Lonnie Freeman, Tom Graham, Dave Gilmour, Paul Hamilton, Bil Hermanson, Jim Hickey, Bill Howes, Ian Huffman, Alex Ivan, Greg Kimmerly, Miike Legros, Mike Lesage, Tom Lundy, Al Mazerall, Matt Moyer, Rick Redwood, Phil Sherwood, Ralph Sparks, Jim Steeves, John Sullivan, Charlie Sutton, Lee Taylor, Bruce Tennant, Kent Wallace, Dean Warren, Mike Whalen, Tony Wice, Dean Willers. **WINDSOR:** Supervisors: Sam Sisco & Harold Pierre. Officials: John Adam, Al Callery, Doug Calhoun, Brian Campbell, Paul Caron, Dave Cassidy, Bob Clifford, Craig Collins, Jim Craig, A.J D'Amico, Kevin Flood, Paul Fortier, Jay Frederick, Gerry Harhden, Jim Hawthorne, Jim Harwood, Mark Hicks, Mike Hobeerg, Harry Hodgson, Tom Kirby, Denis Lemire, Vic Mcmurran, Don Mouck, Chris Muzzin, Dan O'Halloran, Mike Parlette, Robert Pickering, Dave Schofield, Reis Smith, Gord Thompson, Dave Williscraft.

OHA Season 1982-1983
BARRIE: Supervisor: Sandy Proctor. Officials: Ken Bannerman, George Boorman, Alan Caswell, Brian Cormier, Dave Coursey, Bill Earl, Scott Ferguson, Bob Gammon, Terry Gilbert, Bill Heitman, Paul King, David Lee, Charles Maier, John Mcgeown, Wilf Mcquinn, Don Norris, Richard Perry, Sandy Proctor, Rick Ramsay, Brian Reid, Tim Shaughnessy, Jim Stinson, Ken Stevens, Don Stinson, Ernie Warnica, Russ Wright, Bob Zaluski. **BRAMPTON:** Supervisor: Bill Brethauer. Officials: Henry Andrzejewski, Blaine Angus, Bill Barber, Paul Benton, Joe Blake, Paul Bourgard, Kevin Brannon, Al Dawe, Stan Fay, Ken Gordon, Dog Graham, Paul Grant, Bill Hanlon, Darrell Hellowell, John Holder, Gary Johnston, Bob Jones, Garry Kipfer, Brian Landriault, Bob Mackenzie, Paul Maclean, Pat Mccluskey, Bill Prisniak, Doug Robson, Lee Rodgers, Brad Scharf, Larry Skillen, Ken Steen, Wayne Timbers, Bob Strain, Peter Wicklum, Bill Wiles, Justin Winter. **DELHI:** Supervisor: Tony Steyaert. Officials: Randy Allgood, Larry Boden, Jim Carman, Mark Clark, Mike Dukes, Brian Fitzpatrick, Danny Hambleton, Barry Hussey, Jack Harris, Don Mcknight, Jay Mueller, John Muir, Kery Nadalin, Gord Reeves, Doug Robb, Tom Rotchill, Phil Saunders, Pat Steele, Brian Silverthorn.

GUELPH: Supervisors: Lou Maschio & Bill Devorski. Officials: Bill Buys, Angus Campbell, Jim Campbell, Paul Davidson, Mike Deabreu, Bill Devorski, Charlie Dickieson, Bill Dolson, Kevin Donovan, John Evans, Brad Fagan, Jon Fleming, Jeff Good, Rob Good, Bill Granger, Mike Hasler, Brian Haus, Ab Henshaw, Rob Kueber, Brian Laundry, Bob Laurence, Doug Martin, Rick Morphew, Jim Prang, Terry Ryckman, Jim Simmons, Jeff Upton, Larry Van Wyck, Mark Vines, Brain Walsh, Brock Walsh, Steve Wiffen, Doug Wilkinson, Mike Ziegler.
HAMILTON: Supervisor: Bryon Jackson. Officials: Gareth Bond, Jeff Brianard, Don Brockie, Mike Colavecchia, Tom Culp, Cliff Gauthier, George Graham, Bryan Grigsby, Owen Griffiths, Jim Hague, Dave Harlick, Bob Hicks, Greg Higson, Phil Jones, Brian Kelly, Charlie Lennox, Tim Mcwatters, Terry Mcloughlin, Darrell Mills, Peter Moffatt, Bob Morley, Jeff Nicol, Barry O'Hara, Brent Pastor, Shane Patzalek, Ron Preston, Bill Price, Kevin Ryan, Tony Schlegel, Brian Schweitzer, John Searle, Criag Smith, Brent Thompson, Ron Wilkie, Don Williams, Clare Zimmerman. **KINGSTON:** KINGSTON: Larry Norton. Officials: Norm Ball, Garry Buxton, Peter Carroll, John Emerson, Glenn Grice, Ken Harris, Wayne Harrison, Chris Hegarty, John Hitch, Jim Heaphy, Bert Kea, Randy Lambert, Lyle Lloyd, Ray Mcguinness, Frank Robinson, Cam Rundle, Sandy Rutherford, Dave Sullivan, John Thompson, Tim Thompson Dan Wannamaker, Pat Waters. **LONDON:** Supervisors: Hugh McLean & Mel Huctwith. Officials: Rick Baker, Steve Baker, Dave Blake, Mike Calbeck, Dave Cormack, Jon Deactis, Mark Flangan, Brian Mccutcheon, Jim Nanni, Derek Parker, Murray Patterson, Lee Richards, Ray Richards, Keith Rivard, Charlie Roach, Mark Simspon, Marv Simpson, Rick Singleton, Jim Thiorpe, George Tryon, Marcel Vandermark, Bill Walsh, Brad Walsh, Ken Walsh, Dave Whaley, Ed Winkworth, Greg Wright. **NIAGARA:** Supervisor: John Blackwell. Officials: Ron Bazylewski, Russ Bazylewski, Frank Beres, Mel Chupa, Joe Csanyi, Harry Deline, Denis Dignard, Dave Dunsby, Kalvin Forrest, Bob Hanna, Bob Kennedy, Ken Kidd, Mike Macgillivray, John Martin, Don Mcquaig, Al Mecsei, John Norris, Mike Paul, Pat Paul, Yvon Poulin, Ray Prophet,

John Smits, Dave Stortz, Lee Vanhorn. **NORTH-WEST:** Supervisor: Bob Fryday. Officials: Ron Auger, Garry Baker, Dave Black, Pete Chisholm, Mike Churchill, Fred Clendenning, Paul Clock, Don Freeman, Tom Gillespie, Gary Gravett, Don Hughes, Frank Jacobi, Jamie Kearns, Brian Liesemer, Steve Mcallister, John Mccallum, John Mccutcheon, Tom Morgan, Del Neuman, Clarke Pollock, Paul Robson, Graham Shaw, Norm Therrien, Howard Wark, Dave Walliscraft, Pascal Zaitz. **OSHAWA:** Ivan Locke. Officials: Don Abel, Brad Aulthouse, Ian Bell, Gerry Blodgett, John Cane, Bruce Cawker, Dave Chevrier, Mike Collins, Steve Cunningham, Don Daigle, Daniel Gordon, Al Dick, Stephen Gregersen, Gordon Grunwell, Jim Houston, Al Junkin, Bob Kennett, Ron Kroonenberg, Payl Mcgriskin, Mike Mcquade, Gill Nieuwendyk, Mike Passfield, Steve Phillips, Paul Ravary, Ted Reid, Ken Rumble, Alex Rutherford, Dave Scotland, Richard Searle, Ron Shacleton, Bill Simpson, Ken Swales, Berney Turland, Dave Wedlake, Peter Warnica, Barry Yates. **SARNIA:** Supervisor: Ken Werboweski. Officials: Leon Arsenault, Bcb Barnes, Larry Beaton, Dave Bryce, Ivan Bryce, Greg Charpentier, Joe Cowley, Jim Clements, Hugh Devin, Clare Dolan, Les Finch, Bill Leclair, Kevin Mcalpine, Barry Mcfadden, Chuck Nisbet, Bob Ross, John Smith, Randy Smith, Bob Spence, Arnie Ward, Dave Yorke. **TORONTO:** Supervisors: Bob Nadin, Ross Magnus & Tom Brown. Officials: Dale Amos, Peter Balsdon, Randy Bast, Bob Bell, Ted Bisallion, David Blair, David Burton, Norm Carriere, Peter Coleman, Paul Cooke, Ken Cox, Giulio Doria, Mike Duggan, Dan Emerson, Murray Evans, Andre Fauteux, Mike Feeley, Lonnie Freeman, Dave Gilmour, Paul Hamilton, Jim Harwood, Bill Hermanson, Jim Hickey, Bill Howes, Ian Huffman, Greg Kimmerly, Mike Legros, Mike Lesage, Jim Lever, Tom Lundy, Al Mazerall, Matt Moyer, Rick Redwood, Phil Sherwood, Ralph Sparks, Jim Steeves, John Sullivan, Charlie Sutton, Lee Taylor, Bruce Tennant, Mike Whalen, Tony Wice. **WINDSOR:** Supervisor: Sam Sisco & Harold Pierre. Officials: Al Callery, Brian Campbell, Paul Caron, Bob John Cherwak, Clifford, Bill Craig, A.J. D'Amico, Darrell Ellwood, Paul Fortier, Jay Frederick, Kevin Flood, Gerry Harnden, Mark

Hicks, Mike Hoberg, Brad Horton, Tom Kirby, Denis Lemire, Vic Mcmurran, Rick Ofner, Dan O'Halloran, Tim Oliphant, Dale Pare, Bob Pickering, Dave Schofield, Reid Smith, Jim Stitt, Gord Thompson.

OHA Season 1981-1982
BARRIE: Supervisor: Sandy Proctor. Officials: Ken Bannerman, Ted Benninghaus, Robert Bogle, George Boorman, Dave Coursey, Danny Dahmer, Bill Earl, Mike French, Bill Heitman, Paul King, David Lee, John Mcgeown, Wilf Mcquinn, Don Norris, Sandy Proctor, Pete Quennell, Rick Ramsay, Brian Reid, Dave Scott, Earl Scott, Tim Shaughnessy, Jim Stinson, Ken Stevens, Don Stinson, John Thompson, Jim Turner, Kirk Ure, Ernie Warnica, Russ Wright, Ronn Glassford. **BRAMPTON:** Supervisor: Bill Brethauer. Officials: Henry Andrzejewski, Bill Barber, Paul Benton, John Bigelow, Ted Biasaillion, Paul Bourgard, Kevin Brannon, Wendell Brown, Ted Casson, Al Dawe, Stan Fay, Ken Gordon, Doug Graham, Paul Grant, Derek Griffiths, Bill Hanlon, Jim Harwood, Darrell Hellowell, John Holder, Gary Johnston, Bob Jones, Garry Kipfer, Bob Mackenzie, Paul Maclean, Jan Mikkelsen, Dave Penson, Bill Prisniak, Doug Robson, Lee Rodgers, Brad Scharf, Larry Skillen, Ken Steen, Bob Strain, Peter Wicklum, Bill Wiles, Justin Winter. **DELHI:** Supervisor: Tony Steyaert. Officials: Stuart Bisson, Larry Boden, Terry Boughner, Tony Camilleri, Jim Carman, Mark Clark, Harry Clements, Mike Dukes, John Emerson, Jack Harris, Rick Morphew, Tom Rotchill, Phil Saunders. **GUELPH:** Supervisors: Lou Maschio & Jack Fischer. Officials: Randy Bast, Dean Bast, Bill Buys, Angus Campbell, Jim Campbell, Bruce Cherry, Ken Clarkson, Murray Darroch, Paul Davidson, Mike Deabreu, Bill Devorski, Charlie Dickieson, Bill Dolson, Kevin Donovan, John Evans, Jon Fleming, Jeff Good, Rob Good, Bill Granger, Bob Greene, Mike Hasler, Ab Henshaw, John Kuebere, Bob Laurence, Dave Lynch, Doug Martin, Bill Mccreary, Don Moffat, Chris Olinski, Ray Parise, Jim Prang, Terry Ryckman, Jim Simmons, Dave Soper, Dave Taylor, Jeff Upton, Larry Van Wyck, Mark Vines, Brian Walsh, Brock Walsh, Doug Wilkinson, Rick Williams. **HAMILTON:** Supervisor: Bryon Jackson.

Officials: Larry Baxter, Gareth Bond, Don Brockie, Mike Colavecchia, Tom Culp, Jim Drohan, Cliff Gauthier, Greorge Graham, Bryan Grigsby, Jim Hague, Dave Harlick, Bob Hicks, Greg Higson, Pat Hillis, Phil Jones, Brian Kelly, Gene Kusy, Charlie Lennox, Terry Mcloughlin, Tim Mcwatters, Darrell Mills, Bob Morley, Terry Mroz, Barry O'Hara, Brent Pastor, Shane Patzalek, Ron Preston, Doug Robb, Kevin Ryan, Tony Schlegel, John Searle, Mike Sells, Ken Tarling, Gary Ward, Ron Wilkie, Don Williams, Danny Williams, Rick Zbucki, Clare Zimmerman. **KINGSTON:** Supervisor: Larry Norton. Officials: Norm Ball, Garry Buxton, Peter Carroll, Bob Cutler, Richard Derry, John Emerson, Don Goodridge, Mike Graham, Glenn Grice, Ken Harris, Wayne Harison, Chris Hegarty, John Hitch, Bert Kea, Randy Lambert, Richard Landon, Lyle Lloyd, Phil Marshall, Ray Mcguinness, Frank Robinson, Cam Rundle, Sandy Rutherford, Bill Sage, Powell Slimmon, Dave Sullivan, Tim Thompson, Dan Wannamaker. **LONDON:** Supervisors: Hugh McLean & Mel Huctwith. Officials: Dayle Acorn, Rick Baker, Steve Baker, Dave Blake, Mike Calbeck, Paul Coleman, Marshall Coop, Gerald, Hesse, Charles Krieger, Brian Mccutcheon, Jim Nanni, Derek Parker, Murray Patterson, Lee Richards, Ray Richards, Charlie Roach, Marv Simpson, Rick Singleton, Jim Thorpe, George Tryon, Marcel Vandermark, Bill Walsh, Ken Walsh, John Waymann, Dave Whaley, John Wigle, John Willsie, Ed Winkworth, Greg Wright. **NIAGARA:** Supervisor: John Blackwell. Officials: Joe Baldinelli, Russ Bazylewski, Frank Beres, Mel Chupa, Joe Csanyi, Harry Deline, Denis Dignard, Bryan Elliott, Kalvin Forrest, Bob Hanna, Dave Harding, Bob Kennedy, Ken Kidd, Mike Macgillivray, John Martin, Don Mcquaig, John Norris, Mike Paul, Pat Paul, Werner Polsak, Yvon Poulin, Ray Prophet, Mike Quartermain, John Smits, Lee Vanhorn. **NORTH-WEST:** Supervisor: Bob Fryday. Officials: Ron Auger, Garry Baker, John Biehl, Dave Black, Dan Blackburn, Pete Chisholm, Fred Clendenning, Wayne Croft, Ron Forrest, Don Freeman, Burnie Gill, Tom Gillespie, Paul Hamilton, Bill Hatt, Don Hughes, Steve Mcallister, John Mccallum, Bob Mitchell, Tom Morgan, Clarke Pollock, Pete Prophet, Paul Robson, Norm

Therrien, Howard Wark, Dave Williscraft, Pascal Zaitz. **OSHAWA:** Supervisor: Ivan Locke. Officials: Don Abel, Brad Aulthouse, Gerry Blodgett, John Cane, Bruce Cawker, Dave Chevrier, Mike Collins, Paul Cooke, Steve Cunningham, Daniel Gordon, Al Dick, Paul Dinesen, Mike Girard, Steve Gregersen, Gord Grunwell, Cliff Heber, Steve Hogarth, Jim Houston, Al Junkin, Bob Kroonenberg, Terry Landry, John Lucas, Dean Lutz, Paul Mcgriskin, Mike Mcquade, Mike Passfield, Bob Phillips, Mike Rae, Pal Ravary, Ted Reid, Ken Rumble, Alex Rutherford, Bob Scriver, Dave Scotland, Richard Searle, Ron Schackleton, Bill Simpson, Tim Stauffer, Ken Swales, Brent Thompson, Peter Warnica, Dave Wedlake, Foster Williams. **SARNIA:** Supervisor: Ken Werboweski. Officials: Blair Allin, Leon Arsenault, Bob Barnes, Larry Beaton, Ivan Bryce, Jim Clements, Joe Cowley, Hugh Devin, Clare Dolan, Les Finch, Kevin Mcalpine, Barry Mcfadden, Chuck Nisbet, John Smith, Randy Smith, Bob Spence, Arnie Ward, Dave Yorke. **TORONTO:** Supervisors: Bob Nadin, Ross Magnus & Tom Brown. Officials: Dale Amos, Peter Balsdon, Scott Barber, Bill Hermanson, David Blair, Chris Bouchere, Steve Brioux, Dave Burton, Norm Carriere, Peter Coleman, Ken Cox, Grag Darichuk, Giulio Doria, Murray Downs, Mike Duggan, Barry Dunn, Dan Emerson, Murray Evans, Andre Fauteux, Lonnie Freeman, Dave Gilmour, Bill Hermanson, Jim Hickey, Bill Howes, Ian Huffman, Damir Kulas, Brian Landriault, Mike Lesage, Jim Lever, Tom Lundy, Al Mazerall, Matt Moyer, Jim Quigg, Rick Redwood, Gord Reeves, Ralph Sparks, Jim Steeves, John Sullivan, Charlie Sutton, Lee Taylor, Bruce Tennant, Mike Whalen, Tony Wice, Stephen Wiffen. **WINDSOR:** Supervisors: Sam Sisco & Harold Pierre. Officials: Ron Bate, Al Callery, Brian Campbell, Paul Caron, Ron Chittle, Bob Clifford, Luigi Cortese, Angelo D'Amico, Chuck Doherty, Darrell Ellwood, Kevin Flood, Jay Frederick, Don George, Gerry Harnden, Mark Hicks, Mike Hoberg, Harry Hodgson, Brad Horton, Tom Kirby, John Knudsen, Denis Lemire, Gary Martin, Mike Morton, Viv Mcmurran, Richard Ofner, Dennis O'Neil, Dale Pare, Brad Paul, Michael Pierre, Dave Schofield, Reid Smith, Bob Pickering, Jim Stitt, Gord Thompson, Danny Yascheshyn,

OHA Season 1980-1981
BARRIE: Supervisor: Sandy Proctor. Officials: Ken Bannerman, Bill Barber, Ted Benninghaus, John Bigelow, David Blair, Bob Bogle, George Boorman, Ted Casson, Danny Dahmer, Al Dawe, Bill Earl, Bob Gammon, Ken Gordon, Paul Grant, Tom Hall, Paul Kelly, Paul King, Bruce Kitching, Gerald Landers, David Lee, Jim Lowe, Bob Mackenzie, Bruce Magloughlen, John Mcgeown, Wilf Mcquinn, Don Norris, Sandy Proctor, Rick Ramsay, Brian Reid, Doug Robson, Lee Rodgers, Greg St Amant, Dave Scott, Earl Scott, Jim Simpson, Don Stinson, Bob Strain, John Thompson, Kirk Ure, Ernie Warnica, Russ Wright, Pascal Zaitz. **DELHI:** Supervisor: Tony Steyaert. Officials: Larry Boden, Terry Boughner, Tony Camilleri, Jim Carman, Harry Clements, Dave Davey, Mike Dukes, Jack Harris, Richard Jarvis, Rick Morphew, Gord Nisbett, Gord Reeves, Tom Rotchill, Phil Saunders, Reid Smith. **GUELPH:** Supervisors: Lou Maschio Jack Fischer & Ken Bodenistel. Officials: Henry Andrzejewski, Dean Bast, Randy Bast, Ted Basaillion, Wendell Brown, Jim Byrne, Angus Campbell, Jim Campbell, Bruce Cherry, John Clark, Murray Darroch, Mike Deabreu, Bill Devorski, Bill Dolson, Kevin Donovan, John Evans, Jon Fleming, Jeff Good, Rob Good, Doug Graham, Bill Granger, Bob Greene, Pat Halls, Mike Hasler, Darrell Hellowel, Ab Henshaw, John Holder, Roy Howlett, Gary Johnston, Ron Kennedy, Gary Kipfer, Bo Laurence, Dave Lynch, Doug Martin, Bill Mccreary, Bob Mckinnon, Don Moffat, Chris Olinski, Ray Parise, Dave Penson, Jim Prang, Henry Reynen, Doug Robb, Terry Ryckman, Mike Scharf, Larry Skillen, John Smits, Dave Soper, Dave Taylor, Chris Turnbull, Mark Vines, Brian Walsh, Peter Wicklum, Steve Wiffen, Doug Wilkinson, Rick A. Williams. Rick B. Williams. **HAMILTON:** Supervisor: Bryon Jackson. Officials: Larry Baxter, Paul Benton, Gareth Bond, Don Brockie, Bill Brown, Mike Colavecchia, Fletcher Cummons, Greg Darichuk, Jim Drohan, Richard Elop, Andre Fauteux, Stan Fay, Rod Fevreau, Pat Field, Cliff Gauthier, George Graham, Dave Harlick, Dave Henderson, Graham Hern, Bob Hicks, Jim Hopkins, Phil Jones, Charlie Lennox, Terry Mcloughlin, Tim Mcwatters, Darell Mills, Larry Mordue, Bob Morley, Terry Mroz,

Randy Newstead, Kerry Phillips, Ron Preston, Bill Prisniak, Ron Roskovich, Kevin Ryan, Tony Schlegel, John Searle, Mike Sells, Dave Thomas, Gary Ward, Don D. Williams, Don J. Williams, Keith Wilson. **KINGSTON:** Supervisor: Terry Landon. Officials: Norm Ball, Garry Buxton, Peter Carroll, Robert Cutler, Tom Dennis, John Emerson, Rob Fisher, Don Goodridge, Glenn Grice, Ken Harris, Chris Hegarty, Bert Kea, Randy Lambert, Richard Landon, Mike Lesage, Lyle Lloyd, Phil Marshall, Werner Polsak, Dwight Rathwell, Gord Rivoire, Frank Robinson, Cam Rundle, Bill Russell, Sandy Rutherford, Grant Sage, Powell Slimmon, Dave Sullivan, Tim Thompson, Dan Wannamaker. **LONDON:** Supervisors: Hugh McLean & Mel Huctwith. Officials: Dayle Acorn, Al Allain, Greg Allan, Steve Baker, Dave Blake, Jack Bowman, Craig Brown, Paul Coleman, Marshall Coop, John Donley, Doug Leblanc, David Murray, Jim Nanni, Dereck Parker, Murray Patterson, Ken Rielly, Lee Richards, Ray Richards, Keith Rivard, Charlie Roach, Robert Robinson, Rick Singleton, Kelly Smith, Jim Thorpe, George Tryon, Marcel Vandermark, Ken Walsh, Bill Walsh, John Waymann, John Wigle, John Willsie, David Winnegarden, Ed Winkworth, Greg Wright. **NIAGARA:** Supervisor: John Blackwell. Officials: Russ Bazylewski, Ken Clarkson, Harry Deline, Denis Dignard, Dave Dunsby, Kalvin Forrest, Gary Galambos, Bob Hanna, Dave Harding, Bob Kelly, Bob Kennedy, Ken Kidd, Gene Kusy, Mike Macgillivray, John Martin, Don Mcquaig, Mike Paul, Pat Paul, Ray Prophet, John Smits, Ken Tarling, Lee Vanhorn, Ron Wilkie, Rick Zbucki. **NORTH-WEST:** Supervisor: Bob Fryday. Officials: Ron Auger, Garry Baker, John Biehl, John Bright, Fred Clendenning, Paul Clock, Doug Collins, Mark Dahmer, Claude Daw, Ron Forrest, Don Freeman, Burnie Gill, Tom Gillespie, Paul Hamilton, Bill Hatt, Don Hughes, Bob Jones, Bill Krieger, Chris Macdougald, Mark Mackenzie, John Mccallum, Bob Mitchell, Tom Morgan, Ted Mortenson, Clarke Pollock, Pete Prophet, Paul Robson, John Roloson, Steve Scott, Graham Shaw, Roland Vachon, Howard Wark, Dave Williscraft. **OSHAWA:** Supervisor: Ivan Locke. Officials: Bob Armstrong, Glenn Balson, Gus Bambridge, Gerry Blodgett, Bill Buys, John Callaghan, John Cane, Paul

Cooke, Daniel Gordon, Scott Daniels, Don Davis, Al Dick, Paul Dinesen, Jim Dorsett, Rick Gilbert, Mike Girard, Steve Gregersen, Ken Griffin, Gord Grunwell, Steve Hogarth, Jim Houston, Al Junkin, Terry Landry, Dean Lutz, Earle Mccullough, Paul Mcgriskin, Mike Mcquade, Don Moffatt, Mike Passfield, Paul Ravary, Alex Rutherford, Bob Scriver, Ron Shackelton, Jim Spiers, Tim Stauffer, Peter Warnica, Chip Watson, Dave Wedlake, Ed Wells, Foster Williams. **SARNIA:** Supervisor: Ken Werboweski. Officials: Leon Arsenault, Bob Barnes, Larry Beaton, Ivan Bryce, Jim Clements, Joe Cowley, Hugh Devin, Clare Dolan, Les Finch, Kevin Mcalpine, Brian Mccutcheon, Barry Mcfadden, Chuck Nisbet, John Smith, Al Spence, Bob Spence, Mike Van Damme, Arnie Ward. **TORONTO:** Supervisors: Bob Nadin, Ross Magnus & Tom Brown. Officials: Dale Amos, Peter Balsdon, Scott Barber, Bill Beattie, Paul Bourgard, Steve Brioux, Dave Burton, Peter Coleman, Mike Duggan, Dan Emerson, Murray Evans, Mike Feeley, Bill Fox, Lonnie Freeman, Dave Gilmour, Jim Harwood, Bill Hermanson, Jim Hickey, John Hitch, Bill Howes, Ian Huffman, Don Lacombe, John Leonard, Jim Lever, Tom Lundy, Joe Macdonald, Paul Maclean, Peter Mashinter, Al Mazaerall, Jan Mikkelsen, Matt Moyer, Jim Quigg, Rick Redwood, Phil Sherwood, Bill Simpson, Herb Snider, Ralph Sparks, Jim Steeves, Charlie Sutton, Lee Taylor, Tom Taylor, Mike Whalen, Bill Wiles. **WINDSOR:** Supervisors: Sam Sisco & Harold Pierre. Officials: Vic Baillargeon, Ron Bate, Doug Calhoun, Al Callery, Brian Campbell, Paul Caron, Ron Chittle, Bob Clifford, Luigi Cortese, Kim Crapper, Angelo D'Amico, Charles Doherty, Darrell Ellwood, Jay Frederick, Don George, Mark Hicks, Mike Hoberg, Harry Hodgson, Brad Horton, Tom Kirby, Jim Larmond, John Knudsen, Denis Lemire, John Matthew, Vic Mcmurran, Richard Ofner, Dennis O'Neil, Dale Pare, Bob Pickering, Mickey Pierre, Lorne Sanders, Dave Schofield, Gord Thompson, Dan Yascheshyn.

OHA Season 1979-1980
Supervisor: Sandy Proctor. Officials: Dale Amos, Carl Aubrey, Ken Bannerman, Bill Barber, Ted Benninghaus, John Bigelow, Dave Blair, Bob Bogle, George Boorman,

Tom Broderick, Ted Casson, Danny Dahmer, Mark Dahmer, Al Dawe, Jack Bowman, Barry Dunn, Bill Earl, Mike Feeley, Maurice Forget, Robert Gammon, Ken Gordon, Paul Grant, Tom Hall, Tracy Heaslip, John Hitch, Paul Kelly, Paul King, James Kitching, Dave Lee, Jim Lowe, Bob Mackenzie, Bruce Magloughlen, Charles Maier, John Mcgeown, Wilf Mcquinn, Don Norris, Sandy Proctor, Rick Ramsay, Sandy Richmond, Doug Robson, Brian Rodgers, Lee Rodgers, Dave Scott, Earl Scott, Ken St Amant, Don Stinson, Bob Strain, Kirk Ure, Gerrit Vrieswyk, Ernie Warnica, Russ Wright. **DELHI:** Supervisor: Gord Loveday. Officials: Garry Abbey, Gord Anderson, Larry Boden, Terry Boughner, Tony Camilleri, Jim Carman, Dave Davey, Jack Harris, Richard Jarvis, John Maskell, Rick Morphew, Tom Rotchill, Bruce Saunders, Phil Saunders, Reid Smith, Tony Steyaert. **GUELPH:** Supervisors: Lou Maschio, Jack Fischer, Ken Bodendistel & Bill Brethauer. Officials: Norm Adam, Henry Andzejewski, Dean Bast, Ted Bisaillon, Ken Brown, Wendell Brown, Jim Bryne, John Clark, Murray Darroch, Bill Devorski, Bill Dolson, Kevin Donovan, Jim Embling, John Evans, Jon Fleming, Jeff Good, Rob Good, Doug Graham, Bill Granger, B0b Greene, Pat Halls, Mike Hasler, Joe Hislop, John Holder, Roy Howlett, Garry Kipfer, Bob Laurence, Dave Lynch, Frank Martin, Bill Mccreary, Bob Mckinnon, Chris Olinski, Ray Parise, Dave Penson, Jim Prang, Henry Reynen, Doug Robb, Larry Skillen, John Smits, Dave Soper, Bob Tilt, Mark Vines, Brian Walsh, Steve Wiffen, Doug Wilkinson, Foster Williams, Rick Williams, Richard Williams, Mike Wilso., **HAMILTON:** Supervisor: Jack Clancy. Officials: Gareth Bond, Don Brockie, Jim Crawford, Fletcher Cummins, Dave Currie, Greg Darichuk, Jim Drohan, Richard Elop, Rod Fevereau, Pat Field, George Graham, Dave Harlick, Dave Henderson, Graham Hern, Bob Hicks, Pat Hillis, Chuck Keenan, Dennis Kerr, Jim Leblanc, Charlie Lennox, Mark Mackenzie, Ian Mcdonald, Darrell Mills, Larry Mordue, Bob Morley, Terry Mroz, Randy Newstead, Ron Preston, Bil Prisniak, Don Robertson, Ron Roskovich, Kevin Ryan, Tony Schlegel, John Searle, Mike Sells, David Thomas, Harry Vansickle, Gary Ward, Don Williams, Don Wilson, Tony Woitowicz, Clare

Zimmerman. **KINGSTON:** Supervisor: Keith MacDonald. Officials: Norm Ball, Garry Buxton, Peter Carroll, John Emerson, Murray Evans, Don Goodridge, Glenn Grice, Vernon Haggerty, Dale Huyck, Bert Kea, Richard Landon, Mike Lesage, Phil Marshall, Steven Offord, Werner Polsak, Gord Rivoire, Frank Robinson, Cam Rundle, Bill Russell, Sandy Rutherford, Powell Slimmon, Dan Wannamaker. **LONDON:** Supervisors: Hugh McLean & Mel Huctwith. Officials: Al Allain, Greg Allan, Harry Bartley, Glen Beach, Craig Brown, Jim Clark, Paul Coleman, Marshall Coop, John Donley, Mike Dukes, Joe Macdonald, Ron Mercier, David Murray, Jim Nanni, Pat O'Brien, Dereck Parker, Ken Rielly, Lee Richards Ray Richards, Keith Rivard, Charlie Roach, Robert Robinson, Rick Singleton, Kelly Smith, George Tryon, Marcel Vandermark, Bill Walsh, John Wigle, John Willsie, Dave Winegarden. **NIAGARA:** Supervisor: John Blackwell. Officials: Russ Bazylewski, Ken Clarkson, Harry Deline, Harry Deline, Denis Dignard, Dave Dunsby, Marcel Gagne, Gary Galambos, Glen Galambos, Cliff Gauthier, Bob Hanna, Bob Kelly, Bob Kennedy, Ken Kidd, Gene Kusy, Mike Macgillivray, John Martin, Rich Mason, Don Mcquaig, Mike Paul Pat Paul, Peter Prophet, Ray Prophet, John Smits, Lee Vanhorn, Ron Wilkie, Rick Zbucki. **NORTH-WEST:** Supervisor: Clarke Pollock. Officials: Ron Auger, Garry Baker, John Biehl, Dave Black, Harvey Black, John Bright, Wayne Burke, Fred Clendenning, Paul Clock, Doug Collins, Cecil Cowie, Claude Daw, Ron Forrest, Ross Forster, Tom Gillespie, Bruce Griffin, Bill Hatt, Wayne Hopper, Don Hughes, Bill Krieger, Bob Jones, Chris Macdougald, John Macallum, Bob Mitchell, Tom Morgan, Ted Mortenson, Gord Nisbet, Clarke Pollock, Graham Shaw, Paul Robson, Joe Tuohy, Roland Vachon, Howard Wark, Dave Williscraft. **OSHAWA:** Supervisor: Ivan Locke. Officials: Glenn Balson, Gus Bambridge, Gerry Blodgett, Bill Buys, John Callaghan, Angus Campbell, John Cane, Gord Daniel, Don Davis, Al, Dick, Paul Dinesen, Jim Corsett, Bob Edwards, Mike Girard, Richard Gilbert, Ken Griffin, Gord Grunwell, Steve Hogarth, Jim Houston, George James, Al Junkin, Terry Landry, John Levantis, Bob Macdonald, Paul Mcgriskin, Nelson Moffatt, Mike Passfield, Alex

Rutherford, Bob Scriver, Ron Shackelton, Jim Spiers, Peter Warnica, Chip Watson. **SARNIA:** Supervisor: Ken Werboweski. Officials: Bob Barnes, Larry Beaton, Al Bryce, Ivan Bryce, Jim Clements, Joe Cowley, Hugh Devin, Clare Dolan, Les Finch, Doug Lasenby, Brian Mccutcheon, Chuck Nisbet, Al Spence, Bob Spence, Craig Stirtzinger, John Smith. **TORONTO:** Supervisors: Bob Nadin & Ross Magnus. Officials: Peter Balsdon, Scott Barber, Paul Bourgard, Steve Brioux, Tom Brown, Dave Burton, Peter Coleman, Dan Daly, Brian Deakin, Mike Duggan, James Flowers, Bill Fox, Lonnie Freeman, Dave Gilmour, Jim Harwood, Bill Hermanson, Jim Hickey, Bill Howes, Ian Huffman, Don Lacombe, Brian Landriault, Ed Leeds, John Leonard, Jim Lever, Tom Lundy, Paul Maclean, Peter Mashinter, Mike Quartermain, Jim Quigg, Frank Rizzo, Jim Mikkelsen, Pat Shanks, Bill Simpson, Herb Snider, Ralph Sparks, Jim Steeves, Charlie Sutton, Lee Taylor, Tom Taylor, Terry Watson, John Waymann, Mike Whalen, Bill Wiles. **WINDSOR:** Supervisors: Sam sisco & Harold Pierre. Officials: John Adam, Leon Arsenault, Vic Baillargeon, Ron Bate, Doug Calhoun, Paul Chittle, Luigi Cortese, Mike Coutts, Kim Crapper, Angelo D'Amico, Charles Doherty, Jay Frederick, Don George, Mark Hicks, Mike Hoberg, Harry Hodgson, Brad Horton, Tom Kirby, John Knudsen, Jim Larmond, Mike Lefler, Denis Lemire, Albert Macdonald, John Matthew, John Jr Matthew, Don Mathewson, James Mcfadden, Vic Mcmurran, Tim Mifflin, Dennis O'Orien, Dale Pare, Jerry Pateman, Bob Pickering, Mickey Pierre, Lorne Saunders, Bev Suitor, Gord Thompson, Danny Yascheshyn.

OHA Season 1978-1979
BARRIE: Supervisor: Sandy Proctor:. Officials: Dale Amos, Carl Aubrey, Ken Bannerman, Bill Barbere, David Blair, George Boorman, Jack Bowman, Ted Casson, John Clark, Danny Dahmer, Mark Dahmer, Al Dawe, Barry Dunn, Bill Earl, Mike Feeley, Bob Gammon, Paul Grant, Tom Hall, Tracy Heaslip, John Hitch, Dave Lee, Jim Lowe, Bob Mackenzie, Bruce Magloughlen, Charles Maier, Chris Mayne, John Mcgeown, Wilf Mcquinn, Ken Micks, Dave Pollard, Sandy Proctor, Rick Ramsay, Sandy

Richmond, Doug Robson, Lee Rodgers, Dave Scott, Earl Scott, Don Stinson, Bob Strain, Ken St Amant, Kirk Ure, Ralph Vokey, Gerrit Vrieswyk, Ernie Warnica, Stephen Wilde. **DELHI:** Supervisor: Gord Loveday. Officials: Garry Abbey, Gord Anderson, Terry Boughner, Jim Burton, Jim Carman, Keith Cook, Randy Cornellie, Dave Davey, John Easton, Richard Ellins, Terry Glenister, Rob Good, Jack Harris, Doug Jarvis, Richard Jarvis, Peter Korecki, Rick Morphew, Tom Rotchill, Mike Smith, Tony Steyaert, Bill Telfer. **GUELPH:** Supervisors: Lou Maschio & Jack Fischer. Officials: Henry Andrzejewski, Ted Bisaillon, Bill Brethauer, Ken Brown, Wendell Brown, Jim Byrne, John Cecconi, Murray Darroch, Bill Devorski, Jerry Diebold, Bill Dollery, Bill Dolson, Hawley Drone, Brad Edgar, Glen Einwechter, Jim Embling, Jon Fleming, Dave Gilmour, Bill Granger, Ernie Grondin, Pat Haus, Mike Hasler, Ab Henshaw, Joe Hislop, John Holder, Roy Howlett, Jim Hughes, Garry Kipfer, Bob Laurence, Frank Martin, Bill Mccreary, Bob Mckinnon, Clark Mcleod, Chris Olinski, Ray Parise, Lloyd Parkhouse, Dave Penson, Jim Prang, Henry Reynen, Doug Robb, Pat Shanks, Larry Skillen, Frank Slota, John Smits, Dave Soper, Bob Tilt, Foster Williams, Rick Williams, Mike Wilson. **HAMILTON:** Supervisor: Jack Clancy. Officials: Larry Baxter, Gareth Bond, Joe Boylan, Don Brockie, Bill Brown, Jim Crawford, Fletcher Cummins, Dave Currie, John Edwards, Don Fenton, Rod Fevreau, Pat Field, Gary Fitzpatrick, Blair Graham, George Graham, Dave Harlick, Graham Hern, Bob Hicks, Chuck Keenan, Jim Leblanc, Charlie Lennox, Mark Mcelroy, Stewart Mcfarland, Terry Mclean, Darrell Mills, Brent Mordue, Bob Morley, Randy Newstead, Ron Preston, Bill Prisniak, Don Robertson, Bill Rogerson, Ron Roskovich, Steve Ross, Kevin Ryan, Mike Sells, Harry Vansickle, Gary Ward, Don Williams, Keith Wilson, Clare Zimmerman. **KINGSTON:** Supervisor: Pat Hegarty. Officials: Norm Ball, Robert Bogle, Garry Buxton, Peter Carroll, John Emerson, Murray Evans, Don Goodridge, Glenn Grice, Jim Henderson, Dale Huyck, Dennis Jarrell, Bert Kea, Mike Lesage, Keith Macdonald, Phil Marshall, Steven Offord, Rick Ottenhoff, Dean Rice, Gord Rivoire, Frank Robinson, Cam Rundle, Bill Russell, Brock Walsh, Dan Wannamaker, Pat Waters. **LONDON:**

Supervisors: Hugh McLean & Mel Huctwith. Officials: Al Allain, Greg Allan, Harry Bartley, Glen Beach, Gerald Bishop, Richard Bishop, Larry Boden, Barry Brownlee, Murray Butcher, Jim Clark, Paul Coleman, Marshall Coop, Wayne Davey, Mike Dukes, Phil Jones, Joe Macdonald, Mel Macqueen, Earle Mccullough, Ron Mercier, David Murray, Jim Nanni, Pat O'brien, Lee Richards, Ray Richards, Keith Rivard, Charlie Roach, James Robillard, Robert Robertson, Kelly Smith, George Sweeney, Marc Vandermark, Bill Walsh, Ken Werboweski, John Willsie, Ed Winkworth, Claire Wintermute. **NIAGARA:** Supervisor: Jack Clancy. Officials: Levite Beaulieu, Bruce Buckborough, Harry Deline, Denis Dignard, Gary Galambos, Glen Galambos, Cliff Gauthier, Bob Hanna, John Kelly, Bob Kelly, Bob Kennedy, Ken Kidd, Gene Kusy, Mike Macgillivray, Rich Mason, John Martin, Bill Mccann, Glen Mcdonough, Don Mcquaig, Mike Paul, Pat Paul, James Prevost, Ray Prophet, Tony Schlegel, John Smits, Lee Vanhorn, Ron Wilkie, Rick Zbucki. **NORTH-WEST:** Supervisor: Clarke Pollock. Officials: Garry Baker, John Beihl, Harvey Black, John Bright, Craig Brown, Wayne Burke, Fred Clendenning, Paul Clock, Doug Collins, Percy Courtney, Cecil Cowie, Harold Fleet, Ron Forrest, Ross Forster, Frank Garvey, Ron Gibson, Kurt Glover, Don Gravett, Bruce Griffin, Bill Hatt, Wayne Hopper, Don Hughes, Jack Johnston, Bob Jones, Chuck Krieger, Chris Macdougald, John McCallum, Brian Mccutcheon, Bob Mitchell, Bryan Nixon, Bill O'Shea, Clarke Pollock, John Pym, Graham Shaw, Lynn Shewfelt, Howard Wark, Doug Williscraft. **OSHAWA:** Supervisor: Ivan Locke. Officials: Glenn Balson, Gus Bambridge, Ian Bell, Larry Bews, Gerry Blodgett, John Callaghan, John Cane, Scott Daniels, Gerald Davies, Don Davis, Al Dick, Paul Dinesen, Jim Dorsett, Mike Girard, Ken Griffin, Gord Grunwell, Steve Hogarth, Jim Houston, George James, Earl Johns, Terry Landry, Al Junkin, Leo Kelly, Doug Lynch, Paul Mcgriskin, Don Moffatt, Bob Scriver, Ron Shackelton, Jim Taylor, Bill Van Camp. **SARNIA:** Supervisor: Red Graham. Officials: Bob Barnes, Larry Beaton, Al Bryce, Ivan Bryce, Ken Bryce, Jim Clements, Joe Cowley, Hugh Devin, Bruce Douglas, Les Finch,

Charles Kennedy, Rick Macmillan, Chuck Nisbet, Al Spence, Bob Spence, James Young. **TORONTO:** Supervisors: Bob Nadin & Ross Magnus. Officials: Peter Balsdon, Scott Barber, Paul Bourgard, Stephen Branciere, Steve Brioux, Kevin Broughton, Jack Brown, Tom Brown, Bryan Burgess, Dave Burton, Ken Butler, Peter Coleman, Stephen Craig, Bryden Currie, Dandaly, Brian Deakin, Gerry Downes, Mike Duggan, Bill Fox, George Garner, Jim Harwood, Bill Hermanson, Bill Howes, Ian Huffman, Don Lacombe, Don Lamb, Larry Lapointe, Ed Leeds, John Leonard, Jim Lever, Tom Lundy, Mark Mackenzie, Paul Maclean, Peter Mashinter, Jan Mikkelsen, John Morrison, Anders Nielsen, Gord Nisbet, Don Norris, Terry Pierce, James Quigg, Frank Rizzo, Don Robb, Bill Simpson, Ron Smale, Herb Snider, Ralph Sparks, Jim Steeves, Charlie Sutton, Lee Taylor, Tom Taylor, Bruce Toner, Terry Watson, Mike Whalen, Bill Wiles, Ken Wright. **WINDSOR:** Supervisors: Sam Sisco & Harold Pierre. Officials: John Adam, Leon Arsenault, Vic Baillargeon, Ron Bate, Gerald Bocchini, Doug Calhoun, Ian Campbell, Paul Caron, Ron Chittle, Luigi Cortese, Michael Coutts, Kim Crapper, Angelo D;Amico, Charles Doherty, Jay Frederick, Don George, Thomas Gillespie, John Haviland, Mike Hoberg, Harry Hodgson, Brad Horton, Garry Iannicello, Paul King, Tom Kirby, John Knudsen, Jim Larmond, Denis Lemire, Albert Macdonald, Terry Macfarlane, John Matthew, John Jr Matthew, Don Mathewson, Tim Mifflin, Richard Murray, Dale Pare, Mark Pare, Jerry Pateman, Bob Pickering, Mickey Pierre, Ernest Saunders, Bev Suitor, Gord Thompson, Davis White, Danny Yascheshyn, Walter Yascheshyn.

OHA Season 1975-1976
BARRIE: Supervisor: Sandy Proctor. Officials: George Boorman, Jim Coxworth, Walter Borthwick, Don Currie, Scott Earl, John Firth, Bob Gammon, Bill Girard, Ross Kerr, Dave Lee, Jim Lemieux, Ron Marchildon, Peter Marille, Sany Proctor, Rick Ramsay, Archie Rankin, Sandy Richmond, Blaine Smith, Scott Wayne, Ken St Amant, Don Stinson, Ed Tugwell, Ralph Vokey, Ernie Warnica, Wendell White. **DELHI:** Supervisor: Gord

Loveday. Officials: Keith Ayres, Stuart Bisson, Terry Boughner, Andrew Bowden, Jim Burton, Jim Carman, Keith Cook, Dave Douglas, Walt Gardiner, Alan Gaukel, Alan Gillison, Terry Glenister, Doug Jarvis, Paul Kett, John Racher, Tony Steyaert, Bill Telfer. **GUELPH:** Supervisors: Ken Bodendistel & Frank Slota. Officials: Ron Breen, Bill Brethauer, Wendell Brown, John Cecconi, Murray Darroch, Mike Devlin, Bill Devorski, Jerry Diebold, Tom Brennan, Mike Devlin, Glen Einwechter, Jim Embling, John Evans, Bill Fischer, Arden Fischer, Jon Fleming, Bill Franks, Cliff Gauthier, Fred Gillard, Rob Good, Ernie Grondin, Ted Haynes, Ab Henshaw, Joe Hislop, Ian Huffman, Ken Kidd, Ken Kelly, Jerome Kempel, Karl Kiefer, Garry Kipfer, Robert Laurence, George Lazenby, Bruce Lewis, Ken Mcleod, Wayne Marshall, Frank Martin, Clark Mcleod, Bob Mckinnon, Dennis Mooney, Merv Neil, Ray Parise, Lloyd Parkhouse, Brian Peavoy, Henry Reynen, Peter Reynen, Pat Shanks, Frank Slota, John Smits, Dave Soper, Bob Tilt, Murray Wagler, Rick Williams, John Woods, Victor Zboralski. **HAMILTON:** Supervisor: Jack Clancy. Officials: Dennis Adams, Clarke Anderson, Mark Biehler, Ken Boyko, Mike Bray, Don Brockie, Bill Brown, Ray Busby, Al Carpenter, Fletcher Cummins, Robert Delottinville, Dave Denton, Doug Edwards, Bob Elliott, Bernie Ferroni, Don Fenton, Ron French, Blair Graham, Dave Harding, Bill Hermanson, Bob Hickey, Robert Hyslop, Bryon Jackson, Chuck Keenan, Jim Leblanc, Charlie Lennox, Bob Macdonald, Stew Mcfarland, Larry Mordue, Bob Morley, Jeff Nicol, John Penson, Bill Prisniak, Don Robertson, Bill Rogerson, Mike Sanislo, David Slemon, Buddy Thomas, Bruce Thompson, Harry Vansickle, Gary Ward, Charles Waterman, Don Williams, Jim Wolfe. **KINGSTON:** Supervisor: Pat Hegarty. Officials: Norm Ball, Al Black, Bob Bogle, Mike Bukacheski, Dave Descent, John Emerson, Don Goodridge, Orval Gravelle, Terry Gregson, Doug Hayward, Pat Hegarty, Ted Hurst, Herb Latchford, Gary Lavender, Terry Landon, Ted Landon, Don L'Oiseau, John Lyon, Keith Macdonald, Phil Marshall, Tom Mercier, Rick Ottenhof, Dave Publow, Frank Robinson, Tom Scanlon, Joe Smith, Skip Simpson, Cam Rundle, Al Walker, Brock Walsh. **LONDON:** Supervisor:

Hugh McLean. Officials: Larry Appel, Gerald Bishop, Rick Bishop, Barry Brownlee, Murray Butcher, Jim Byatt, Don Clark, Paul Coleman, Jim Cressman, Don Dixon, Gene Doyle, Bob Dueck, Mike Dukes, Pat Fox, George Garner, Kendal Hislop, Brad Horton, Jim Houze, George Jamieson, Phil Jones, David Mcleod, Tim Mcfadden, Melvin Macqueen, Bill Melville, Ron Mercier, Rick Morphew, Evan Donley, Pat O'Brien, Wayne Pethick, Lee Richards, Ray Richards, James Shurrie, Rick Singleton, John Slota, Paul Slota, R. Stevenson, George Sweeney, Gary Taylor, George Thomas, Ken Walsh, John Willsie, Ed Winkworth, Clare Wintermute, Bob Young. **NIAGARA:** Supervisor: Jack Clancy. Officials: Joe Bedard, Joe Boylan, Bob Cole, Harry Deline, Alex Diomin, Jim Dodds, Jim Garrett, Gary Galambos, Don Hull, Joe Kirchlechner, Craig Lawson, Mike Macgillivray, Rich Mason, Bill Mcmartin, Don Mcquaig, Pat Paul, Jim Prevost, Ray Prophet, Howard Stayzer, Russ Steinburg, Lee Vanhorn, Rick Zbucki. **NORTH-WEST:** Supervisor: Bob Fryday. Officials: Dave Anstett, Paul Clock, Bruce Collins, Cecil Cowie, Jack Crozier, Paul Curle, Barry Dunn, Dave Fawcett, Don Fludder, Frank Garvey, Pat Gaudet, Tom Gillespie, Bruce Griffin, Terry Hockley, Roy Howlett, Bob Jones, Ken King, Paul Martin, Eric Mastin, John Mccutcheon, Bob Mitchell, Frank Pearce, Clarke Pollock, Lynn Shewfelt, Terry Watson, Ken Werboweski. **OSHAWA:** Supervisor: Ivan Locke. Officials: Glenn Balson, Gus Bambridge, Bob Barnes, Gerry Blodgett, Steve Craig, Gerald Davies, Don Davis, Al Dick, Al Fenton, Kent Gilliam, Gord Grunwell, Al Junkin, Leo Kelly, Terry Landry, Wayne Mcgowan, Paul Mcgriskin, Trevor Meek, Don Moffatt, Jim Orr, Doug Parkin, Doug Reilly, Bob Scriver, Ron Shackleton, Jim Walker, Al White. **SARNIA:** Supervisor: Red Graham. Officials; Cyril Addley, Ken Bryce, Ivan Bryce, Joe Cowley, Hugh Devin, Bruce Douglas, Jim Goodhand, Ken Gould, Paul Jackson, Mike Killby, Ron Lemarsh, Larry Lasenby, Don Mathewson, John Matthew, John Munro, Chuck Nisbet, Herb Parker, Jerry Pateman, Mike Phipps, Ray Simard, John Smith, Al Spence, Bev Suittor, Larry Tomchick, Bill Walrath, Arnie Ward, Doug White. **TORONTO:** Supervisors Bob Nadin, Ross Magnus & Larry Regan.

Officials: Peter Balsdon, Bill Barry, Larry Blight, Paul Bourgard, Stephen Branciere, Tom Brown, Bryan Burgess, Dave Burton, Andy Closs, Peter Coleman, Brian Coles, Doug Cowan, Bayden Currie, Bill Dewan, Rick Finkbeiner, Bob Firth, Mike Fox, Rick Carson, Dunc Godfrey, Jim Cox, Scott Dowle, Doug Graham, Dave Harlick, Jim Hickey, Don Hopkins, Bill Howes, Jim Hughes, Graham Knight, Ed Leeds, Jim Lever, Joe Lofranco, Tom Lundy, Paul Maclean, Ross Maclean, Peter Mashinter, John May, Ralph Maze, Steve Mccasey, Earle Mccullough, Gary Moroney, John Morrison, Don Norris, Gord Patterson, Doug Robb, Bill Simpson, Ron Smale, Herb Snider, Ralph Sparks, Robert Starrett, Jim Steeves, Charlie Sutton, Lee Taylor, Tom Taylor, Jeff Watson, Mike Whalen, Paul Willard, Mike Wilson, Scott Wonnell, Doug Woods, Frederick Yates, Rod Yorke. **WINDSOR:** Supervisor: Sam Sisco. Officials: Ron Bate, Gerald Bocchini, Mel Brunet, Bill Chalmers, Ron Chittle, Ivan Clark, Luigi Cortese, Kim Crapper, Earl Dafoe, Angelo D'Amico, Charles Doherty, Ron Earl, Bill Haggitt, Ron Hickey, Terry Hickey, Mike Hoberg, Harry Hodgson, Gary Ianicello, Daler Jones, Charles Kennedy, John Kennedy, Pat Kennedy, John Koelln, Jim Larmond, Fred Maindonald, Miro Martinello, Richard Murray, Brian O'Orien, Danny Ouellette, Norm Petryshyn, Bill Ruiter, Sam Sisco, Brian Thompson, Dave Turner, Kevin Weatherby, Danny Yascheshyn, Waler Yascheshyn.

OHA Season 1958-1959
CHATHAM: Frank Uniac, Bill Doyle, GALT: Bill Brethauer, Wes Lillie, GUELPH: Lou Maschio, Larry Lewin, HAMILTON: Bev Hamilton, Jack Clancy, Hugh McLean, KITCHENER: Frank Slota, Jerry Olinski, Ed Melcheski, Merle Glassford, Jim Muldoom, LONDON: Ken McFadden, Gord Houghton, George Higgins, George Robertson, Gil Robertson, Russ Evon, Fred Hewson, SARNIA: Fred Fellows, Pete Glaab, STRATFORD: Don Schram, Len Leinweber, TORONTO: Gord Fevereau, Bill Balmer, Jack Schropshire, WINDSOR: Harold Pierre.

OHA Season 1957-1958
CHATHAM: Frank Uniac, Bill Doyle, GALT: Bill Brethauer, Wes Lillie, GUELPH: Lou Maschio, Larry Lewin, HAMILTON: Bev Hamilton, Jack Clancy, Hugh McLean, KITCHENER: Frank Slota, Jerry Olinski, Ed Melcheski, Merle Glassford, Jim Muldoom, LONDON: Ken McFadden, Gord Houghton, George Higgins, George Robertson, Gil Robertson, Russ Evon, Fred Hewson, SARNIA: Fred Fellows, Pete Glaab, STRATFORD: Don Schram, Len Leinweber, TORONTO: Gord Fevereau, Bill Balmer, Jack Schropshire, WINDSOR: Harold Pierre.

Area: **OHA (Early Years)** Season: **1948 - 1949** Supervisor: Officials: BALA: Gordon Ing, BARRIE: J.F.Dobson, Cecil Coon, BELLEVILLE: Speedy St Loius, E.Watts, Toots Holway, BLENHEIM: Stanley St Clair, BRACEBRIDGE: Frank Suter, E.A.Walker, BRAMPTON: Howard Teasdale, Jack H.Scott, BRANTFORD: Robert Riley, Gordon Boyd, Fred Robins, Anthony Torti, BOWMANVILLE: Jas Crombie, CALEDONIA: Ken Baird, Hugh Shea, COBOURG: Lorne Cane, COLLINGWOOD: E.V.Beatty, A.Wilson, CREEMORE: David Smith, DELHI: W.E.McLeod, FREGUS: E (Rusty) White, GALT: John J.Liscombe, J.T.Hogan, D.Watkins, GUELPH: James Kelly, P.W.Burke, Reg W.Hutton, HAMILTON: Wm R.Towns, A.E.Danes, Les V.Kirkpatrick, Robert Gray, Don Roberts, Jack Ewan, Pat J.Maloney, Gord Gerrard, Donald J.Goodrow, Clarence Shillington, Allen J.Sanderson, Hugh Barlow,, HARRISTON: Nels Young, HAGERSVILLE: Grant Kett, Harry Thomas, INGERSOLL: J.W (Nip) Henderson, Thos Lussons, KINGSTON: Harry Radley, Geo Patterson, Bill Steen, Mike Rodden, Stan Scrutton, Bill Mortimer, KINCARDINE: J.A.Graham, KITCHENER: Frank Udvari, Alen Tehrenbach, Wilf Hoch, LAMBETH: Tom R.Burgess, V.H.Burgess, LUCKNOW: Chas Webster, LANGSTAFF: Les Markle, LONDON: Clare Van Horne, Harry Rockey, Harold Hyatt, LEASIDE: Phil Stein, MILTON: Cliff Houston, Dave Brush, MIDLAND: A.D.Wilson, Bruce Holt, Jack Symonds, MT DENNIS: Gordon Cliffe, MILLGROVE: Hugh Barlow, Mt Brydges: A.Calvert, MIMICO: Al Promaine, MARKHAM: Max Reesor,, NEWMARKET: Maurice Walsh, Robert Peters,

NELLES CORNERS: Jack Mehlenbacher, OWEN SOUND: Wm McArthur, J.F.McArthur, James Boddy, ORILLIA: W.M.McGill, Earl Johnson, OSHAWA: Wm R.Morrison, Harry T.Dyas, Norm Allan, Doug Calhoun, PT COLBORNE: F.W.Moore, Jack Cuthbert, PT ELGIN: Norman Locking, PETERBOROUGH: Herb Payne, J.R.Quimet, PRESTON: C.Eby, Robt Homuth, George Jones, Bob Hamilton, PENETANG: Jack Symons, PT DOVER: G.Karges, RICHMOND HILL: Jas Grainger, ST GEORGE: Dell Robinson, STIRLING: Harry Ingram, ST CATHARINES: Wm Mocha, Jack Boyd, STRATROY: Clarence Gibson, Duncan Galbriath, Wm Gough, STRATFORD: Harold Baird, Pat Gardner, MIckey McQuade, Stan Smith, Robert McCully, Peter M.Nigh, SUTTON-WEST: C.E.Carpenter, F.L.Smth SEAFORTH: Chas Reeves, Ralph McFadden, Norman Hubert, Gordon Muir, C.Lemon, SIMCOE: P.R.Mauthie, Herb Hause, TORONTO: Ken Holmeshaw, C.F.Patterson, James Primeau, J.A.Wood, Gordon Scott, Eddie Morris, Pearcey Allen, A.B.Grant, Lloyd Gardiner, Randy Anderson, Wm Cooper, Dave Appleton, Ewart P.Pinder, Jas Casburn, Wm Chriss, H.Morrison, Al Roberts, C.J.kelly, F.C.Moat, Lorne Britton, W.A.Wilson, Jack McKay, W.J.Palmer, Ernie Wortley, Art Seafred, W.Dyer, A.Bourrassa, Harvey Jackson, L.D.Markle Bernia Lemaitre, Melvin (Spark) Vail, THOROLD: Chas Thompson, TAVISTOCK: Wm Mathies, TRENTON: F/L S.E. Martin, WHITBY: L.H.Effreing, John Heard, WATERLOO: E(Honey) Kuntz, WINDSOR: Lorne Loree, Gordon J.Parsons, Robert Paterson, Douglas Young, Godon Porter, WALKERTON: Frank Cordick, J.Raybould, WOODSTOCK: George Bennett, Cecil Mooney, WESTON: G.Cliffe, WELLAND: Frank Chase, WINGHAM: Alf Lockridge, WOODBRIDGE: Gary Evans

Area: **OHA (Early Years)** Season: **1947 - 1948**
Supervisor: Officials: AJAX: J.G.Wood, ALVINSTON: Alex McLachlin, Alex McTaggart, ARTHUR: Lorne Dingman, BRANTFORD: R.Riley, Fred Robus, K.M.Campbell, Thomas King, Anthony Torti, Gordon Boyd, BLENHEIM: Stan Clair, BRAMPTON: Howard Teasdale, BURK'S FALLS: Allan Quirt, BRIDGEPORT: Carl Schmidt,

BOWMANVILLE: Jos Crombie, BRACEBRIDGE: Frank Suter, Russell Salmon, BELLEVILLE: Speedy St.Louis, Toots Holway, Don Lee, Vern Goyer, BARRIE: C.R.Farrell, John F.Dobson, Cecil Cook, G.H.Kashner, CALEDONIA: Ken Baird, CREEMORE: Deverde Smith, CAYUGA: Earl Dyte, COBOURG: Lorne W.Cave, COLLINGWOOD: E.Beatty, DUNNVILLE: Tom Roddy, Soggy Green, DELHI: Wm. McLeod, John Passmore, FISHERVILLE: Jack Mehlenbacher, GALT: John J.Liscombe, Newton Kenney, J.T.Hogan, GLENCOE: Stan Humphries, Art Stinson, H.Anderson, GUELPH: James Kelly, P.W.Burke, GRAVENHURST: Fred Barnes, GRIMSBY: Rev B.A.O'Donnell, HAGERSVILLE: Grant Kett, Harry Thomas, HESPELER: Fred Shepherd, HASTINGS: Jack Crowley, HAMILTON: Wm Towns, Hugh McLean, James (Red) Dunn, L.V.Kirkpatrick, A.E.Danes, Robert Gray, D.S.Brown, Jack Ewan, A,J. (Bud) Duffy, Thos A.Conney, Pat Maloney, Fred Partridge, Jack McCully, A.J.Sanderson, Douglas Runions, Donald J.Goodman, John Miller, HARRISTON: Nelson Young, Jack Ward, Percy Bean, INGERSOLL: J.W. (Nip) Henderson, Earl Thornton, Jack Smith, KINGSTON: M.J.Rodden, W.(Bill) Watts, W.(Bill) Steen, Harry Radley, W.Reason, KITCHENER: Geo Hainsworth, Frank Udvari, Wilfrid Hoch, LAMBETH: T.R.Burgess, LISTOWEL: Grant Bitton, LONDON: Wm.Van Horne, Harry Rockey, N.R.McDougall, Clare Van Vorne, Manford Boyd, LINDSAY: Don F.Dart, Lou Walker, Ralph Wakelin, Max Aldous, MILVERTON: Elmer Appel, MOUNT FOREST: Clifford Donald, MIDLAND: Wm.McArthur, Bruce Holt, Herb Payne, C.L.Wilcox, MARKHAM: Douglas James, Max Reesor, MIMICO: H.Mooney, NORTH BAY: Geo.O.Frankus, NIAGARA FALLS: Cst J.R.Brunker, NEWMARKET: Robert Peters, M.Walsh, OMEMEE: Art Jamieson, OSHAWA: Wm.R.Morrison, Harry Dyas, Norm Allan, Douglas Love, Chas Webster, Ted McComb, OWEN SOUND: J.T.McArthur, OSHWEKEN: Cliff Lickers, ORILLIA: Earl Johnson, Walter Varty, PORT DALHOUSIE: E.W.(Red) Reynolds, PORT COLBORNE: F.W.Moore, John Cuthbert, PALMERSTON: J.Nicoll, PRESTON: Harold F.Hanlon, Robert Homuth, PORT PERRY: Wm.Taylor, PORT DOVER: Gerald Karges, PORT HOPE: Stan

Crossett, Gerald Rowden, Bernie Hodgetts, PETERBORO: Jack Begley, W.P.Calladine, Herb Payne, James C.Ellis, A.G.Weir, J.R.G.(Dick) Ouimet, POINT EDWARD: Charles Levan, PARIS: Dick Emerson, PICTON: H.D.Hyatt, PENETANG: J.Symons, RICHMOND HILL: James Grainger, ST THOMAS: Leonard Binns, STRATHROY: Duncan Galbraith, Clarence Gibson, SEAFORTH: Gordon Muir, Ralph McFadden, Norman Hubert, SIMCOE: T.E.Carnochan, P.R.Mauthe, Herb Hause, STRATFORD: H.W.Baird, P.K.Gardner, Mickey McQuade, Stan Smith, SUTTON: Ellis Pringle, F.L.Smith, ST CATHARINES: Frank Elliott, Leo Sargent, Wm.Mocha, STIRLING: Ralph Utman, STOUFFVILLE: Chas Webster, SARNIA: Len Rutter, Scrap Perry, TAVISTOCK: Wm.Matthies, TORONTO: Andy Bellemer, C.F.Patterson, D.A.Houston, Ken Holmeshaw, Jas.Primeau, Eddie Mepham, Garney Large, Eddie Morris, Lloyd Gardiner, C.J(Cy)Kelly, Bernia LeMaitre, Jack McEachren, Ernie Wortley, Harry Hawker, J.A.Wood, Wm.(Bill)Roberts, Wm.(Bill)Thoms, Pearcey Allen, Robt.N.Davidson, A.J.Bourass, Chas R.Good, Ralph Adams, Gordon Scott, Ab Grant, Ed Hodgson, Gord Gerrard, Art Seafred, F.C.Moat, E.Armstrong, Max Hackett, Ralph Anderson, Ewart G.Pender, Fred Page, Peter Chromyshyn, K.Braithwaite, Eddie Burke, Walter Dyer, Harry Morrison, Howard Harvey, A.W.Roberts, Rex Millard, D.B.Caswell, Fred Heintzman, Wm.S.Palmer, Dutch Cain, Phil Stein, F.J.Woodrow, Wm.Chriss, WALKERTON: H.G.Doughty, Frank Cordick, WATERLOO: E.(Honey)Kuntz, Jack Hogan, Geo Cassidy, WHITBY: Lawrence Heffering, WATFORD: Howard Jenkins, WESTON: Gordon Cliffe, WINGHAM: Alf Lockridge, WINDSOR: Norval Fitzgerald, Bernard Hartford, R.Paterson, Gordon J.Parsons, Douglas Young, WOODSTOCK: Geo J.Bennett, Cecil Mooney, WATERFORD: Ted Scott.

Area: **OHA (Early Years)** Season: **1946 - 1947** Supervisor: Officials: ALVINSTON: Alex McLachlin, Alex McTaggart, AURORA: Ewart G.Pinder, BRANTFORD: R.Riley, Fred Robus, K.M.Campbell, BRIDGEPORT: Carl Schmidt, BRADFORD: N.E.Colling, T.A.Woodcock, BOWMANVILLE: Jos Crombie, BRACEBRIDGE: Frank

Suter, Russell Salmon, BELLEVILLE: Speedy St.Louis, Toots Holway, BARRIE: C.R.Farrell, John F.Dobson, E.E.Burke, G.H.Kashner, CAMP BORDEN: Fred R.Clark, COPETOWN: Wm.G.Wood, COBOURG: Lorne W.Cave, COLLINGWOOD: E.Beatty, CALEDONIA: Ken Bair, FRANKFORD: D.Smith, GALT: Jack Liscombe, GLENCOE: Stan Humphries, Art Stinson, H.Anderson, GUELPH: James Kelly, P.W.Burke, GRAVENHURST: Fred Barnes, GRIMSBY: Rev.B.A.O'Donnell, HAGERSVILLE: Grant Kett, Jack Melhanbacker, HESPLER: Fred Shepherd, HASTINGS: Jack Crowley, HAMILTON: Wm Towns, HUGH McLean, James (Red) Dunn, L.V.Kirkpatrick, A.E.Danes, Robert Gray, D.S.Brown, Jack Ewan, A.J.(Bud)Duffy, Thos A.Conney, Pat Maloney, Fred Partridge, Jack McCully, A.J.Sanderson, HARRISTON: Nelson Young, Jack Ward, Percy Bean, INGERSOLL: J.W. (Nip) Henderson, Earl Thornton, KINGSTON: M.J.Rodden, W (Bill) Watts, W (Bill) Steen, Harry Radley, Max Jackson, Al Campbell, R.Dougall, LISTOWEL: Grant Bitton, LONDON: Wm Van Horne, Russ Evon, Harry Rockey, N.R.McDougall, LAKEFIELD: T.H.Junkin, LINDSAY: Don F.Dart, Lou Walker, Ralph Wakelin, Max Aldous, MILVERTON: Elmer Appel, MOUNT FOREST: Clifford Donald, MIDLAND: Wm McArthur, Bruce Holt, MARKHAM: Max Reesor, NIAGARA FALLS: Cst J.R.Brunker, NEWMARKET: Robert Peters, OMEMEE: Art Jamieson, OSHAWA: Wm Morrison, Earl (Peg) Hurst, Douglas Love, Nibs McCrombie, ORONO: Roy Winters, ORILLIA: Earl Johnston, PORT DALHOUSIE: E.W. (Red) Reynolds, PORT COLBORNE: F.W.Moore, John Cuthbert, PALMERSTON: J.Nicoll, PRESTON: Harold F.Hanlon, PORT PERRY: Wm Taylor, PORT DOVER: Jerry Karges, PORT HOPE: Lorne Williams, Stan Crossett, PETERBORO: Jack Begley, W.P.Calladine, Herb Payne, James C.Ellis, A.G.Weir, RICHMOND HILL: James Grainger, ST THOMAS: Leonard Binns, STRATHROY: Duncan Galbraith, Clarence Gibson, SEAFORTH: Gordon Muir, SIMCOE: Herb Hawes, STOUFFVILLE: Chas Webster, ST CATHARINES: Frank Elliott, Wm Mocha, SARNIA: Roy Brown, Len Barry, Chas Kelch, STRATFORD: Stan Smith, Bob McCully, Mickey McQuade, TAVISTOCK: Wm Matthies, THOROLD: Chas

E.Thompson, F.A.Doherty, TRENTON: Bruce Robinson, Capt Walter Bowen, Al LaMorre, TORONTO: Andy Bellemer, C.F.Patterson, D.A.Houston, Ken Holmeshaw, Jas Primeau, Eddie Mepham, Garney Large, Eddie Morris, Lloyd Gardiner, C.J.(Cy) Kelly, Bernie Le Maitre, Jack McEachern, Ernie Wortley, Maurice Walsh, Harry Hawker, J.A.Wood, Wm (Bill) Roberts, Wm (Bill) Thoms, Pearcey Allen, Rex Millard, Webber Transom, D,B,Caswell, Fred Heintzman, Wm Palmer, Dutch Cain, Phil Stein, F.J.Woodrow, Gord Gerrard, Harry Morrison, WALKERTON: H.G.Doughty, Frank Cordick, WATERLOO: E. (Honey) Kuntz, WHITBY: Lawrence Heffering, WATFORD: Howard Jenkins, WINGHAM: Alf Lockridge, WINDSOR: Norval Fitzgerald, Bernard Hartford, R.Paterson, Gordon J.Parsons, Doug Young.

Area: **OHA (Early Years)** Season: **1945 - 1946** Supervisor: Officials: ALVINSTON: Alex McLaughlin, AURORA: Edward G.Pinder, ARTHUR: Morley Wright, Norbert Hefferman, BRACEBRIDGE: George Suter, Russell Salmon, BARRIE: C.R.Farrell, J.F.Dobsoon, E.E.Burke, BRANTFORD: R.Riley, Al Levoy, Murray Cinnamon, BELLEVILLE: Speedy St Louis, Walt Gerow, H.P.Holway, Don Lee, A.R.Holway, BOWMANVILLE: Jas Crombie, CHATHAM: Roy Reynolds, CAMP BORDEN: Sgt J.E.Gibbs, CLINTON: Red Rath, DURHAM: R.L.Saunders, Norman Dean, FERGUS: Reg Bartlett, FOREST: Stan Newton, GLENCOE: Stan Humphrey, Ab Anderson, GALT: Ab Kilgour, Ted Elmes, GUELPH: Johnny Jones, James Kelly, GRAVENHURST: Fred Barnes, GRIMSBY: Jerry Carson, Rev B.A.O'Donnell, HAMILTON: Wm Towns, Hugh McLean, John (Red) Dunn, Al Kirpatrick, Douglas Runions, HARRISTON: Nelson Young, Jack Ward, Percy Bean, INGERSOLL: George Hayes, JEFFERSON: Jack Bennett, KINGSTON: C.W.Steen, M.J.Rodden, W.J.Watts, Harry Radley, LINDSAY: Lou Walker, Ralph akelin, Everett T.Reeves, LISTOWEL: Grant Bitton, LONDON: Wm Van Horne, Clare Van Horne, MOUNT FOREST: Clifford Donald, MARKHAM: Max Reesor, MILVERTON: Elmer Appel, MIDLAND: W.A.McArthur, Jack Ridyard, Bruce Holt, NEWMARKET: Capt D.B.Caswell, C.H.Gibney, Robert Peters, T.E.Myers,

OWEN SOUND: J.F.McArthur, OSHAWA: Wm R.Morrison, Earl Hurst, OMEMEE: G Art Williamson, ORILLIA: Earl Johnston, PETERBORO: Red Creighton, Jas C.Ellis, Herb Payne, Max Board, PORT COLBORNE: F.W.Moore, Jack Cuthbert, PORT HOPE: Ditty Rowden, Stan Crossett, Bernard Hodgetts, RICHMOND HILL: Jas Grainger, SEAFORTH: Gordon Muir, STRATFORD: Stan Smith, Bob McCully, Ken Sanders, SIMCOE: Maurice Schnarr, ST CATHARINES: Frank Eliott, E.W.Reynolds, Wm Mocha, TRENTON: W.M.Bowen, Bruce Robertson, THOROLD: Chas F.Thompson, TORONTO: Andy Bellemer, C.F.Patterson, D.A.Houston, Ken Holmeshaw, Jas Primeau, Eddie Mepham, Garney Large, Eddie Morris, Lloyd Gardiner, W.R.Henderson, C.J.(Cy) Kelly, Bernie Le Maitre, Jack McEachern, Ernie Wortley, Maurice Walsh, Harry Hawker, Bert Hedges, J.A.Wood, Wm (Bill) Roberts, Wm (Bill) Thoms, Pearcy Allen, Rex Millard, Art Jackson, Webber Transom, WOODSTOCK: John Bell, Cecil Wray, C.N.Mooney, WATFORD: Howard Jenkin, WINDSOR: Doug Young, WATERLOO: Honey Kuntz, WINGHAM: Alf Lockridge, John Brent, WALKERTON: Harry Doughty, Frank Cordick, Lou Schnurr

Area: **OHA (Early Years)** Season: **1944 - 1945** Supervisor: Officials: ALVINSTON: Alex McLaughlin, AURORA: Edward G.Pinder, W.R.Henderson, BRANTFORD: Chas LeLafrainer, Gordon Boyd, Dick W.Riley, Murray Cinnamon, BARRIE: C.R.Farrell, J.F.Dobson, BELLEVILLE: Speedy St Louis, CAMP BORDEN: R.S.M.eddie Burke, CHATHAM: Roy Reynolds, FORE#ST: Stan Newton, FORT ERIE WEST: Roy D.Smith, GLENCOE: Stan Humphreys, A.Gould, GALT: A.C.Kilgour, Reir Buck, Newton Kenny, GUELPH: Johnny Jones, HAMILTON: Wm Towns, Hugh McLean, Gordon McKay, John (Red) Dunn, P.J.Maloney, Wm Sherry, L.Kilpatrick, Len Godin, INGERSOLL: George Hayes, KINGSTON: C.W.Steen, M.J.Rodden, KITCHENER: Jack Vrooman, Alex Fehrenback, Honey Kuntz, MARKHAM: Max Reesor, MIDLAND: W.A.McArthur, NEWMARKET: Robt Peters, T.E.Myers, OSHAWA: Wm M.Morrison, LINDSAY: Wm Bryan, OWEN SOUND: J.F.McArthur, PORT COLBORNE: Muir McGowan, F.W.Moore,

PETERBORO: Herb Payne, SEAFORTH: Gorden Muir, STRATFORD: Stan Smith, Rob McCully, ST CATHARINES: Frank Elliott, E.W.Reynolds, Wm Mocha, THOROLD: Chas Thompson, TORONTO: Andy Bellemer, C.F.Patterson, D.A.Houston, Ken Holmeshaw, Jas Primeau, Eddie Mepham, Garney Large, Eddie Morris, Lloyd Gardiner, Bernie LeMaitre, Jack McEachren, Ernie Wortley, Maurice Walsh, Jock Bennett, Harry Hawker, W.Fred Hall, H.S.Bourassa, Bert Hedges, J.A.Wood, Bert McCaffrey, WINDSOR: Harold Wellwood, WATERLOO: Honey Kuntz, Stan Clare,

Area: **OHA (Early Years)** Season: **1943 - 1944** Supervisor: Officials: AURORA: Edward G.Pinder, BARRIE: C.R.Farrell, J.F.Dobson, BELLEVILLE: Speedy St Louis, J.Don Lee, BRANTFORD: M.Cinnamon, CHATHAM: Roy Reynolds, CLINTON: Grant Rath, Ross McEwen, FORT ERIE WEST: Roy D.Smith, GALT: Dave Johnston, A.C.Kilgour, Edward Ambois, GODERICH: Don McKay, GUELPH: Johnny Jones, HAMILTON: Wm Towns, Hugh McLean, Gordon McKay, Jame dunn, INGERSOLL: George Hayes, KINGSTON: C.W.Steen, KINCARDINE: Tory Gregg, LUCKNOW: Chas Webster, MIDLAND: Wm McArthur, MOUNTAIN VIEW: Sgt J.W.(Dutch) Cain, MARKHAM: Max Reesor, NEWMARKET: T.E.Myers, Robt Peters, ORILLIA: Wm J.Houston, OSHAWA: Wm Morrison, PETERBORO: Herb Payne, PORTSMOUTH: Gus Marker, PORT DOVER: Gerald S.Karges, PARRY SOUND: Wilf Sutcliffe, PORT COLBORNE: F.W.Moore, Muir McGowan, Jack Cuthbert, Vincent Upper, SEAFORTH: Gordon Muir, Archie Hubert, STRATFORD: Robt McCully, Stan Smith, ST CATHARINES: Jack Boyd, Wm Mocha, Frank Elliott, THOROLD: Charles Thompson, TORONTO: Ernie Wortley, James Primeau, Bert McCaffrey, Bert Hedges, Jock Bennett, lloyd Gardiner, D.A.Houston, Eddie Mepham, Ken Holmeshaw, C.F.Patterson, Garney Large, Mike Rodden, Bernie J.LeMaitre, Jack McEachren, Edward Morris, J.A.Wood, Lou Walker, C.Burns, C.J.Kelly, Chas J.Zeagman, Edward Gill, A.R.(Buck) Thomas, J.E."Al" Gibbs, S.W.Sadler, H.S.Bourassa, Maurice Walsh, Jow White, WINDSOR: H.P.Allin, Gordon Parsons,

Area: **OHA (Early Years)** Season: **1942 - 1943** Supervisor: Officials: AJAX: Leo McElroy, AURORA: Edward G.Pinder, BARRIE: C.R.Farrell, J.F.Dobson, BELLEVILLE: Speedy St Louis, Albert (Toots) Holway, BOLTON: O.J.Hardwick, BRANTFORD: M.Cinnamon, BRACEBRIDGE: Russell Salmon, CHATHAM: Roy Reynolds, CLINTON: Grant Rath, Ross McEwen, EXETER: Flying Officer McCaa, FORT ERIE WEST: Roy D.Smith, Wm Holmes, GALT: Dave Johnston, A.C.Kilgour, GRIMSBY: Father B.A.O'Donnell, GODERICH: Don McKay, GUELPH: Johnny Jones, HAMILTON: Wm Towns, Hugh McLean, Gordon McKay, James Dunn, H.Marsh, Edward Ambis, INGERSOLL: George Hayes, KINGSTON: C.W.Steen, W.Watt, KINCARDINE: Tory Gregg, MARKHAM: Max Reesor, NEWMARKET: Robert Peters, OSHAWA: A.W.Armstrong, Wm Morrison, PETERBORO: Herb Payne, PORT COLBORNE: F.W.Moore, Muir McGowan, Jack Cuthbert, PRESTON: Charles Tabot, SEAFORTH: Gordon Muir, STRATFORD: Bob McCully, Stan Smith, THOROLD: Charles Thompson, TRENTON: F.O. W.Stan Jackson, TORONTO: Ernie Wortley, James Primeau, Bert McCaffrey, Bert Hedges, Jock Bennett, Lloyd Gardiner, D.A.Houston, Eddie Mepham, Ken Holmeshaw, Gordon Kerr, C.F.Patterson, Garney Large, Mike Rodden, Ralph Adams, Bernie J.LeMaitre, Jack McEachren

Area: **OHA (Early Years)** Season: **1941 - 1942** Supervisor: Officials: ALVINSTON: Norman Trenouth, AURORA: Edward G.Pinder, BARRIE: John F.Dobson, C.R.Farrell, BELLEVILLE: H.P.Holway, M.J.Rodden, BOLTON: O.J.Hardwick, BOWMANVILLE: M.Breslin, BRANTFORD: M.Cinnamon, T.Ivanoff, R.Riley, Albert Amos, BRACEBRIDGE: Russell Salmon, BRADFORD: N.Collings, COBOURG: P.E.Gibson, CALEDONIA: Ken Baird, CAYUGA: Tony Murphy, CHATHAM: Roy Reynolds, COLLINGWOOD: Britton Burns, DUNNVILLE: E.G.Hastings, FENELON FALLS: Max Aldous, FORT ERIE WEST: W.H.Bogardis, GALT: A.C.Kilgour, Lorne McDonald, Dave Johnston, GANANOQUE: Buzz Robertson, GODERICH: Stewart Grant, H.Murney, GRAVENHURST: William LaRoche, GRIMSBY: Bob Hillier,

GUELPH: Johnny Jones, Evan Brill, HAMILTON: Bill Towns, Hugh McLean, Gordon McKay, INGERSOLL: George Hayes, JEFFERSON: Jock Bennett, KINGSTON: C.W.Steen, J.Smith, W.Watt, Charles Funnell, James Walshe, Roy Dougall, KITCHENER: James Cullen, George Hainsworth, Carl Schmidt, KINCARDINE: Tory Gregg, LAKEFIELD: John Sabatino, LONDON: Harry Switzer, W.H.Legge, MARKHAM: Max Reesor, MIDLAND: Alfred Brodeur, MILTON: D.Brush, MITCHELL: Charles Stoneman, NEW HAMBURG: W.Bowman, NEWMARKET: Stan Smith, NIAGARA FALLS: Alex Weir, Gordon Peterkin, Gordon Smeaton, W.Prestia, Geo Massecar, Cliff McGillivray, ORILLIA: Norman Cook, OWEN SOUND: William Garbutt, OSHAWA: Hap Hamel, A.Armstrong, Wm Morrison, J.W.Chappell, POWASSON: J.A.McCormack, PAISLEY: Hal McArthur, PORT ELGIN: Reg Padden, PALMERSTON: J.R.Auld, PETERBORO: Cliff Houston, P.Weir, Max Board, Herb Payne, PORT COLBORNE: Muir McGowan, Vince Upper, W.F.Moore, Geo Hudson, Jack Cuthbert, PORT HOPE: V.H.Harwood, PRESTON: Charles Talbot, PARRY SOUND: John McConvey, John Forbes, RIPLEY: S.Bowers, SOUTHAMPTON: Robert Piper, SEAFORTH: Gordon Muir, STAYNER: Clarence Wood, SIMCOE: Russell Oatman, J.M.Roxburgh, SUTTON: Ellis Pringle, ST CATHARINES: Wardie Wright, Ken Baird, Roger Stewart, STRATFORD: Stan Smith, Jack McCully, L.J.Appel, STRATHROY: C.S.Withers, SUNDRIDGE: Gordon Rennie, THOROLD: Charles Thompson, TORONTO: Jack Draper, Frank O'Brien, Ernie Wortley, James Primeau, Bert McCaffrey, Bert Hedges, D.A.Houston, E.A.Mepham, Ken Holmeshaw, Gordon Kerr, Leo Bruyea, Al Roberts, Sonny Wilson, C.F.Patterson, Garney Large, W.A.Sutcliffe, Paul McNamara, WOODSTOCK: Cecil Mooney, WHITBY: Clarence Rice, WALKERTON: Ray Bruder, Ken Ginshinski, WINGHAM: Len Nicholls, Ken Somers, WATERLOO: J.Hemphill,

Area: **OHA (Early Years)** Season: **1940 - 1941** Supervisor: Officials: ACTON: Dude Lindsay, ALVINSTON: Norman Trenouth, AURORA: Edward G.Pinder, Chas Sweeney, BRIGHTON: Alex Weir,

BARRIE: John F.Dobson, C.R.Farrell, BEAMSVILLE: Harry Reid, BELLEVILLE: H.P.Holway, E.W.Whelpton, Leo Barrett, BOBCAYGEON: George Johnson, BOLTON: O.J.Hardwick, W.Leavens, BOWMANVILLE: M.Breslin, Hugh Cameron, BRAMPTON: Howard Teasdale, J.J.Burrell, BRANTFORD: M.Cinnamon, T.Ivanoff, R.Riley, Albert Amos, BRACEBRIDGE: Russell Salmon, C.Ecclstone, BRADFORD: N.Collings, COBOURG: P.E.Gibson, CALEDONIA: Ken Baird, CAYUGA: Tony Murphy, CHATHAM: Roy Reynolds, CLINTON: D.Thorndyke, P.McEwen, R.Rath, COLLINGWOOD: Alex Wilson, Britton Burns, Roy Burmister, DUNNVILLE: E.G.Hastings, Tex White, DURHAM: Ken Wilson, Harry Dean, DELHI: Ross Mills, ELMIRA: H.O.Weichel, A.Seiling, FERGUS: F.O.Moon, Rusty White, FENELON FALLS: Max Aldons, FORT ERIE: W.H.Bogardis, F.A.Filmore, Stan Jackson, GALT: A.C.Kilgour, Lorne McDonald, Dave Johnston, Reid Buck, GANANOQUE: Buzz Robertson, GEORGETOWN: P.F.Blackburn, GODERICH: Stewart Grant, Harold Murney, Donald McKay, Nicholas Burnside, GRAVENHURST: William LaRoche, GRIMSBY: Bob Hillier, Harry Reid, GUELPH: Johnny Jones, Evan Brill, HAGERSVILLE: Dr Harry Whitehead, Maurice Winger, HAMILTON: Hugh McLean, William Towns, Jack Beemer, Gordon Mckay, HAVELOCK: Douglas Brennan, HANOVER: C.Van Slyke, INGERSOLL: H.Riseboro, JEFFERSON: Jock Bennett, KINGSTON: C.W.Steen, J.Smith, Roy Dougall, W.Watt, Max Jackson, KITCHENER: T.Hillman, R.A.Reinhart, Jamess Cullen, Werner Schnaar, George Hainsworth, R.Fellbaum, KINCARDINE: Tory Gregg, Mel Riggin, LISTOWEL: F.W.Kemp, LUCKNOW: H.Agnew, Leo Schnurr, LAKEFIELD: John Sabatino, Michael Gorham, LINDSAY: Everett Reeves, Ralph Wakelin, LONDON: Harry Switzer, Tom Munro, Fred Ollson, Dr Janes, W.H.Legge, LANSDOWNE: A.W.Edwards, MARKHAM: Max Reesor, MIDLAND: Alfred Brodeur, Wm McArthur, R.Dodds, C.Simpson, MILTON: D.Brush, P.H.McMullen, MITCHELL: W.C.Thorne, Charles Stoneman, NEW HAMBURG: W.Bowman, NEWMARKET: Stan Smith, Robert Peters, NORTH BAY: Wilfred Denham, NIAGARA FALLS: J.Gordon Smeaton, W.Prestia, George Massecar,

411

Wm Hunter, Gordon Peterkin, Cliff Mcgillivray, ORILLIA: Norm Cook, Hugh Kelly, Bill Curan F.Suter, OWEN SOUND: Bill Garbutt, A.McIntyre, OSHAWA: Hap Hamel, A.M.Armstrong, Peg Hurst, W.M.Morrison, OAKWOOD: Peter McIntyre, POWASSON: J.A.McCormack, PAISLEY: George Grant, Hal McArthur, PORT ELGIN: Reg Padden, James Parr, PALMERSTON: J.R.Auld, W.R.Johnston, PETERBORO: Walter Jackson, Cliff Houston, Bob Creighton, Max Board, L.LeBarr, F.J.Miller, Herb Payne, PORT COLBORNE: George Hudson, Jack Cuthbert, George Wade, F.W.Moore, Vince Upper, Muir McGowan, PORT HOPE: V.H.Harwood, Gerald Rowden, PRESTON: Charles Talbot, PARRY SOUND: John Forbes, Ken Buchan, Melville Wylie, RIPLEY: S.Bowers, SARNIA: Norm Perry, Roy Brown John Neale, SOUTHAMPTON: Robert Piper, SEAFORTH: Gordon Muir, Cyril Flannery, STAYNER: Clarence Woods, R.J.Somerville, Peter Woods, SIMCOE: Russell Oatman, J.M.Roxburgh, SUTTON: Ellis Pringle, Leon Smith, ST CATHARINES: M.V.Corrigan, Wardie Wright, STRATFORD: Stan Smith, Jack McCully, B.Norfolk, L.W.Appel, STRATHROY: C.S.Wilkie, SUNDRIDGE: Gordon Rennie, TORONTO: R.M.Ecclestone, Jack Draper, Frank O'Brien, L.T.Walker, Ernie Wortley, James Primeau, Bert mcCaffrey, Bert Hedges, D.A.Houston, Geo Ewens, M.Young, E.Mepham, Ken Holmeshaw, Leo Bruyea, Gordon Kerr, George Walsh, H.P.Allen, C.F.Patterson, Gerald LeGrave, Corp Frank Finnigan, Fred Heintzman, Norbert Mueller, John McConvey, Pte R.W.Green, W.A.Sutcliffe, H.P.Allen, M.J.Rodden, TWEED: Sam Curry, THOROLD: C.E.Thompson, TRENTON: B.R.York, WATFORD: L.W.Harper, WOODSTOCK: Dr Norman Douglas, Cecil Mooney, WHITBY: Clarence Rice, Jack Sleightholm, WELLAND: J.A.Lenehan, WALKERTON: Raymond Bruder, Ken Ginskinski, WINGHAM: Ken Powers, Jack Gard, Cy Proctor, Len nicholls, Ken Somers, WATERLOO: Honey Kuntz.

Area: **OHA (Early Years)** Season: **1939 - 1940** Supervisor: Officials: ALVINSTON: Norman Trenouth, AURORA: Edward G.Pinder, BRIGHTON: Alex Weir, BARRIE: John F.Dobson, Gordon Meeking, C.R.Farrell,

BEAMSVILLE: Harry Reid, BELLEVILLE: H.P.Holway, E.W.Whelpton, Leo Barrett, BOBCAYGEON: George Johnson, BOLTON: O.J.Hardwick, W.Leavens, BOWMANVILLE: M.Breslin, Hugh Cameron, BRAMPTON: Howard Teasdale, J.J.Burrell, BRANTFORD: M.Cinnamon, T.Ivanoff, R.Riley, BRACEBRIDGE: Russell Salmon, C.Ecclestone, BRADFORD: Ellis Pringle, N.E.Collings, COBOURG: P.E.Gibson, CALEDONIA: Ken Baird, CAYUGA: Tony Murphy, CHATHAM: Roy Reynolds, CLINTON: Doug Thorndyke, COLLINGWOOD: Alex Wilson, Britton Burns, Roy Burmister, CRYSTAL BEACH: William Holmes, DUNNVILLE: E.G.Hastings, Tex White, DURHAM: R.L.Saunders, Duke Shutz, DELHI: Ross E.Mills, ELMIRA: H.O.Weichel, A.Seiling, FERGUS: F.O.Moon, FENELON FALS: Max Aldons, FORT ERIE: W.H.Bogardis, F.A.Filmore, Stan Jackson, GALT: A.C.Kilgour, Lorne McDonald, Dave Johnston, GANANOQUE: Buzz Robertson, GEORGETOWN: P.F.Blackburn, GODERICH: Stewart Grant, Harold MUrney, Donald McKay, Nicholas Burnside, GRAVENHURST: Wm LaRoche, GRIMSBY: Harry Reid, Hap Hilier, GUELPH: Johnny Jones, HAGERSVILLE: Dr Harry Whitehead, Maurice Winger, HAMILTON: Hugh McLean, William Towns, Jack Beemer, Gordon McKay, Jack Worthy, HARRISTON: Lawson Burrow, HAVELOCK: Douglas Brennan, HANOVER: C.Van Slyke, INGERSOLL: H.Riseboro, KINGSTON: Joe Smith, C.W.Steen, Roy Dougall, W.Watt, Max Jackson, KITCHENER: Tee Hilman, R.A.Reinhart, James Cullen, Werner Schnarr, George Hainsworth, R.Fellbaum, Honey Kuntz, KINCARDINE: Tony Gregg, Mel Riggin, LISTOWEL: F.W.Kemp, LUCKNOW: W.Agnew, LAKEFIELD: John Sabatino, LINDSAY: Everett Reeves, LINDSAY: Everett Reeves, LONDON: Tom Munro, W,H.Legge, Harry Switzer, Dr.J.M.Janes, Dave Johnson, MARKHAM: Max Reesor, Pete Reesor, MIDLAND: Alfred Brodeur, William McArthur, R.Dodds, C.Simpson, MILTON: D.Brush, P.H.McMullen, MITCHEll: W.G.Thorne, Charles Stoneman, NEW HAMBURG: W.Bowman, Hap Hamel, NEWMARKET: Stan Smith, NORTH BAY: Wilfred Denham, NIAGARA FALLS: W.Prestia, George Massecar, ORILLIA: Norm Cook, Hugh Kelly, Bill Curran, George

Ross, OWEN SOUND: W.Garbutt, A.McIntyre, OSHAWA: A.M.Armstrong, Ralph McAlpine, Peg Hurst, OAKWOOD: Peter McIntyre, PAISLEY: George Grant, Hal McArthur, PORT ELGIN: Reg Paddon, Jas Parr, PALMERSTON: J.R.Auld, W.R.Johnston, PARIS: H.M.Fair, PETERBORO: Walter Jackson, Cliff Houston, P.Weir, Bob Creighton, L.LeBarr, Max Board, PORT COLBOURNE: George Hudson, Jack Cuthbert, George Wade, F.W.Moore, PORT HOPE: V.H.Harwood, Gerald Rowden, PRESTON: Chas Talbot, PARRY SOUND: John Forbes, SARNIA: Norm Perry, Roy Brown, John Neale, SOUTHAMPTON: Robert Piper, Happy Rogers, Mike Huska, SEAFORTH: Gordon Muir, Cyril Flannery, STAYNER: Clarence Woods, J.Somerville, SIMCOE: Russell Oatman, ST CATHARINES: M.V.Corrigan, STRATFORD: Reg Reid, Jack McCully, STRATHROY: C.S.Wilkie, SUNDRIDGE: Gordon Rennie, STAYNER: Peter Woods, TORONTO: C.H.Day, Norman Lamport, Frank O'Brien, L.T.Walker, Ernie Wortley, James Primeau, Jock Bennett, Bert MCaffery, Dutch Cain, Bert Hedges, D.A.Houston, James McPherson, Ken Holmeshaw, Leo Bruyea, Gordon Kerr, George Walsh, Murray Payne, George Ewens, H.P.Allen, Bro Silvin, Bing Caswell, Harold Farlow, TWEED: Sam Curry, THOROLD: C.Thompson, TRENTON: B.R.York, WATFORD: L.W.Harper, WOODSTOCK: Dr Norman Douglas, Cecil Mooney, Fred Marsden, WHITBY: Clarence Rce, Jack Sleightholm, WELLAND: J.A.Lenehan, WALKERTON: Raymond Bruder, H.Doughty, WINGHAM: Ken Powers, Jack Gard, Cy Proctor, Alf Lockeridge,

Area: **OHA (Early Years)** Season: **1938 - 1939** Supervisor: Officials: ALVINSTON: Norman Trenouth, AURORA: Edward G.Pinder, BRIGHTON: Alex Weir, BARRIE: john F.Dobson, Wm.Blogg, Gordon Meeting, C.R.Farrell, BEAMSVILLE: Harry Reid, BELLEVILLE: H.P.Holway, E.W.Whelpton, Leo Barrett, Ken Colling, BOBCAYGEON: George Johnson, BOLTON: O.J.Hardwick, W.Leavens, BOWMANVILLE: M.Breslin, Hugh Cameron, BRAMPTON: Howard Teasdale, J.J.Burrell, BRANTFORD: M.Cinnamon, R.Riley, Tommy Ivanoff, BRACEBRIDGE: Russell Salmon, BRADFORD: Norman E.Collings, COBOURG: P.E.Gibson, CALEDONIA: Ken Baird,

CAYUGA: Tony Murphy, Tom McSorley, CHATHAM: Roy Reynolds, CLINTON: Doug Thorndyke, Carl Draper, COLLINGWOOD: Alex Wilson, Britton Burns, Lloyd Young, CRYSTAL BEACH: Bill Holmes, DUNNVILLE: E.G.Hastings, Tex White, DURHAM: R.L.Saunders, DELHI: Ross E.Mills, ELMIRA: H.O.Weichel, A.Seiling, FERGUS: F.A.Filmore, FENELON FALLS: Max Aldous, FORT ERIE: W.H. Babe Bogardis, Stan Jackson, GALT: A.C.Kilgour, Thos DuValle, Lorne McDonald, Hugh Cassidy, GEORGETOWN: P.F.B ackburn, GRAVENHURST: Wm.LaRoche, GRIMSBY: Harry Reid, Hap Hillier, GUELPH: Johnny Jones, Clayton Lindsay, HAGERSVILLE: Dr.Harry Whitehead, Maurice Winger, HAMILTON: Johnny Mitchell, Gordon McKay, Jack Beemer, Jack Worthy, W.R.Towns, Fred Partridge, HARRISTON: Lawson Burrow, HAVELOCK Douglas Brennan, Ben Hagerman, INGERSOLL: H.Riseboro, KINGSTON: A.Stollery, Joe Smith, KITCHENER: Tee G.Hillman, Werner Schnarr, Geo Hainsworth, R.Fellbaum, Edward Kuntz, Burton Lederman, James Cullen, KINCARDINE: Tony Gregg, LISTOWEL: F.W.Kemp, LAKEFIELD: John Sabatino, LINDSAY: Everett Reeves, W.D.Hyatt, LONDON: Tom Munro, W.H.Legg, Fred Olson, Dr.J.M.Janes, Dave Johnson, LANGTON: T.McDonald, MARKHAM: Max Reesor, Pete Reesor, MEAFORD: Ernie J.Smith, MIDLAND: Alfrec Brodeur, Wm.McArthur, MILTON: D.Brush, MITCHELL: W.C.Thorne, Chas Stoneman, NEW HAMBURG: W.Bowman, Hap Hamel, Edward Kalbfleisch, NEWMARKET: Stan Smith, NIAGARA FALLS: W.Prestia, George Massecar, J.G.Smeaton, NEW TORONTO: A.H.Johnston, ORILLIA: Norm Cook, Hugh Kelly, OSHAWA: A.M.Armstrong, Harry Lott, Peg Hurst, Wm.Morrison, PALMERSTON: J.R.Auld, W.R.Johnston, PARIS: H.M.Fair, PETERBORO: Walter Jackson, CLiff Houston, E.Jackson, W.Wright, Archie Weir, Bob Creighton, Lou LeBarr, PORT COLBORNE: George Hudson, Jack Cuthbert, William Mountain, F.W.Moore, PORT HOPE: V.H.Harwood, Gerald Rowden, PRESTON: Charles Talbot, PENETANG: Bert Corbeau, SARNIA: Gordon Paterson, Norm Perry, Roy Browm, John Neale, SEAFORTH: A.W.Dick, Gordon Muir, STAYNER: Clarence Woods, R.J.Somerville, SIMCOE: Russell Oatman,

ST.CATHARINES: M.V.Corrigan, STRATFORD: Deane Gee, Reg Reid, Chick Appel, Jack McCully, E.B.Norfolk, STRATHROY: C.S.Wilkie, SUNDRIDGE: Gordon C.Rennie, TORONTO: C.H.Day, M.J.Rodden, Norman Lamport, Frank O'Brien, Ernie Wortley, Bert MCaffrey, E.C.Johnston, Dutch Cain, Bert Hedges, Whitney Field, D.A.Houston, J.H.McPherson, James Primeau, Ted Gregory, J.W.Davidson, E.Corbeau, Lloyd Percival, Fred Wright, Harold Allen, Ken Holmeshaw, H.W.Farlow, Leo Bruyea, Gordon Kerr, TWEED: Sam Curry, WATFORD: L.W.Harper, WOODSTOCK: Dr.Norman Douglas, Cecil Mooney, Fred Marsden, WHITBY: Clarence Rice, Jack Sleightholm, WELLAND: J.A.Lenahan.

Area: **OHA (Early Years)** Season: **1937 - 1938** Supervisor: Officials: ALVINSTON: Norman Trenouth, AURORA: Edward G.Pinder, BARRIE: John F.Dobson, Wm Blogg, BEAMSVILLE: Harry Reid, BELLEVILLE: Alex Weir, H.P.Holway, E.W.Whelpton, Leo Barrett, Ken Colling, BOBCAYGEON: George Johnson, BOLTON: O.J.Hardwick, W.Leavens, BOWMANVILLE: M.Breslin, Hugh Cameron, BRAMPTON: Howard Teasdale, J.Burrell, BRANTFORD: M.Cinnamon, J.Albert Amos, T.Ivanoff, BRACEBRIDGE: Russell Salmon, CALEDONIA: Ken Baird, CAYUGA: Tony Murphy, Tom McSorley, CHATHAM: Roy Reynolds, CLINTON: Doug Thorndyke, Carl Draper, COLLINGWOOD: Alex Wilson, Britton Burns, Lloyd Young, CRYSTAL BEACH: Bill Holmes, DUNNVILLE: E.G.Hastings, Tex White, DURHAM: R.L.Saunders, E.Schutz, ELMIRA: H.O.Weichel, A.Seiling, FERGUS: F.A.Filmore, FENELON FALLS: Max Aldous, FORT ERIE: Babe Bogardis, Stan Jackson, GALT: A.C.Kilgour, Thos DuValle, H.Slack, Lorne McDonald, Hugh Cassidy, Dave Johnston, GEORGETOWN: P.F.Blackburn, GRAVENHURST: Wm.LaRoche, GRIMSBY: Harry Reid, GUELPH: Johnny Jones, HAGERSVILLE: Maurice Winger, Dr,Harry Whitehead, HAMILTON: Johnny Mitchell, Gordon McKay, Jack Beemer, H.A.Quinney, Jack Worthy, H.Sparling, W.R.Towns, C.R.Farrell, Fred Partridge, HARRISTON: Lawson Burrow, HAVELOCK: Douglas Brennan, Ben Hagerman, INGERSOLL: H.Riseboro, KINGSTON: A.Stollery, Joe Smith, KITCHENER: Ted

Hillman, WernerSchnarr, Geo Hainsworth, John Schnaar, R.Fellbaum, KINCARDINE: Tony Gregg, LISTOWEL: F.W.Kemp, LAKEFIELD: John Sabatino, LINDSAY: Everett Reeves, Harold Fever, W.D.Hyatt, LONDON: Tom Munro, W.H.Legg, Fred Olson, Dr.J.M.Janes, Harry Pettinger, MARKHAM: Max Reesor, Pete Reesor, MEAFORD: Ernie J.Smith, MIDLAND: Alfred Brodeur, Robert Dods, Wm.McArthur, MILTON: D.Brush, MITCHELL: W.C.Thorne, Chas Stoneman, NEW HAMBURG: W.Bowman, Hap Hamel, Edward Kalbfleisch, NEWMARKET: Stan Smith, NIAGARA FALLS: W.Prestia, Cliff MacGillivray, George Massecar, J.G.Smeaton, ORILLIA: Norm Cook, George Ross, Hugh Kelly, OSHAWA: A.M.Armstrong, Harry Lott, PALMERSTON: J.R.Auld, W.R.Johnston, PARIS: H.M.Fair, PETERBORO: Walter Jackson, Ray Rose, Cliff Houston, W.E.Jackson, PORT COLBORNE: George Hudson, Jack Cuthbert, William Mountain, Bert Corbeau, PORT HOPE: V.H.Harwood, PRESTON: Charles Talbot, SARNIA: Norm Perry, Roy Brown, John Neale, SEAFORTH: A.W.Dick, Gordon Muir, STAYNER: Clarence Woods, SIMCOE: Russell Oatman, ST.CATHARINES: M.V.Corrigan, STRATFORD: Reg Reid, Chick Appel, Jack McCully, C.H.Brothers, E.B.Brothers, E.B.Norfolk, STRATHROY: C.S.Wilkie, TORONTO: M.J.Rodden, DR.Frank McCurry, Eddie Rodden, Norman Lamport, Frank O'Brien, Fred Waghorne Jr, Ernie Wortley, Bert McCaffrey, Jack Bennett, E.C.Johnston, Dutch Cain, Tracey Shaw, Bert Hedges, Pearcey Allen, Wally hern, John Ross Roach, Al Wood, Whitey Field, A,H,Johnston, D.A.Houston, Robert Porter, J.H.McPherson, Jas Primeau, Ted Gregory, Redge Scott, TWEED: Sam Curry, WATFORD: L.W.Harper, WOODSTOCK: Dr.Norman Douglas, Cecil Mooney, Fred Marsden, Beatty Washer, WHITBY: Clarry Rice.

Area: **OHA (Early Years)** Season: **1936 - 1937** Supervisor: Officials: ALVINSTON: Norman Trenouth, AURORA: Edward G.Pinder, BARRIE: John F.Dobson, A.H.Clarke, BEAMSVILLE: Harry Reid, BELLEVILLE: Alex Weir, H.P.Holway, Ernest W.Whelpton, Leo Barrett, Ken Collins, BOBCAYGEON: George Johnson, BOLTON: O.J.Hardwick, W.Leavens, BOWMANVILLE: M.Breslin,

Hugh Cameron, BRAMPTON: Howard Teasdale, Jack Burrell, BRANTFORD: Earl Balkwell, W.E.Jackson, M.Cinnamon, Albert Amos, R.Riley, BRADFORD: N.E.Collings, CALEDONIA: Ken Baird, Cayuga: Tony Murphy, Tom McSorley, CHATHAM: Roy Reynolds, CLINTON: Doug Thorndye, A.McEwan, Carl Draper, COLLINGWOOD: Alex Wilson, DUNNVILLE: E.G.Hastings, Tex White, DURHAM: R.L.Saunders, ELMIRA: H.O.Weichel, A.Seiling, FERGUS: F.A.Fillmore, FENELON FALLS: Max Aldous, FORT ERIE: Stan Jackson, Babe Bogardis, GALT: A.R.Oliver, A.C.Kilgour, Thos DuVale, GEORGETOWN: P.F.Blackburn, GODERICH: H.Murney, GRAVENHURST: Bruce Finlay, GRIMSBY: Dad Farrell, Harry Reid, Happy Hillier, GUELPH: Johnny Jones, HAGERSVILLE: Maurice Winger, Dr.Harry Whitehead, HAMILTON: John Mitchell, Gordon McKay, Jack Beemer, H.A.Quinney, Tom Moore, Jack Worthy, H.Sparling, W.R.Towns, Guy Smith, Douglas G.Horne, HARRISTON: D.A.Houston, Lawson Burrow, HAVELOCK: Douglas Brennan, INGERSOLL: H.D.Riseboro, KINGSTON: C.Devlin, Art Casterton, William Watts, F.Bellringer, Arthur Stollery, KITCHENER: Jack Hemphill, Paddy Farrell, Ted Hillman, Werner Schnaar, Dave Schneider, Nelson Seibert, F.W.Marsden, Geo Hainsworth, KINCARDINE: Tony Gregg, LISTOWEL: F.W.Kemp, LAKEFIELD: john Sabatino, LINDSAY: Everett Reeves, H.Rogers, LONDON: Tom Munro, W.H.Legg, MARKHAM: Max Reesor, Pete Reesor, MEAFORD: Ernie Smith, MIDLAND: Alfred Brodeur, William McArthur, MILTON: D.Brush, MITCHELL: W.C.Thorne, Chas Stoneman, NEW HAMBURG: W.Bowman, Hap Hamel, Edward Kalbfleisch, NEWMARKET: W.P.Epworth, H.E.Gilroy, Stan Smith, NIAGARA FALLS: W.Prestia, Cliff MacGillivray, W.J.Hunter, J.G.Smeaton, OAKVILLE: Dr.Deans, ORILLIA: Norm Cook, George Ross, Hugh Kelly, OSHAWA: A.M.Armstrong, Harry Lott, PALMERSTON: J.R.Auld, W.R.Johnston, C.W.Kells, PARIS: Russell Sandercock, PETERBORO: Walter A.Jackson, Ray Rose, Cliff Houston, Lewis J.LeBarr, PORT COLBORNE: George Hudson, Jack Cuthbert, William Mountain, Bert Corbeau, Arthur Clark, PORT HOPE: Stan Crossett, V.H.Harwood, PORT PERRY: J.Boe, PRESTON: Charles Talbot, SARNIA:

N.Perry, Roy Brown John Neale, SEAFORTH: A.W.Dick, Gordon Muir, STAYNER: Clarence Wood, SIMCOE: Russell Oatman, ST CATHARINES: M.V.Corrigan, STRATFORD: Wm Easson, Reg Reid, L.W."Chick" Appel,, E.B.Norfolk, Jack McCulley, STRATHROY: C.S.Wilkie, TWEED: Sam Curry, Jim Quinn, TORONTO: M.J.Rodden, Dr.Frank McCurry, Eddie Rodden, Bert Clayton, Ernie Wortley, Lou Walker, Charles Delahay, Bert McCaffrey, Norm Lamport, Jock Bennett, E.C.Johnston, George McEwens, Dutch Cain, Tracy Shaw, Percy Topping, Bert Hedges, Herb Gibbs, Robert Armstrong, Bruce Paul, Pearcy Allen, Clare McIntyre, Bob Crosby, John Ross Roach, Reg Noble, Ted Gregory, Al Wood, Jack Marks, Whitey Field, WATFORD: L.W.Harper, WOODSTOCK: Harry King, Dr.Douglas

Area: **OHA (Early Years)** Season: **1935 - 1936** Supervisor: Officials: ALVINSTON: Norman Trenouth, AURORA: Lorne Lee, Edward G.Pinder, Herb Holman, BARRIE: Clifford Jemmett, John Dobson, A.H.Clarke, BEAMSVILLE: Harry Reid, BELLEVILLE: W.Green, H.P.Holway, Leo Barrett, Ken Colling, S.R.Burrows, BOBCAYGEON: George Johnson, BOLTON: Albert Kennedy, S,Cameron, O.J.Hardwick, W.Levans, BOWMANVILLE: W.A.Edgar, M.Breslin, Hugh Cameron, BRAMPTON: Howard Teasdale, Jack Burrell, BRANTFORD: Earl Balkwell, Stanley Verner, W.E.Jackson, M.Cinnamon, Albert V.Amos, R.Riley, BURLINGTON: E.E.Summers, E.W.Smith, CALEDONIA: John Morrison, Ken Baird, CAYUGA: Tony Murphy, J.L.Murdoch, CHATHAM: Roy Reynolds, CLINTON: Carl Draper, Doug Thorndike, COLDWATER: Wilfred Manning, COLLINGWOOD: Jos Belcher, Edgar Fryer, Clarence Wood, CAMP BORDEN: W.G.Robinson, DUNNVILLE: E.G.Hastings, J.W.Edwards, George Karges, Tex White, D.A.Houston, DURHAM: E.R.Shultz, R.L.Saunders, ELMIRA: H.O.Weichel, A.Seiling, ELORA: Robert Fisher, Alex Karges, George Hills, FENELON FALLS: Max Aldons, FORT ERIE: Stan Jackson, H.O.Taylor, Babe Bogardis, FERGUS: F.W.Marsden, GALT: George Himes, Fred George, A.R.Oliver, A.C.kilgour, D.Johnston, GEORGETOWN: P.F.Blackburn, GODERICH: H,Murney,

GRAVENHURST: Bruce Findlay, GRIMSBY: Dad Farrell, Les Farrell, John R,McVicar, Harry Reid, Happy Hillier, GUELPH: Earl Brill, Johnny Jones, HAGERSVILLE: Maurice Winger, Dr.Harry Whitehead, HAMILTON: John Mitchell, Gordon McKay, George Redding, Jack Beemer, H.A.Quinney, Tom Moore, Jack Worthy, H.Sparling, W.R.Towns, Guy Smith, HARRISTON: Lawson Burrow, John D.Ward, INGERSOLL: H.D.Riseboro, KINGSTON: C.Devlin, Joe L.Smith, R.Fougall, A.Casterton, Fred Brown, William Watts, Ab Stinson, Jas P.Walsh, F,Bellringer, KITCHENER: Jack Hemphill, Paddy Farrell, Ted Hillman, Maurice Schnarr, Bobby Fellbaum, Dave Schneider, LAKEFIELD: John Sabatino, LINDSAY: Everett Reeves, LONDON: Tom Munro, W.H.Legg, Pick Hines, Borden Armstrong, MARKHAM: Dr.R.G.Cowie, Max Reesor, Peter Reesor, MEAFORD: Ernest Smith, Thos.Riley, George Bell, MIDLAND: Clarence Simpson, Alfred Brodeur, MILTON: D.Brush, MITCHELL: W.C.Thorne, D.Eizerman, Chas Stoneman, NEW HAMBURG: W.Bowman, Hap Hamel, NEWMARKET: W.P.Epworth, C.Harman, NIAGARA FALLS: W.Prestia, OAKVILLE: Dr.Deans, ORILLIA: Norm Cook, George Ross, OSHAWA: A.M.Armstrong, OWEN SOUND: Bill Garbutt, PALMERSTON: J.R.Auld, J.Barton, W.R.Johnston, R.E.Root, PARIS: Russell Sandercock, PENETANG: Bert Corbeau, PETERBORO: Walter Jackson, Ray Rose, M.Board, Grover Halpin, Cliff Houston, PORT COLBORNE: George hudson, Frank Smith, A.P.McAvoy, Jack Cuthbert, William Mountain, PORT HOPE: Stanley Crossett, V.H.Harwood, PORT PERRY: J.Boe, PRESTON: Charles Talbot, SARNIA: N.Perry, Roy Brown, John Neale, SEAFORTH: A.W.Dick, SIMCOE: Elmer V.Ramey, Jack Barrett, Russell Oatman, C.E.Watts, Chas Mitchell, ST CATHARINES: M.V.Corrigan, STRATFORD: William Easson, Reg Reid, H.W.Jamieson, ChickAppel, Walter Kelterborn, E.B.Norfolk, Jack McCully, STRATHROY: C.S.Wilkie, TWEED: Sam Curry, Jim Quinn, WALKERTON: Joseph Raybold, WHITBY: Bert Smith, Charles Lavery, Clarry Rice, WINDSOR: A.W.Bruce, R.M.Bert Foote, WOODSTOCK: Harry King, Chilton Childs, Dr.Douglas, WATFORD: L.W.Harper, TORONTO: M.J.Rodden, Dr.Frank McCurry, Eddie Rodden, Bert

Clayton, Ernie Wortley, Lou Walker, Harold Farlow, Charles Delahay, Bert McCaffery, Norm Albert, N.Lamport, Jock Bennett, E.C.Johnston, George Ewens, W.J.Buchanan, Dutch Cain, J.D.Christie, Tracy Shaw, Percy Topping, Frank Sullivan, W.J.Walshe, Ralph Adams, Jack Tackaberry, W.Graham, Bert Hedges, Douglas Lough, Herb Gibbs, Robert Armstrong, Eddie Mepham, Bruce Paul, Harold Frost, J.K.Wheeler, Pearcy Allen, Clare McIntyre, Fred W.Hall, Glen Smith, Garney Large, Jimmy MacPherson, Mac McCarthy.

Area: **OHA (Early Years)** Season: **1934 - 1935** Supervisor: Officials: ACTON: Gordon Huffman, ALVINSTON: R.Conner, S.Williams, Norman Trenouth, AMHERSTBURG: W.H.Timmins, Glen C.Hamilton, Jack R.Hamilton, ARTHUR: Dennis O'Neill, W.Reilly, AURORA: Lorne Lee, Ewart G.Pinder, Herb Holman, BARRIE: Clifford Jemmett, Gordon Meeking, Lou Vair, John Dobson, C.B.Brown, F.Rayner, BEAMSVILLE: Harry Reid, BELLEVILLE: W.Green, H.P.Holway, Leo Barrett, K.J.Colling, Allan Meagher, C.E.Thompson, BOBCAYGEON: George Johnson, BOLTON: Albert Kennedy, S.Cameron, O.J.Hardwick, W.Levans, BOWMANVILLE: H.Osborne, J.Chartrand, Gordon Chartrand, W.A.Edgar, M.Breslin, BRACEBRIDGE: Elmer E.Line, Earl Walker, Murt Dunn, Russell E.Salmon, BRADFORD: C.Evans, BRAMPTON: Howard Teasdale, Jack Burrill, BRANTFORD: Earl Balkwill, StanleyVerner, W.E.Jackson, M.Cinnamon, Albert V.Amos, BURLINGTON: H.E.Sheppard, E.E.Summers, E.W.Smith, CALEDONIA: John Morrison, Ken Baird, CAMPBELLFORD: Frank Whitton, Fred Ingram, Perry Saunders, Charles Holmes, Clifford Weston, B.Whilton, Ken Davis, CAYUGA: Tony Murphy, CHATHAM: Red Curran, Roy Reynolds, CHESLEY: J.C.McDonald, H.C.Blohm, CLINTON: John Nediger, Douglas Kennedy, Carl Draper, R.McEwen, Doug Thorndike, Grant Rath, Cecil Van Horne, COBOURG: Kent Payne, John Lloyd, Clarence Thompson, COLDWATER: Wilfrid Manning, COLLINGWOOD: Josh Belcher, Edgar Fryer, W.G.Robinson, DUNNVILLE: E.G.Hastings, J.W.Edwards, George Karges, Tex White, DURHAM: E.R.Shultz,

R.L.Saunders, A.C.Clements, ELMIRA: H.O.Weichel, A.Seiling, ELORA: D.A.Houston, Robert Fisher, Alex Karges, George Hills, FENEON FALLS: Max Aldous, FERGUS: Elmer Lovell, FOREST: S.Newton, FORT ERIE: Stan Jackson, H.O.Taylor, Babe Bogardis, GALT: George Hines, Fred George, A.R.Oliver, GANANOQUE: H.McCartney, Arthur Robertson, Ian Beresford, Kenneth Lasha, GEORGETOWN: A.Duncan, P.F.Blackburn, Lakefield Ford, H.Tost, H.Scott, GODERICH: H.Murney, P.Oliver, Pete Turner, M.Wark, Harold Murphy, Donald McKay, GRAVENHURST: Wm Christenson, Roy Christenson, Bruce Findlay, GRIMSBY: Dad Farrell, Les Farrell, John R.McVicar, Harry Reid, GUELPH: Earl Brill, Johnny Jones, H.Sparling, Dick Carroll, HAGERSVILLE: Maurice Winger, Maynard Slack, Percy Hoag, Dr.Harry Whitehead, Ken Lampman, Karl Davidson, HAMILTON: Johnny Mitchell, Gordon McKay, Percy LeSueur, George Redding, Jack Beemer, H.A.Quinney, Tony Murphy, W.Dunkerly, Leo Reise, Tom Moore, A.R.Galbraith, Pat Maloney, W.R.Towns, Jack Worthy, HARRISTON: Lawson Burrow, John D.Ward, HUNTSVILLE: B.Ganton, Hermaan Cole, Ray Ball, Gene Fraser, KINGSTON: C.Devlin, Joe L.Smith, R.Dougall, A.Casterton, Fred Brown, William Watts, Ab Stinson, Jas P.Walsh, F.Bellringer, KITCHENER: Jack Hemphill, Paddy Farrell, Ted Hillman, Nels Siebert, Jack White, Ike Masters, Maurice Schnarr, Bobby Fellbaum, LAKEFIELD: John Sabatino, Braden Blewett, LINDSAY: Buster Martin, Everett Reeves, Leo Begley, H.Rogers, LONDON: James Haldane, Gordon Donaldson, Scottie Bruce, Tom Munro, W,H,Legg, W.Starkings, Bob Armstrong, Pick Hines Gregg House, MADOC: James Watson, Tom Rupert, MARKDALE: C.Burnside, H.H.mercer, MARKHAM: Dr.R.G.Cowie, P.M.Reesor, Pete Reesor, MEAFORD: Ernest Smith, MIDLAND: Clarence Simpson, Alfred Brodeur, MILTON: H.V.Peacock, D.Brush, Clifford Houston, Dr.Beacock, MITCHELL: W.C.Thorne, D.Eizerman, Chas. Stoneman, NAPANEE: E.Watts, Ray Wilson, Fred Bently, NEW HAMBURG: R.C.Puddicombe, H.Grundenburger, W.Bowman, Hap Hamel, NEWMARKET: W.B.Epworth, C.Harman, Fred Thompson, Bob Peters, NIAGARA FALLS: James Smeaton, George Pennie, W.Prestia,

OAKVILLE: Dr. Deans, ORILLIA: Norm Cook, George Ross, ORONO: C.M.Bresln, OSHAWA: A.M.Armstrong, Ed Mulligan, W.S.Hancock, OWEN SOUND: W.Garbutt, Albert Whinfield, Alvin Moore, PAISLEY: George Grant, Orville Burns, PALMERSTON: J.R.Auld, J.Barton,W.R.Johnston, R.E.Root, PARIS: Russell Sandercock, PENETANG: Bert Corbeau, PETERBORO: Walter Jackson, Ray Rose, M.Board, Grover Halpin, Cliff Houston, PETROLIA: L.Gleason, PORT COLBORNE: George Hudson, Frank Smith, A.P.McAvoy, Jack Cuthbert, William Mountain, PORT DOVER: J.J.Parker, M.E.Gilbert, L.D.Kelly, J.McDonald, PORT ELGIN: David Wilson, PORT HOPE: J.Rowden Stanley Crossett, Royland Jex, Alex Hills, PRESTON: Charles Talbot, Lionel Arnott, Buck Bowman, Stan Miers, Cecil Mader, SARNIA: N.Perry, Howard Jenkin, Roy Brown, SEAFORTH: G.Muir, A.W.Dick, S.Ronnie, Cecil Van Horne, F.Bullard, Russell Holmes, SIMCOE: Elmer V.Ramey, Jack Barrett, Russell Oatman, C.E.Watts, ST CATHARINES: Joe Chatteron, Bruce Burns, I.M.V.Corrigan, George Hastle, Borden Armstrong, A.A.Morrisson, STAYNER: Clarence Wood, SCARBORO: W.J.Davis, STIRLING: C.E.Thompson, STRATFORD: William Easson, Reg Reid, Charles Lightfoot, H.W.Jamieson, Chick Appel, Walter Kelterborn, E.B.Norfolk, Jack McCully, STRATHROY: C.S.Wilkie, THORNHILL: J.O.Oliver, TILLSONBURG: Delos Hicks, TRENTON: A.Mitchell, C.R.Heeney, Charles Allore, Harold Bleakely, Ross Burtt, Rube Schensel, TWEED: Sam Currie, Jim Quinn, UXBRIDGE: Bun Willis, WALKERTON: Joseph Raybold, Harris B.Rife, F.C.Sherrer, WALKERVILLE: W.Y.Shaw, Herb Smith, WATFORD: Norman Trenouth, M.McIntosh, WELLAND: George Falls, William Davis, WHITBY: Bert Smith, Charles Laverty, Clarry Rice, WIARTON: Allan Ashley, Fred Gildner, WINDSOR: Paddy Farrell, Puss Traub, Robert Foote, Glenn Smith, A.W.Bruce, Frank McGuire, WINGHAM: H.C.MacClean, H.Summers, A.Lockeridge, WOODSTOCK: Harry King, Chilton Childs, Dr.Douglas, A.Parker, WOODVILLE: Alex Cameron, WATERFORD: Nelson Govelock, TORONTO: R.W.Hewitson, M.J.Rodden, Dr.Frank McCurry, A.Mollenhauer J.R.Tackaberry, Eddie Rodden, Bert Clayton, Ernie Wortley, Louis Walker,

Harold Farlow, Charley Delahay, Bert McCaffery, Norm Albert, Vern Forbes, W.A.Dawson, N.Lamport, Jock Bennett, Harry Meeking, E.J.Collett, Jerry Denoird, E.C.Johnston, George Ewens, W.J.Buchanan, Dutch Cain, J.K.Wheeler, F.E.Horton, H.J.Walker, F.G.Cubbidge, C.H.johnston, H.G.Peacock, George Coulter, J.D.Christie, Tracy Shaw, Harold Frost, Percy Topping, Frank Sullivan, W.J.Walshe, Ralph Adams, Mac McCarthy, Corbett Denneny, Gus Ryder, W.graham, Bert Hedges, Bab Dye, Douglas Lough, Doug Smith, H.A.Dixon, Herb Gibbs, Lou Walker, Robert Armstrong

Area: **OHA (Early Years)** Season: **1933 - 1934** Supervisor: Officials: ACTON: Gordon Huffman, ALVINSTON: R.Connor, S.Williams, AMHERSTBURG: W.H.Timmis, C.Hamilton, Jack R.Hamilton, ARTHUR: Dennis O'Neill, W.Reilly, AURORA: lorne Lee, Ewart G.Pinder, BARRIE: Clifford Jemmett, Gordon Meeking, Lou Vair, John Dobson, BEAMSVILLE: Harry Reid, BELLEVILLE: W.Green, H.P.Holoway, Leo Barrett, K.J.Colling, Allan Meager, BOBCAYGEON: George Johnson, BOLTON: Albert Kennedy, S.Cameron, BOWMANVILLE: W.A.Edger, Gordon Chartrand, H.Osborne, Jumbo Chartrand, BRACEBRIDGE: Elmer E.Line, Earl Walker, Murt Dunn, BRADFORD: C.Evans, BRAMPTON: Howard Teasdale, Jack Burrill, BRANTFORD: Earl Balkwill, Stanley Verner, W.E.Jackson, M.Cinnamon, BURLINGTON: H.E.Sheppard, E.E.Summers, CALEDONIA: Ken Baird, CAMP BORDEN: Capt H.Gill, CAMPBELLFORD: Frank Whitton, Fred Ingram, Perry Saunders, Charlie Holmes, Clifford Weston, CAYUGA: Tony Murphy, CHATHAM: Red Curran, Roy Renolds, CHESLEY: J.C.McDonald, H.C.Blohm, CLINTON: John Nediger, Douglas Kennedy, Carl Draper, R.McEwen, COBOURG: Kent Payne, John Lloyd, Clarence Thompson Blake Street, COLDWATER: Wilfrid Manning, COLLINGWOOD: Josh Bilcher, Ernie Fryer, W.G.Robinson, DUNDAS: J.E.Lesage, DUNDALK: Charles Murcar, DUNNVILLE: E.G.Hastings, J.W.Edwards, George Karges, Tex White, DURHAM: E.R.Schultz, R.L.Saunders, A.C.Clements, ELMIRA: H.O.Weichel, A.Seiling, ELORA: D.A.Houston, Robert Fisher, Alex Karges, George Hills,

FENELON FALLS: Max Aldous, FERGUS: Elmer Lovell, FOREST: S.Newton, FORT ERIE: Stan Jackson, H.O.Taylor, GALT: George Himes, A.R.Oliver, GANANOQUE: H,McCartney, GEORGETOWN: A.Duncan, P.F.Blackburn, Lakefield Ford, H.Tost, GODERICH: H.Murney, P.Oliver, Pete Turner, M.Wark, GRAVENHURST: Wm Christerson, Roy Christenson, GRIMSBY: Dad Farrell, Les Farrell, GUELPH: Earl Brill, Johnny Jones, H.Sparling, HAGERSVILLE: Maurice Winger, Maynard Slack, PercyHoag, Dr Harry Whitehead, HAMILTON: Johnny Mitchell, Gordon McKay, Percy LeSueur, George Redding, Jack Beemer, H.A.Quinney, Tony Murphy, W.Dunkerley, Leo Reese, Tom moore, A.R.Galbraith, Pat Maloney, W.R.Towns, HARRISTON: Lawson Burrow, John D.Ward, HENSALL: R.Shoddick, KINGSTON: C.Devlin, R.Boyer, N.Derry, Joe Smith, R.Dougall, A,Casteron, Tim Brennan, Fred Brown, William Watts, Ab Stinson, KITCHENER: Jack Hemphill, Paddy Farrell, Ted Hillman, Nels Siebert, Jack White, Maurice Schnarr, Bobby Fellbaum, LAKEFIELD: John Sabatino, Braden Blewett, LINDSAY: Buster Martin, Everett Reeves, Leo Begley, LONDON: James Haldane, Gordon Donaldson, Scottie Bruce, Tom Munro, W.H.Legg, W.Starkings, B.Armstrong, Pick Hines, Gregg House, MADOC: James Watson, Tom Rupert, MARKDALE: C.Burnside, H.H.Mercer, MARKHAM: Dr R.G.Cowie, P.M.Reesor, Pete Reesor, MIDLAND: Clarence Simpson, Stan Burgoyne, MILTON: H.V.Peacock, D.Brush, Clifford Houston, Dr Babcock, MITCHELL: W.C.Thorne, D.Elizerman, L.Sawyer, NAPANEE: E.Watts, NEW HAMBURG: R.C.Puddicombe, H.Grundenberger, W.Bowman, Hap Hamel, NEWMARKET: W.B.Epworth, C.Harman, Fred Thompson, NIAGARA FALLS: James Smeaton, George Pennie, W.Prestia, OAKVILLE: Dr Deans, ORILLIA: Norm Cook, George Ross, ORONO: M.Breslin, OSHAWA: A.M.Armstrong, Ed Mulligan, OWEN SOUND: W.Garbutt, Albert Whinfield, Alvin Moore, PAISLEY: George Grant, Orville Burns, PALMERSTON: J.R.Auld, J.Barton, W.R.Johnston, R.E.Root, PARIS: Russell Sandercock, PENETANG: Bert Corbeau, PETERBORO: Walter Jackson, Ray Rose, M.Board, Grover Halpin, PETROLIA:

L.Gleason, PORT COLBORNE: George Hudson, Frank Smith, A.P.McAvoy, Jack Cuthbert, PORT DOVER: J.J.Parker, M.E.Gilbert, L.D.Kelly, PORT ELGIN: David Wilson, PORT HOPE: J.Rowden, Stanley Crossett, Royland Jex, PRESTON: Charles taylor, Lionel Arnott, Buck Bowman, SARNIA: N.Perry, SEAFORTH: G.Muir, A.W.Dick, S.Ronnie, F.Bullard, SIMCOE: Elmer V.Ramey, Jack Barrett, Russell Oatman, ST CATHARINES: Joe Chatteron, Bruce Burns, I.M.V.Corrigan, STAYNER: Clarence Wood, STIRLING: C.E.Thompson, STRATFORD: William Easson, Reg Reid, Charles Lightfoot, H.W.Jamieson, Chick Appel, Walter Keiterborn, E.B.Norfolk, STRATHROY: C.S.Wilkie, THORNHILL: J.O.Oliver, TILLSONBURG: Delos Hicks, TRENTON: H.A.Mitchell, C.R.Heaney, Charles Allore, Harold Bleakley, Ross Burtt, Rube Schensel, TWEED: Sam currie, UXBRIDGE: Bun Willis, WALKERTON: Joseph Raybould, Harris S.Rife, F.C.Sherrer, WALKERVILLE: W.Y.Shaw, WATFORD: Norman Trenouth, M.McIntosh, WELLAND: George Falles, Wm Davis, WELLESLEY: Elwood Foulhafer, WESTON: Lorne Bartlett, E.G.Farr, WHITBY: Bert Smith, Charles Lavery, Clarry Rice, WIARTON: Allan Ashley, Fred Gilder, WINDSOR: Paddy Farrell, Puss Traub, Robert Foote, Glenn Smith, A.W.Bruce, WINGHAM: H.C.MacLean, WOODSTOCK: Harry King, Chilton Childs, Dr Douglas, A.Parker, ZURICH: L.O'Brien, TORONTO: R.W.Hewitson, M.J.Rodden, Harry Watson, Dr Frank McCurry, Lou E.Marsh, Jack Tackaberry, Gordon Mitchell, A,Mollenhauer, Eddie Rodden, Bert Clayton, Ernie Wortley, Steve Vair, Loius Walker, Harold Farlow, Charley Delahey, Bert McCaffrey, Norman B.Albert, Vern Forbes, W.A.Dawson, Norman Lamport, Jack Cameron, Jock Bennett, Harry Meeking, J.Douglas Thorndike, C.E.Thompson, E.J.Collett, Jerry Deniord, E.C.Johnston, George Ewens, W.J.Buchanan, Dutch Cain, J.K.Wheeler, F.E.Horton, H.J.Walker, F.G.Cubbidge, C.H.Johnston, H.G.Peacock, George Coulter, J.D.Christie, Tracy Shaw, Harold Frost, Percy Topping, Frank Sullivan, Gordon Mitchell, W.J.Walshe, Ralph Adams, Mac McCarthy, Gus Ryder, W.Graham, Bob Armstrong, Bert Hedges, Ross Paul.

Area: **OHA (Early Years)** Season: **1932 - 1933**
Supervisor: Officials: AURORA: Ewart G.Pinder, ARTHUR: Dennis O'Neill, W.Reilly, AMHERSTBURG: W.H.Timmis, Glen C.Hamilton, Jack R.Hamilton, ACTON: Gordon Huffman, BELLEVILLE: W.Green, H.H.Jacobs, H.P.Holway, Leo Barrett, K.J.Colling, Allan Meager, BARRIE: Clifford Jemmett, Gordon Meeking, Ernie Thompson, Lou Vair, John Dobson, BOBCAYGEON: G.W.Johnson, BRANTFORD: Earl Balkwill, Stanley Verner, W.E.Jackson, M.Cinnamon, BOWMANVILLE: W.A.Edger, Gordon Chartrand, BEAMSVILLE: Harry Reid, BRAMPTON: Jack Burrell, H.J.Teasdale, BRACEBRIDGE: Earl Walker, Murt Dunn, Bud Fisher, BURLINGTON: H.E.Sheppard, E.E.Summers, BOLTON: Albert Kennedy, S.Cameron, COLLINGWOOD: Josh Bilcher, Ernie Fryer, W.G.Robinson, COLDWATER: Wilfrid Manning, CAP BORDEN: Capt H.Gill, CAMPBELLFORD: Frank Whitton, Fred Ingram, Perry Saunders, Charlie holmes, Clifford Weston, CLINTON: John Nediger, Douglas Kennedy, Carl Draper, COBOURG: Clarence E.Thompson, CHATHAM: Red Curran, Roy Reynolds, Pick Hines, CAYUGA: Tony Murphy, CHESLEY: J.C.McDonald, H.C.Blohm, CALEDONIA: Ken Baird, DUNDAS: J.E.Lesage, DURHAM: E.R.Schultz, R.L.Saunders, A.C.Clements, DUNNVILLE: E.G.Hastings, J.W.Edwards, George Karges, Tex White, DUNDALK: Charles Murcar, ELMIRA: H.O.Weichel, A.Seiling, ELORA: D.A.Houston, Robert Fisher, Alex Karges, George Hills, EXETER: Goldie Cochrane, Dick Shaddoe, Leroy O'Brien, FERGUS: Elmer Lovell, FENELON FALLS: Max Aldous, FORT ERIE: Stan Jackson, Garney Lderman, H.O.Taylor, GALT: A.R.Oliver, Fred George, GODERICH: H.Murney, P.Oliver, Pete Turner, GEORGETOWN: A.Duncan, P.F.Blackburn, Lakefield Ford, H.Tost, GRIMSBY: Dr.James Robson, C.A.Dad Farrell, Robert Hillier, Les Farrell, GANANOQUE: H.McCartney, GUELPH: Earl Brill, Johnny Jones, GRAVENHURST: Wm.Christenson, Roy Christenson, HARRISTON: Lawson Burrow, John D.Ward, HUNTSVILLE: Ernie Doyle, HAGERSVILLE: Maurice Winger, Maynard Slack, Percy Hoag, HAMILTON: Gordon McKay, Johnny Mitchell, Percy LeSueur, George Redding, Jack Beemer, H.A.Quinney, Tony Murphy, W.Dunkerley,

Leo Reese,, Tom Moore, A.R.Galbraith, Pat Maloney, INGERSOLL: Jack Cross, KINGSTON: J.A.Casterton, Roy Dougall, W.Watts, T.Brennan, Joe Smith, C.Devlin, KITCHENER: Paddy Farrell, Ted Hillman, Nels Siebert, Maurice Schnaar, Jack White, LINDSAY: Elwood Coombs, Leo Begley, LONDON: James Haldane, Gordon Donaldson, Scottie Bruce, Tom Munro, W.H.Legg, W.Starkings, MILTON: H.V.Peacock, D.Brush, Dr.Babcock, MIDLAND: Dr.George Westman, C.German, MARKHAM: Dr.R.G.Cowie, P.M.Reesor, MARKDALE: C.Burnside, H.H.Mercer, MITCHELL: W.C.Thorne, D.Eizerman, MANILLA: Doug Thorndike, MADOC: James Watson, Tom Rupert, NAPANEE: E.Watts, NEWMARKET: W.B.Epworth, NEW HAMBURG: R.C.Puddicombe, H.Grundenberger, W.Bowman, Hap Hamel, NIAGARA FALLS: James Smeaton, George Pennie, W.Prestia, OWEN SOUND: W.Garbutt, Albert Whinfield, OAKVILLE: Dr.Deans, OSHAWA: A.M.Armstrong, Ed Muligan, ORILLIA: Norm Cook, George Ross, Ken McNabb, PORT COLBORNE: A.H.Jamieson, W.Francis Moore, Frank Smith, A.P.McAvoy, PRESTON: Charles Talbot, Lionel Arnott, Buck Bowman, PARIS: Russell sandercock, PALMERSTON: J.R.Auld, J.Barton, W.R.Johnston, R.E.Root, PETERBORO: W.A.Jackson, PENETANG: O.L.Dubeau, PORT HOPE: John Rowden, PORT DOVER: J.J.Parker, M.E.Gilbert, L.D.Kelly, ROUGE HILLS: E.C.johnston, SARNIA: Harry Prout, Norman Geary, ST MARY'S: L.Lavelle, R.Tuer, SUDBURY: Alex McKinnon, STRATFORD: William Easson, Reg Reid, Charles Lightfoot, H.W.Jamieson, Chick Appel, Walter Kelterborn, E.b.Norfolk, STAYNER: Clarence Wood, SEAFORTH: Nelson Govenlock, A.W.Dick, Dalton Reid, ST CATHARINES: J.B.Burns, SIMCOE: Elmer V.Ramey, Jack Barrett, STIRLING: C.E.Thompson, STRATHROY: C.S.Wilkie, TRENTON: C.R.Heaney, Charles Allore, Harold Bleakely, Ross Burtt, Rube Schensel, TILLSONBURG: Delos Hicks, THORNHILL: J.O.Oliver, WALKERTON: Joseph Rayboud, Harris S.Rife, F.C.Sherrer, WIARTON: Allan Ashley, WINDSOR: Puss Traub, Robert Foote, Glenn Smith, A.W.Bruce, Pick hines, WOODSTOCK: Harry King, Chilton Childs, Dr.Douglas, A.Parker, WINGHAM: H.C.MacLean,

WELLAND: George Falles, Wm Davis, WELLESLEY: Elwood Foulhafer, WESTON: Lorne Barlett, E.G.Farr, WATFORD: N.Trenouth, L.E.Harper, WALKERVILLE: W.Y.Shaw, WHITBY: Bert Smith, Charles Lavery, Clarry Rice, WATERLOO: Jack Hemphill, Ernie Parkes, Honey Kuntz, TORONTO: Norman Albert, Norman Lamport, Alf Skinner, Frank J.McCurry, Art Smith, Ernie Wortley, Ross Paul, Corbett Denneray, Gerald Deniord, J.A.Wood, Jesse Spring, Harold Frost, M.J.Rodden, Frank Allen, Lou E,Marsh, E.A.Bennett, Doug Smith, Gordon Mitchell, Jack Christie, Jack Cain, A.Mollenhauer, Harry Meeking, Harry Watson, Frank Sullivan, Bert Burry, W.Graham, Lou Walker, Harold Farlow, H.G.Peacock, Milton Burt, W.J.Walshe, Ralph Adams, Stan Burgoyne, T.P.(Perc)Topping, D.Pollock, Mac McCarthy, Tracy Shaw Eric Leckley, Gordon Grant, Bert Hedges, Lou LeBarr, E.C.Johnston, E.J.Collett, Bob Armstrong, E.H.Goudie, Len Cook, Jack Tackaberry

Area: **OHA (Early Years)** Season: **1931 - 1932** Supervisor: Officials: ARTHUR: Joseph Pindergast, James C.O'Neill, AMHERSTBURG: W.H.Timmis, C.Hamilton, Ed Eckert, BOWMANVILLE: W.A.Edger, BLENHEIM: Harry Riseborough, BRACEBRIDGE: Earl Walker, Dr.L.N.Ryan, BRAMPTON: Jack Burell, S.R.Dennis, H.J.Teasdale, BELLEVILLE: Vernon Weir, C.E.Thompson, W.D.Green, Leo Barrett, Ken Colling, Harry Drew, Claude Tice, BURLINGTON: Elmer E.Summers, H.C.Sheppard, BRANTFORD: Stanley Verner, Earl Balkwin, BARRIE: Gordon Meeking, C.Jemmett, Lou Vair, CANNINGTON: Hugh Wilson, CALEDONIA: Ken Baird, COLLINGWOOD: J.Belcher, Walter Robinson, CLINTON: Caryl Draper, CAMPBELLFORD: C.S.Weston, Jack Cowell, CAYUGA: Thomas McSorley, Tony Murphy, COBOURG: Ken Payne, CHATHAM: Glen Crouchmon, J.E.Curren, Henry Blackwell, Roy Reynolds, R.E.Smalley, DURHAM: R.L.Saunders, Clarence McGirr, DUNNVILLE: J.W.Edwards, George Karges, DUNDAS: J.E.Lesage, ELORA: D.A.Houston, Bob fisher, Alex Karges, George Hillis, EXETER: Goldie Cochrane, R.H.Sayers, FENELON FALLS: Max Aldons, FERGUS: Elmer Lovell, GALT: Fred

George, Reid Oliver, GODERICH: P.Turner, GRIMSBY: Robert Hillier, Dad Farrell, GRAVENHURST: W.B.Findlay, Roy Christenson, GEORGETOWN: Angus Duncan, H.Ford, GUELPH: Johnny Jones, Sandy Little, HAMILTON: Fred (Beano) Wright, William Dunkerly, W.A.H.Sparling, Johnny Mitchell, Ivan W.Girvani, Gordon McKay, J.Worthy, A,K.Galbraith, Percy Lesuer, HARRISTON: L.H.(Doc) Burrows, HAGERSVILLE: Maurice Winger, HUNTSVILLE: W.N.MacDonald, Andrew Kellock Jr, KITCHENER: Tee Hillman, Nelson Seibert, Werner Schnaar, KINGSTON: H.Hartley, R.Dougall, Art Purdy, Clair Devlin, Harry Batstone, Jos Smith, LISTOWEL: Cully Rocher, F.W.Kemp, B.McIntyre, LINDSAY: Elwood Coombs, LONDON: Gordon Donaldson, Tom Munro, Fred Ollson, Wm Starkings, Scottie Bruce, W.H.Legg, LAKEFIELD: John Sabatino, MEAFORD: George Long, MILVERTON: Gordon Meyer, Wilot Kelterbord, MANILLA: Doug Thorndike, MIDLAND: Clarence Simpson, MILTON: Cliff Houston, D.Brush, MITCHELL: W.C.Thorne, D.Eigerman, NEW HAMBURG: Herb Hamel, R.Puddicombe, H.W.Grundenberg, NEWMARKET: E.A.Doyle, H.B.Epworth, NIAGARA FALLS: George Pennie, Victor Prestia, Arthur Kinghorn, OAKVILLE: Dr.F.M.Deans, Arthur Hillmer, ORILLIA: Norman Cooke, OWEN SOUND: Alex MacIntyre, William Rogers, OSHAWA: Harvey Lott, R.W.Armstrong, PETERBORO: Walter Jackson, J.O.Kennaley, Lewis LeBarr, B.E.Park, Maxwell Board, PARIS: Russell Sandercock, PALMERSTON: James Auld, Walter Barton, PORT HOPE: J.Rowden, PRESTON: Charles Talbot, Lionel Arnott, Buck Bowman, A.T.Kinder, PORT COLBORNE: Frank Smith, F.W.Moore, PORT DOVER: M.Gilbert, J.Parker, PARRY SOUND: Fred Thompson, STAYNER: Clarnece Woods, Ike Moore, STRATFORD: William Easson, N.Norfolk, J.McCully, C.Lightfoot, Chic Appel, SUDBURY: George A.Duncan, SANDWICH: Paddy Farrell, SIMCOE: Elmer Ramey, J.Barrett, H.Evans, Laurence Kelly, STRATHROY: C.S.Wilkie, SEAFORTH: Artie Dick, TRENTON: Ross Burtt, Charles Allore, WHITBY: Bert Smith, C.Rice, WALKERVILLE: Sid Rankin, WATERLOO: Ernie Parkes, Jack Hemphill, Honey Kuntz, WAKERTON: Bernard Scheerer, WINDSOR: Ivan Corrigan, Puss Traub,

WOODSTOCK: Harry King, Dr.Norman Douglas, Chilton Childs, Doug Marshall, TORONTO: M.J.Rodden, Rogers Plaxton, Tracy Shaw, W.J.Walshe, Stewart Ferguson, Ross Paul, Jack Christie, H.H.Jacobi, Harry Meeking, J.A.Dick, Bert Hedges, Jack Cameron, Thos Gaye, Bob Armstrong, Harry Watson, D.F.Pollock, Lawson Whitehead, Herb Matthews, Fred Denning, Frank Sullivan, Steve Rice, Gordon Mitchell, Ernie Wortley, J.A.Wood, Fred Heintzman, Harold Farlow, Clare Hoose, Gus Ryder, A.A.Mollenhauer, H.A.Applegath, Herb gibbs, Mac McCarthy, Ernie Collett, W.Graham, Corbett Dennenay, W.G.Bell, L.W.Chambers, Len Cook, Lou Walker, Norman Albert, T.P.Topping, Lou Carrell, Gerald Deniord, Graham Peacock, Harold frost, E.A.Bennett, James McFadyen, Fred Rose, Jesse Spring,

Area: **OHA (Early Years)** Season: **1929 - 1930** Supervisor: Officials: AYR: James O.Oliver, AMHERSTBURG: W.H.Timmis, AURORA: Dr E. Underhill, BELLEVILLE: K.J.Colling, William Green, BOBCAYGEON: G.W.Johnson, BRANTFORD: Earl Balkwill, Stanley Vener, BOWMANVILLE: W.A.Edger, Allan Campbell, BEAMSVILLE: Harry Reid, BRAMPTON: Jack Burrell, H.J.Teasdale, BRACEBRIDGE: Earl Walker, Murt Dunn, BARRIE: Lou Vair, Jack Armstrong, Bus Clarke, BURLINGTON: H.E.Sheppard, BOLTON: Albert Kennedy, CLINTON: J.D.Thorndike, COBOURG: Clarence E.Thompson, COLLINGWOOD: J.John Belcher, Lawrence Cain, CHATHAM: Roy Reynolds, CAYUGA: H.K.Parson, CHESLEY: J.C.McDonald, H.C.Blohm, COLDWATER: E.Rawson, CALEDONIA: Ken Baird, DURHAM: R.L.Saunders, A.C.Clements, DUNNVILLE: L.H.Burrows, J.A.H.Jamieson, DUNDALK: Charles Murcar, ELMIRA: H.O.Weichel, ELORA: Robert Fisher, Alex Karges, George Hills, EXETER: Goldie Cochrane, FERGUS: Elmer Lovell, GALT: Fred George, A.R.Oliver, GODERICH: N.P.Flarity, Ed Merklinger, B.Chase, H.Murney, GEORGETOWN: Dr A.Duncan, P.F.Blackburn, GRIMSBY: Dr James Robson, C.O. (Dad) Farrell, GANANOQUE: H.McCarney, GUELPH: Earl Brill, Johnny Jones, Sandy Little, GRAVENHURST: Wm Christenson, Roy Christenson, HAMILTON: John Mitchell, Gordon McKay, Dr Charlie Stewart, Guy Smith,

Tony Murphy, HAGERSVILLE: Murphy Slack, INGERSOLL: Joseph Richardson, HARRISTON: John D.Ward, KINGSTON: Harry Batstone, Chick Mundell, A.Brouse, Clare Devlin, J.Smith, H.Nicholson, Prof J.F.Gelley, Bubs Britton, KITCHENER: T.G.Hillman, Isaac Masters, George Karges, Dr Robert Ferguson, Jack Hemphill, Nelson Seibert, LISTOWEL: Cully Rocher, B.L.Bamford, LONDON: D.R.Mallen, GERALD Goodman, W.H.Legg, J.George Arthurs, J.A.Greer, Charles Slater, O.L.Gendron, Milton Burt, MIDLAND: Capt Clarence Simpson, LINDSAY: Elwood Coombs, Charles Board, MOUNT FOREST: E.Murphy, MILVERTON: W.J.Kelterborn, Gordon Meyer, MILTON: H.V.Peacock, D.Brush, MIDLAND: Dr George Westman, C.German, MARKHAM: Dr R.G.Cowie, P.M.Reesor, MARKDALE: C.Burnside, H.H.Mercer, MITCHELL: W.C.Thorne, D.Eizerman, NAPANEE: E.Watts, NEW HAMBURG: Harry Grundenberger, R.C.Puddicombe, Walter Bowman, Leslie Bowman, Newmarket: W.B.Epworth, NIAGARA FALLS: George Pennie, ORILLIA: P.L.Thompson, Frank Doyle, Norman Cook, OSHAWA: Jack Bond, Sam Lowe, A,H,Kincaid, OAKVILLE: Dr.F.M.Deans, OWEN SOUND: Ambrose Whinfield, PARIS: P.S.Gill, Ernie Doyle, Russell, Sandercock, PAISLEY: George Grant, PORT ROWAN: Fred McMillan, J.J.Parker, M.E.Gilbert, PORT HOPE: John Rowden, PETERBORO: B.E.Park, J.O.Kennaley, William E.Jackson, Walter Jackson, Maxwell Board, Lewis LeBarr, K.Collings, PORT CREDIT: H.C.Thompson, PALMERSTON: W.R.Johnston, G.A.Laurence, PRESTON: Buck Bowman, A,H.Schlegel, Charles Talbot, ST MARY'S: L.Lavelle, R.Tuer, SUDBURY: Alex McKinnon, STRATFORD: William Easson, Reg Reid, Charles Lightfoot, H.W.Jamieson, STAYNER: Clarence Wood, SEAFORTH: Nelson Govenlock, A,W.Dick, I.L.Reid, SIMCOE: Elmer V.Ramey, STIRLING: C.E.Thompson, STRATHROY: C.S.Wilkie, TRENTON: C.R.Heaney, TAVISTOCK: Chick Appel, TILLSONBURG: Delan Hicks, WALKERTON: Joseph Raybould, WIARTON: Allan Ashley, WATERLOO: Leo Quinn, WINDSOR: Roy Hinsperger, Art Leaver, Brother Selvin, Red Curran, WOODSTOCK: Harry king, Chilton Child, WINGHAM: H.C.MacLean, WELLAND: T.H.Jones, Frank Lambert, WELLESLEY: Elwood Foulhafer,

WESTON: Lorne Barlett, E.G.Farr, WATFORD: N.Trenouth, F.R.Rogers, WALKERVILLE: W.Y.Shaw, WHITBY: bert Smith, Charles Lavery, TORONTO: Ernie Parks, Dalt A.Lowry, M.J.Rodden, Rogers Plaxton, James Loftus, James McFadyen, Wally Hern, John Gallagher, Ernest Collett, H.B.Lockhart, Stuart Ferguson, Ed Chatfield, Fred Morrell, Robert Armstrong, Russell Henley, Bert Hedges, A.Mollenhauer, W.E.Stoddard, D.F.Pollock, Ernie Wortley, Norman Albert, Mac McCarthy, Harry Watson, Robert Hewitson, Ross Taylor, Jack Potter, Percy Lesueur, Gene Dupp, W.Lymn, W.J.Walshe, W.Graham, Frank Sullivan, Charles Delahey, Frank Fisher, Ross Paul, Gus Ryder, Vic Draper, Jock Bennett, Harold Farlow, H.H.Jacobi, Wally Taylor, W,Cumming, H.M.Townsend, Frank Knight, Thos Gaye, J.F.Gain, Roy Cheetham, H.Graham, W.A.Taylor, E.H.McCutcheon, Frank Allen, Tracy Shaw, J.M.McCluskey.

Area: **OHA (Early Years)** Season: **1929 - 1930** Supervisor: Officials: AYR: James O.Oliver, AMHERSTBURG: W.H.Timmis, AURORA: Dr E. Underhill, BELLEVILLE: K.J.Colling, William Green, BOBCAYGEON: G.W.Johnson, BRANTFORD: Earl Balkwill, Stanley Vener, BOWMANVILLE: W.A.Edger, Allan Campbell, BEAMSVILLE: Harry Reid, BRAMPTON: Jack Burrell, H.J.Teasdale, BRACEBRIDGE: Earl Walker, Murt Dunn, BARRIE: Lou Vair, Jack Armstrong, Bus Clarke, BURLINGTON: H.E.Sheppard, BOLTON: Albert Kennedy, CLINTON: J.D.Thorndike, COBOURG: Clarence E.Thompson, COLLINGWOOD: J.John Belcher, Lawrence Cain, CHATHAM: Roy Reynolds, CAYUGA: H.K.Parson, CHESLEY: J.C.McDonald, H.C.Blohm, COLDWATER: E.Rawson, CALEDONIA: Ken Baird, DURHAM: R.L.Saunders, A.C.Clements, DUNNVILLE: L.H.Burrows, J.A.H.Jamieson, DUNDALK: Charles Murcar, ELMIRA: H.O.Weichel, ELORA: Robert Fisher, Alex Karges, George Hills, EXETER: Goldie Cochrane, FERGUS: Elmer Lovell, GALT: Fred George, A.R.Oliver, GODERICH: N.P.Flarity, Ed Merklinger, B.Chase, H.Murney, GEORGETOWN: Dr A.Duncan, P.F.Blackburn, GRIMSBY: Dr James Robson, C.O. (Dad) Farrell, GANANOQUE: H.McCarney, GUELPH:

Earl Brill, Johnny Jones, Sandy Little, GRAVENHURST: Wm Christenson, Roy Christenson, HAMILTON: John Mitchell, Gordon McKay, Dr Charlie Stewart, Guy Smith, Tony Murphy, HAGERSVILLE: Murphy Slack, INGERSOLL: Joseph Richardson, HARRISTON: John D.Ward, KINGSTON: Harry Batstone, Chick Mundell, A.Brouse, Clare Devlin, J.Smith, H.Nicholson, Prof J.F.Gelley, Bubs Britton, KITCHENER: T.G.Hillman, Isaac Masters, George Karges, Dr Robert Ferguson, Jack Hemphill, Nelson Seibert, LISTOWEL: Cully Rocher, B.L.Bamford, LONDON: D.R.Mallen, GERALD Goodman, W.H.Legg, J.George Arthurs, J.A.Greer, Charles Slater, O.L.Gendron, Milton Burt, MIDLAND: Capt Clarence Simpson, LINDSAY: Elwood Coombs, Charles Board, MOUNT FOREST: E.Murphy, MILVERTON: W.J.Kelterborn, Gordon Meyer, MILTON: H.V.Peacock, D.Brush, MIDLAND: Dr George Westman, C.German, MARKHAM: Dr R.G.Cowie, P.M.Reesor, MARKDALE: C.Burnside, H.H.Mercer, MITCHELL: W.C.Thorne, D.Eizerman, NAPANEE: E.Watts, NEW HAMBURG: Harry Grundenberger, R.C.Puddicombe, Walter Bowman, Leslie Bowman, Newmarket: W.B.Epworth, NIAGARA FALLS: George Pennie, ORILLIA: P.L.Thompson, Frank Doyle, Norman Cook, OSHAWA: Jack Bond, Sam Lowe, A,H,Kincaid, OAKVILLE: Dr.F.M.Deans, OWEN SOUND: Ambrose Whinfield, PARIS: P.S.Gill, Ernie Doyle, Russell, Sandercock, PAISLEY: George Grant, PORT ROWAN: Fred McMillan, J.J.Parker, M.E.Gilbert, PORT HOPE: John Rowden, PETERBORO: B.E.Park, J.O.Kennaley, William E.Jackson, Walter Jackson, Maxwell Board, Lewis LeBarr, K.Collings, PORT CREDIT: H.C.Thompson, PALMERSTON: W.R.Johnston, G.A.Laurence, PRESTON: Buck Bowman, A,H.Schlegel, Charles Talbot, ST MARY'S: L.Lavelle, R.Tuer, SUDBURY: Alex McKinnon, STRATFORD: William Easson, Reg Reid, Charles Lightfoot, H.W.Jamieson, STAYNER: Clarence Wood, SEAFORTH: Nelson Govenlock, A,W.Dick, I.L.Reid, SIMCOE: Elmer V.Ramey, STIRLING: C.E.Thompson, STRATHROY: C.S.Wilkie, TRENTON: C.R.Heaney, TAVISTOCK: Chick Appel, TILLSONBURG: Delan Hicks, WALKERTON: Joseph Raybould, WIARTON: Allan Ashley, WATERLOO: Leo Quinn, WINDSOR: Roy Hinsperger, Art Leaver, Brother

Selvin, Red Curran, WOODSTOCK: Harry king, Chilton Child, WINGHAM: H.C.MacLean, WELLAND: T.H.Jones, Frank Lambert, WELLESLEY: Elwood Foulhafer, WESTON: Lorne Barlett, E.G.Farr, WATFORD: N.Trenouth, F.R.Rogers, WALKERVILLE: W.Y.Shaw, WHITBY: bert Smith, Charles Lavery, TORONTO: Ernie Parks, Dalt A.Lowry, M.J.Rodden, Rogers Plaxton, James Loftus, James McFadyen, Wally Hern, John Gallagher, Ernest Collett, H.B.Lockhart, Stuart Ferguson, Ed Chatfield, Fred Morrell, Robert Armstrong, Russell Henley, Bert Hedges, A.Mollenhauer, W.E.Stoddard, D.F.Pollock, Ernie Wortley, Norman Albert, Mac McCarthy, Harry Watson, Robert Hewitson, Ross Taylor, Jack Potter, Percy Lesueur, Gene Dupp, W.Lymn, W.J.Walshe, W.Graham, Frank Sullivan, Charles Delahey, Frank Fisher, Ross Paul, Gus Ryder, Vic Draper, Jock Bennett, Harold Farlow, H.H.Jacobi, Wally Taylor, W,Cumming, H.M.Townsend, Frank Knight, Thos Gaye, J.F.Gain, Roy Cheetham, H.Graham, W.A.Taylor, E.H.McCutcheon, Frank Allen, Tracy Shaw, J.M.McCluskey.

Area: **OHA (Early Years)** Season: **1928 - 1929** Supervisor: Officials: AMHERSTBERG: W.H.Timmis, AYR: James O.Oliver, BEAMSVILLE: Hatty N.Reid, BRAMPTON: James Burrell, Jack Burrell, H.J.Teasdale, J.O.Adams, BOWMANVILLE: W.A.Edgar, Allan Campbell, BROCKVILLE: A.A.Birks, E.C.Higgins, William Simmons, J.Sandercock, BRACEBRIDGE: Earl Walker, Murt Dunn, BARRIE: Lou Vair, Jack Armstrong, BRANTFORD: Stan Verner, Lawson White, BOLTON: Albert Kennedy, E.Ingram, BURLINGTON: H.E. Sheppard, COLDWATER: E.Rawson, CAYUGA: A.C.Murphy, W.Barry, B.J.Hammond, CHESLEY: J.C.McDonald, H.C.Blohm, CORNWALL: John Dennenay, R.Mallett, V.Silmser, COLLINGWOOD: John Belcher, Josh Belcher, Oscar Bernhardt, CALEDONIA: Ken Baird, CLINTON: J.D.Thorndike, G.R.Patterson, C.Draper, DURHAM: R.L.Saunders, A.C.Clements, DUNNVILLE: William McBrien, L.H.Burrows, Earl Knight, ELMIRA: A.Seiling, A.Allgier, ELORA: Robert Fisher, George Hills, Alex Karges, EXETER: Goldie Cochrane, DUTTON:

D.A.Houston, GALT: A.R.Oliver, W.Marsh Preston, GODERICH: Ed Merklinger, N.P.Flarity, GUELPH: J.Jones, Sandy Little, Nelson Henry, John Jones, GEORGETOWN: Wakefield Ford, A.Duncan, Roy F.King, GRIMSBY: C.O.(Dad) Farrell, GANANOQUE: H.McCarney, GRAVENHURST: Wm Christenson, Roy Christenson, HAMILTON: F.H.Duckett, F.R.Lishman, Guy Smith, Gordon McKey, James Stewart, Ernie Smith, George Walsh, HAGERSVILLE: Murphy Slack, INGERSOLL: Joseph Richardson, HARRISTON: John D.Ward, KINGSTON: Harry Batstone, Chick Mundell, A,Brouse, Clare Devlin, J.Smith, H.Nicholson, Prof J.F.Gelley, KITCHENER: T.G.Hillman, Isaac Masters, George Karges, Dr Robert Ferguson, Jack Hemphill, LISTOWEL: Cully Rocher, B.L.Bamford, LONDON: D.R.Mallen, Fred George, Gerald Goodman, Tom Munro, W.H.Legg, J.George Arthurs, Sid Rankin, J.A.Greer, Charles Slater, O.L.Gendron, LINDSAY: Elwood Coombs, Charles Board, MOUNT FOREST: E.Murphy, MILVERTON: W.J.Kelterborn, Earl Meyers, MORRISBURG: Ken Mallen, MILTON: H.V.Peacock, D.Brush, MIDLAND: Capt Clarence Simpson, Dr George Westman, C.German, MARKHAM: Dr R.G.Cowie, P.M.Reesor, MARKDALE: C.Burnside, H.H.Mercer, MITCHELL: W.C.Thorne, D.Eizerman, NIAGARA FALLS: George Pennie, NEW HAMBURG: R.C.Puddicombe, Walter Bowman, Leslie Bowman, ORILLIA: P.L.Thompson, Frank Doyle, Norman Cook, OSHAWA: Jack Bond, Sam Lowe, OAKVILLE: Dr F.M.Deans, OWEN SOUND: Ambrose Whinfield, PAISLEY: George Grant, PORT HOPE: John Rowden, PETERBORO: William E.Jackson, Walter Jackson, Maxwell Board, PORT CREDIT: H.C.Thompson, PALMERSTON: Charles Murcar, W.R.Johnston, G.A.Lawrence, PRESTON: Buck Bowman, A.H.Schlegel, SARNIA: H.B.Crouchman, ST MARY'S: L.Lavelle, R.Tuer, STRATFORD: William Easson, Reg Reid, Charles Lightfoot, H.W.Jamieson, STAYNER: Clarence Wood, SEAFORTH: Nelson Govenlock, A.W.Dick, SIMCOE: Elmer V.Ramey, STIRLING: Clarence E.Thompson, TRENTON: C.R.Heaney, TAVISTOCK: Chick Appel, WALKERTON: Joseph Raybould, Harris S.Rife, WIARTON: Allan Ashley, WATERLOO: Leo Quinn, WINDSOR: Roy

Hinsperger, W.Y.Shaw, Art Leaver, Brother Selvin, WOODSTOCK: Harry King, Chilton Childs, WINGHAM: H.C.MacLean, WELLAND: T.H.Jones, Frank Lambert, George Forbes, WESTON: Lorne Barlett, E.G.Farr, WATFORD: N.Trenouth, F.R.Rogers, WALKERVILLE: W.Y.Shaw, Sid Rankin, WHITBY: Bert Smith, Charles Lavery, TORONTO: Lou E.Marsh, M.J.Rodden, R.W.Hewitson, D.A.Lowry, Harry Watson, Ross Taylor, Jack Porter, Gene Dopp, Ernest Parkes, W.Lymn, Norman B.Albert, Ernie Wortley, Ed Chatfield, Jack Carmichael, Nip Dwan, H.G.Peacock, Mac McCarthy, A,Mollenhauer, R.H.Bailey, Bob Armstrong, W.Graham, Thomas Gaye, Norman R.Mann, Ernie Collett, H.P.Lockhart, H.H.Jacobi, J.R.Mooney, Frank Sullivan, J.J.Riordan, Gus Ryder, Charles Delahey, Frank Fisher, Glen Armstrong,

Area: **OHA (Early Years)** Season: **1927 - 1928** Supervisor: Officials: AYR: James O.Oliver, BRACEBRIDGE: Murt Dunn, Earl Walker, BARRIE: Jack Armstrong, Louis Vair, Frank Doyle, BRANTFORD: Stan Verner, E.Balkwell, M.Cinnamon, BROCKVILLE: William Simmons, J,Sandercock, BELLEVILLE: Bill Greene, Leo Barrett, Stan Nurse, Clayton Frechette, BOLTON: Albert A.Kennedy, E.Ingram, BURLINGTON: H.E.Sheppard, BOWMANVILLE: W.A.Edger, Allan Campbell, BRAMPTON: J.O.Adams, Jack Burrell, H.J.Teasdale, CAYUGA: A.C.Murphy, W.Barry, B.J.Hammond, CHESLEY: J.C.McDonald, H.C.Blohm, CORNWALL: John Dennenay, R.Mallett, V.Silmser, COLLINGWOOD: John Belcher, Josh Belcher, Oscar Bernhardt, CALEDONIA: Ken Baird, DURHAM: R.L.Saunders, DUNNVILLE: William McBrien, H.Burrows, Earl Knight, ELMIRA: A.Seiling, A.Allgeier, ELORA: Robert Fisher, George Hills, Alex Karges, EXETER: Goldie Cochrane, GALT: A.R.Oliver, W.Clayton Hoffmans, GUELPH: J.Jones, Sandy Little, Nelson Henry, John Jones, GEORGETOWN: Wakefield Ford, A.Duncan, Roy F.King, GRAVENHURST: Wm Christenson, Roy Christenson, HAMILTON: F.H.Duckett, F.R.Lishman, Guy Ernest Smith, Guy Smith, Gordon McKay, James Stewart, Arthur Jones, Marsh Preston, HAGERSVILLE: Murphy Slack, INGERSOLL: Joseph Richardson, JORDAN:

V.A.Alexander, D.A.Farrell, KITCHENER: T.G.Hillman, Isaacs Masters, George Karges, Dr Robert Ferguson, Jack Hemphill, KINGSTON: Joseph Smith, Harry Batsone, Chick Mundell, Harry McNeill, A.Brouse, LISTOWEL: Cully Rocher, F.C.Kelly, B.L.H.Bamford, LONDON: Fred George, Gerald Goodman, Tom Munro, W.H.Legg, J.George Arthurs, Sid Rankin, D.R.Mallen, J.A.Greer, LINDSAY: Elwood Coombs, Charles Board, MOUNT FOREST: E.Murphy, MARKDALE: H.H.Mercer, MILVERTON: W.J.Kelterborn, Earl Meyers, MORRISBURG: Ken Mallen, MILTON: H.V.Peacock, D.Brush, MIDLAND: Dr George Westman, C.German, MARKHAM: Dr R.G.Cowie, P.M.Reesor, MITCHELL: W.C.Thorne, Dr Sawyer, W.Ratz, NIAGARA FALLS: George Pennie, W.Eugene Fraser, NEWMARKET: Ernie Doyle, Bert day, NEW HAMBURG: Walter Bowman, R.C.Puddicombe, OWEN SOUND: Earl Hicks, OSHAWA: James McFadyen, Charles Hall, Jack Smith, ORILLIA: P.L.Thompson, Norman Cooke, OAKVILLE: Dr A.M.Deans, PORT COLBORNE: A.P.McAvoy, D.A.Dixon, Frank Smith, PALMERSTON: W.R.Johnston, Charles Kells, James Auld, Stan Burns, PARIS: L.G.Cook, Russell Sandercock, PICTON: Earl Croft, Burt Burns, PORT DOVER: M.E.Gilbert, J.H.Misner, D.McDonald, PORT HOPE< Wilfrid Hills, PRESTON: Buck Bowman, Alvin Schlegel, Allan Kinder, PARRY SOUND: Jack Capbell, PETERBORO: William E.Jacjson, Walter Jackson, SIMCOE: E.Ramey, STAYNER: Clarence Wood, STRATFORD: William Easson, H.W.Jamieson, W.Heard, K.Easson, Wally Hern, Charles Lightfoot, SEAFORTH: Dot reid, A.W.Dick, SARNIA: Harry Prout, William McCart, ST MARY'S: L.Lavelle, R.Tuer, ST CATHARINES: D.E.Bawtinheimer, Bruce Burns, TAVISTOCK: L.W.Appel, TILLSONBURG: Delos Hicks, TRENTON: Ross Burtt, C.Allore, UXBRIDGE: G.Crosby, WIARTON: Robert Simmie, Allan Ashley, WATERFORD: Ford Wilson, WOODSTOCK: Dr Norman Douglas, Harry King, Chilton Childs, WINGHAM: H.C.MacLean, WELLAND: T.H.Jones, Frank Lambert, WESTON: Lorne Barlett, WATFORD: N.Trenouth, F.R.Rogers, WINDSOR: Lawson Whitehead, WALKERTON: Joe Raybould, WALKERVILLE: W.Y.Shaw, Sid Rankin, WHITBY: Bert Smith, TORONTO: Lou

E.Marsh, Harold Farlow, R.W.Hewitson, M.J.Rodden, Herb Matthews, D.A.Lowry, Harry Watson, S.W.Hall, A.J.Halliwell, Norman Albert, Ernie Wortley, Thomas Gaye, James McFadyen, A.Mollenhauer, Gene Dopp, Ernest Collett, Frank (Dutch) Cain, Douglas Peacock, Jack Carmichael, Ernest Parkes, J.C.Cameron, Jack Nettlefield, Stan Burgoyne, Ed Chatfield, H.H.Jacobi, Glen Sullivan, James Green, Louis Walker, Frank Sullivan, H.J.Keenan, Murray Walsh, Murray Rutherford, J.D.Stewart, N.E.Stoddard, Andy Kyle, Robert Armstrong, Eugene Sidley, H.Lynn Hudson, George S.Currie, Dr R.T.Smylie, H.G.Peacock, Steve Vair, W.Lynn, Mac McCarthy

Area: **OHA (Early Years)** Season: **1926 - 1927** Supervisor: Officials: Aurora: Dr Eugene Underhill, AYR: James O.Oliver, BARRIE: Jack Armstrong, Loius O.Vair, Frank Doyle, BOWMANVILLE: W.A.Edgar, Allan Campbell, BROCKVILLE: William Simons, BOLTON: E.Ingram, BRAMPTON: J.O.Adams, J.A.Burrell, H.J.Teasdale, BRANTFORD: Stan Verner, BELLEVILLE: Stan Nurse, Clayton Frechette, William Green, L.Barrett, COLLINGWOOD: Josh Belcher, CAYUGA: W.Barry, COBOURG: Ken Payne, H.C.Higginbotham, CORNWALL: John Dennenay, R.Mallett, CALEDONIA: Ken Baird, CHESLEY: J.C.McDonald, DUNNVILLE: Earl Knight, William McBrien, DURHAM: R.L.Saunders, ELORA: Alex Karges, ELMIRA: L.Ruppel, H.Weichel, GEORGETOWN: A.Duncan, GUELPH: Sandy Little, Charles Ogg, Nelson Henry, John Jones, GALT: A.R.Oliver, GRIMSBY: L.J.Farrell, Nick Burnside, HAMILTON: Ernest Smith, Oren Frood, Guy Smith, Gordon McKay, James Stewart, Marsh Preston, Arthur Jones, HAGERSVILLE: Murphy Slack, INGERSOLL: Joseph Richardson, KINGSTON: Harry Batstone, C.Mundell, W.P.Hughes, A.Brouse, KITCHENER: Jack Hemphill, Isaac Masters, George Hiller, George Karges, Dr Robert Ferguson, LISTOWEL: Cully Rocker, Frank Kemp, Frank Kelly, LINDSAY: Elwood Coombs, Charles V.Board, LONDON: Tom Munro, W.H.Legg, J.George Arthurs, Jerry Goodman, FredGeorge, Sid Rankin, MILTON: H.V.Peacock, D.Brush, MIDLAND: C.German, MARKHAM: Dr R.G.Cowie,

P.M.Reesor, MITCHELL: W.Ratz, Dr Sawyer, W.C.Thorne, NIAGARA FALLS: George Pennie, NIAGARA FALLS NY: D.V.McLean, NEWMARKET: Ernie Doyle, Bert Day, NEW HAMBURG: Robert Puddicombe, Walter Bowman, OWEN SOUND: Earl Hicks, OAKVILLE: Dr F.M.Deans, OSHAWA: Charles Hall, Jack Smith, ORILLIA: P.L.Thompson, Norman C.Cook, PARIS: Russell Sandercock, A.Fraser, PETERBORO: Walter Jackson, PORT DOVER: J.H.Misner, D.McDonald, PORT HOPE: J.Rowden, PALMERSTON: Stanley Burns, W.R.Johnston, W.E.Root, W.Kells, James Auld, PRESTON: Buck Bowman, Alvin Schlegel, Allan Kinder, PICTON: Bert Burns, PARRY SOUND: Jack Campbell, PORT COLBORNE: H.Taylor, Frank Smith, A.P.McAvoy, PAISLEY: George Grant, RICHMOND HILL: B.Cooke, STRATFORD: W.Heard, K.Easson, H.W.Jamieson, Wally Hern, Charles Lightfoot, SEAFORTH: Dot Reid, A.W.Dick, SIMCOE: E.V.Ramey, George Currie, SARNIA: Harry Prout, William McCart, ST MARY'S: L Lavelle, ST CATHARINES: D.E.Bawtinheimer, Bruce Burns, STAYNER: Oscar Bernhardt, TILLSONBURG: Delos Hicks, TAVISTOCK: L.W.Appel, UXBRIDGE: G.Crosby, WIARTON: Robert Simmie, Allan Ashley, WHITBY: Bert Smith, WATERFORD: Ford Wilson, WOODSTOCK: Dr Norman Douglas, Harry King, Chilton Childs, WINGHAM: H.C.MacLean, WELLAND: Norman Burmister, T.H.Jones, Frank Lambert, WESTON: lorne Barlett, E.G.Farr, WATFORD: N.Trenouth, F.R.Rogers, TORONTO: Lou E,Marsh, Harold Farlow, R.W.Hewitson, Mike J.Rodden, Harold Mitchell, Herb Matthews, D.A.Lowry, Norman Albert, Ernest Wortley, S.W.Hall, A.J.Halliwell, Ernest Collett, Louis Walker, Frank Sullivan, H,J,Keenan, Murray Walsh, Murray Rutherford, Steve Vair, Ernest Parkes, James R,Green, J.D.Stewart, N.E.Stoddard, Andy Kyle, Robert Armstrong, Eugene Sidley, Mac McCarthy, Jack Carmichael, Jack Cameron, H.Lynn Hudson, James McFayden, George S.Currie, Dr.R.T.Smylie,

Area: **OHA (Early Years)** Season: **1925 - 1926** Supervisor: Officials: AURORA: Dr Eugne Underhill, BARRIE: Jack Armstrong, Louis O. Vair, Frank Doyle, BEAMSVILLE: H.Reid, BOWMANVILLE: W.A.Edger, Allan

Campbell, BROCKVILLE: William Simons, Charles Swayze, BOLTON: E.Ingram, BRAMPTON: J.O.Adams, J.A.Burrell, H.J.Teasdale, BRANTFORD: Stan Verner, BRADFORD: O.McKinstry, BELLEVILLE: Stan Nurse, C.Frechette, L.Barrett, COLLINGWOOD: Josh Belcher, CHESLEY: John C.McDonald, CAYUGA: W.Barry, COBOURG: Ken Payne, H.C.Higginbothan, CORNWALL: John Dennenay, DUNNVILLE: Earl Knight, William McBrien, ELORA: Alex Karges, R.Fisher, GEORGETOWN: A.Duncan, GUELPH: Sandy little, Charles Ogg, Nelson Henry, Johnny Jones, GALT: Marsh Preston, A.R.Oliver, GRIMSBY: A.Clark, G.Foulis, W.R.Fisher, HAMILTON: Guy Smith, James Stewart, Fred Naylor, Ernie Smith, Harry Lucky, HAGERSVILLE: Murphy Slack, INGERSOLL: James Richardson, KITCHENER: Isaac Masters, George Hiller, George Karges, Jack Hemphill, Dr Robert Ferguson, KINGSTON: Harry Batstone, W.P.Hughes, Jack McKelvey, Joe Smith, Arthur Brouse, Dr R.P.Millan, LISTOWEL: Cully Rocker, Frank Kemp, Frank Kelly, LONDON: Fred George, Tom Munro, W.H.Legg, Sid Rankin, Teddy Graham, Roy Briscoe, MILTON: H.V.Peacock, D.Brush, MIDLAND: C.German, W.H.Duncan, MARKHAM: Dr R.G.Cowie, P.M.Reesor, MITCHELL: W.Ratz, Dr Sawyer, NIAGARA FALLS: George Pennie, Eugene Fraser, NEWMARKET: Ernie Doyle, Bert Day, NEW HAMBURG: Robert Puddicombe, Walter Bowman, OWEN SOUND: Earl Hicks, OAKVILLE: Dr F.M.Deans, OSHAWA: Charles Hall, Jack Smith, ORILLIA: P.L.Thompson, Norman C.Cook, PARIS: Russell Sandercock, A.Fraser, PETERBORO: Walter Jackson, Percy Bond, PORT DOVER: J.H.Misner, D.McDonald, PORT HOPE: J.Rowden, PALMERSTON: Lloyd White, Stanley Burns, W.R.Johnston, W.E.Root, W.Kells, James Auld, PRESTON: Buck Bowman, Alvin Schlegel, Allan Kinder, PICTON: Bert Burns, Earl Croft, PARRY SOUND: Jack Campbell, RICHMOND HILL: B.Cooke, RENFREW: Oren Frood, STRATFORD: John Seebach, Walter Hern, Charlie Lightfoot, SEAFORTH: Dot Reid, A.W.Dick, Ken Easson, H.W.Jameson, SIMCOE: E.V.Ramey, W.Piett, SARNIA: Harry Prout, William McCart, ST MARY'S: L.Lavelle, ST CATHARINES: D.E.Bawtinheimer, Bruce Burns, TRENTON: Ross Burtt, TILLSONBURG:

A,B,Stanley, Delos Hicks, UXBRIDGE: G.Crosby, WIARTON: Robert Simmie, Allan Ashley, WHITBY: Bert Smith, WATERFORD: GFord Wilson, WOODSTOCK: Harry King, Dr Norman Douglas, Chilton Childs, WELLAND: Norman Burmister, T.H.Jones, Frank Lambert, WESTON: Lorne Barlett, E.G.Farr, WINDSOR: E.G.Lowery, Percy LeSueur, W.C.Montgomery, Patrick Farrell, George Walsh, WATFORD: N.Trenouth, F.R.Rogers, TORONTO: Lou E,Marsh, M.J.Rodden, Harold Mitchell, Harold Farlow, R.W.Hewitson, Steve Vair, Herb Matthews, Andy Kyle, Bob Armstrong, E.B.Sidley, Mac McCarthy, Nip Dwan, D.A.Lowry, Norman Albert, Ernest Wortley, S.W.Hall, Jack P.Walwyn, Stan Burgoyne, Jock Bennett, Jack Cameron, Jack Carmichael, Ernie Cook, Frank Sullivan, Murray Rutherford, H.A.McNeill, Art Halliwell, W.M.Cumming, Ernie parkes, F.C.Waghorne, James McFayden, Dr W.J.Laflamme, Ed Chatfield, H.Lynn Hudson

Area: **OHA (Early Years)** Season: **1924 - 1925** Supervisor: Officials: AURORA: Dr Eugene Underhill, AYR: C.Bain, James Oliver, BUFFALO: W.V.Adams, BRAMPTON: J.O.Adams, BRANTFORD: C.L.Kaufman, S.Verner, BRADFORD: O.McKinstry, BURLINGTON: Percy Lesueur, BOWMANVILLE: W.A.Edger, Allen Campbell, BELLEVILLE: Stan Nurse, C.Frechette, L.Barrett, BROCKVILLE: Wm Simons, Charles Swayze, BARRIE: Frank Doyle, L.O.Vair, COLLINGWOOD: Josh Belcher, Walter Robinson, J.A.Bell, CHESLEY: John C.McDonald, C.B.Hoeflin, CLINTON: Carl Draper, CAYUGA: W.Barry, A.C.Murphy, COBOURG: Kent Payne, CAMPBELLFORD: C.Holmes, CORNWALL: John Dennenay, DUNNVILLE: W.McBrien, Earl Knight, EXETER: Goldie Cochrane, ELORA: Alex Karges, GUELPH: Sandy Little, I.M.Corrigan, Charles Ogg, Nelson Henry, T.Arnold Elliott, GODERICH: B.H.Chase, L.G.Young, GEORGETOWN: P.F.Blackburn, GRIMSBY: L.J.Farrell, GALT: John Brackenborough, A.Kilgor, A.R.Oliver, GLENCOE: J.E.Weaver, HAMILTON: Ernie J.Smith, J.J.L.Stewart, Fred Naylor, Guy Smith, HAGERSVILLE: Murphy Slack, INGERSOLL: James Richardson, Robert Henderson, KITCHENER: George Hiller, George Karges,

Ike Masters, Jack Hemphill, Robert Ferguson, KINGSTON: Harry Batstone, W.P.Hughes, Jack McKelvey, Joe Smith, George Van Horne, Arthur Brouse, Dr R.P.Millan, LISTOWEL: Cully Rocher, Frank Kemp, Frank Kelly, LONDON: Tom Munro, Ken Mallen, Rene Fournier, Fred George, Murray Shoe, A.G.Stirrett, Sid Rankin, W.H.Legg, MONTREAL: Walter Smaill, MIDLAND: Jack Armstrong, C.German, MITCHELL: W.Ratz, D.Eizerman, Dr L.Sawyer, NIAGARA FALLS: Steve Rice, NEWMARKET: E.A.Doyle, MEAFORD: A.M.Pillgrem, NEW HAMBURG: R.C.Puddicome, Walter Bowman, OWEN SOUND: Earl Hicks, OSHAWA: Charles Hall, PARIS: Russell Sandercock, A.Fraser, PORT DOVER: J.H.Misner, D.MacDonald, PORT HOPE: J.Rowden, PALMERSTON: Lloyd White, Stanley Burns, PETERBORO: Walter Jackson, Percy Bond, PRESTON: Alvin Schlegel, A.T.Kinder, PORT CREDIT: H.C.Thompson, PICTON: Bert Burns, RICHMOND HILL: B.Cook, STRATFORD: John Seebach, Charles Lightfoot, SEAFORTH: A.W.Dick, Dot Reid, H.Johnstone, STAYNER: Neil Pearson, SARNIA: W. McCart, H.B.Crouchman, ST THOMAS: Spence McLean, SIMCOE: L.Cratt, Elmer Ramey, W.Piette, ST MARYS: L.B.Avery, S.Wilson, L.Lavelle, TORONTO: Lou E.Marsh, Mike J.Rodden, R.W.Hewitson, Dr W.J.Laflamme, H.H.Jacobi, L.Runhardt, Norman B.Albert, Herbert Matthews, Robert Armstrong, Harold Mitchell, Harold Farlow, D.A.Lowry, Jack Carmichael, Andy Kyle, G.F.Evans, Jimmy Green, Russell Henley, Dave Smith, S.W.Hall, Eugene Sidley, Glenn Sullivan, Murray Rutherford, W.W.Cumming, J.B.Nettelfield, Ernie Wasson, James McFadyen, Ernest Cook, Nip Dwan, F.M.Bradfield, E.J.Collett, Ernie Wortley, A.J.Halliwell, Glen Smith, Charlie Brown, H.R.Polson, Stanley E.Wade, M.S.McCarthy, F.Allen, Alan Skaith, Jack Burrill, F.C.Waghorne Sr, Frank Sullivan, Harry McNeill, George Maunder, TRENTON: Ross Burtt, TILLSONBURG: Delos Hicks, UXBRIDGE: F.G.Crosby, WIARTON: Robert Simmie, Allan Ashley, WHITBY: Bert Smith, WATERFORD: Ford Wilson, WOODSTOCK: Harry King, Dr N.Douglas, Chilton Childs, WELLAND: N.E.Burmister, WESTON: Loren Barlett, WILLOWDALE: O.Smith.

Area: **OHA (Early Years)** Season: **1923 - 1924**
Supervisor: Officials: AURORA: Dr Eugene Underhill, AYR: C.Bain, BRAMPTON: J.A.Burrell, J.O.Adams, BRANTFORD: S.Verner, BURLINGTON: Percy Lesueur, BOWMANVILLE: Allen Campbell, BROCKVILLE: William Simon, Daniel Street, Charles Swayze, Sheldeon Burt, BELLEVILLE: S.Nurse, L.Barrett, C.Frechette, CALEDONIA: B.French, Alfred Atkinson, CAYUGA: W.Barry, CHESLEY: William Davison, Alex Lustig, COLLINGWOOD: Bernard Brophy, Walter Robinson, COBOURG: Norman Derry, CORNWALL: John Dennenay, ELORA: Alex Karges, GUELPH: Sandy Little, Charles Ogg, M.Corrigan, GEORGETOWN: James Clark, Everett Cole, H.J.Clark, GODERICH: L.G.Young, GLENCOE: J.E.Weaver, GRIMSBY: Dr W.J.Carson, GALT: A.Kilgour, HAMILTON: John Brackenborough, Corbett Dennenay, Fred Naylor, Ernie Smith, J.L.Stewart, Dr Charles Stewart, HAGERSVILLE: M.Winter, Maynard Slack, INGERSOLL: James Richardson, Robert Henderson, John Cross, KITCHENER: A.J.Leroux, Geoorge Hiller, Doc Merrick, Geo Karges, KINGSTON: Harry Batstone, Joe Smith, Jack Powell, George Van Horne, LONDON: J.A.Greer Jr, W.Legg, Sid Rankin, R.M.Briscoe, LISTOWEL: Cully Rocker, C.C.Cavell, F.Kelly, MILTON: Roy Chisholm, MONTREAL: Walter Smaill, MIDLAND: Aberdeen McGill, Dick Semple, C.German, MITCHELL: D.Eizerman, NIAGARA FALLS: Stephen Rice, Earl Jamieson, NEW HAMBURG: R.C.Puddicombe, A.H.Coombs, OWEN SOUND: E.T.Hicks, J.R.Dier, OSHAWA: Charles Hall, OAKVILLE: R.Taylor, Dr F.M.Dean, ORANGEVILLE: Bert Booth, Wally Hopkins, PALMERSTON: S.Burns, W.R.Johnston, R.Horning, E.Root, PETERBORO: Walter Jackson, J.Percy Bond, PARIS: Russell Sandercock, PRESTON: A.T.Kinder, Alvin Schlegel, ST. CATHARINES: William Lynn, ST MARY'S: L.B.Avery, SARNIA: W.McCart, SEAFORTH: Dot Reid, Reg Reid, A.W.Dick, STAYNER: William Clark, ST THOMAS: Spence McLean, SIMCOE: L.Cratt, Dr Burt, WOODSTOCK: Chilton Childs, Arthur Parker, Stanley Wade, Harry King, Dr Douglas, TILLSONBURG: Delos Hicks, TORONTO: Lou E.Marsh, Steve Vair, Harold Farlow, Harold Mitchell, R.W.Hewitson, Charles

Dinsmore, B.J.Hughes, Norman Albert, Dalton Lowry, Cecil Wagner, Nip Dwan, Beattie Ramsay, H.H.Jacobi, Bob Armstrong, J.B.Nettlefield, Andy Kyle, Glen Smith, Alex Romeril, Cecil Dye, William Cumming, E.S.Heaton, Lawson Whitehead, Jack Marshall, H.Bee, R.E.Henley, Jack Carmichael, Jack Marks, R.H.Bailey, Murray Rutherford, Basil Harinfton, D.A.Carey, M.J.Rodden, Gordon Mitchell, Ernie Wortley, Herb Matthews, George Westman, Hugh Fox, C.F.Cumming, WIARTON: Allan Ashley, M.J.Gildner, E.Miers, WHITBY: Bert Smith, WATERFORD: A.Maddiford, Ford Wilson, ZURICH: Lee Hoffman.

Area: **OHA (Early Years)** Season: **1922 - 1923** Supervisor: Officials: AYR: J.Oliver, C.Bain, AURORA: Jack Brown, ALVINSTON: A.McEachern, Simon Williams, BRAMPTON: J.O.Adams, Jack Burrell, Rod Anderson, BOWMANVILLE: Alan Campbell, BELLEVILLE: Leo Barrett, BURLINGTON: Stan Coates, BRACEBRIDGE: Murt Dunn, BOLTON: C.D.Norton, S.Cameron, L.Gould, BRANTFORD: Stanley Verner, Ken Mallen, BROCKVILLE: Charles Swayze, John Murray, W.H.Simmon, CAMPBELLFORD: Clifford Weston, COBOURG: Kent Payne, CANNINGTON: George Halward, COLLINGWOOD: Josh Belcher, Jack Burns, CORNWALL: John Dennenay, J.Keenan, CLINTON: Carl Draper, CAYUGA: A.Murphy, COLDWATER: John R.Watson, DUNNVILLE: W.White, EXETER: Goldie Cochrane, ELMIRA: H.O.Weichel, GUELPH: T.R.Doyle, J.R.Kennedy, GALT: A.Kilgor, Clayton Hoffman, GLENCOE: Jacob weaver, Art Davenport, GODERICH: Ray Marchand, GRAVENHURST: E.Walker, GEORGETOWN: E.Cole, A.Duncan, HAMILTON: Goldie Prodgers, Ernie Smith, C.J.Davey, Dr Charles Stewart, Carson Cooper, E.Runnion, E.Garfield, HUNTSVILLE: A.Kellock Jr, HAGERSVILLE: T.Winger, KITCHENER: George Hillier, Leo Quinn, George Hainsworth, William Uffelman, Doc Merrick, George Karges, Roy Anderson, KINGSTON: George Van Horne, Jack Powell, Dr Rupert Millan, Harry Batstone, LAKEFIELD: Reg Murdoff, LISTOWEL: Cully Rocher, C.C.Cavell, F.C.Kelly, LINDSAY: Art Carew, LONDON: John A.Greer, Tom Munro, W.H.Legg, MITCHELL:

D.Eizerman, J.Otto, John Rodger, MILVERTON: W.J.Bundscho, MILTON: G.Farlow, D.Brush, MIDLAND: Clarence Simpson, Charles German, NEWMARKET: Ernie Doyle, NIAGARA FALLS: Eugene Fraser, NEW HAMURG: Robert Puddicombe, Walter Bowman, MONTREAL: Walter Smaill, OWEN SOUND: E.T.Hicks, ORANGEVILLE: Bert Booth, OSHAWWA: Charles Hall, ORILLIA: Norman Cook, OAKVILLE: B.W.Hillmer, Dr F.M.Deans, PARIS: Percy Gill, PICTON: E.G.Hudgin, PRESTON: Alvin Schlegel, Allan Kinder, Buck Bowman, Stan Burgoyne, PORT HOPE: J.Rowden, PETERBORO: Grover Halpin, J.Percy Bond, PORT DOVER: Lawrence Kelly, PORT COLBORNE: Alan German, STAYNER: Oscar Bernhardt, STRATHROY: H.Munroe, W.H.Chambers, H.Parlow, SARNIA: Harry Prout, Jas Brady, William McCart, N.L.LaSueur, SIMCOE: L.C.Cratt, Weber Piette, STRATFORD: William Easson, E.P.Edmunds, SEAFORTH: Dot Reid, Reg Reid, ST CATHARINES: J.B Burns, A.E.Mix, E.H.Lancaster, SHELBURNE: Dr Zinn, ST THOMAS: Spencer McLean, TILLSONBURG: Dellos Hicks, TRENTON: Joe Freeman, Ross Burt, TORONTO: Lou E.Marsh, Robt Hewitson, D.A.Lowry, Noran B.Albert, Harvey Sproule, W.A.McCord, Mike Rodden, Wm Cumming, Alex Romerill, Andy Kyle, Harold Farlow, D'Arcy Smith, H.H.Jacobi, Bob Armstrong, H.F.Smith, Steve Vair, Russel Henley, Arthur J.Halliwell, Lonel Conacher, Gordon Mitchell, Mac McCarthy, Murray Rutherford, R.E.Chisholm, Jas McFadgen, Jack Carmichael, W.J.Killackey, Ernest Wortley, Jack Moxon, R.H.Bailey, WOODSTOCK: Russell Sandercock, Harry king, Stanley Wade3, Clarence Gorrie, WHITBY: Bert Smith, WATFORD: Fred Rodgers, A.Elliott, N.Trenough, WATERFORD: Ford Wilson,

Area: **OHA (Early Years)** Season: **1921 - 1922** Supervisor: Officials: ALVINSTON: Simon Williams, Clarence Reid, AURORA: Jack Brown, BOLTON: Stuart Cameron, BELLEVILLE: W.P.Allen E.Laing, Clayton, Frechette, BURLINGTON: Stan Coates, BRAMPTON: J.O.Adams, J.A.Burrell, BOWMANVILLE: Reg Jones, BRACEBRIDGE: Murt Dunn, BRANTFORD: E.C.Gould, Stanley Verner, BROCKVILLE: Charles Swayze, John

Murray, CANNINGTON: George Halward, COLDWATER: John R.Watson, COLLINGWOOD: Josh Belcher, CLINTON: Carl Draper, COBOURG: Kent Payne, CORNWALL: John Dennenay, DUNDALK: C.A.Farrell, DURHAM: James McLaughlin, Robert Saunders, DUNNVILLE: W.White, EXETER: Goldie Cochrane, L.W.Hoffman, C.A.Hoffman, GALT: Wylie Wilkinson, James fraser, H.O.McGuire, Percy LeSueur, G.J.Gravelle, GLENCOE: A.Davenport, T.E.weaver, GODERICH: J.Wiggins, Roy McDonald, GRAVENHURST: E.Walker, GUELPH: T.R.Doyle, Charles E.Ogg, HARRISTON: R.W.Ward, HAMILTON: Goldie Prodgers, W.H.Pym, HUNTSVILLE: A.Kellock Jr, KINGSTON: George Van Horne, H.A.MacKenzie, J.Powell, Roy Marchand, Dr Rupert Millan, KITCHENER: W.M.Box, Bert Leroux, George Hillier, W.Uffelman, Doc merrick, LAKEFIELD: Reg Murdoff, LONDON: Tom Munro, J.A.Greer, W.H.Legg, Sid Rankin, Lee Walden, George McCallum, LINDSAY: D.Lowry, MITCHELL: D.Eizerman, J.Otto, MILTON: R.E.Chisholm, MIDLAND: Aberdenne McGill, MARKDALE: H.H.Mercer, NEWMARKET: Ernie Doyle, NIAGARA FALLS: E.Eugene Fraser, NEW HAMBURG: Robert Puddicombe, Walter Bowman, OWEN SOUND: J.Herbert, PORT COLBORNE: A.German, PARIS: P.S.Gill, A.D.Fraser, PRESTON: Allan Kinder, Alvin Schlegel, PORT DOVER: Laurence Kelly, STAYNER: Oscar Bernhardt, SEAFORTH: Dot Reid, SIMCOE: Len Cratt, STRATFORD: E.P.Edmunds, Wm Easson, SARNIA: W.McCant, Stewart D.Simpson, B.H.McCreath, TORONTO: Lou E.Marsh, Steve Vair, Robert Hewitson, H.A.MacLennan, F.C.Waghorne, Jas Etherington, F.Harvey Sproule, H.H.Jacobi, W.A.McCord, James Labett, Mike Rodden, Jack Carmichael, Harold W.Falow, F.B.Fenney, Ernie Broderick, Mac McCarthy, Dutch Brophy, Bob armstrong, Stan Burgoyne, Murray Rutherford, Lionel Conacher, Corbett Dennenay, R.A.Barker, Len Cook, Peck Wright, W.J.Kellackey, Ernie Cook, H.W.Mitchell, R.G.Gordon, Nip Dwan, WESTON: Lorne R.Barlett, WIARTON: Allan Ashley, WOODSTOCK: Harry King, Russell Sandercock, Reg Stone, Jame Gunn, C.N.Gorrie, WATFORD: Fred Rodgers, Alex Elliott,

WELLAND: C.W. Book, James Herbert, A.McLeod, Frank Best

Area: **OHA (Early Years)** Season: **1920 - 1921**
Supervisor: Officials: A list of officials for the OHA 1920-1921 season is not available. We have looked at the 1919-20 list and the 1921-22 list and deducted that anyone on both lists would have been there in 1920-21. The list is as follows: BOLTON: Stuart Cameron, BELLEVILLE: W.P.Allen, E.Laing, Clayton Frechette, BURLINGTON: Stan Coates, GALT: Jas Fraser, GLENCOE: A.Davenport, T.E.Weaver, GODERICH: J.Wiggins, KINGSTON: George Van Horne, KITCHENER: A.Leroux, LONDON: Tom Munro, J.A.Greer, W.H.Legg, Sid Rankin, MITCHELL: D.Eizerman, NEW HAMBURG: R.C.Puddicombe, Walter Bowman, PARIS: P.S.Gill, A.D.Fraser, PRESTON: Allan Kinder, Alvin Schlegel, STRATFORD: E.P.Edmunds, W.Easson, SARNIA: W.McCart, Stewart D.Simpson, TORONTO: Lou E.Marsh, Steve Vair, F.Harvrey Sproule, H.H.Jacobi, F.C.Waghorne, W.A.McCord, James Labett, Robert Hewitson, H.W.Mitchell, Mike Rodden, F.B.Fenney, H.A.MacLennan, G,N,Gorrie, WOODSTOCK: Reg Stone, James Gunn, Welland: C.W. Book, James Herbert

Area: **OHA (Early Years)** Season: **1919 - 1920**
Supervisor: Officials: BOLTON: Stuart Cameron, BELLEVILLE: W.P.Allen, E.Lang, Clayton Frechette, BURLINGTON: Stan Coates, BLENHEIM: A,B,Shillington, BRAMPTON: Irving Ardagh, Dr O.A.Peaker, COLLINGWOOD: Ernie Fryer, ELMIRA: M.Weichel, GALT: Jas Fraser, GODERICH: J.Wiggins, GLENCOE: A.Davenport, T.E.Weaver, KINGSTON: Geo Van Horne, KITCHENER: E.L.Parkes, Doc Merrick, L.Kreuger, Nelson Gross, A.Leroux, W.M.Boll, LONDON: Tom Munro, J.A.Greer, W.H.Legg, Sid Rankin, MITCHELL: D.Eizerman, MILVERTON: Sid Spencer, NEW HAMBURG: R.C.Puddicome, Walter Bowman, NIAGARA FALLS: E.Eugene Fraser, PARIS: P.S.Gill, A.D.Fraser, PRESTON: Allan Kinder, Alvin Schelgel, SEAFORTH: A.W.Dick, Joe Sills, STRATFORD: E.P.Edmunds, Wm Easson, SARNIA: W.McCart, Stewart D.Simpson, ST CATHARINES: Geo

Hiller, SIMCOE: W.Piett, THAMESVILLE: T.J.Davidson, C.Willis, TORONTO: P.H.LeSueur, Lou E.Marsh, Steve Vair, B.J.Murphy, W.P.Irving, O.F.Burkart, C.N.Gorrie, F.Harvey Sproule, J.Douglas Stewart, Wilfred Stratton, Peter G.Campbell, H.H.Jacobi, Wm Marsden, Willard Box, Lawson Whitehead, Dr W.J.Laflamme, F.C.Waghorne, W.A.McCord, James Labbett, C.L.Querrie, Robert Hewitson, Leonard Smith, H.W.Mitchell, Mike Rodden, W.M.Tackberry, F.B.Fenney, F.D.McLure, F.H.Moxon, P.A.Lowry, H.A.MacLennan, J.M.O'Brien, WESTON: Lorne R.Barlett, A.R.Smith, WOODSTOCK: Reg Stone, Jas Gunn, WATERLOO: Wm Uffelman, WELLAND: Geo Foulis, C.W.Book, Jas Herbert

Area: **OHA (Early Years)** Season: **1918 - 1919** Supervisor: Officials: BRACEBRIDGE: Murt Dunn, CLINTON: W.Johnston, ELMIRA: H.Weichel L.Ruppel, GALT: Robert Broomfield, F.George, GUELPH: Wm Drone, Wm Craven, W.Squirrel, H.S.Gaundier, GODERICH: R.Rumball, GRAVENHURST: W.Howard, HUNTSVILLE: W.McDonald, INGERSOLL: George Mason, Charles Woolson, KINGSTON: George Van Horne, KITCHENER: A.Leroux, E.Parkes, George Hillier, LONDON: Tom Munro, H.H.Ferguson, NIAGARA FALLS: E.Eugene Fraser, NEW HAMBURG: R.C.Puddicombe, Alex Hahn, PARIS: A.Fraser, PORT COLBORNE: Dan MacDonald, PRESTON: A.T.Kinder, A.H.Schlegel, SIMCOE: L.Cratt, STRATFORD: William Easson, Charlesw Lightfoot, E.P.Edmunds, SEAFORTH: Dalton Reid, A.W.Dick, TORONTO: Sergt-Major P.H.LeSueur, Lou E.Marsh, Steve Vair, B.J.Murphy, W.P.Irving, O.F.Burkhart, J.Lewis Brown, C.N.Gorrie, F.Harvey Sproule, Glenn Smith, Harry Meeking, Lawson Whitehead, Dr W.J.Laflamme, F.C.Waghorne, W.A.McCord, Stan Burgoyne, James Labett, C.L Querrie, Robert Hewitson, Leonard Smith, B.H.McCreath, W.Graham, H.W.Mitchell, Mike Rodden, W.M.Tackberry, F.B.Feeney, TRENTON: Charles Croft, WESTON: Lorne r.Barlett, WELLAND: William McAuliffe, WOODSTOCK: Reg Stone

Area: **OHA (Early Years)** Season: **1917 - 1918**
Supervisor: Officials: BRADFORD: O.G.Bernhardt, BELEVILLE: E.Laing, BRANTFORD: E.C.Gould, COBOURG: Herb Payne, L.S.Barr, J.Sprague, GALT: James Fraser, Robt Broomfield, GODERICH: Roy McDonald, HAMILTON: S.McKeon, INGERSOLL: George Mason, Charles Woolson, George Gregory, KITCHENER: W.Knell, Ernie Parkes, A.Leroux, O.Siebert, George Hainsworth, KINGSTON: George Van Horne, LONDON: Tom Munro, Clarence Armstrong, W.H.Legg, Sergt J.H.Foster, NIAGARA FALLS: A.G.Code, NEW HAMBURG: A.Hahn, T.Brodeur, OSHAWA: W.Fair, C.Hall, J.Etherington, PORT HOPE: John Rowden, Wm McMillan, PARIS: A.Fraser, PRESTON: A.Kinder, W.Dennis, SARNIA: James Brady, J.Adams, W.McCart, William Twaits, STRATFORD: Charles Lightfoot, Toad Edmunds, TORONTO: Sergt-Major Percy H.LeSueur, Major Lou E.Marsh, D.Raymond Mallen, Sergt Steve Vair, R.W.Robinson, B.J.Murphy, Leuit J,Mac Sheldon, W.P.Irving, O.F.Burkart, H.H.Ferguson, J.Lewis Brown, C.Rocher, C.N.Gorrie, F.H.Sproule, Lawson Whitehead, Dr W.J.Laflamme, F.C.Waghorne, W,A.mcCord, Stan Burgoyne, Jas Labatt, C.L.Querrie, A.N.Hunter, Rbert hewitson, Leonard Smith, B.H.McCreath, W.Graham, Fred McLure, Pte Ernie Williams, Earl Gustin, WESTON: Lorne R.Barlett, WHITBY: Bert Smith, WOODSTOCK: Sergt R.H.Sandercock, Charles Davidson, R.A.Stone

Area: **OHA (Early Years)** Season: **1916 - 1917**
Supervisor: Officials: AURORA: W.Hancock, BRADFORD: O.G.Bernhardt, BLENHEIM: Messrs McQuaig and Rutherford, BELLEVILLE: E.Laing, BOWMANVILLE: F.Williams, Roy Jones, BARRIE: Gren Caldwell, BRANTFORD: E.C.Gould, COBOURG: Kent Payne, ELMIRA: H.Weichel, Ernie Otto, GALT: Jas Fraser, W.F.Trivett, GLENCOE: Messrs Weaver and Davenport, INGERSOLL: Chas Woolson, George Mason, Dr R.A.Williams, KITCHENER: O.Siebert, Albert Leroux, E.Roscchman, KINGSTON: A.G.Brouse, Geo Van Horne, Bert Hunt, Reg Crawford, A.Cook, LONDON: Tom Munro, NEWMARKET: E.A.Doyle, OSHAWA: Lient H.H.Jacobi, OTTAWA: W.M.Tackberry, PETERBORO: J.P.Bond, Lieut

Cameron, PRESTON: Allan T.Kinder, W.Dennis, I.H.Bowman, A.H.Schlegel, ST THOMAS: Lieut O.B.Brown, Lieut Thompson, SARNIA: James Brady, STRATFORD: Wally Hern, Toad Edmunds, Chas Lightfoot, D.Forbes, TORONTO: F.H.Sproule, Lawson Whitehead, H.H.Ferguson, Ellerby Farr, R.McWhirter, R.W.Robinson, B.J.Murphy, W.J.Laflamme, F.C.Waghorne, W.A.McCord, Stan Burgoyne, Frank Rankin, Jas Labatt, C.L.Querrie, A.N.Hunter, Jack Moxon, Robt Hewitson, W.W.Davidson, Leonard Smith, B.H.McCreath, Bert Darlington, THAMESVILLE: Messrs Caine and Davidson, WOODSTOCK: R.H.Sandercock, WATERLOO: Eddie Engle, WHITBY: Bert Smith

Area: **OHA (Early Years)** Season: **1915 - 1916** Supervisor: Officials: ALVINSTON: C.W.Williams, Cherry Wahl BROCKVILLE: George Warwick, BRADFORD: O.G.Bernhardt, BARRIE: Gren Caldwell, Harry Riddell, BERLIN: Oliver Seibert, BELLEVILLE: Ernie T.Lang, W.J.Matheson, BOLTON: E.H.Elliott, S.H.Cameron. BRANTFORD: Jack Kelly, E.C.Gould, BRACEBRIDGE: C.Russell. COLLINGWOOD: J.Belcher. CORNWALL: Angus McMillan.DETROIT: A.N.Hunter, GODERICH: Harry Belcher, GALT: Jas Fraser, H.H. Jacobi. GRAVENHURST: M.Dunn. HAMILTON: Bert McKenzie, Sid Rankin. INGERSOLL: Geo Mason, Chas Woolson, Dr R.A.Williams, G.Gregory. KINGSTON: Reg Crawford, H.H.Ferguson, B.N.Steacy, A.G.Brouse, Dr Blakslea. LINDSAY: Alfred Gamble. LONDON: Tom Munroe, W.H.Rhodes, Lieut N.L.LeSuer. MITCHELL: Wilfred Morenz. MILTON: Bob Fleming. MARKHAM: Harry Stewart. MIDLAND: E.English, MADOC: Dr Gunn, NEWMARKET: Henry Rachine, OTTAWA: W.M.Tackberry, ORILLIA: J.A.Sinclair, OWEN SOUND: Lieut W.D.Mercer, W.S.Hancock, PRESTON: Allan T.Kinder, W.Dennis, PETERBORO: J.P.Bond, PARIS: Lorne Fraser, A.D.Fraser, SEAFORTH: G.J.Sills, STRATFORD: Wally Hern, Toad Edmunds, Jas Preston, Dave Forbes, SARNIA: J.M.Brady, Wm McCart, TORONTO: L.A.Whitehead, C.G.(Chad) Toms, F.H.Sproule, W.A.McCord, Frank Rankin, A.W.Dunkley, P.Curzon, Stanley Burgoyne, Walter G.Trivett, W.W.Davidson, Dr W.J.Laflamme,

F.C.Waghorne, Jack Moxon, Lou E.Marsh, J.B.McArthur, Robt Hewitson, B.J.Murphy, P.H.LeSueur, Jas Labatt, A.G.Davis, J.A.Burrell, W.H.Williams, Frank Doyle, N.E.Irving, J.M.Kerran, UXBRIDGE: Dr G.E.Gilfillan, WIARTON: Allan Ashley, G.Porter, WATERLOO: Eddie Engle, E.Schlosser, WOODSTOCK: R.H.Sandercock, A.Allen Hall, James Gunn, WINDSOR: A.N.Hunter.

Area: **OHA (Early Years)** Season: **1914 - 1915**
Supervisor: Officials: ALVINSTON: J.Bartholomew, AYR: A.Brohman, ALLANDALE: Harry Riddell, BOLTON: E.H.Elliott, S.H.Cameron, BRADFORD: O.G.Bernhardt, BERLIN: L.Kreuger, O.Seibert, Albert Leroux, BRANTFORD: Eddie Gould, Roy Brown, Jack Kelly, R.Robbins, BARRIE: Steve Vair, BRACEBRIDGE: Archie Yeomans, BELLEVILLE: Bert Allen, Ernie T.Lang, COLLINGWOOD: John A.Belcher, DRUMBO: H.Baxter, GALT: James Fraser, GODERICH: H.Belcher, John Wiggins, GRAVENHURST: H.Ditchburn, HAMILTON: Tom Phillips, T.Moran, Frank Robbins, Percy K.Teeter, INGERSOLL: George Mason, Charles A.Wilson, LONDON: Sid J.Rankin, S.Munroe, MEAFORD: Jas Hair, MITCHELL: D.Eizerman, NIAGARA FALLS: Frank Logan, NEW HAMBURG: Harry Beck, ORILLIA: J.A.Sinclair, PORT HOPE: Count Bunny, PRESTON: A.T.Kinder, PETERBOROUGH: J.P.Bond, PT COLBORNE: Robt. Willson, PARIS: Lorne Fraser, Percy Gill, W.Gill, STAYNER: R.J.Gartlan, STRATFORD: E.P.Edmunds, Wally Hern, F.H.Baker, Charles Lightfoot, ST MARYS: A.Wilson, W.Lavelle, TORONTO: L.A.Whitehead, C.G Chad Toms, F.H.Sproule, W.A.McCord, Frank Rankin, W.M.Tackaberry, A.W.Dunkley, P.Curzon, Ernie Cook, Stanley Burgoyne, Walter G.Trivett, W.W.Davidson, Dr W.J.Laflamme, F.C.Waghorne, Lew Brown, Jack Moxon, J.A.Burrell, A.G.Davis, Lou E.Marsh, J.B.McArthur, W.M.Gladish, WELLAND: George A.Peart, Charles Coulson, WATERLOO: Wm Uffelman, WOODSTOCK: James Gunn, Redge Stone, G.Ellis, WATFORD: C.E.Dodds.

Area: **OHA (Early Years)** Season: **1913 - 1914**
Supervisor: Officials: ALLENDALE: Harry Riddell,

BELLEVILLE: James Connolly, Sanford Burrows, Dr W.L.Gilbert, BRANTFORD: G.B.Gordon, Roy Brown, Duff Adams, J.J.Kelly, BARRIE: Gren. Caldwell, BRADFORD: O.G.Bernhardt, BERLIN: L.Kreuger, CLINTON: H.Twitchell, R.Rumball, GODERICH: J.Wiggins, D.McDonald, GALT: Jas Fraser, Dr Broomfield, GUELPH: W.J.Squirrel, H.Gandier, HAMILTON: Ralph Ripley, Tom Phillips, T.Moran, INGERSOLL: George Mason, KINGSTON: Reg Crawford, LONDON: R.Penny, A.E.Carruthers, J.Rankin, H.Leckey, LISTOWEL: Wm Zinkham, Stan J.Kemp, MITCHELL: D.E.Eiserman, NEW HAMBURG: H.Beck, NIAGARA FALLS: John Urquhart, W.A.Fraser, OSHAWA: Dr Rowley Young, Leo Quinn, PRESTON: A.T.Kinder, W.Werlich, PICTON: Chas Bedborough, Earl Croft, PARIS: Percy Gill, Lorne Fraser, W.Gill, A.Fraser, W.Peebles, St Marys: DLavelle, R.M.Northgraves, STRATFORD: Frank Baker, Dave Forbes, Wally Hern, E.Edmunds, SIMCOE: Lorne Munroe, Lynn Cratt, SARNIA: Dr Sangster, ST THOMAS: Charlie Johns, TORONTO: W.S.Hancock, C.G.(Chad) Toms, F.H.Sproule, W.A.McCord, O.F.Burkart, Frank Ranklin, W.M.Tackberry, A.W.Dunkley, P.Curzon, Ernie Cook, S.T.Burgoyne, Harry Burgoyne, Walter G.Trivett, W.W.Davidson, Dr W.J Laflamme, F.C.Waghorne, J.L.Brown, Jack Monon, W.P.Irving, TILLSONBURG: L.Weatherwax, TRENTON: E.V.Illsey, Jas A.Cumming, WATERLOO: E.Engle, E.A.Slosser, WATFORD: Fred Rogers, C.C.Dodds, WOODSTOCK: James Gunn

Area: OHA (Early Years) Season: **1912 - 1913** Supervisor: Officials: AYR: A.G. Laurie. ALVINSTON: Simeon Williams. BARRIE: Gren. Caldwell, Steve Vair. BERLIN: Nelson Gross, Loius Kreuger, Oliver Seibert. BELLEVILLE: J.Connlly. BRANTFORD: J.J.Kelly, Duff Adams, Roy Brown. CHATHAM: Tim Phillips. CLINTON: W.Johnson, H.Twitchell. ELMIRA: G.L.Zeigler. GUELPH: D.Kilgour, W.J.Tisdale, Champ Herder. GALT: James Fraser. GODERICH: Dan McDonald, Harry Belcher. HAMILTON: Ralph Ripley, D.M.Cameron, A.Morden, T.Morin, E.W.Gustin. HESPELER: Roy Johnson, Wallace Craig, Wm Rutledge. INGERSOLL: DR. Ralph Williams. KINGSTON: George Van Horne, John Powell, Noble

Steacy, E.Elliott, E.O.Sliter. LONDON: Sidney Rankin, A.E. Carruthers. LISTOWEL: B.Bamford. MITCHELL: J.Eizerman. PICTON: E.Croft, W.Burns. PETERBORO: George Lynch. PRESTON: A.T.Kinder, Werlich Dennis. PARIS: A.Fraser, L.Fraser, W.Peebles. STRATFORD: James Preston, Dave Forbes, H.J.Coghill, Wally Hern, Redge Rankin. ST MARYS: O.Schultz. SEAFORTH: Dalton Reid, Gerald Case. TORONTO: O.F.Burkart, A.W.Dunkley, F.J.Giroux, P.Curzon, W.S.Hancock, Ernie Cook, W.A.McCord, S.F.Burgoyne, Harry Burgoyne, Lou E. Marsh, Dave Drohan, Walter G.Trivett, W.W.Davidson, F.H.Sproule, Dr. W.J.Laflamme, F.C.Waghorne, Alex Maclean, J.L.Brown, W.J.O'Brien. TRENTON: E.V.Illsey, H.N.Armstrong. WATFORD: Fred Rogers. WOODSTOCK: James Gunn.

Index

Adams, Charles, 64
Amell, Derek, 2, 35, 36, 67, 122, 123 295
Anderson Brent, 90
Anderson, Mike, 300
Angus, Blaine, 95, 118, 289
Apps, Syl, 65
Armstrong, Neil, 66, 110
Ashley, George, 296
Ashley, John, 139
Asselstine, Ron, 6, 34, 42, 129, 263, 298

Baker, Steve, 88, 164
Baker, Ted, 77, 79
Ball, Norm, 1, 33, 35, 118
Balsdon, Peter, 32
Bambridge, Gus, 5, 33, 176
Bannerman, Ken, 1, 21-28, 117, 118, 161, 208
Bannerman, Kevin, 21, 22, 161
Bannerman, Korey, 21, 22, 27, 161
Baxter, Larry, 43
Beam, Toby, 300
Beatty, Bob, 297
Beer, Brad, 294
Bell, Bob, 87, 299
Biljetina, Mike, 220
Blackwell, John, 5, 21, 59, 61, 131, 139
Blackwell Awards, 114
Blodgett, Gerry, 4
Boddy, Jim, 126
Bodendistel, Ken, 166
Boorman, George, 4
Boscariol, Steve, 463
Bouchard, Butch, 142
Bower, Johnny, 67
Bradshaw, James, 89

Branch, David 66, 75
Brethauer, Bill, 6, 32, 301
Brown, John, 165
Brown, Tom, 32, 118, 158
Brudz, Jim, 89
Bryce Family, 297
Buffey, Vern's mother, 49
Burchell, Darcy, 118, 156
Bush, Eddie, 152
Butler, Ed, 6, 76, 165

Callaghan, John, 130
Campbell, Clarence, 142
Campbell, Greg, 6
Cane, John, 36
Caplan, Jeff, 32, 130
Carroll, Ryan, 118
Casselman, Brent, 32, 67
Casterton, Art, 117
Chase, Frank, 117
Cheevers, Gerry, 125
Cherrey, Scott, 296
Clancy, Jack, 21, 36, 131, 139
Clancy Awards, 115
Clark, Larry, 33, 66, 116, 145
Clark, Mark, 139
Clayton, Ma, 126
Coburn, John, 163
Coles, Brian, 32, 165
Connor, Art, 3, 35
Constant, Guy, 118
Coopman, Todd, 87
Coubertin Pierre de, 8
Craig, Ben, 7, 36
Crichton, Brian, 60
Cruickshank, Steve, 90
Cunningham, Rick, 148

Daigle, Don, 4, 32

D'Amico, John, 66, 73, 139
Dawe, Al, 1, 33, 118, 280
Dawson, Darryl I, 36 118
Deline, Harry, 4
Devorski, Bill, 33, 80-82, 117, 130, 160
Devorski, Greg, 82, 160, 291
Devorski, Paul, 82, 160
Dick, Al, 33
Dick, Steve, 4
Dionne, Marcel, 11
Dobson, John, 86
Doherty, Pat, 81
Dolbear, Tim, 5
Doolittle, Loring, 123, 126
Downs, Neil, 66
Driscoll, Scott, 2, 34, 35, 67, 157, 159, 291, 302
Duggan, Mike, 5, 34, 269
Dumesnil, Mark, 36
Duncan, Briant, 139

Edgar, Bryan, 5
Edwards, Jeff, 4
Ellwood, Darrell, 139
Emerson, Dan, 118
Etcher, Arnold, 38

Fagan, Brad, 297
Fallis, Terry, 66
Farkas, Chuck, 3, 5
Ferguson, John, 67
Ferguson, Scott, 118
Ferreira, Chris, 44
Ferris, Steve, 66
Fevreau, Gord, 11, 32, 33, 35, 61, 117, 139, 144-146
Finn, Ron, 42, 43, 291
Forrest, Kalvin, 2
Foster T.J., 118
Foster Tim, 118
Fraser, Barry, 66
Fraser, Kerry, 001

French, Archie, 144, 146
French, Chris, 2
Friday, Bill, 162

Gainey, Bob, 147
Garbutt, Terry, 33
Gardner, Dave, 149
Gauthier, Cliff, 118
Gauthier, Dave, 118
Gavin, Ted, 46
Gibbs, Darren, 95
Glaspell, Alan, 122
Goodridge, Don, 36
Gordon, Gus, 7
Goyer, Vern, 117
Graham, Blair, 33, 65, 117, 118, 139, 147-149, 157
Graham, George, 139
Grant, Danny, 65
Gravelle, Red, 31, 139
Gregson, Terry, 75, 117, 302
Gretzky, Wayne, 23, 158
Grice, Glen, 33
Griffen, Ken, 4
Guidolin, Bep, 149

Hache, Conrad, 166
Hagarty, Pat, 35
Hainsworth, George, vi
Hanley, Bill, 65, 66, 130, 147
Harasymchuk, Brian, 3
Harris, Bill, 123
Harris, Ken, 203
Harris, Wally, 32, 33
Harvey, Doug, 17
Hawthorne, Jim, 5, 118
Hayes, George, 66, 67, 139 292
Hayward, Doug, 79
Henderson, Paul, 132
Hickey, Jim, 139
Hoberg, Mike, 299

Hoberg, Scott, 299
Hobor, Terry, 118, 156
Hodges, Bob, 3, 24, 298
Hoggarth, Ron, 162, 291
Holdsworth, Brent, 118, 156 255
Hood, Bruce, 33, 77
Hornsby, Dave, 4, 31
Horton, Tim, 17
Houston, Jim, 118
Howe, Gordie, 151, 162
Howes, Bill, 301
Hubbard, Andrew, 94
Huctwith, Mel, 104, 117, 276
Hull, Bobby, 150
Hutchinson, Ryan, 75
Hutchinson, Scott, 50, 76-78, 85, 118, 163, 164

IIHF Worlds, 119-121
Ion, Mickey, 79
Izerman, Steve, 23

Jackson, Bryon, 3, 36
Jagr, Jaromir, 157
Jones, Davey, 7
Jones, Paul, 5, 54
Jukes, Tom, 6, 88

Kalar, John, 1
Kea, Bert, 301
Kharlumov, Valeri, 46
Kilrae, Brian, 39
Kimmel, Al, 294, 298
Kimmerly, Greg, 118, 296
King, Jim, 2, 35, 130
Knight, Bobby, 46
Koharski, Don, 5, 6,
Kostyk, Pete, 118, 164
Kovachik, Brad, 162, 295
Koziel, Dave, 163
Kusy, Gene, 34

Lach, Elmer, 142
Lacroix, Andre, 65
Ladds, Brent, 27, 50 66, 142
LaFleur, Guy, 11
LaFranco, Joe, 165
Landon, Terry 34
Langdon, Bob, 302
Lavendor, Scott, 6
LeBlanc, Jim, 5, 34, 118, 158
Lemieux, Mario, 159
Lennox, Charlie, 7, 34, 43, 51-54, 56, 66, 116, 123, 225
Lever, Jim, 2, 4, 32, 33, 35 37-39, 117, 118, 129, 134, 157
Lewis, Alyson, 69
Lewis Bryan, 4, 69-73, 76, 116, 117, 168
Lewis, Dave, 118, 122, 123, 164
Lewis, Duane, 69, 73
Lewis, Janelle, 69, 73
Lloyd, Lyle, 7, 31
Locke, Ivan, 2, 95, 116, 122-127, 130, 282
Locke Awards, 114
Loicq, Paul, 8
Lucas, Mike, 3, 35, 118, 130
Lundy, Tom, 2, 33, 289
Luxmore, T.J., 91, 118, 164
Lynch, Dave, 35, 118, 299

MacLean, Ron, 68, 290
MacLeish, Rick, 65
MacMillan, John, 149
Madill, Greg, 42, 122, 139
Magnus, Ross, 116
Maitland, Jim, 199
Makita, Stan, 150
Manor Matt, 3
Marley, Mike, 118, 289

Marouelli, Dan, 75, 77
Marsh, Lou, vi, 65
Marshall, Brian, 298
Martin, Doug, 35
Martinello, Metro, 35
Maschio, Lou, 32, 117, 139, 148, 301
Matthews, Darryl, 6, 35
May, John, 7, 31, 139 286
Maybury, Deb, 293
McCauley, John, 76, 117, 139
McCauley, Wes, 290
McCreary, Bill, 67, 291
McCutcheon, John, 7, 33, 214
McDonald, Wayne, 3, 260
McKellar, Bob, 85
McLean, Hugh, 2, 5, 21, 32, 35, 38, 82, 113, 116, 117, 122, 123, 126, 139, 141-143, 148, 292
McLean Awards, 114
McLoughlin, Rick, 149
McQuigge, Sean, 118, 159
Mepham, Eddie, 142
Mikolasek, Dave, 3, 34
Miller, Ken, 76-79, 118, 125, 289
Miller, Steve, 162, 294, 302
Mills, Rob, 51, 75
Miron, Ray, 90
Montgomery, Dave, 7, 34, 273
Moore, Dinty, 116
Morley, Bob, 35, 66, 117, 118, 131-136, 158, 183
Morley, Rob, 133
Moroney, Gary, 110, 116, 122, 301
Morphew, Rick, 6, 31, 118, 180
Morrison, Scotty, 6, 33

Morton, Dean, 122, 123, 162, 296

Nadin, Bob, 8-12, 32-35, 39, 65, 75-78, 91, 116-118, 126, 134, 141, 157, 189
Neely, Aaron, 43
Neill Mike, 300
Neilson, Roger, 147, 152-155
Neuwendyk, Gil, 32
Nichols, Ian, 2, 36
Nicholson, Kendrick, 118
Nomi, Mike, 3
Norris, Will, 5, 31, 41, 66, 81, 117, 125, 129, 295

Oakman, Scott, 91 93, 118, 159, 289
Ogilvie, Dave, 4, 35, 118, 299
O'Halloran, Dan, 296
Olinski, Jerry, 117, 297
Orr, Bobby, 65, 150, 162
Osborne, Mitch, 35

Padt, Rob, 88
Palin, Sarah, 72
Pallett, Howard, 72
Palm, Rob, 164
Paolini, Joe, 246
Pare, Mark, 248
Park, Joe, 118
Parish, Dennis, 75
Pasma, Rod, 73
Pateman, Jerry, 237
Paterson, Pat, 2, 4
Pavelich, Matt, 66, 110, 117, 292
Pearce, Mike, 93, 118, 156, 243
Peel, Tim, 118, 291
Percy, Steve, 3
Phillips, Cliffe, 122

Phillips, Dwayne, 2
Pollock, Clarke, 2, 31-33, 41, 118, 293
Pollock, Kevin, 162, 293
Porteous, Martin, 6
Primeau, Jim, 142
Proctor, Sandy, 6, 24, 33, 118, 289
Proudfoot, Jim, 42
Pryde, Mike, 122, 123
Punchard, Brett, 163

Quinn, Pat, 162

Racicot, Pierre, 67
Rasenberg, Scott, 6
Reese, Leo, 142
Reeve, Ted, 49, 51
Ragan Dave, 118
Regan, Larry, 146
Reid Ted, 4
Reid, Sean, 118, 166
Rennie, Brian, 66
Richard, Maurice, 17, 142
Richards, Bryan, 33, 41
Richmond Bill, 122
Robb, Doug, 4, 35, 118, 134, 218
Roberts, Lance, 172
Robinson, Dick, 80
Robinson, Frank, 2, 34, 116
Rundle, Cam, 139
Russell, Scott, 79
Ryan, Kevin, 3

Sauve, Jeanne, 142
Sawchuk, Terry, 17
Scapinello, Ray, 66, 67, 302
Scarlett, Pat, 79
Schaly, Rick, 78, 118
Shewchyk, Mark, 296
Schlegel, Tony, 4
Schwippl, Eric, 32
Searle, John, 5

Seitz, Lyle, 95
Sherwood, Glenn, 2, 166
Shropshire, Jack, 35
Sinclair, Christine, 65
Singleton, Rick, 118, 194
Sisco, Sam, 35, 45-47, 75, 77, 117, 125, 129, 267
Skov, Art, 3, 73
Slota, Frank, 116, 117, 139, 150
Smith, Niall, 88
Smith, Tom, 7
Spada, Craig, 95-97, 118, 252
Sparks, Helen, 59, 60
Sparks, Ralph, 31-34, 58-61, 117, 118, 165, 257
Spence, Bob, 5, 34, 129, 265
Stackhouse, Ron, 153
Steeves, Jim, 3, 32
Stefan, Brent, 20
Stephenson, John, 118
Stewart, Barb, 90
Steyaert, Tony, 301
Stickle, Leon, 231
Stiles, Ken, 91
Storey, Red, 292
Stortz, Dave, 2, 4, 35
Sullivan, John, 32, 43, 78
Sundin, Matt, 96

Taylor, Scott, 85
Taylor, Tom, 5, 32
Town, Colin, 6
Traub, Matt, 300
Tretiak, Vladislov, 46

Van Hellemond, Andy, 3, 31, 34, 111
Van Massenhoven, Don, 33, 34, 118, 290, 293, 302
Vance, Bob, 90
Vines, Mark, 1, 31

Visconti, Lou, 144

Waddell, Rob, 139
Waghorne, Fred C., 116
Walkom, Stephen, 67, 68, 75, 117, 118, 291, 293, 298
Wareham, Brian, 77
Warren, Dean, 118, 299
Warren, Jay, 87
Webb, Steve, 87
Whaley, Dave, 139

Wicks, Ron, 78
Wiffen, Steve, 118
Willsie, John, 1, 5, 33, 35, 118, 134, 165
Wilson, Ben, 82, 160
Wilson, Garey, 66, 85, 165
Wilson, George, 7, 76, 129, 297
Wilson, Ryan, 82, 160
Winter, Justin, 32, 118, 293
Wright, Dave, 118

Acknowledgments

Thanks to Scott Farley and the Ontario Hockey Association for allowing me to compile this book which is small part of the OHA's officiating history.

Thanks to Gary Wren for permission to use his cartoon design for the front cover. It was originally a Christmas present from past President Brent Ladds.

Thank you to writer Mike Dodd, of Orillia Today for permission to use his wonderful story of Ken Bannerman's retirement.

Thanks to the NHL for allowing me to use the media pictures of former OHA officials who graduated to the NHL.

Thanks to the Hockey Hall of Fame for helping me with some pictures of old time OHA officials.

Thanks to all the past and present officials who answered the officiating questionnaires and for sending in their pictures. This book could not have been completed without their input.

To the twelve veteran referees who responded to the "Where are they Now" interview questions giving me some insight into their officiating careers. Thank you: Bob Nadin, Ken Bannerman, Jim Lever, Sam Sisco, Ralph Sparks, Bryan Lewis, Bill Devorski, Craig Spada, Mel Huctwith, Matt Pavelich, Ivan Locke, and Bob Morley for your input.

Thanks to Steve Bosciarol who wrote the awesome introduction for my Crystal Puck Award which I have used here as a history of my officiating career.

Thanks to Lindsey Huckabee and Brittany Lavin of Infinity Publishing for all their help in getting me onside to complete my goal.

To my friend Bob Nadin, who kept me on track with his officiating expertise from his many years supervising in Canada and in Europe.

A special thanks to my wife Diane and daughter Susan and future son-in-law, Rick Pomerleau, for their ongoing support throughout the entire process.

About the Author Charlie Lennox

Often overlooked but always appreciated the referees and officials in the sport of hockey make the game work. Without them the game is lost, with them the game produces some of the most exciting and creative plays in all of sport. For over 44 years, Charlie Lennox has proven without a doubt that officiating is a crucial part of the greatest game on earth.

On Friday evening November 27, 2009 in Oakville, the OHA honoured Charlie with a pre-game ceremony which both celebrated and outlined his many contributions to the OHA. Upon receiving the coveted Crystal Puck Award for outstanding service to the OHA, Charlie made sure to thank those who have made his OHA career a successful and positive experience.

Charlie began his OHA career in the Metro JrB League in 1957 playing for the Leaside Rangers and then, he captained the Woodbridge Dodgers hockey team for his final two years. Playing as a defenseman his love for the game would last well after his playing career was over.

In 1967 he began a 15-year career as an OHA official. In his first year, he worked the Memorial Cup between Niagara Falls and Estavan Bruins. He worked another Memorial Cup in 1970 in Ottawa and two Allan Cups in 1969 and 1971 in Cambridge. In 1979 he refereed the Canada Winter games in Brandon, Manitoba. His career as an official ended on October 22, 1982, when his 16 year old son was tragically killed in a car accident while he was away refereeing a JrB game in Guelph.

Two years later in 1984, Charlie took over the job of OHA Supervision Co-Ordinator from Ross Magnus. It was here that Charlie developed computerized Supervision Reports, which were used until 2011.

In 1985, Charlie became an OHA Supervisor, a title he held for four years and two more after his retirement.

In 1989, he was named to replace Will Norris as the OHA Referee Assignor. A full time position he held for 22 years until his retirement in 2011.

Outside of the OHA, Charlie's officiating has transpired into other sports including Lacrosse and Ball Hockey. He was the Referee-in-Chief for the North York Hockey League from 1972-1974 and he was the Referee-in-Chief of the Minor Oaks Hockey Association in Oakville from 1979-1981. He was the Referee-in-Chief of the Toronto Ball Hockey Association from 1974-1986. He later became the Referee-in-Chief of the Ontario Ball Hockey Association from 1979-1981. In 1998, Charlie was inducted into the Ontario Ball Hockey Hall of Fame.

Story by Steve Boscariol, OHA Development Co-Ordinator

CPSIA information can be obtained at www.ICGtesting.com
Printed in the USA
BVOW04*0935290713

327087BV00003B/3/P

9 780741 497031